Contents

This guide was prepared in collaboration with

Guías Turísticas Banamex, S.A. de C.V.

REFORMA N° 155 3ᵉʳ PISO, LOMAS DE CHAPULTEPEC CP. 11000 MEXICO. D.F. TEL. 540.64.21

MAP OF PRINCIPAL SIGHTS

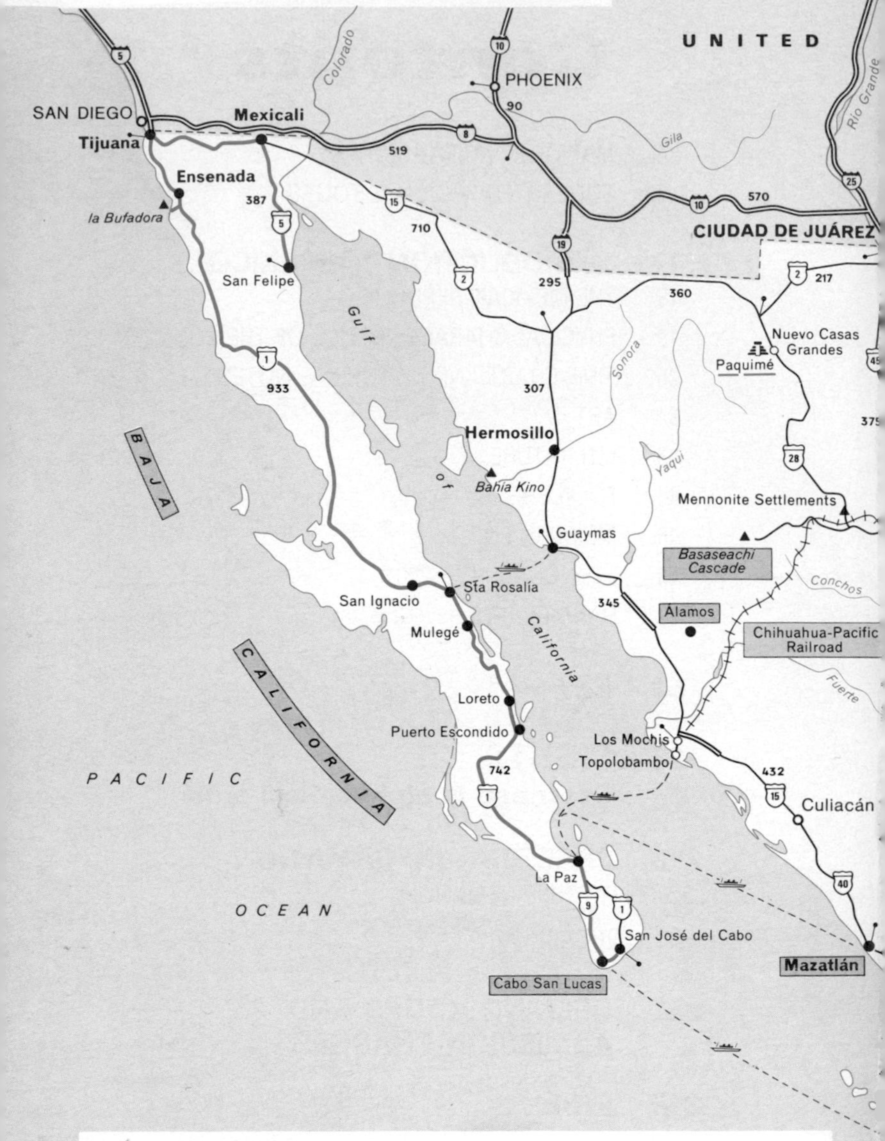

UNITED

PHOENIX

SAN DIEGO
Tijuana
Mexicali
519
Ensenada
387
la Bufadora
San Felipe
933
San Ignacio
Mulegé
Loreto
Puerto Escondido
742
La Paz
Cabo San Lucas
San José del Cabo

Colorado
Gila
90
10
8
15
2
295
710
307
Hermosillo
Bahía Kino
Guaymas
Sta Rosalía
345
Yaqui
Sonora

CIUDAD DE JUÁREZ
217
Nuevo Casas Grandes
Paquimé
375
28
Mennonite Settlements

Basaseachi Cascade
Álamos
Chihuahua-Pacific Railroad
Conchos
Fuerte
Los Mochis
Topolobampo
432
Culiacán
15
40
Mazatlán

Rio Grande
570
360
45

B A J A

C A L I F O R N I A

G u l f   o f   C a l i f o r n i a

P A C I F I C   O C E A N

Key to Symbols

Worth the trip	★★★
Worth a detour	★★
Interesting	★

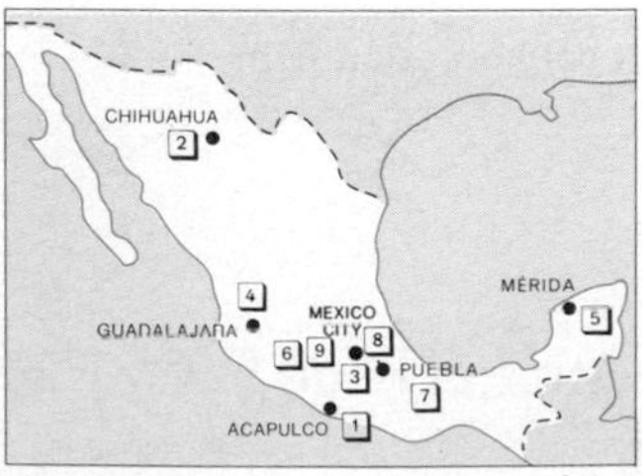

The names in black type face indicate the cities and sights described in this guide. See Index.

- ● Place described
- ✝ Religious building
- ⛏ Archeological site
- ∩ Grotto

━━━ Route described
═══ Superhighway
─── Highway
150 Road distances (in km)

▲ Other Points of Interest

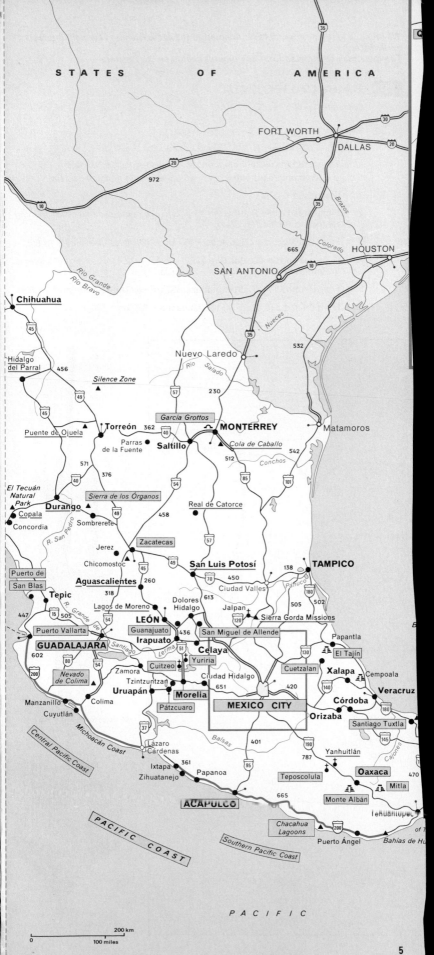

We propose 11 regional tours, to be adapted to the circumstances and main interests of each visitor.
The tours may be initiated from any overnight stop on the itinerary.

1 BAJA CALIFORNIA

Description p 60

2 NORTHWEST – CHIHUAHUA, HERMOSILLO and CIUDAD JUÁREZ

Itinerary leaving from Chihuahua on the Chihuahua-Pacific Railroad.
6 days – approximately 1 840 km – 1 143 miles and 14 hours on the train.

1. Chihuahua★ *(p 70)*.

2. Chihuahua-Pacific Railroad★★★ *(p 71)* – 14 hours by train *(see Opening Hours and Admission Charges)*.

3. From Los Mochis to Guaymas – *450 km – 280 miles:* Alamos★★ *(p 59)*.

4. Guaymas and San Carlos Bay *(p 92)* – *20 km – 12.4 miles* – from Guaymas to Hermosillo *(p 92)* – *140 km – 87 miles*.

5. From Hermosillo to Ciudad Juárez – *850 km – 528 miles:* Paquimé★ *(p 159)*.

6. From Ciudad Juárez *(p 74)* to Chihuahua – *380 km – 236 miles*.

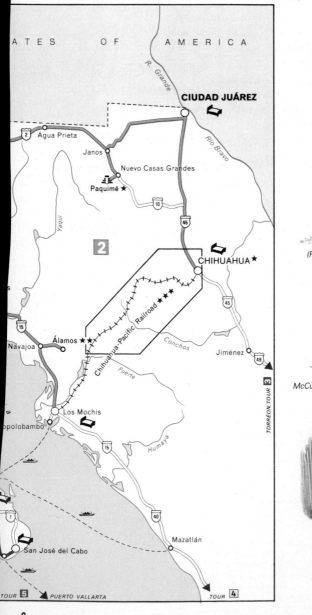

(From photo by G. Sioen/ C.E.D.R.I./Paris)

(From photo by S. McCutcheon/RAPHO/Paris)

(From photo by Hayon/ PITCH/Paris)

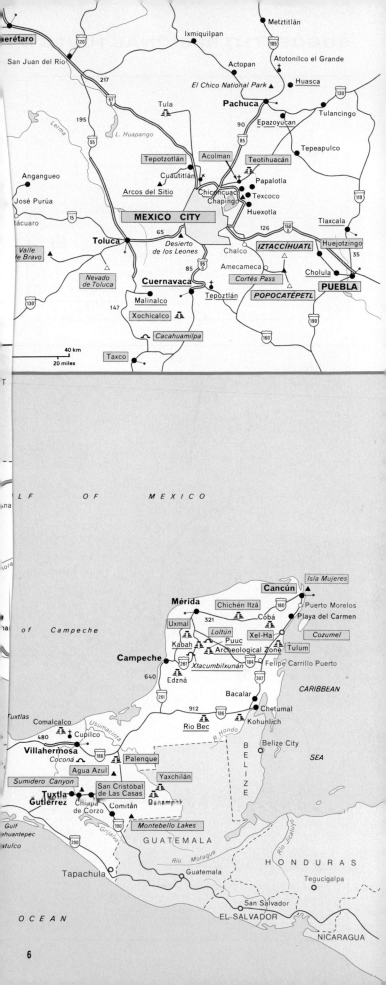

SUGGESTED REGIONAL TOURS

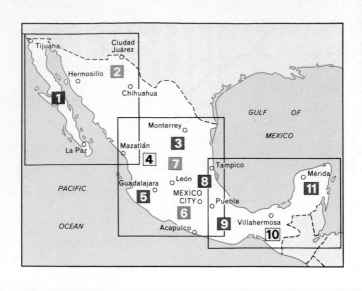

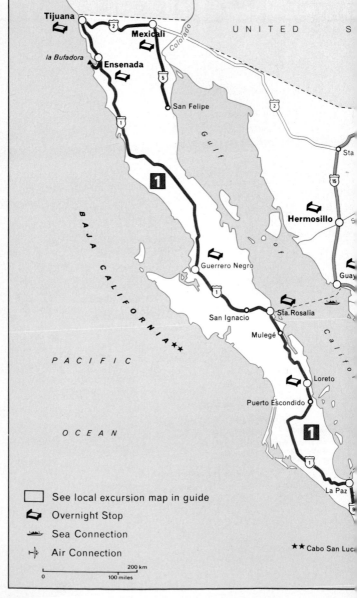

See local excursion map in guide

Overnight Stop

Sea Connection

Air Connection

★★ Cabo San Lucas

200 km
0   100 miles

3 NORTHEAST – ZACATECAS, TORREÓN, MONTERREY and SAN LUIS POTOSÍ

Itinerary starts in Zacatecas.
8 days – approximately 1 760 km – 1 094 miles.

1. Zacatecas★★ and Chicomostoc Ruins *(p 224)* – *95 km – 59 miles.*
2. From Zacatecas to Torreón *(p 207)* – *380 km – 236 miles.*
3. From Torreón to Saltillo – *345 km – 214 miles:* Parras de la Fuente *(p 159).*
4. From Saltillo *(p 175)* to Monterrey – *140 km – 87 miles:* García Grottos★★ *(p 143)* – Huastec Canyon★ *(p 142).*
5. Monterrey *(p 141).*
6. From Monterrey to Real de Catorce★ *(p 176)* and Matehuala – *400 km – 249 miles.*
7. From Matehuala to San Luis Potosí★ *(p 179)* – *200 km – 124 miles.*
8. From San Luis Potosí★ *(p 179)* to Zacatecas – *200 km – 124 miles:* Convent of Guadalupe★ *(p 224).*

4 CENTER – ZACATECAS, GUADALAJARA, MAZATLÁN, DURANGO

Itinerary starts in Zacatecas.
13 days – approximately 1 740 km – 1 081 miles.

1. Zacatecas★★ and Convent of Guadalupe★ *(p 224)* – *12 km – 8 miles.*
2. From Zacatecas to Aguascalientes★ *(p 57)* – *130 km – 81 miles.*
3. From Aguascalientes to Guadalajara★★ *(p 82)* – *250 km – 155 miles.*
4.5.6. Guadalajara★★ *(p 82).*
7. From Guadalajara to Tepic – *270 km – 168 miles:* Tequila *(p 86)* – Ixtlán del Río Archeological Site *(p 197)* – Ceboruco Volcano and Lake Santa María *(p 197).*
8. Tepic *(p 196)* and excursion to Puerto de San Blas★★ *(p 197)* – *140 km – 87 miles.*
9. From Tepic to Mazatlán★★ *(p 98)* – *300 km – 186 miles.*
10. Mazatlán★★ *(p 98).*
11. From Mazatlán to Durango – *320 km – 199 miles:* Concordia *(p 99)* – Copala★ *(p 99).*
12. Durango★ *(p 81)* and Villa del Oeste *(p 82)* – *20 km – 12 miles.*
13. From Durango to Zacatecas – *305 km – 190 miles:* Sierra de los Órganos★★ *(p 185)* – Sombrerete *(p 185).*

5 GUADALAJARA AND CENTRAL PACIFIC COAST

Itinerary leaving from Guadalajara.
8 days – approximately 1 250 km – 777 miles.

1.2.3. Guadalajara★★ *(p 82).*
4. From Guadalajara to Tepic – *270 km – 168 miles:* Tequila *(p 86)* – Ixtlán del Río Archeological Site *(p 197)* – Ceboruco Volcano and Lake Santa María *(p 197).*
5. Tepic *(p 196)* and excursion to Puerto de San Blas★★ *(p 197)* – *140 km – 87 miles.*
6. From Tepic to Puerto Vallarta★★ *(p 172)* – *170 km – 106 miles:* Guayabitos *(p 172)* – Peñita de Jaltemba★ *(p 172).*
7. From Puerto Vallarta to Manzanillo *(p 98)* – *270 km – 168 miles:* Chamela *(p 155)* – Barra de Navidad *(p 155).*
8. From Manzanillo to Guadalajara – *400 km – 249 miles:* Cuyutlán and El Paraíso *(p 98)* – Colima *(p 75)* – Jocotepec, Ajijic and Lake Chapala *(p 87)* – *see local excursion map p 87.*

6 MEXICO CITY AND SOUTHERN PACIFIC COAST

Itinerary starts in Mexico City.
11 days – approximately 1 330 km – 827 miles.

1. to 4. Mexico City★★★: visit to the principal sights
1. Plaza de la Constitución★★★ *(p 105)* – Metropolitan Cathedral★★★ *(p 106)* – Metropolitan Tabernacle *(p 110)* – Great Temple *(p 110)* – National Palace★★ *(p 112)* – House of Tiles★ *(p 118)* – Monastery of Saint Francis *(p 119)* – Iturbide Palace★★ *(p 119)* – La Profésa Church *(p 119)* – Minería Palace★★ *(p 120)* – Central Post Office★ *(p 120)* – National Art Museum★ *(p 120)* – Palace of Fine Arts *(p 121)* – Arts and Crafts Museum *(p 121)* – Franz Mayer Museum★★★ *(p 122).*

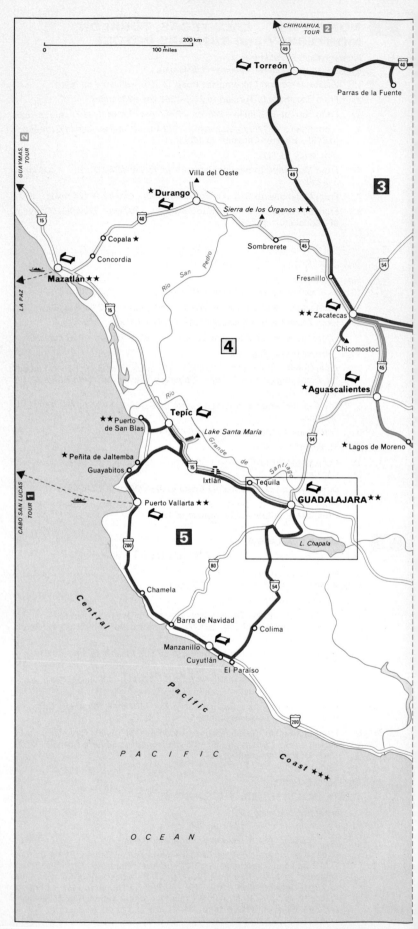

García Grottos ★★
MONTERREY
Saltillo
57
54
Linares
★ Real de Catorce
Matehuala
85
3
Conchos
TAMPICO
San Luis Potosí ★
Ciudad Valles
Pánuco
70
57
7
85
Concá
Sierra Gorda Missions ★
LEÓN
Dolores Hidalgo
Jalpan
Landa de Matamoros
★ Atotonilco
★★★ Guanajuato
San Miguel de Allende ★★
8
180
Irapuato
Querétaro ★★
Ixmiquilpan
Poza Rica
Celaya
San Juan
del Río
Actopan
130
Lerma
† Yuriria ★★
Tula
★★★ El Tajín
★★ Cuitzeo †
Acámbaro
Pachuca
Tulancingo
Morelia ★★
57
Epazoyucan ★
PÁTZCUARO ★★★
MEXICO CITY ★★★
15
150
Toluca
15
95
† Tepoztlán ★
134
★★ Xochicalco
Cuernavaca ★
Ciudad Altamirano
6
Taxco ★★★
Balsas
Atoyac
95
Ixtapa Zihuatanejo
Papanoa
200
ACAPULCO ★★★
Southern
Pacific
Coast ★★
200

MEXICO

GULF OF

VERACRUZ ▶

PUEBLA, TOUR **9**

OAXACA, TOUR **9**

2. National Anthropological Museum★★★ *(p 125)* – National Historical Museum★★ *(p 128)*.

3. Coyoacán★★: Avenida Francisco Sosa★ *(p 131)* – Plaza de la Conchita *(p 131)* – Frida Kahlo Museum★ *(p 131)* – San Ángel★: Plaza de San Jacinto *(p 132)* – Casa del Risco *(p 132)* – Diego Rivera Studio Museum *(p 132)* – University Campus★ *(p 132)* – Cuicuilco Archeological Site *(p 133)* – Xochimilco: Canal Tour★★ *(p 133)*; San Bernardino Parish Church *(p 134)*.

4. Popocatépetl – Iztaccíhuatl Volcanoes★★★ *(p 164)* – *178 km – 111 miles*: Tlalmanalco.

5. From Mexico City to Toluca *(p 203)* – *65 km – 40 miles*.

6. From Toluca to Ixtapa and Zihuatanejo *(p 156)* – *350 km – 218 miles*.

7. From Zihuatanejo to Acapulco★★★ *(p 54)* – *240 km – 168 miles*: Papanoa *(p 156)*.

8. Acapulco★★★ *(p 54)*.

9. From Acapulco to Taxco★★★ *(p 190)* – *270 km – 168 miles*.

10. From Taxco to Cuernavaca★ *(p 76)* – *120 km – 75 miles*: Xochicalco Archeological Site★★ *(p 220)*.

11. From Cuernavaca to Mexico City – *105 km – 65 miles*: Ocotepec Cemetery★ *(p 77)* – Tepoztlán★ *(p 199)* – *see local excursion map p 77*.

7   CENTER – QUERÉTARO, ZACATECAS, GUANAJUATO, MORELIA

Itinerary starts in Querétaro.
16 days – approximately 1 400 km – 870 miles.

1. Querétaro★★ *(p 173)*.

2. From Querétaro to San Miguel de Allende★★ *(p 182)* – *100 km – 62 miles*: Celaya *(p 176)*.

3. From San Miguel de Allende to San Luis Potosí – *200 km – 124 miles*: Atotonilco Sanctuary *(p 184)* – Dolores Hidalgo *(p 80)*.

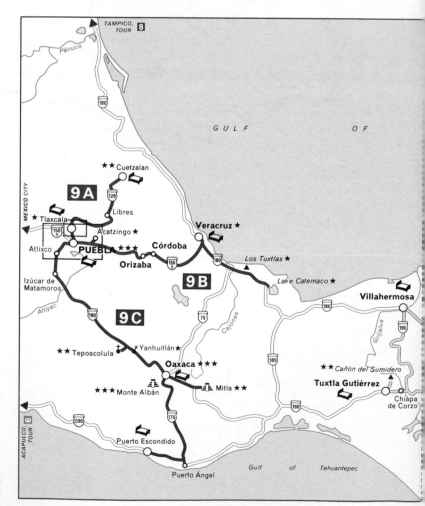

8 CENTRAL GULF – QUERÉTARO, TAMPICO, EL TAJÍN

Itinerary starting in Querétaro.
10 days – approximately 1 690 km – 1 050 miles.

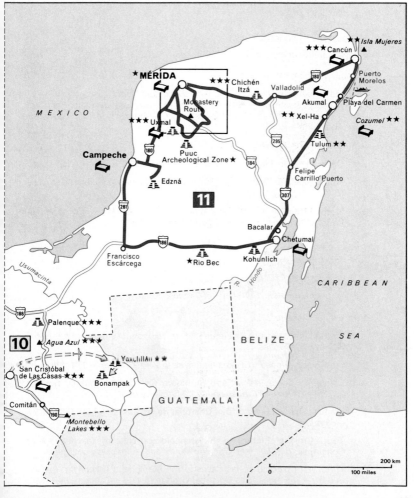

5. From San Luis Potosí to Tampico – *540 km – 336 miles*: Sierra Gorda★ (Concá, Jalpan, Landa de Matamoros) – *(p 184)*.

6. Tampico *(p 189)*.

7. From Tampico to Poza Rica – *280 km – 174 miles:* El Tajín★★★ *(p 186)*.

8. From Poza Rica to Pachuca – *200 km – 124 miles*: Tulancingo *(p 154)* – Epazoyucan★ *(p 154)*.

9. Pachuca *(p 153)*.

10. From Pachuca to Querétaro – *370 km – 230 miles:* Tula Archeological Site *(p 207)* – Actopan *(p 154)* – Ixmiquilpan *(p 154)* – San Juan del Río *(p 176)*.

9   SOUTHEAST – PUEBLA, OAXACA, VERACRUZ

A. Puebla – Tlaxcala

5 days – 235 km – 146 miles – see local excursion maps pp 170 and 171.

1. 2. 3. Puebla★★★ *(p 165)*.

4. From Puebla to Tlaxcala★ *(p 200)* – *35 km – 22 miles:* Sta. Inés Zacatelco *(p 201)* – Tepeyanco de las Flores *(p 201)*.

5. From Tlaxcala to Cuetzalan★★ *(p 79)* – *200 km – 124 miles:* Tizatlán *(p 202)* – Atlihuetzía★ *(p 202)* – Yauhquemecan *(p 202)* – Huamantla *(p 202)* – Libres *(p 80)*.

B. Puebla – Veracruz

6 days – approximately 600 km – 373 miles.

1. 2. 3. Puebla★★★ *(p 165)*.

4. From Puebla to Veracruz – *280 km – 174 miles:* Acatzingo★ *(p 170)* – Orizaba *(p 152)* – Córdoba *(p 153)*.

5. Veracruz★ *(p 215)*.

6. From Veracruz to Lake Catemaco★ *(p 211)* – *320 km – 199 miles:* Los Tuxtlas★ *(p 211)*.

C. Puebla – Oaxaca

9 days – approximately 900 km – 559 miles.

1. 2. 3. Puebla★★★ *(p 165)*.

4. From Puebla to Oaxaca – *440 km – 273 miles:* Tlaxcalancingo *(p 73)* – San Francisco Acatepec *(p 73)* – Atlixco *(p 171)* – *see local excursion map p 170* – Teposcolula★★ *(p 152)* – Monastery of Yanhuitlán★ *(p 152)* – San Pedro Apóstol Etla *(p 152)*.

5. 6. Oaxaca★★★ *(p 148)*.

7. Oaxaca★★★ *(p 148)* and Monte Albán★★★ *(p 138)* – *20 km – 12 miles.*

8. From Oaxaca to Mitla★★ *(p 136)* – *100 km – 62 miles:* Tlalixtac de Cabrera *(p 151)*.

9. From Oaxaca to Puerto Escondido *(p 156)* – *330 km – 205 miles*: San Bartolo Coyotepec *(p 151)* – Puerto Ángel *(p 156)*.

10   SOUTHEAST – VILLAHERMOSA, SAN CRISTÓBAL DE LAS CASAS

7 days – approximately 1 110 km – 690 miles.

1. Villahermosa *(p 218)*.

2. From Villahermosa to Palenque★★★ *(p 156)* and Agua Azul★★★ *(p 57)* – *400 km – 249 miles.*

3. From Villahermosa to Tuxtla Gutiérrez *(p 210)* – *280 km – 174 miles.*

4. Chiapa de Corzo *(p 210)* and Sumidero Canyon★★: Tour by boat★★★ *(p 186)* – *34 km – 21 miles and 2 1/2 hours by boat.*

5. From Tuxtla Gutiérrez to San Cristóbal de las Casas★★★ *(p 178)* – *85 km – 53 miles.*

6. Tour by plane (1 hour) to the archeological sites of Yaxchilán★★ and Bonampak *(p 221)* – (see Opening Hours and Admission Charges).

7. From San Cristóbal de las Casas to the Montebello Lakes★★★ *(p 141)* – *300 km – 186 miles:* San Cristóbal Grottos *(p 179)* – Comitán *(p 141)*.

11 SOUTHERN PENINSULA – MÉRIDA, RÍO BEC, CANCÚN

Itinerary starting in Mérida
15 days – approximately 1 860 km – 1 156 miles.

(Photo PIX/Paris)

Bark painting

15

THE STATES OF THE MEXICAN REPUBLIC

STATE	ABBREVIATION	CAPITAL
Aguascalientes	**Ags.**	Aguascalientes
Baja California Norte	**BCN**	Mexicali
Baja California Sur	**BCS**	La Paz
Campeche	**Camp.**	Campeche
Coahuila	**Coah.**	Saltillo
Colima	**Col.**	Colima
Chiapas	**Chis.**	Tuxtla Gutiérrez
Chihuahua	**Chih.**	Chihuahua
Distrito Federal (Federal District)	**D.F.**	
Durango	**Dgo.**	Durango
Guanajuato	**Gto.**	Guanajuato
Guerrero	**Gro.**	Chilpancingo
Hidalgo	**Hgo.**	Pachuca
Jalisco	**Jal.**	Guadalajara
México	**Méx.**	Toluca
Michoacán	**Mich.**	Morelia
Morelos	**Mor.**	Cuernavaca
Nayarit	**Nay.**	Tepic
Nuevo León	**NL**	Monterrey
Oaxaca	**Oax.**	Oaxaca
Puebla	**Pue.**	Puebla
Querétaro	**Qro.**	Querétaro
Quintana Roo	**Q. Roo**	Chetumal
San Luis Potosí	**SLP**	San Luis Potosí
Sinaloa	**Sin.**	Culiacán
Sonora	**Son.**	Hermosillo
Tabasco	**Tab.**	Villahermosa
Tamaulipas	**Tamps.**	Ciudad Victoria
Tlaxcala	**Tlax.**	Tlaxcala
Veracruz	**Ver.**	Jalapa
Yucatán	**Yuc.**	Mérida
Zacatecas	**Zac.**	Zacatecas

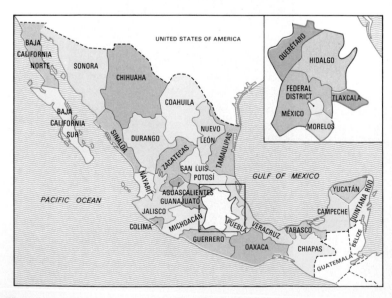

Introduction
to Mexico

From the Pacific Ocean to the Caribbean Sea, from desert lands to tropical jungles, from plateaus to snow-covered volcanoes, Mexico offers an incredible variety of light, color and landscapes. At the same time, Mexico has forged a strong sense of national unity, adapting to progress while preserving the roots of its ancient cultures with dignity.
No other country in the "New World" offers the traveler greater riches: delicious cuisine, impressive archeological sites, folklore, colonial art and, above all, a proud, forceful, happy and friendly people who appreciate their illustrious past and the beauty of their land.

(Photo Guillermo Aldana/Mexico)

Popocatépetl and Iztaccíhuatl Volcanoes

The symbol ⊙ placed in the left margin beside a sight description indicates that specific visitor information can be found in the Opening Hours and Admission Charges section at the end of this guide.

The sights are listed alphabetically in this section either under the place – town, village or area – in which they are situated or under their proper name.

17

THE MEXICAN REPUBLIC

The United Mexican States constitute a Democratic and Federal Republic. Its system of government is composed of three branches: the Executive (president), the Legislative (senators and representatives) and the Judicial (Supreme Court and lower courts).

The territory is composed of 31 states and the Federal District, which is the capital of the Mexican Republic. Mexico is located in the southwestern part of North America, with an area of 1 972 547 km^2 – 758 136 square miles, of which 5 000 km^2 – 2 071 square miles are islands. It has 10 000 km – 6 320 miles of seacoast, the second longest coast in the Americas. Mexico is the fifth largest country in the Western Hemisphere, after Canada, the United States, Brazil and Argentina.

Mexico's boundaries are: to the north, the United States; to the south, Guatemala and Belize; to the east, the Gulf of Mexico and the Caribbean Sea; and to the west, the Pacific Ocean.

In Mexico, there are three **time zones:** central standard time (most of the country falls within this zone), mountain standard time (states of Nayarit, Sinaloa, Sonora and Baja California Sur) and Pacific standard time (Baja California Norte).

The official language is Spanish, although indigenous tongues and dialects are still spoken.

While there is freedom of worship, the country is overwhelmingly Catholic.

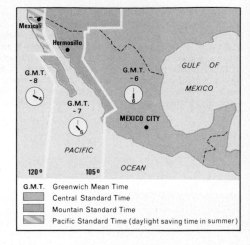

G.M.T.   Greenwich Mean Time
          Central Standard Time
          Mountain Standard Time
          Pacific Standard Time (daylight saving time in summer)

A Country of Contrasts. –

Mexico offers dramatically contrasting features. Its landscapes combine lofty snow-capped volcanoes, the deserts of the central and northern regions; the high mountain ranges that run across its territory; countless beaches with white sands and many-hued waters; wide valleys, forests and jungles; rivers and waterfalls. These varied landscapes sustain a rich flora and fauna.

The pre-Hispanic past, the *mestizaje* or racial intermingling that began with the Spaniards' arrival, and the North American and French invasions have contributed to endow the country and its people with a life style, as well as with artistic and cultural expressions that are uniquely Mexican.

The archeological sites, the convents, monasteries, cathedrals and residences of the colonial period, the French influence in the 19C, the mural painting of the 20C, along with its exceptional contemporary architecture, provide an overview of Mexico's cultural evolution.

However, there are some places where time seems to stand still; in their farming, their markets and their festivals, the Mexican people reveal their attachment to tradition, despite the uncertainties of their present condition.

The Mexicans. – The diversity of regions and climates and the mixture of Indian and European strains have produced the Mexican people. It is fascinating to get to know the Mexicans. They are generally happy-go-lucky, hospitable, resourceful, outgoing and informal. In sum, they may be disorganized, but they are highly creative human beings. The Mexican has his own notion of time; often one hears *"ahorita"* or *"al ratio"*, "in a little while" which could indicate minutes, days or an indefinite wait. It might be said that Mexico is the country of the unexpected; not in vain did André Breton describe it as surrealist.

Respect the environment.
Drive cautiously on country roads.
Smokers, be careful in wooded areas!

PHYSICAL CHARACTERISTICS OF THE COUNTRY

Mexico's location between the 14th and 32nd parallels places the country under the influence of two great climatic belts of the Northern Hemisphere: the desert in the north and the tropics in the south. However, these conditions are modified by the uneven topography, as well as by the sea air from the Pacific on the west and the Gulf of Mexico on the east. Both these factors cause numerous changes in climate *(see below)* and vegetation, making Mexico a veritable mosaic of contrasting natural regions.

TOPOGRAPHY

The erratic physiognomy of the country resembles an inverted triangle, stretched from the northwest to the southeast and narrowed down at the **Isthmus of Tehuantepec.**
Two oddly-shaped peninsulas protrude from the northern and southern extremes of this great land mass. These are linked to the rest of the country by narrow strips of land less than 150 km – 93 miles wide. To the northwest is Baja California, bathed by the Pacific and by the Gulf of California (also known as the Sea of Cortés), formed by a narrow belt of mountainous terrain over 1 000 km – 621 miles long and averaging 100 km – 62 miles in width. At Mexico's southeastern end, lies the rhomboid-shaped Yucatan Peninsula, made up of an enormous lime-based plateau over 100,000 km^2 – 38 462 square miles in size, surrounded by the Gulf of Mexico and the Caribbean Sea.
These features result in a very irregular territory with abrupt changes in altitude, making for a variety of landscapes ranging from the alpine type with snow-capped peaks and evergreens to inhospitable sandy deserts.

Mountains. – The Mexican landscape, viewed from above, looks like wrinkled paper, with hundreds of landslides running between the mountain folds, deep canyons caused by faults or fractures, as well as cliffs molded by erosion, where unexplored regions are still to be found. This sort of landscape covers 60% of the Mexican territory and is due to three continental mountain ranges, formed geologically by Tertiary period foldings and by volcanic activity at the beginning of the Quaternary period. These ranges are, in order of importance: **Sierra Madre Occidental** (Western Sierra Madre), **Sierra Madre del Sur** (Southern Sierra Madre), **Sierra Madre Oriental** (Eastern Sierra Madre) and **Sierra Volcánica Transversal** (Transversal Volcanic Range) *(p 22)*. The latter has the highest elevations, including such snow-covered volcanoes as **Pico de Orizaba,** the highest (alt 5 610 m – 18 406 ft), Popocatépetl (alt 5 465 m – 17 930 ft), Iztaccíhuatl (alt 5 230 m – 17 159 ft), Nevado de Toluca (alt 4 690 m – 15 387 ft) and Nevado de Colima (alt 4 240 m – 13 911 ft).

Rocks, Lava and Fire. – At the beginning of the 19C, the renowned German scientist **Alexander von Humboldt** carried out natural science research in the New World. In his work in Mexico, he highlighted the importance of the Sierra Volcánica Transversal. Located between the two arms of the Sierra Madre, this range forms a natural east-west barrier. Despite its location in the subtropical latitudes, there are snow-capped volcanoes towering over exuberant jungles, which in turn border on desert regions like the Balsas Depression.
Another of Humboldt's interesting conclusions was that the ancient Mesoamericans located their cities and sanctuaries along universal axes related to geographic, bio-geographic and astronomic phenomena. Humboldt also reckoned that Náhuatl myth-ology used these criteria for calendar and cosmogonic calculations. One example of this is the Cholula Pyramid *(p 73)*, the location (on the 19th parallel) and orientation of which coincide twice a year with the sun at its highest point (May 25th and July 15th). On these dates the sun rises behind the Citlaltépetl (Pico de Orizaba) Mountain of the Dawn and sets behind the Xinantécatl (Nevado de Toluca) Mountain of the Sunset, passing between the Iztaccíhuatl and Popocatépetl volcanoes, precisely above Otzumba on the Summit of the Sun Road (Cima del Camino del Sol).

> *"How beautiful are the Mexican mountains – those cones covered with majestic snow, which rise amidst luxuriant tropical vegetation – like the crest of the Orizaba, observatory of such a prodigious geology, that seems to shake its crown of snow to soften the tropical ardors of the Gulf of Mexico".*
>
> Alexander von Humboldt

Plains and Plateaus. – Between the great mountain ranges mentioned lie two enormous plateaus: the **Mexican High Plateau** (Altiplanicie Mexicana) (alt 2 000 to 2 500 m – 6 562 to 8 201 ft) in the north central part; and to the south, enclosed by some offshoots of the principal ranges, the **Meseta del Anáhuac** with similar altitudes. Among the less extensive lower plains are the coastal plains of the Gulf and of the Pacific, which correspond to the outer slopes of the Sierra Madre Oriental and Occidental respectively.

CLIMATE

The country's climate ranges from alpine to tropical, from temperate humid to desert dry, including Mediterranean-like weather.

Arid and Temperate Zones. – From the extreme north to the Tropic of Cancer, desert and semi-desertic regions are interspersed with rainy temperate zones in the steep mountains that cover principally the northern states with an average yearly rainfall of 100 to 700 mm – 4 to 28 inches; monthly mean temperatures that fluctuate between 12°C (54°F) and 18°C (64°F) in the high temperate zones and from 18°C (64°F) to 22°C (72°F) in the low desert zones, with hot summers and freezing winters.

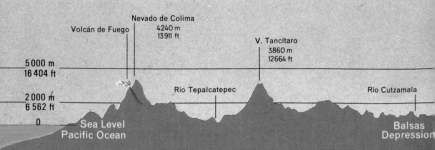

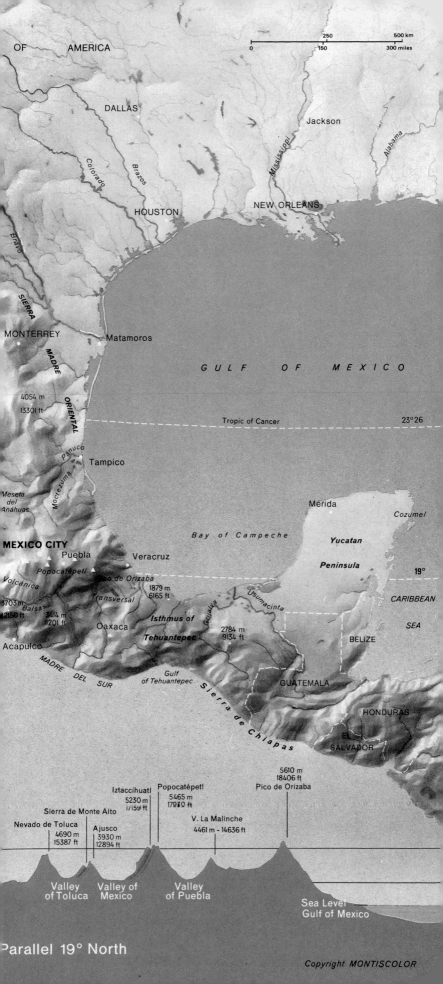

Tropical Zone. – South of the Tropic of Cancer, where the Meseta del Anáhuac and the Valley of Mexico are located, the weather varies from temperate to semitropical and hot tropical pockets occur on the outer slopes of the Sierra Madres and some sections of the interior, especially in the depressions south of the volcanic range. In the tropical areas, like Tabasco, Chiapas, and the south Yucatan Peninsula, the annual rainfall varies from 800 to 3 000 mm – 30 to 120 inches, with very slight temperature variations from 22°C (72°F) to 24°C (75°F). With rare exceptions, there are no sudden temperature changes or frosts in this zone. In the summer season, the humid winds coming from the oceans cross the mountains, which act as a weather-tempering barrier, producing abundant rain on the plateau, especially when they bring hurricanes and cyclones from the Atlantic, Carribean or Pacific. The Nortes is a mass of damp winter air originating in

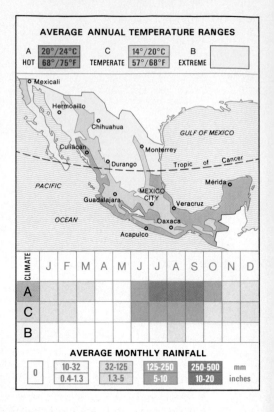

North America and causing substantial drops in temperature on plateaus and mountain ranges, where occasional snowfalls are reported.

NATURAL REGIONS, PLANTS AND ANIMALS

See map p 23.

Mexico can be divided into six great natural regions with landscapes that have common geological, climatic and botanical features.

Baja California Peninsula, and the Mountains and Deserts of the Northwest (1). – The peninsula landscape is dominated by the mountain ridge that runs its full length, with broad rocky deserts where xerophilous vegetation, such as spiny saguaro and cereus cacti, rubber-producing *gobernadoras* and, in the upper reaches of the mountains, small pine woods, grow.
In the states of Sonora and Sinaloa, facing the Gulf of California *(see map pp 20-21)*, deserts – in some cases sandy, like the Altar Desert – spread across the wide coastal plains at the foot of the Sierra Tarahumara (alt 3 000 m – 9 843 ft). This range has an imposing configuration and majestic gorges, such as the Barranca del Cobre (Copper Canyon) *(p 71)*, where there are rich pine and oak forests.
Towards the south (Sinaloa-Nayarit), a change from semi-desertic to sub-tropical environments is noticeable. Here are savannahs, spiny low jungles and, further south, the beginning of semi-jungle heralded by the presence of ceiba and palm trees.

The Mexican High Plateau (Altiplanicie Mexicana) (2). – This broad, arid region covered by grasslands and dwarf evergreen oak thickets (chaparrales), mixed with prickly-pear trees and century plants, has large livestock grazing areas, broken by isolated mountain elements, such as rocky outcroppings (bufas) strangely shaped by erosion – a landscape especially typical of Chihuahua, Coahuila, Durango and Zacatecas.

Eastern Highlands and Gulf Coastal Plains (3). – This is a region of great contrasts caused by the Sierra Madre Oriental (alt 3 000 to 3 500 m – 9 843 to 11 483 ft), on the slopes of which lies the subregion called Huastecas, extending over Potosí, Tamaulipec and Hidalgo. Numerous rivers run across these slopes, and sudden drops in altitude account for the formation of waterfalls and deep canyons. This rough terrain produces evergreen woods as well as mesophyte forests (forests that grow under medium conditions of moisture), which are fog-bound most of the year. The mountain slopes finally sink into the tropical jungles on the coast.

Meseta del Anáhuac and the Volcanic Range (4). – The Anáhuac plateau comprises wide plains with some minor mountain outcroppings as well as the lake basins of Chapala, Yuriria and Cuitzeo. These include the Bajío region, with a great variety of farming activities, and the largest cities and industrial complexes of the country. Outstanding examples of the latter are Mexico City, Guadalajara, Toluca and León, and of the former, the irrigated lands of the Lerma and Tula Rivers – vital for the country's agriculture. Towards the south rises the imposing Sierra Volcánica Transversal, with its numerous volcanic cones and basalt overflows.

Southern Depressions, Southern Ranges and Pacific Coastal Plain (5). – This region of Mexico is formed by the Balsas and Central Chiapas Depressions, with surrounding ranges that make up the Isthmus of Tehuantepec, formerly called the Mixtec Knot (Nudo Mixteco), on account of its complex geological origin.

The part that corresponds to the Sierra Madre del Sur has jagged summits covered with oaks and mixed forests, whereas the Pacific slopes are blanketed with low jungle vegetation of mangrove trees and bulrushes surrounding lake formations such as Cuyutlán *(p 98)*, Coyuca *(p 55)* and Chacahua *(p 156)*. This region extends over the southern part of the states of Jalisco, Michoacán, Guerrero, Oaxaca and Chiapas.

Yucatan Peninsula (6). – This region consists of an enormous, basically homogeneous plain, entirely devoid of mountains, geologically constituted of lime soils with no superficial faults. This is due to filtrations that dissolved the carbonated rock, forming the cenotes or wells, and constituting a vast underground drainage system. The soil is carpeted with vegetation consisting, in the north, of low jungle and, in the south, of medium jungle, largely unexplored. The shores of this region have lakes interconnected with the sea, both underground and on the surface.

Animal Life. – There are two principal animal habitats in America: the Nearctic and the Neotropical. The Mexican boundary between these habitats lies near the volcanic range and the southern depressions – a region that specialists call the Mexican Transitional Zone. In this zone, the two habitats overlap, forming a complex zoographic combination. The outstanding mammals from the Nearctic group include bears, elks, wolves and coyotes; among the Neotropical fauna are a variety of monkeys, tapirs, deer, jaguars and armadillos. Those that belong to both regions are the pumas, ocelots, lynxes and the so-called ring-tailed cats (cacomixtles), as well as a great variety of reptiles, such as the caiman in the coastal lake areas, and birds with beautiful plumage like the *quetzal*, flamingo and parrot.

National Parks. – This wealth of flora and fauna has led to the establishment of a large number of national parks. Not all of them are equipped with camping facilities, since their main purpose is to protect wild life, prevent the extermination of species, regulate hunting and control lumbering, especially in the case of precious tropical woods. At present, Mexico has more than sixty national parks and wildlife reserves. Their number is continuously increasing, because ecological protection has lately gained great importance in the government's plans. In addition to these wildlife sites, areas with archeological remains, historic relics, grottos and zones of geological interest have been designated national parks.

COASTLINES AND WATER SYSTEMS

(see map pp 20-21)

One of the main attractions of the Mexican coastline is its great variety. On the Pacific coast, in contrast with the Gulf of Mexico, high cliffs and mountainous bays alternate with extensive coastal plains, lakes, tidelands and reefs. Among the most important water systems are those of the southeast and the Gulf basin (Grijalva, Usumacinta, Papaloapan and Coatzacoalcos). They result from the region's high average rainfall and provide the setting for Mexico's largest hydraulic works *(p 186)*. In the center and west, the Lerma-Santiago River is particularly important, determining the economic activities of the Bajío, and watering land as far as its mouth on the Pacific at San Blas, Nayarit. Other significant rivers are the Balsas, which flows through the states of Guerrero and Michoacán and is essential for generating electric power; the Moctezuma Pánuco, which rises at the north of the Valley of Mexico and empties into the Gulf of Mexico, and, in the north, the Bravo, which forms part of the border between Mexico and the United States.

ECONOMIC ACTIVITY

During the first decades of the present century, Mexico continued to be a predominantly rural country. A few cities had grown up around mining centers, and others became commercial, administrative and service hubs for the rural areas. In the 1940s, the country began to change. Economic policies favoring industrialization gained priority; industry, trade and services now account for the largest share of the national product.

These dynamic industrialization and urbanization processes were accompanied by rapid demographic growth, resulting in a predominantly young population. Mexico's population reached 67 000 000 in 1980, with a density of 34.1 inhabitants per km^2 – 88.4 inhabitants per square mile. Although a substantial proportion of the rural population still lives in the thousands of small hamlets scattered throughout the country, the majority of Mexicans live in a few cities in the center and the north of the country. Among these, Mexico City, Monterrey and Guadalajara are the largest.

Agriculture

Despite the economic changes described above, agriculture and cattle raising continue to provide the main livelihood for the Mexican people; two fifths of the economically active population are engaged in these pursuits. However, their overall productivity is low, a fact which is reflected in their modest contribution to the national product (9%).

Agriculture in Mexico is highly diversified, comprising products from tropical, temperate and cold zones. It depends largely on the intensity and regularity of the rainfall. Mexico's leading agricultural products are: corn, beans, wheat, sugar cane, coffee and sorghum. Half of the cultivated land is devoted to the first two, since they are the basis of the nation's diet. Wheat and sugar cane are items of general consumption. Coffee, on the other hand, is the major agricultural export, while sorghum has become a crucial product for chicken and pig farming – industries which have developed greatly in recent years. These agricultural and livestock activities fall into two categories: on one hand, there are enterprises which have abundant resources, modern technology and high productivity; and, on the other, enterprises with rudimentary technology, low returns and limited acreage, which induces the continuous migratory flow from the rural areas towards the main urban centers within the country and abroad.

The structure of land ownership in Mexico is a consequence of the land reform which was initiated by the 1910 Revolution. The Mexican State reserved the power to regulate the size of private farms and to restore to the peasant communities *(ejidos)* the lands that had been taken away from them prior to the Revolution. In this way, private property and *ejido* property were established and regulated in Mexico. Each of these two categories of land ownership accounts for approximately 50% of the farm land.

Livestock

The ecological conditions in almost every region of Mexico are favorable to livestock raising and, throughout the country, farms with diverse technological resources engage in this industry.

Cattle raising is economically the most important stock-breeding activity and is mainly concentrated in the north of the country, with Chihuahua, Durango, Sonora and Zacatecas producing one fourth of the national stock, a large share of which is exported to the United States on the hoof. In the center of the country and on the tropical plains of Veracruz, Tabasco and Chiapas, livestock raising is mainly geared to the national market.

Fishing

The country has an extended coastline and a rich fishing potential, at present under-developed, which makes only a slight contribution to the national product. It is vital, however, for the employment of the inhabitants of the 10 000 km – 6 320 mile seacoast. The most productive zone for fishing resources is the northwest coast, where great quantities of sardines, tuna, shrimp, clams and lobsters, among other species, are found. Shrimps amount to over one third of the value of the national catch and rank first among fishing exports.

The general conditions under which fishing is carried out – small boats, outdated technology, inadequate refrigeration facilities in the ports and insufficient means of transportation – in addition to the eating habits and the marketing practices, which inflate prices, have all contributed to low domestic consumption levels.

Mining

The traditional mining wealth of Mexico is determined by its geological makeup. The leading mining centers are located in the mountainous regions in the north of the country. Although the relative importance of this activity has waned, Mexico is still the largest producer of silver in the world and is one of the five leading producers of zinc, mercury, fluorite and sulphur.

Petroleum. – Petroleum and gas are the most important resources within Mexico's mining industry and are a decisive factor in the nation's economic growth. These products are large foreign currency earners (amounting to two thirds of exports) and contribute significantly to government income, employment and demand for industrial inputs.

Since the nationalization of Mexico's oil industry in 1938, the government controls petroleum and natural gas production and marketing through Petróleos Mexicanos (PEMEX), the largest Mexican company.

The discovery of new petroleum reserves at the end of the 1970s placed Mexico among the five leading petroleum-exporting countries in the world.

At present, the main drilling areas are situated in the south of the country, in the region between the states of Tabasco and Chiapas and on the continental shelf of Campeche, which, together with the coastal zone of the Gulf, Tamaulipas and Veracruz, constitute the Great Petroleum Zone of Mexico.

Industry

The industrial sector accounts for the second largest share of the national product – two fifths of the total – and employs one fourth of the country's economically active population.

In the post-Revolutionary period, the Mexican government created favorable conditions for industrial development, by nationalizing the petroleum and electric power industries, establishing financial institutions, encouraging foreign investment and participating directly through government corporations in virtually every sector of the national economy. Under these conditions, industry grew considerably. At the outset, it followed import substitution policies for consumer goods and before long textile, food, iron and steel factories, among others, were set up in such urban centers as Mexico City, Monterrey, Guadalajara, Puebla and Veracruz. Later on, industry was diversified according to the country's development requirements, and major factories were set up to manufacture transport equipment, chemical products and machinery. However, Mexican imports of intermediate products and capital goods are still high.

This industrial growth concentrated in certain regions: the metropolitan areas of Mexico City, Monterrey and Guadalajara are responsible for two thirds of national manufacturing. The remaining cities in the country register low degrees of industrial development, and their productive structures are scarcely diversified, focusing mainly on food, clothing and non-durable consumer goods.

The industrial infrastructure is made up of many small and medium-sized establishments and a limited number of large enterprises, which represent a substantial share of total production.

The Assembly and Finishing Industries (La industria maquiladora). – In recent years, the establishment of *maquiladora* enterprises has flourished in the main northern border cities. These concerns come principally from the United States, and they assemble or transform raw materials and intermediate goods that are temporarily imported into Mexico and then returned to the country of origin as a finished product.

In the last few years, the *maquiladoras* have expanded further into Mexico, although those established near the border continue to predominate. The leading products processed in this way include electrical appliances, clothing and transportation equipment.

Trade and Services

Mexico's most important economic activities are trade and services (more than fifty percent of the total national product), which provide employment to one third of the economically active population of the country.

In the majority of Mexico's cities, activities pertaining to the service sector predominate. The distinctive feature of the trade and services sectors is the great number of small and medium-size enterprises, scattered throughout the country, whereas the large modern enterprises are concentrated in the main cities.

The Tourist Trade. – The tourist trade plays an important part in the economic growth of the country. The government coordinates the activities related to this sector, grants financial support and develops infrastructure through government enterprises.

The annual flow to Mexico of visitors from abroad reaches nearly five million, coming principally from its northern neighbor, the United States. In the main tourist areas, Mexico has developed an adequate network of hotels and services.

TIME CHART AND HISTORICAL NOTES

Origins

50 000 BC	The first settlers of America arrive from Asia across the Bering Strait.
12 000	The Tepexpan Man. The oldest human remains found in Mexico.
9 000	The domestication of corn.
7 000	Probable beginning of settlements and agriculture.

Pre-Hispanic Era

1800-200 BC **Preclassic Period**

Communities engaged in fishing, gathering, hunting and incipient agriculture. Appearance of ceremonial centers and fertility cults. Development of the **Olmec culture** (main ceremonial centers: La Venta, Tres Zapotes and San Lorenzo), which exerted a powerful influence throughout Mesoamerica. Settlement of the Mayan lowlands begins and the foundations of Monte Albán are laid.

200 BC-900 AD **Classic Period**

High level of urbanization, formation of theocratic ruling castes. Apogee of pre-Hispanic civilizations, flourishing of Mesoamerican art, ceramics, writing and the calendar. Multiplication of deities. Splendor of Teotihuacán, Monte Albán (Zapotec), Mitla (Zapotec), Uxmal, Palenque, Tajín, Cobá, Bonampak, Yaxchilán; fall of the great cities of Cacaxtla and Xochicalco.

900-1521 **Post-classic Period**

Militarization of the theocratic societies; metallurgy appears. Mesoamerica reaches its greatest expansion. Great development of the Toltecs in Tula. Peak of Mitla (Mixtec) and Monte Albán (Mixtec).

1325 **Foundation of México-Tenochtitlán,** beginning of the Mexica domination within the Mesoamerican territory and beyond.

1511 The shipwrecked crew of a Spanish boat is captured near Jamaica by the Yucatan Mayas. Among the Spaniards is **Gerónimo de Aguilar,** who eventually becomes Cortés' interpreter.

1517 Exploratory expedition of **Hernández de Córdoba** along the Yucatan coast.

1518 **Juan de Grijalva** sails from Cozumel Island to Cape Roxo on the Tamiahua Lagoon, along the Mexican coast, gathering the first impression of the splendor of Mesoamerica.

1519 Population of Mesoamerica: 25 000 000 inhabitants. **Alfonso Alvarez Pineda** sails along the Gulf Coast from Florida to the Pánuco River.

Feb. 1519 The Governor of Cuba, Diego de Velázquez, sends **Hernán Cortés** to the Yucatan coast.

Apr. 1519 Cortés founds the first Spanish town, **Villa Rica de la Vera Cruz** *(see p 215),* scuttles his ships and begins exploring the hinterland.

Nov. 1519 Arrival of the Spaniards at Tenochtitlán. **Moctezuma II** receives them peaceably, lodges them in the Palace of Axayácatl, and bestows honors on them. A few days after their arrival, Moctezuma II is emprisoned.

1520 Upon learning that Pánfilo de Narváez has arrived with orders to replace him, Cortés leaves Tenochitlan to encounter Narvaez in combat, leaving Pedro de Alvarado in command of the city. A religious celebration ends in the battle known as the **Great Temple Slaughter.** The besieged Spaniards are attacked while trying to escape and many die during the so-called **Noche Triste** or Sad Night.

May 1521 The Spaniards begin the siege of Tenochtitlán, which lasts 75 days, after conquering other Aztec fortifications.

Aug. 1521 **Fall of Tenochtitlán** *(p 104).*

Colonial Era

1524 Twelve Franciscan friars arrive in New Spain (Mexico).

1528 Charles V of Spain established in New Spain the first *Audiencia,* a government institution with judicial and executive powers.

1531 The second *Audiencia* was established, thus beginning the consolidation of Royal Authority, a task that is continued by the first two Viceroys: Mendoza and Velasco.

1522-1536 A series of expeditions is organized with a view to strengthening and expanding Spanish power: Cortés to Pánuco; Gonzalo Sandoval to Coatzacoalcos; Luis Marín to Oaxaca and Chiapas; Pedro de Alvarado to Guatemala; Olid to Zacatula and Michoacán; Nuño de Guzmán to the northwest, (the future kingdom of New Galicia).

1539	The first printing press in Mexico is established.
1551	Opening of the Royal and Pontifical University of Mexico, with the same privileges as Salamanca University in Spain, including five Faculties.
1566	Conspiracy of Martín Cortés. The Conquistadors revolt against the authority of Madrid.
1571	The Court of the Holy Office (Inquisition) is established.
1651	Birth of Sor Juana Inés de la Cruz, the renowned Mexican poetess, in San Miguel Nepantla.
1692	**Insurrection in Mexico City.** The mobs burn the Viceroy's Palace and City Hall.
1767	Expulsion of the Jesuits ordered by Charles III of Spain.
1809	The Valladolid conspiracy of Captain García Obeso, Lieutenant Mariano Michelena and Padre Vicente de Santa María, attempt to form an assembly to govern Mexico in the name of Ferdinand VII of Spain.
1810	**Querétaro Conspiracy** *(p 173)*. The conspirators of this city, with the support of the mayor, Miguel Domínguez, and his wife, María Josefa Ortiz, meet to discuss their plans for independence. Aldama and Allende attend these meetings and the latter informs the priest, Miguel Hidalgo y Costilla.
Sept. 1810	**The War of Independence** (1810-1821). El Grito de Dolores (Cry of Dolores): Hidalgo proclaims Mexico's independence in Dolores; taking the banner of the Virgin of Guadalupe, he is followed by the populace in arms.
1811	In the Puente de Calderón battle, the revolutionists are defeated and their leaders forced to go north in search of help, but Elizondo ambushes them in Acatita de Baján. Hidalgo, Allende, Aldama and Abasolo are tried and all except for Abasolo, are condemned to death. **José María Morelos** becomes Hidalgo's successor in the fighting and, in an early campaign, conquers nearly all the territory of the present state of Guerrero. He is joined by the Galván and Bravo brothers as well as by Vicente Guerrero.
1814	The Apatzingán Constitution, inspired by the French Constitution of 1793 and the Spanish Constitution of 1812, is announced by Congress but never implemented.
1817	Fighting by Francisco Xavier Mina, Mier y Terán, and Vicente Guerrero y Torres continues.
1821	**Agustín de Iturbide** proclaimes the Iguala, or Three Guarantee, Plan: one religion, solidarity among all social groups, and Mexican independence under a constitutional monarchy.
Aug. 1821	Viceroy Juan O'Donojú signs the Córdoba Treaty, ratifying the Iguala Plan.
Sept. 1821	Mexican independence is sealed with the triumphal entrance into Mexico City of the **Three-Guarantee Army** (Ejército Trigarante) led by Iturbide.

Independent Mexico

1822-23	**First Empire:** Iturbide is crowned Emperor Agustín I. At the beginning of 1823 **Antonio López de Santa Anna** launches the project of a Republic for Mexico, with the support of the former revolutionaries and royalists. Iturbide abdicates.
1824	Adoption of the **Constitution of Mexico,** establishing the Federal Republic.
1836	Texas, New Mexico and California declare their independence from Mexico *(see map p 31)*.
1846-48	Under the presidency of General López de Santa Anna, war with the United States breaks out. This conflict ends with the signature of the Treaty of Guadalupe, according to which Mexico recognizes the independence of Texas, New Mexico and California.
1858-61	Under Benito Juárez, the **Reform War** was fought between liberals and conservatives.
1859	The **Reform Laws** *(see p 31)* establish the nationalization of Church properties, civil marriage, a national registry office, cemeteries under municipal control, and freedom of worship.
1862	The **Battle of May 5th** (Batalla del 5 de Mayo), Puebla *(see p 165)*: the French are defeated by the national army.
1864	Second Empire: **Maximilian of Habsburg** is crowned emperor of Mexico. He signs the Treaty of Miramar according to which he must pay Napoleon III the exorbitant costs of the French invasion.
1867	Maximilian loses French protection and attempts to resign from the throne. However, the conservatives persuaded him to remain in power. He is attacked by the republicans and withdraws to Querétaro *(see p 174)*. Finally he is taken prisoner and shot on Cerro de Las Campanas. The Republic is reinstated, with Juárez as president.
1873	Under the regime of Lerdo de Tejada, the so-called Cristeros Rebellion begins in Guanajuato and Jalisco, as a protest against the Reform.

Under the rule of General **Porfirio Díaz,** Mexico achieves economic progress and expands its oil and mining industries; important public works are carried out and foreign investment is attracted.

1908 The Díaz-Creelman Interview *(see p 32)*; Díaz declares that his legitimate successor will be chosen in free and open elections. His words prompt the establishment of political opposition parties.

1910 **Francisco I. Madero** proposes the Plan of San Luis Potosí *(see p 32)*.

The Revolution

1910-20 The overthrow of President Porfirio Díaz. The military campaign of the Revolution.

1911 Emiliano Zapata proclaimed the Ayala Plan for agrarian reform, with his slogan: "Land and Liberty" ("Tierra y Libertad"). Madero accedes to the presidency.

1913 The **Ten Tragic Days** (Decena Trágica). During these ten days, Mexico City is under seige; Victoriano Huerta betrays Madero, by signing the Pact of the Citadel or of the Embassy. Madero and Vice President Pino Suárez are forced to resign and Pedro Lascurain is named interim president; Madero and Pino Suárez are taken prisoners and murdered two days later.

1917 The new constitution is adopted and Venustiano Carranza is elected president.

1919 Emiliano Zapata is assassinated.

1920 Congress appointes Adolfo de la Huerta provisional president of the Triumphant Revolution.

Contemporary Mexico

1929 Establishment of the first official political party, National Revolutionary Party (Partido Nacional Revolucionario), today the Institutional Revolutionary Party (Partido Revolucionario Institucional).

1938 President Lázaro Cárdenas decrees the expropriation of the foreign oil companies and nationalizes the petroleum industry (creating the Campania Exportadora del Petroleo Nacional). The railroads are nationalized and, one year later, are turned over to the railway workers' union.

1968 Violent university student demonstrations.

1982 President José López Portillo nationalizes the banking institutions.

1986 Sharp decline in petroleum prices. Mexico becomes a member of GATT (General Agreement on Tariffs and Trade).

(Photo GIRAUDON/Paris)

Illustration from *History of the Indians* by Durán, 1579

Approximately fifty thousand years ago the first settlers of the American continent came from Siberia across the Bering Strait, when the Wisconsin glaciation created a land bridge linking eastern Asia and western Alaska.

Preclassic Period. – Large agricultural communities engaged in cultivating corn, beans, hot peppers, and squash were established in the 18C BC in the middle of the continent, a region called Mesoamerica. The **Olmecs**, at the southern part of the Gulf of Mexico, started the construction of irrigation canals and raised platforms of earth and mud to worship the jaguar, which symbolized night and death. They also created systems of writing and numbering that soon were adopted by other communities.

Classic Period. – The emergence of highly populated cities in the 1C and 2C AD facilitated the priestly class's rise to political power. They imposed complex **polytheistic religions** that encompassed every aspect of life. Sanctuaries atop monumental pyramids overlooking broad plazas proliferated.
These **theocracies** remained in power for centuries, owing to extensive commercial networks and the production of ceramic and stone objects. The religious elite engaged in the study and practice of magic, religion, medicine, mathematics and astronomy.
Around the 7C AD, the social structure began to break down. Population growth without innovations in agricultural technology, impoverishment of the peasants, ever more dissatisfied with the established order, and invasions by nomadic groups from the north seem to have been the primary causes for this collapse.

Post-Classic Period. – The crisis unleashed was only brought under control two centuries later, through the emergence of **militaristic governments** that encouraged the worship of blood-thirsty divinities that demanded human sacrifices. The rapidly gained wealth of these new cities was based on heavy tributes exacted from the weaker tribes; this gave rise to tensions that increased under the **Aztec** or **Mexica** rule as of 1325.
The astonishing vitality, power and maturity of the Mesoamerican cultures, composed of nearly 25 million people in the 16C, were suddenly interrupted by the **Spanish Conquest** (1521), but their imprint still lingers, not entirely unchanged, in the indigenous population of Mexico.

(Photo Michelin)

Palenque. Temple of the Inscriptions

COLONIAL PERIOD

In 1519, **Hernán Cortés** reached the Mexican coast and rescued an old shipwreck survivor, **Gerónimo de Aguilar,** who lived among the Mayas in Yucatan. As he moved north, Cortés made contact with other indigenous peoples: in Tabasco he was offered twenty maidens, among them **la Malinche** who, along with Aguilar, was to be a key to the conquest of Mexico, since Aguilar spoke Spanish and Maya and Malinche was fluent in Maya and Nahuatl. Later Cortés founded Villa Rica de la Vera Cruz, where he established the first Spanish royal government on the American continent. From there he penetrated the hinterland, defeating the Tlaxcaltecs and converting them into powerful allies against the Mexica empire. **Moctezuma Xocoyotzin** welcomed him to México-Tenochtitlán, thus initiating the process that eventually led to his downfall *(p 104)*.
The Spanish soldiers who conquered México-Tenochtitlán were dissatisfied with their share of the booty and, although they were later given land, they did not consider that this was a proper reward for the services rendered to the king, since they had risked their lives and undergone untold hardships. Tilling the soil, they thought, was not a worthy occupation for men accustomed to the perils of war; they required wealth that would free them from farm work.

During the military campaign, the soldiers had discovered that there was abundant gold in the country, and they set out to in search of wealth. New soldiers and adventurers arrived during this century, and gold was the great attraction that impelled them to explore the northern regions, peopled by the savage and ferocious Chichimec tribes. Along with these adventurers went an imposing indigenous army that formed new settlements – Tlaxcaltec soldiers, who not only conquered but also populated cities and mixed with the indigenous Indians.

The Indians and the Spanish soldiers together developed the north, creating a new source of wealth more valuable than gold or silver, that is, agriculture and livestock raising. A key element in this conquest were the **missionaries**. The first to arrive were the Franciscans, followed by the Dominicans and, finally, the Agustinians. These missionaries performed a gigantic task: they dealt directly with the local peoples, learned their tongue, earned their trust and thus laid the groundwork for the fusion of these cultures.

INDEPENDENCE AND FIRST EMPIRE

On the morning of September 16th, 1810, in the atrium of the Dolores parish church in Guanajuato, **Miguel Hidalgo**, the town priest, called his parishoners to rise up in arms against the Spanish government and conquer their independence. With a handful of followers, he marched to Mexico City, accompanied by Ignacio Allende, Juan Aldama, Mariano Jiménez and Mariano Abasolo. They went by Atotonilco, where Hidalgo took the banner of the Virgin of Guadalupe as their flag, since nothing united the indigenous population more than their devotion to King Ferdinand VII of Spain or to the Virgin of Guadalupe, the Mexican Virgin.

In Guanajuato, Governor Riaño, a man interested in social issues, refused to surrender the city and took refuge in the Alhóndiga of Granaditas. This building was captured in a bloody battle by the rebels, who by then numbered over 30 000 – an utterly undisciplined horde of men, women and children, devoid of military leadership and training.

On the Mountain of the Crosses (Monte de las Cruces) beyond Toluca, in the immediate vicinity of Mexico City, a new battle was waged against the royalist forces and was won at the cost of a great many casualties. Nonetheless, Hidalgo did not dare to seize Mexico City, which, unprotected, was awaiting the revolutionaries' entrance. He instead decided to go to the United States of America to seek support for the Revolution.

However, once it had recovered from the inital surprise, the Spanish government sent General **Félix María Calleja del Rey** in pursuit of the revolutionaries. He had hastily raised an army in San Luis Potosí, which he trained around the clock in the Hacienda de la Pila. The confrontation took place in the town of Aculco, where the royalist army, though infinitely smaller in number, roundly defeated the disorganized and poorly led revolutionaries. The rebels scattered: Allende went to Guanajuato where he was again beaten, while Hidalgo moved to Guadalajara, where he declared the abolition of slavery, distributed land and suppressed the tributes paid by the Indians and destitute social groups, or *castas*. But Calleja caught up with Hidalgo there and inflicted a scathing defeat on him at Puente de Calderón. What was left of the revolutionary army was just a band of fugitives, seeking safety in the United States.

They passed through Zacatecas and went on to Saltillo, penetrating into the desert in an exhausting and hopeless operation. The royalist, **Ignacio Elizondo,** pretending to join the revolutionaries, betrayed them at Acatita de Baján, captured their leaders and shot them. By that time the fighting, carried on by a large number of revolutionaries, had devastated the countryside. Most of them had been leaders in Hidalgo's army, like Amo Torres in New Galicia, the priest José María Mercado in Nayarit, José María González Hermosillo in Sonora, Rafael Iriarte in Zacatecas, and the most brilliant of all, the priest **José María Morelos** in the south.

From the army organized by Morelos would emerge the chiefs of the second phase of the War of Independence: Mariano Matamoros, the Galeano and Bravo brothers and **Vicente Guerrero.** The latter was one of the few important leaders who would see independence consolidated on the 21st of September of 1821.

On September 27th of the same year, the Three Guarantee Army (Religion, Union and Independence) triumphantly entered Mexico City, headed by **Agustín de Iturbide.** The first independent government of Mexico was formed forthwith. The Constituent Congress was obliged to elect Iturbide as emperor, with the title of Augustine I. He was crowned in the Metropolitan Cathedral on July 21st, 1822, emperor of a territory that stretched from Oregon and the Colorado River to Panama.

In January of 1823, **Antonio López de Santa Anna** devised the **Plan of Casa Mata,** a project to establish a republic in Mexico. The plan was supported by the former revolutionaries, as well as by the Bourbonists of the Conservative Party, and put an end to the empire on March 19th of that year. Iturbide was exiled to Livorno, Italy and the old Captaincy General of Guatemala, together with the Central American States, decided to secede from Mexico and become independent.

REFORM AND SECOND EMPIRE

In December of 1855, **Ignacio Comonfort** became the surrogate president of Mexico. The times of anarchy and chaos, when Antonio López de Santa Anna had repeatedly governed, with the resulting loss of more than half of the Mexican territory to the United States, were left behind. In 1856 the implementation of reforms was initiated, with a view to separating church and state. In 1857 the Constitution was promulgated; under its provisions Ignacio Comonfort was elected president and Benito Juárez, vice president. Soon the Conservative Party rebelled and proclaimed the so-called Plan of Tacubaya, which was led by General Félix Zuloaga. In an effort to bring about peace in the country, Comonfort annulled the Constitution, thereby splitting his own Liberal Party. Under the leadership of **Benito Juárez,** this party joined the struggle for legality, albeit with an improvised and ill-equipped army.

The Conservative Party had professionally trained military leaders with broad experience in combat, among whom were outstanding generals such as Luís G. Osollo, Leonardo Márquez, Tomás Mejía, Miguel Miramón and Severo del Castillo, who forced Juárez to flee. After reaching the western coast at Mazatlán, Juárez sailed to Panama, crossed the isthmus, reached New Orleans, and thereupon returned to Veracruz, where he established his government. Meanwhile, the fighting was turning civilians into trained soldiers. Such was the case of Santos Degollado, Jesús González Ortega, Porfirio Díaz, Carlos Pacheco and many others. During three years they fought the Conservative forces, who had appointed General Miguel Miramón president of the Republic.

In Veracruz, Benito Juárez enacted the **Reform Laws** (Leyes de Reforma), whereby, among other measures, church property was nationalized, national registers under government control were instituted, the church was separated from the state, and cemeteries were placed under government administration. The Catholic Church protested, but by that time the Liberal Party was on its way to winning the war. As a result, leading members of the Conservative Party went to Europe in search of help, or even intervention, with the aim of bringing a European prince to rule Mexico. They believed that the civil war would not end unless a foreign power intervened. Both parties signed treaties: the Liberals with the United States (the McLane-Ocampo Treaty) and the Conservatives with Spain (the Mon Almonte Treaty). The former was never put into effect because the US Senate did not ratify it; and the latter was invalidated by the Conservatives' loss of the war. However, it did open the door to foreign intervention.

José María Gutiérrez de Estrada, Juan N. Almonte, and José Manuel Hidalgo worked actively to persuade a European power to intervene in Mexico. The opportunity arose when Eugenia de Montijo married Napoleon III, because, through her friendship with the Mexican conspirators, **Ferdinand Maximilian of Habsburg** accepted the then nonexistent Mexican crown. Thus Maximilian, with the support of France came to rule Mexico.

Meanwhile, after three years of civil war and the chaotic period that had preceded it, Mexico had fallen into a deep economic slump, compelling President Juárez to suspend payment on the public debt. The creditor nations – France, England and Spain – met in London, where they declared that they sought only a guarantee of payment of the Mexican debt and that Mexico's national integrity would be respected.

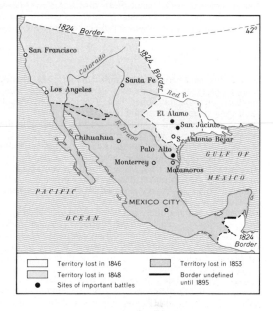

Territory lost in 1846
Territory lost in 1848
● Sites of important battles
Territory lost in 1853
━ Border undefined until 1895

As the expeditionary forces landed in Mexico, meetings were held with the Mexican government and the Soledad Treaties were signed. According to their provisions, England and Spain withdrew from Mexico, but France refused to do so and the invasion continued. On **May 5th, 1862** a fierce **battle** broke out in Puebla, which the Mexicans won; only one year later were the Napoleonic forces able to break through the resistance in that area.

President Juárez abandoned the capital of the Republic and started a long pilgrimage that took him as far as the northern border. In Paso del Norte (today Ciudad Juárez) he established his government, remaining there until the end of the Second Empire.

Groups of patriots sprang up everywhere to support the rebellion against the French army, Maximilian's government and his Mexican collaborators, until Napoleon III, under Prussian threat, was finally compelled to withdraw his troops from Mexico.

Maximilian of Habsburg, thus abandoned by his ally, chose to fight on against the Mexican forces, repatriating for this task Generals Miramón and Márquez, whom he had sent to Europe.

The Juárez forces kept on defeating the armies of the empire, finally trapping them in Querétaro, where he forced them to surrender. Maximilian and Generals Miramón and Mejía were taken prisoners and, after a military trial, were shot on June 29th, 1867. Juárez returned to Mexico City on July 15th, 1867, whereby the Republic was restored.

PORFIRISMO

In 1884, General **Porfirio Díaz** became president of the Mexican Republic for the second time. His main task was to maintain peace within the nation, for which he had to subdue various bands of highway robbers, as well as the few leaders who still harbored rebellious intentions. He organized a rural police force, known as the *rurales,* some of whom were social misfits or former delinquents, who found in this type of occupation a means of reestablishing themselves, or of obtaining a pardon. After numerous attempts at reform, this body was finally disbanded.

Peace and order in the countryside soon resulted in economic expansion, which was furthered by the introduction of modern farm implements and machinery.

As some of his fellow soldiers died or retired to private life, Díaz was able to place in his cabinet men who were unrelated to the military campaigns that had carried Díaz and his confederates to power; such was the case of **José Ives Limantour**, appointed Minister of Economy, who reorganized the public finances so as to leave an unprecedented surplus in the Treasury.

The relations between the Díaz government and the Catholic Church were amicable, although in order to maintain a spirit of submission in the clergy, the Reform Laws were left in abeyance; thus they were neither abolished nor implemented.

In international affairs Díaz tried to secure the friendship of all states and peoples, since after the death of Maximilian of Habsburg, ties with various European governments had been interrupted. His idea was that by seeking European help in political and economic affairs, he could counterbalance United States influence. This policy, however, proved costly in certain respects. For example, to obtain England's recognition of his government, Díaz was obliged to cede a part of Mexican territory, which was added to Belize in 1893. France became his closest and most influential ally. During Porfirio Díaz's regime, Mexican life followed French trends, to the extent of adopting a mansard-type architecture with slanted roofs in a country where it never snows.

Fashions, literature, military technology, agricultural manuals and such, all came from France, although, naturally, these **Frenchifying trends** only affected the middle and upper classes, since the common man remained untouched by their impact.

The pervasive paternalism of General Díaz's dictatorship did not prevent censorship and abuses perpetrated against the press, dispossession of peasants' land, with their resulting servitude to the hacienda system, unlimited working hours and the like – all of which caused groups to gradually seek political and social change.

REVOLUTION

In 1908, President Porfirio Díaz granted the journalist, James Creelman, a press interview, in which he asserted that he was firmly resolved to relinquish power at the end of his mandate, and that he hoped that a political party would be able to set up a truly democratic government at that time.

The interview aroused a veritable wave of euphoria in the populace, and groups were immediately formed with the intention of participating in the forthcoming political elections. Among the most enthusiastic was **Francisco I. Madero**; however, out of respect for the outgoing president, Madero originally intended to run for vice president. Nevertheless, in a meeting with Díaz, Madero lost all respect for him, and therefore decided to run for president. He was persecuted by the government and fled to the United States, taking refuge in Texas. In exile he launched the **Plan of San Luis Potosí** which called for an uprising on November 20th.

In the south several groups rose in arms *(see map below)*; in Guerrero state, the Figueroa brothers seized the capital, Chilpancingo, in 1911; and in Morelos state, Emiliano Zapata, the revolutionary leader who best understood the peasants' demands, succeeded in taking the cities of Cuautla and Cuernavaca in 1917. Victory came for the Revolution with the capture of Ciudad Juárez in the north. When President Díaz heard the news, wishing to avoid further bloodletting, he decided to give up the presidency and to sail for Europe, leaving Francisco León de la Barra as president. The latter signed with Madero the Treaties of Ciudad Juárez, whereby the revolutionary army was disbanded, leaving the federal army intact. Shortly after Madero assumed power as president, General **Victoriano Huerta** overthrew him in a bloody coup d'etat.

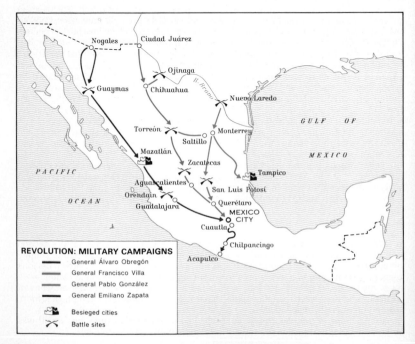

REVOLUTION: MILITARY CAMPAIGNS
General Álvaro Obregón
General Francisco Villa
General Pablo González
General Emiliano Zapata
Besieged cities
Battle sites

Madero could do little to prevent it, since all the revolutionary groups were clamoring for the immediate satisfaction of the demands that had originally roused them to arms – an impossible task to accomplish in a few months' time. Upon Huerta's accession to power as president, violence broke out anew; several attempts were made to overthrow the usurper and to avenge the deaths of President Madero and Vice President Pino Suárez. **Venustiano Carranza,** as the first constitutionally elected head of state, attacked Huerta *(plan p 32),* seconded by leaders like Alvaro Obregón, who directed the western campaign; **Pablo González,** in the east; and **Francisco Villa,** in the center. The latter, as head of the Northern Division, fought the most heroic battles against the Federal army, which was finally defeated at Zacatecas, thus leaving open the road to Mexico City.

(Photo GIRAUDON/Paris)

Emiliano Zapata

Nevertheless, schisms were appearing among the revolutionary forces: Carranza was not recognized by the Aguascalientes Convention, which nominated three different presidents. These proved incapable of commanding the respect required to rule the country.

Carranza escaped to Veracruz, where he established his government. **Alvaro Obregón's** military skills and strategy enabled him to overshadow Francisco Villa, whose army was destroyed on the fields of Celaya. Meanwhile, **Emiliano Zapata** was gathering strength in the Morelos mountains, although he was no immediate threat to the Carranza followers.

In 1917 Carranza enacted the new **Constitution,** which reflected the feelings of the revolutionary rank and file, thus satisfying the hopes of those who had fought against Díaz and the usurper, Huerta. It guaranteed an eight-hour working day and freedom of education, among other rights.

Upon finishing his term of office, Carranza wished to leave as his successor a person of his choice. This caused armed uprisings once more. The president was forced to flee and was assassinated while escaping. Emiliano Zapata and Francisco Villa were also murdered shortly thereafter.

CONTEMPORARY MEXICO

Starting with Adolfo de la Huerta as acting president, the process of national reconstruction began, a task to which later presidents also contributed. Plutarco Elías Calles completed the process, not only establishing peace, but also consolidating the political party which had emerged from the Revolution.

Under President **Lázaro Cárdenas's** regime (1934-1940), the undeclared civil war, which had begun in 1910, came to an end. He made peace with the *Cristeros,* defeated the rebel General Saturnino Cedillo and had him put to death. Peace allowed for larger resources to be allocated to education and culture. New primary schools for nearly 2 million children were built. In order to improve higher education, the National Polytechnic Institute (Instituto Politécnico Nacional), the Teachers' Training College (Escuela Normal Superior) and the Physical Education School (Escuela de Educación Física) were established. A Department of Indian Affairs was also set up in an effort to assimilate the Indian population into the mainstream of national development. The nationalist feelings awakened by the petroleum expropriations were strengthened by the creation of the National Institute of Anthropology and History, which began its work with the exploration of the Malinalco and Tajín archeological sites.

On these general bases, the post-Revolutionary governments established the policies that have shaped present-day Mexico.

Michelin Green Tourist Guides
Picturesque scenery, buildings
Attractive routes
Touring Programs
Plans of towns and buildings.

ART

Pre-Hispanic

In pre-Hispanic settlements, **ceremonial centers** played a prominent role. In these centers, surrounded by broad esplanades for public worship and open-air market installations, imposing tiered or pyramidal foundations were constructed, with temples on the top, some of them made of perishable materials. Only the nobility and the ruling elite could enter these small sacred chambers, which were decorated with striking symbols designed to inspire awe among the populace.

The location of the vast majority of these ceremonial centers was determined by the orientation of the temples and roads, in relation to the sunrise or the sunset in accordance with a series of complex astronomical calculations, some of which have yet to be fully elucidated by specialists of pre-Hispanic civilizations.

This monumental stone architecture, a product of collective effort and imagination, was designed to dominate the natural landscape through stunning interplays of volumes and spaces. Construction materials generally included adobes, precisely cut stone blocks and mortar.

Owing to the custom of using ancient mounds as a foundation for new structures, the part of the ruins that is visible today constitutes the last construction phase of a superimposed structure. This system managed to preserve the variety of Mesoamerican aesthetic components, which are all the more impressive in the light of its technological limitations, such as the lack of beasts of burden, the wheel and metal tools. In recent years, archeological explorations have focused on these great constructions, because the painting, sculpture and artifacts found in them reflect the customs and beliefs of the pre-Hispanic cultures. Sumptuous residences belonging to judges, rich merchants, leaders and priests, as well as government buildings, surround these centers. Some walls and the roofs of these palaces, formerly supported by wooden beams, have now almost entirely disappeared. The principal facades were generally painted, as were the statues and the floors, since color was especially meaningful in their peculiar vision of the world. Red represented blood and eternal life, black the netherworld and shadows. With a surprising feel for composition and movement, they used drawing to express the poetic language of the intellectuals on stelae, walls and **codices** *(see p 43).*

Toward the end of the Classic period, ritual **ball games** *(juegos de pelota)* appeared. This quasi-religious ceremony, not yet fully understood by specialists, was usually performed in double T-shaped fields. The ball players attempted to pass a rubber or wooden ball, symbolizing the sun, through the stone rings which generally were built into the ball court walls. In some cultures the ritual ended in the sacrifice of one of the contenders.

Through these expressions of Mesoamerican art, archeologists have inferred a sophisticated polytheistic religion, which acted as an integrating force. The whole world of forms that the potters masterfully rendered in the **ceremonial ceramics,** has a deep spiritual dimension, from the graceful feminine figurines, associated with fertility, to the elaborate multicolored vessels used to accompany the dead into the other world.

The ancient Mexicans had a complex understanding of inner life in which divine mercy was essential for survival. To venerate their deities they fashioned offerings of wood, bone, rock crystal and, in later eras, of gold, silver and copper, in which the craftsmen's skills and art are outstanding.

The reliefs with which they covered the stones were so fine that they appeared to be made of plasterwork. Their many sculptures are delightful for the profusion of fretwork, scrolls and details which portray realistically and accurately their most important gods, rulers and historical events.

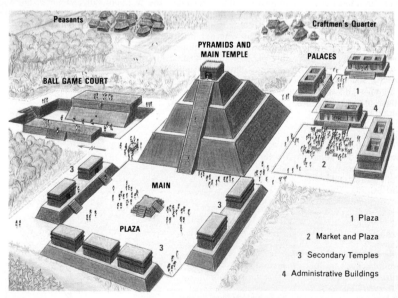

Components of a ceremonial center

Teotihuacán. View from the Pyramid of the Moon

Stucco modeling was also developed into a fine art, especially in the regions where stone was scarce, in which case this mixture of lime, sand and water was employed to adorn friezes, pillars and stairways.

On the periphery of the great ceremonial centers, the craftsmen lived and worked in one particular district; the peasants, on the other hand, were more widely distributed, living in modest huts made of adobe and straw near their farmlands. Few examples of these constructions have come down to us intact.

Cultural Regions of Mesoamerica

The West. – Since the Preclassic period, different peoples have inhabited the region between the south of Sinaloa and the state of Guerrero. As time went by, they constituted a geographic corridor, parallel to the Pacific Ocean, which facilitated the exchange of diverse cultural expressions from the southwestern United States to Ecuador and Colombia.

The better-known artistic works that have reached us come from the **Purépechas,** settlers in the area of Michoacán, whom the Spaniards called **Tarascos.** Compared with their contemporaries, they were very advanced from a technological point of view; their use of copper for decoration and for arms manufacture, made them one of the most difficult groups to subdue during the pre-Hispanic era.

In the field of architecture they achieved monumental proportions, as can be seen in their splendid capital, **Tzintzuntzan** *(p 211)*. Their excellent ceramics adopted abstract plant forms with a fine brilliantly colored finish.

In the present-day states of Colima and Nayarit, domestic animals were used as models in their various forms of artistic expression. Such was the case of the plump dogs that were an important part of the people's diet.

Central Plateau (Altiplano Central). – The abundant natural resources and the strategic advantages derived from occupying a central location have made this plateau the seat of the most powerful groups in Mexican history.

During the Preclassical period, the simple rural towns became the first ceremonial centers. In places like **Tlatilco,** they modeled statuettes related to agriculture and in other places, such as **Cuicuilco** *(see table p 36)*, the first great stone foundations were built.

In the Classic period, one of the most formidable religious metropolis of the ancient world flourished at **Teotihuacán** *(p 193)* – the cultural capital of Mesoamerica. From the monumental temples built atop artificial mountains, which blend in with the peaks on the distant horizon, the priestly leaders devised ideas and cults that extended as far as Guatemala.

The austere spirit of the era was expressed in architecture by the **talud-tablero** configuration, consisting of a series of sloping walls *(taludes)* surmounted by vertical panels *(tableros)*, which became a characteristic feature of the pyramid constructions in the region.

Political instability, war and famine may have caused the fall of this City of the Gods in the 8C AD. This collapse did not bring down Cholula or Cacaxtla and caused the subsequent rebirth of **Xochicalco** *(p 220)*, where one of the most famous *taludes* of Mesoamerica was carved.

At the beginning of the post-Classic period, Tula *(p 207)* started to exercise its power, exalting military values that were expressed architecturally in **warrior-shaped columns,** defensive walls and tombstones with representations of animals eating hearts. However, nomadic invasions put an end to this development, whereupon the Toltec population emigrated to the south, settling in faraway Chichén Itzá, a site where the Mayas masterfully interpreted the religion of the plateau.

After burning Tula, the Chichimecs from the north moved on to **Tenayuca** *(p 134)* and later to Texcoco, where they created a powerful kingdom.

CULTURAL REGIONS

1	WEST	**3**	GULF OF MEXICO	**5**	MAYA
2	CENTRAL PLATEAU	**4**	OAXACA	**6**	NORTH

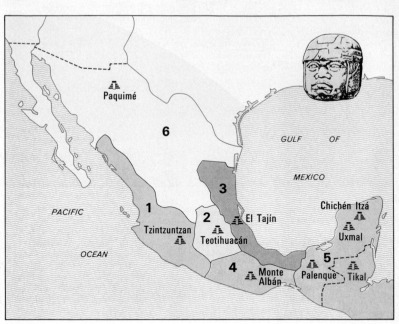

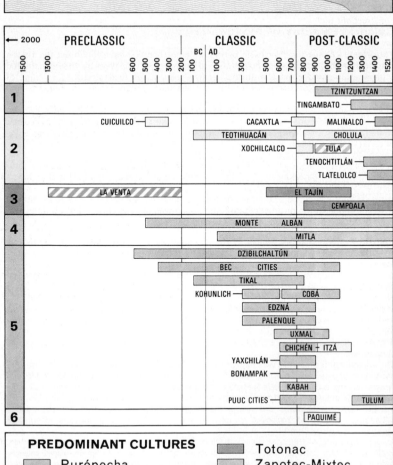

PREDOMINANT CULTURES

- Purépecha
- Aztec
- Teotihuacán
- Toltec
- Totonac
- Zapotec-Mixtec
- Olmec
- Maya
- Others

36

In 1325 the **Mexicas,** or **Aztecs,** founded the greatest religious, administrative and cultural center of pre-Columbian America, **México-Tenochtitlán** *(p 104).* Its powerful stone sculpture reveals a strong temperament: carved vases to contain sacrificial blood; reliefs of the sun with burning torches shaped like serpents; gods wearing the skin of their victims or covering their faces with tragic masks – all these constituted part of their broad repertory. The 13th of August, 1521, after a 72-day siege, the Spaniards took the city, thus initiating the colonial period.

Gulf of Mexico. – The Gulf basin, with a richly varied flora and fauna, witnessed three highly developed civilizations during the pre-Hispanic era.

Olmec. – Having laid down the basis for cultural development in Mesoamerica, the Olmec is considered the mother culture. It was established (1800 BC) in the region with the heaviest rainfall, between the basins of the Papaloapan and Grijalva Rivers. In this location, only a few poorly preserved archeological remains have survived. They produced monumental sculpture with astonishing **colossal heads.** The jaguar was their principal god. It was the first culture to carve a stone calendar. By concentrating power and knowledge in a single social group, they created rigid hierarchies. The leading ceremonial centers of the Olmec culture were San Lorenzo, La Venta and Zapotes.

Veracruz Center. – It flourished during the Classic period, after the construction of the city of **El Tajín** *(p 186),* when the **Totonacs** settled in the area. This group furthered trading with the plateau settlements. Also they carved astounding yokes, palms and funereal axes, which contrast with the infectious merriment of their **little smiling faces** (caritas sonrientes) modeled in clay.

Huastec. – The apogee of this group occurred in the post-Classic period in the northern part of the Gulf, where there was continuous fighting against the Mexicas. Their relative independence allowed them to concentrate their religious beliefs on fertility, producing sculptures of figures with prominent sexual organs and gods related to agriculture.

Oaxaca. – In the mountainous state of Oaxaca, numerous communities existed without common cultural links, a fact that can still be observed in their ethnic variety. In pre-Hispanic times the **Zapotecs** in the southeast, and later the **Mixtecs** in the northeast, predominated. Both located their principal ceremonial center in the heart of **Monte Albán** *(p 138),* **Mitla** *(p 136)* and **Yagul** *(p 137).* Monte Albán is the most interesting, because of its ingenious construction plan atop a hill and also because it was used both as a city and as a cemetery.

In the whole region, great architectural innovations appeared. One was the massive constructions that tended to horizontality, thus harmonizing with the terrain. Another was the use of the **tablero escapulario,** originated in Teotihuacán, and consisting of a vast panel on which moldings in the form of simple frets were applied as decorations; the play of light created a chiaroscuro effect. In the centuries immediately preceding the Spanish Conquest, **goldsmithing** was also highly developed in this region, noted for its extremely fine filigree. Other decorative arts using feathers, clay sculpture and stone carving bear witness to the creativity of local craftsmen.

Maya. – The Mayas, one of the most surprising peoples of the ancient world, inhabited the present-day Mexican states of Yucatán, Quintana Roo, Campeche, Tabasco and Chiapas and the countries of Belize, Guatemala, Honduras and El Salvador. Their admirable adaptation to an inhospitable climate is further evidence of their brilliant artistic and cultural development.

Constant observation of the stars' movements in the heavens, along with the enigmatic environment in which the Maya lived, may have contributed to enhance their acute perceptiveness and interpretative skills, which continue to astound and perplex researchers. Amidst these exuberant settings, the monumental ceremonial centers of **Uxmal** *(p 213),* **Palenque** *(p 156)* and **Yaxchilán** *(p 221)* remain as silent examples of the rich imagination evidenced in their mural paintings, stucco masks, decorated building facades with sober frets and elaborate cresting that lighten the overall appearance of the structures. Their ingenuity is demonstrated by the creation of the **false or Maya arch,** a triangular-shaped arch consisting of corbeled stone slabs meeting at the summit in a point or a slight curve. This skillful architectural solution allowed for the dome-shaped roofings that covered the temples. Special mention should be made of the exceptional **calendar glyphs** and sculptures, as well as their richly stylized and decorated ceramics.

In some cases the ceremonial centers were complemented with numerous **processional roadways** which the Mayas extended to connect different cities, thus building an ample network of roads, or **sacbés,** that promoted trade in the Yucatan Peninsula.

One of the most splendid ceremonial centers of the Maya culture was Tikal in Guatemala, characterized by its very lofty and imposing architecture.

Northern Cultures

The aridity of northern Mexico was one of the main hardships confronting its inhabitants, the **Chichimecs,** a semi-nomadic group that lived by gathering and hunting. The so-called Desert Cultures led such precarious existences that only in sites like **Paquimé** *(p 159)* did they achieve outstanding cultural expressions, as seen in their **ceramics,** decorated with very simple aquatic and plant motifs, and in their basketwork.

From the end of the Classic period, the Chichimec invasions of Mesoamerica fostered their cultural and ethnic mixing, radically changing the future of the Central Plateau settlers, who were subsequently obliged to defend their vulnerable northern frontier.

GODS IN PRE-HISPANIC MYTHOLOGY

PRINCIPAL ATTRIBUTE	NAME	CULTURAL ZONE	ICONOGRAPHY
Agriculture	Quetzalcóatl	Central Plateau	Feathered Serpent
	Kukulcán	Maya	Feathered Serpent linked to the wind
Heaven	Itzamná	Maya	Two-headed Lizard
Creator	Hunab Kú	Maya	Unrepresented
Fire	Huehuetéotl	Plateau & Gulf	Old Man holding a brazier
War	Huitzilopochtli	Aztecs	Hummingbird
	Tezcatlipoca	Aztecs	Jaguar claws on a foot
Moon	Coyolxauhqui	Aztecs	Bells on the cheek
Rain, Thunder	Tláloc	Central Plateau	Goggles and tusks
	Chac	Maya	Large-nosed mask
	Cocijo	Zapotecs	Goggles
	Tajín	Totonacs	Goggles and mustache guard
Corn	Xilonen	Aztecs	Woman adorned with corn ears
	Yum Kaax	Maya	Ear of corn in the hand
	Pitao Cosobi	Zapotecs	Ear of corn on the chest
Death, Darkness	Mictlantecuhtli	Plateau, Oaxaca	Thinness
	Ah Puch	Maya	Fleshless head
Renovation	Xipe Totec	Plateau, Mixtecs	Hide covering
Sun	Tonatiuh	Aztecs	Blond, with knife-shaped tongue
	Curicaveri	Tarascos	Old bent-over man with a brazier
Earth	Coatlicue	Aztecs	Skirt of serpents
Venus	Tlahuizcalpantecuhtli	Toltecs & Huastecs	Ascending god with claws
Wind	Ehécatl	All cultures in post-Classic period	Wearing a mouth mask shaped like a duck's bill
	IK	Maya	Letter T

(Photo Muller/C.E.D.R.I./Paris)

Presentation of offerings to the goddess of the sea

COLONIAL ART

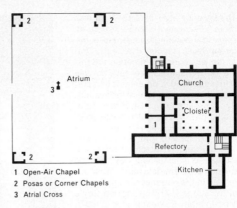

Sixteenth Century. – Colonial art in this century developed from the introduction of European customs in Mexico. In its evangelizing zeal, the Catholic Church promoted all the arts; as a result, non-religious arts, except for architecture, were negligible in colonial Mexico.

Under the friars' direction, convents and monasteries were built, along with structures unknown in Europe, such as the **atrium** to accommodate hundreds of Indian worshippers out in the open. Three types of **open-air chapels** (capilla abierta) were designed for celebrating mass. In the first one, the altar was set up at the church entrance, under the widest and tallest arch. The second type, called balcony style, was raised, as a rule, above the entrance and the facade panel. And the third, called the *exenta,* was provided with all the necessary installations to function independently of the church.

1 Open-Air Chapel
2 Posas or Corner Chapels
3 Atrial Cross

(From photo by Antonio Mercado/Mexico)

Calpan. – Corner chapel

Another innovation was the **posas** or **corner chapels** (capillas posas) used during processions to give The Most Holy (Santísimo) a pause. Since the processions were held in the open air, within the confines of the atrium, these were also called corner chapels because they were built in each corner of the atrium. The *posas* are, in fact, small rooms furnished with two entrances so as to go in by one door, carry out the established ritual, and exit through the other, directly facing the next chapel. Fortress-like churches were built with a single nave, as basilicas, in a mixture of styles: Romanesque, Gothic and Renaissance. The **Plateresque style** (the term is derived from the Spanish word for silversmith, *platero*) is characterized by finely carved ornamental motifs.

The cloisters also vary in style and in many of them mural paintings have been preserved, on such subjects as the New Testament or the saints.

As for sculpture, gigantic wooden altarpieces were carved and then gilded and adorned with Mannerist images *(estofadas)*, as well as oil paintings on wood. Painters such as **Simón Pereyns,** Andrés de la Concha, Juan de Arrué, the **Baltazar Echaves,** and others produced these works of medieval tone with Flemish or Italian influences.

The Baroque Period. – At the end of the 16C, architecture in Mexico underwent a radical transformation, when the secular clergy replaced the traditional priests, and more parish churches were founded.

The massive conventual structures were replaced by more modest constructions, adopting the Latin cross as the standard design, wherein the single nave is bisected by a transept, separating it from the presbytery. At the intersection, there was a cupola resting on pendentives. This allowed for the *cuadrante* or registry room (where marriages and baptisms were registered) and the sacristy to be placed on either side of the front wall. The priests' quarters *(casa cural)* generally flanked one side of the nave. Another innovation was the establishment of **nuns' convents,** in which there was no main portal, but rather two lateral entrances, to accommodate the high altar and the choirs – high and low – at opposite ends of the interior. The cloisters were generally very spacious – veritable women's villages – since it is believed that some convents accommodated over 300 nuns, in addition to the servants who attended them.

1 Registry Room
2 Sacristy
3 Priests' Quarters

(From photo by Antonio Mercado/Mexico)

Mexico City. The Metropolitan tabernacle

39

The Baroque style in New Spain was more decorative than structural, since few buildings presented a different basic layout. The early baroque was considered sober, moderate or transitional, because it was rather subdued in ornamentation and limited in terms of formal innovation. By approximately 1640, the Solomonic phase – so called because of its helicoidal, or spiral, columns – began to spread. Another characteristic baroque architectural form, the **estípite** – a pilaster with an inverted truncated pyramidal shape – first appeared in the altarpiece of the Chapel of the Kings (1718) in Mexico City's Metropolitan Cathedral *(see p 107)*. The 18C witnessed the introduction and development of a sumptuously ornate baroque variant called the **Churrigueresque style,** named after the renowned Spanish family of architects, the Churrigueras.

Civil architecture was prominent particularly in the beautiful city palaces, almost all built on a single design: a central patio, surrounded by four bays. By the 18C, these acquired a second floor, so that the ground floor was used for servants' rooms and rental space, leaving the second floor for the owner's house. These edifices gave an elegant air to the cities of that era.

(Photo Damm/ZEFA FRANCE)

Acolman Monastery. Facade

NINETEENTH CENTURY

From the middle of the 18C, various artists became interested in the novelties of neoclassical art and even attempted to found an academy, but lack of support from the Spanish and Viceroyal authorities foiled their plans. Nevertheless, neoclassical forms began to appear in their works, as was the case with the painter, **Miguel Cabrera,** and the architect, **Ortiz de Castro.** However, in point of fact the purity of the Greco-Roman styles never materialized, since the pervasive baroque influence persisted in the neoclassical style.

In 1785, the Royal Academy of Fine Arts of Mexico was founded, under the auspices of the Spanish King Charles III. This prestigious institution was subsequently renamed the **Academy of San Carlos** (Academia San Carlos) in honor of its royal founder. Among the European professors chosen to instruct the students were the sculptor and architect **Manuel Tolsá,** the painter **Rafael Ximeno y Planes,** and the metal engraver Jerónimo Antonio Gil.

Tolsá played an important role in Mexican architecture, both civil and religious. He is credited with the completion of the Metropolitan Cathedral, the Mining School (Escuela de Minería) and the plans for the Cabañas Hospice, to mention only a few.

Among the more famous architects of this period, **Francisco Eduardo Tresguerras** (1759-1833) was notable; besides being an architect, he was a painter, a sculptor, a musician and a poet. He exercised great influence in central Mexico, planning and building many works, such as the Carmelite church at Celaya in Guanajuato state.

In the painting of this period, only **Ximeno y Planes** contributed with substantial work, including the mural dedicated to the Virgin of Guadalupe that he created for the chapel of the Mining School.

From 1810 on, New Spain was in a state of war, so that artistic production diminished sharply. Many artists participated in the War of Independence, and more than a few died for the cause, as was the case with José Luis Rodríguez Alconedo, painter and goldsmith, who was killed while serving in the army of José María Morelos. In 1821, Mexico gained independence from Spain, but the war did not end. Many of the groups involved in that combat took up new banners, and the fighting continued.

This situation was exacerbated by two French military interventions and one more from the United States. Only in 1884, when General Porfirio Díaz became president of the Republic for the first time, was peace reestablished, allowing artistic endeavors to flourish anew.

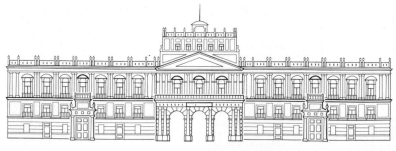

Mexico City. Minería Palace. Main facade

Meanwhile, in 1847 the Academy was reorganized, and a new group of European artists came to Mexico to teach various courses. Prominent among them were the painters **Pelegrín Clavé** and **Eugenio Landesio**. Clavé managed to form a large group of students who in time became fine artists: among them Santiago Rebull, José Salomé Pina, Felipe Gutiérrez and José Obregón are to be noted. From this same period, **Juan Cordero,** who had studied in Rome but left the most important part of his work in Mexico, today on exhibit in the National Art Museum *(p 120),* should be mentioned. Landesio's best student was **José María Velasco,** a famous landscapist with exceptional gifts as a draftsman and colorist, and whose works are also on display at the National Art Museum.

A second group emerged years later, with artists like Felipe Soho, Luís Coto and Martín Soriano. Their works can also be found at the National Art Museum.

Independently from the Academy of San Carlos, **Agustín de Arrieta** worked in Puebla; **Hermenegildo Bustos,** in Guanajuato; and **José María de Estrada** in Guadalajara.

As for sculpture, the Spanish master, Manuel Vilar, directed the School of Sculpture, but without Clavé's success. *The Tlahuicole, a Traxcaltec warrior,* by Vilar is preserved in the National Art Museum.

Also outstanding as a sculptor was **Miguel Noreña,** to whom we owe the sculpture of Cuauhtémoc, at present on Paseo de la Reforma.

In architecture, the period was not particularly notable. While Javier Cavallari lectured at the Academy, he did not succeed in producing a large number of outstanding students. **Lorenzo de la Hidalga** was the most prominent; among his many works, the cupola of the church of Santa Teresa la Antigua, on the east side of Plaza de la Constitución, and the pedestal of the sculpture called *El Caballito (p 120),* are famous.

Among the Romantic school painters, in the last years of the 19C, the following are worthy of mention: **Germán Gedovius,** an excellent European-trained painter; and **Joaquín Claussel,** the only Mexican Impressionist, whose studio in the House of the Counts of Calimaya includes remarkable examples of his work. **Julio Ruelas** was a genuine representative of Romanticism and an extraordinary draftsman, who produced not only paintings but also engravings. However, his work is difficult to find, since it is scattered in many private collections. **Saturnino Herrán,** a forerunner in the treatment of Mexican themes, must also be cited; he was the first to exalt the indigenous population and the humble people, thus becoming the immediate predecessor of the great Mexican muralists.

(Photo Guillermo Aldana/Mexico)

Guadalajara. Father Hidalgo as depicted
in the mural by Orozco
in the Government Palace

TWENTIETH CENTURY

Diego Rivera was the founder of the Mexican school of mural painting, which included great figures like **José Clemente Orozco** and **David Alfaro Siqueiros**. The idea was to teach Mexican history through painting. **Rufino Tamayo,** their contemporary, worked independently.

In the shadow of these painters, another distinguished group was formed, that included Pablo O'Higgins, Fernando Leal, Alfredo Zalce and many others, and more recently, Francisco Toledo, Francisco Corzas, **José Luís Cuevas** and **Pedro** and **Rafael Coronel.**

Since the time of General Lázaro Cárdenas, architecture has taken an innovative path, with the use of concrete and glass, creating novel forms and spaces. The architects **Luís Barragán,** Ricardo Legorreta, Teodoro González de León, Abraham Zabludovsky and especially **Pedro Ramírez Vázquez,** are all internationally known.

In the field of sculpture, Mexico has produced few great national artists, but Ignacio Asúnsolo and more recently, **Francisco Zúñiga,** Baltazar Martínez and Julián Martínez Sotos should be mentioned.

In recent years, interest in handicrafts has increased considerably and in response to this, state institutions have been set up to ensure the conservation of traditional forms and techniques and to promote quality crafts and new designs. This policy has been applied particularly in the state of Michoacán.

(Photo Benser/ZEFA FRANCE)

Mexico City. University Campus –
mural by Siquieros

Mexico	Date	Other Civilizations
	BC	
First settlers on the American continent.	**50 000**	
	30 000	Paleolithic period. Rupestrian paintings in southwest France and northern Spain.
	3000-1750	Babylonia flourishes. Pyramids of Giza and the Great Sphinx.
Olmecs flourish.	**1820-200**	
Archaic cultures: Copilco, Cuicuilco.	**1520-200**	
Monte Albán begins. Maya	**800**	Olympic Games in Greece.
lowlands begin to be settled.	**500**	
	447-432	Parthenon constructed in Athens.
Foundation of Teotihuacán.	**200-150**	
	AD	
	Approx. 72-80	Construction of the Coliseum in Rome.
Climax of Teotihuacán.	**200-500**	
Peak of Maya culture.	**300-900**	
	313	Edict of Milan.
	330	Founding of Constantinople.
Great development of Monte Albán.	**400-800**	
	532-537	Hagia Sophia is built in Constantinople.
Splendor of Xochicalco.	**800**	Charlemagne is crowned emperor in Rome.
Maturity of Toltec culture: Tula.	**1000**	
	1000-1150	Romanesque period.
Flourishing of stone sculpture in the Huastec culture. Founding of Tenochtitlán.	**1100-1400**	
	1163-1235	Notre-Dame Cathedral built in Paris.
Under Moctezuma I, stone buildings following an overall plan are constructed.	**1469**	
	1492	Columbus discovers America.
	1508-1512	Michelangelo paints the Sistine Chapel.
Hernández de Córdoba explores the Yucatan coast.	**1517**	Luther's Protestant Reformation.
Cortés arrives in Veracruz.	**1519**	Mannerism flourishes.
Fall of Tenochtitlán.	**1521**	
	1527	Pizarro discovers the Inca Empire.
	1540	Foundation of the Society of Jesus. The Portuguese arrive in Japan.
With the discovery of Zacatecas, a mining boom starts.	**1545-1563**	Council of Trent; Counter Reformation.
The Inquisition.	**1547**	
	1598	Construction of the Escorial Monastery in Spain.
	1656	Diego de Velázquez paints *Las Meninas*.
	1661-1710	Palace of Versailles.
Measures taken by the Bourbon government in Spain provoke discontent among the Spanish Americans which leads to the War of Independence from Spain.	**1740**	
Jesuits expelled from New Spain.	**1767**	Jesuits expelled from Spain and her empire.
	1776	The United States of America gains independence from England.
	1789	French Revolution.
Iturrigaray captured by government agents.	**1808**	Napoleonic invasion of Spain.
War of Independence	**1810-1821**	Bourbon monarchy restored in Spain. Napoleon abdicates at Fontainebleau.
Independence is achieved with the Iguala Plan by Iturbide.	**1821**	Greek War of Independence against the Turks.
Empire of Agustín de Iturbide	**1822-1823**	Absolutism reestablished in Spain.
Guadalupe Victoria, first President of Mexico.	**1824-1829**	
Loss of Texas, New Mexico and California, under the presidency of Santa Anna.	**1836**	Peak of Industrial Revolution. Proclamation of the French Republic. Marx and Engels publish *The Communist Manifesto*.
Reform Laws	**1859**	Darwin: *The Origin of the Species*.
French Intervention, Battle of May 5th in Puebla.	**1862**	
Maximilian of Habsburg, Emperor of Mexico.	**1864**	
	1865	End of the American Civil War. Lincoln assassinated in USA.
The Republic is reestablished with Juárez.	**1867**	Marx: *Das Kapital*
	1874	First exhibit of Impressionist painting.
Porfirismo.	**1877-1910**	End of the Carlista War in Spain. Setting up of the Triple Alliance and the Triple Entente.
First industrial strikes.	**1906**	
	1907	Pablo Picasso paints *Les Demoiselles d'Avignon*.
Mexican Revolution.	**1910-1920**	First World War. Russian Revolution. Futurism and Dadaism.
Manifest of the Painters' and Sculptors' Union, starting point of muralism.	**1922**	
	1924	Surrealist Manifesto in Paris.
Foundation of the Partido Nacional Revolucionario (later, PRI).	**1929**	The Great Depression.
Presidency of Lázaro Cárdenas. Expropriation of foreign oil companies.	**1934-1940**	Spanish Civil War; Second World War.

LITERATURE

Pre-Hispanic Period. – The literature of Mesoamerica reflects the world view, the socio-political evolution, the philosophical thinking and the history of the pre-Hispanic peoples. It is expressed through pictographic, ideographic and, in some cases, oral means. During the colonial period, friars and Indian and mestizo historians started the ambitious task of analyzing and interpreting such varied works – an endeavor that continues to the present day.

In the Maya culture there are two fundamental works: the **Book of Popol Vuh,** which is an epic narration about the origins of the Mayas and the **Book of Chilam Balam,** which is a series of chronicles written by priests.

In the Náhuatl culture, there are many well-preserved documents: *The Twenty Hymns of Tepeapulco; the Poem of Quetzalcóatl,* and the *Mexican Codices and Songs,* where myths, legends, proverbs and riddles codes are treated.

Colonial Period. – Once the Conquest was over, the chronicle *(crónica)* was the first genre to be cultivated. The best examples are: the **Letters Reporting the Discovery and Conquest of New Spain by Hernán Cortés** *(Cartas de Relación de Hernan Cortés) (see p 104)*; and *The True History of the Conquest of New Spain (La Historía Verdadera de la Conquista de la Nueva España)* by **Bernál Díaz del Castillo.** The missionaries **Sahagún** *(see p 154),* **Motolinía** and **Fray Bartolomé de las Casas,** among others, recorded the native customs to understand the Indian peoples in order to teach them the new religion.

The theater was used mainly as a means of propagating the Catholic faith, in many cases, staging *autos sacramentales* – religious mystic plays – and presenting works written by the friars themselves. In the context of this new colonial society, the plays of **Juan Ruíz de Alarcón** were remarkable. He developed an original style for his theater of characters, as seen in his play, *The Truth Suspected (La Verdad Sospechosa).*

Nevertheless, in the 17C, there was a change of outlook; literature came under the strong influence of Gongorism, meshed with Conceptism, which became ever more extreme and extravagant in its pursuit of refinement and culture.

Sor Juana Inés de la Cruz *(p 118),* a nun with great intellectual gifts and sensitivity, succeeded in breaking with the contrived literary style of the period. She wrote with equal mastery poetry, *Quatrains and Sonnets (Redondillas y Sonetos);* prose, *Reply to Sor Filotea (Carta a Sor Filotea de la Cruz);* and theater, *The Obligations of a Home (Los Enredos de una Casa).* Of no less importance is the work of **Carlos de Sigüenza y Góngora,** a historian, poet, scientist and prominent personality of his time.

(Photo Ignacio Urquiza/Mexico)

Portrait of Sor Juana Inés de la Cruz

In the 18C, a reaction led by the Jesuits **Landívar, Clavijero** and **Alegre** broke out against the literary decadence that continued to predominate. They cultivated good Latin poetry and translated the classics. The latter two were also excellent historians.

Nineteenth Century. – During the first decade, political pamphlets became the main literary instrument, both for the royalists (with a refined and cultivated style) and for the rebels (with a plain and natural style).

José Joaquín Fernández de Lizardi, editor of the weekly, *El Pensador Mexicano,* wrote in those years the first profoundly Mexican novel: *El Periquillo Sarniento,* in which a feeling of social moralizing prevails.

In 1836, **José María Lacunza** and **Rodríguez Galván** founded the Academy of Saint John Lateran (Academia de San Juan de Letrán), giving a new impulse to literature through the study of grammar, versification, serious criticism and new theses.

The political confrontations continued and, from this , a literary division arose. On the one hand, Romanticism, with revolutionary tendencies, was initiated by **Fernando Calderón,** followed by **Guillermo Prieto** and culminated in the tragic figure of **Manuel Acuña.** On the other hand, Classicism was represented by **José Joaquín Pesado,** in poetry, and **Ignacio Ramírez,** in the novel – both humanists of refined culture and exquisite style.

The political peace achieved during the era of Porfirio Díaz is echoed in the periodical *El Renacimiento,* where writers of the most diverse ideological currents collaborated, such as **Manuel Payno, Roa Bárcenas, Justo Sierra** and others.

The novel as an artistic form was infused with nationalistic feelings and themes in the works of **Ignacio Manuel Altamirano, Emilio Rabasa, José López Portillo Rojas, Rafael Delgado** and **Federico Gamboa.**

Modernism arrived in Mexico with **Gutiérrez Nájera, Salvador Díaz Mirón** and **Amado Nervo** who contributed to the periodical *Azul,* and reached its peak with *Revista Moderna,* which published pieces by leading writers including **Olaguíbel.**

Twentieth Century. – The Mexican Revolution (1910) was a major source of inspiration for novels and stories in the years following the fighting. Two notable works were *The Underdogs (Los de Abajo)* by **Mariano Azuela** and *The Eagle and the Serpent (El Aguila y el Serpiente)* by **Martín Luís Guzmán.**

Mention must also be made of the work of three important writers: the influential humanist and philosopher **José Vasconcelos,** author of *A Creole Ulysses (Ulises Criollo);* the critic, **Alfonso Reyes,** who wrote *The Demarcation (El Deslinde);* and essayist **Antonio Caso,** renowned for his work entitled *The Human Being (La Persona Humana).*

The various tendencies of the last decades surfaced in periodicals like *Contemporáneos,* which seeks to introduce Mexican literature into the European avant-garde trends and to promote the stylistic renovation begun by the poet, **López Velarde,** author of *Suave Patria.* To this group belong **Jorge Cuesta, Rodolfo Usigli** and the great poet, **Carlos Pellicer.**

Another periodical is *Taller* in which poets and novelists led by **Octavio Paz,** author of *The Labyrinth of Solitude (El Laberinto de la Soledad),* met to combat the aestheticism of the periodical *Contemporáneos.*

In mid-century, the revolutionary novel reappeared with *The Edge of the Storm (Al Filo del Agua)* by **Agustín Yañez,** precursor and professor of the present generation of writers: **Rosario Castellanos, Carlos Fuentes, Jorge Ibargüengoitia,** and **Juan Rulfo,** father of Magic Realism as exemplified by his work, *Pedro Páramo.*

Among the playwrights, the following should be highlighted: **Vicente Leñero, Emilio Carballido** and **Luisa Josefina Hernández;** among the short story writers, **Edmundo Valadés** and **Francisco Rojas González;** and among the poets, **Ali Chumacero, Efraín Huerta** and **José Emilio Pacheco,** who also writes short stories.

Further Reading. – *See page 228.*

FOLKLORE

Mexico is a country with traditions that are rooted in the merry and religious character of its people. These traditions cover all aspects of Mexican life; festivities, art, work and business are all deeply immersed in popular feelings.

Festivals and Fairs. – *See also table p 45.* Most of these festivals and fairs have a religious origin, for they celebrate the patron saint or commemorate an important date in the liturgical calendar. Sometimes they coincide with events of local life such as harvesting, planting, livestock or industrial fairs.

Religious Events. – Some religious celebrations reveal the merry character of the Mexican people. Such is the case with the *Pastorelas,* which can be traced back to the theatrical performances organized by Catholic friars in colonial times. However, in other cases utmost solemnity surrounds the religious experience as during Holy Week celebrations.

Music and Dances. – Mexican music and dances constitute veritable feasts for the eyes and ears, on account of the colorful costumes worn by the participants and the population at large; the rhythms and dances performed include the waltzes and polkas of the north, the mariachi music of Jalisco, the merry *sones* from Veracruz and Huasteca, the nostalgic marimba music from the Isthmus and the romantic *trova* of Yucatan.

Tianguis and Markets. – *Tianguis* are handicraft fairs whose origins date back to pre-Hispanic times. European-style markets were introduced during the colonial period. In many regions throughout Mexico, the visitor will discover these bustling centers of activity with their fabulous display of arts and crafts, fruits, flowers, as well as a wide range of industrial products.

Charrería. – Mexican horsemen, *charros,* constitute a fundamental part of the national folklore. Their feminine counterpart is *Adelita,* a renowned personality of the Revolution. The contest in which they attempt a series of daring feats of horsemanship, reminiscent of hacienda life in pre-Revolutionary times, is called *Jaripeo.*

(Photo Grathwohl/ZEFA FRANCE)

Matachines Dancers

FESTIVALS AND FAIRS

DATE AND PLACE	TYPE OF EVENT
January	
18 **Taxco** (Gro.)	Birthday songs *(mañanitas)* and typical dances in honor of the Patroness, Santa Prisca
20 **Chiapa de Corzo** (Chis.)	Festival of Saint Sebastian. Dance of the *Parachicos*. Reenactment of a battle on the Grijalva River with fireworks.
22 **Tehuantepec** (Oax.)	Parade of the brides or single girls in lovely costumes. In the evening and night, a torchlight parade.
February or March	
Mardi Gras *(Carnaval)*	
San Juan Chamula (Chis.)	The natives leap over a barrier of fire to purify themselves. They cover their bodies with monkey fur.
Huejotzingo (Pue.)	Various events. Representation of a battle between the French and the Mexicans, and the abduction of the famous bandit, Agustín Lorenzo.
Mazatlán (Sin.)	The best in the north. Parade of floats, costume balls.
Veracruz (Ver.)	One of the liveliest. Parade of floats. Costume balls. Election of the King of the Mummers.
Ash Wednesday	
Amecameca (Mex.)	Solemn procession with the Christ of the Holy Mountain *(Sacromonte)* during the night. Meanwhile the *Chinelo* dancers perform.
Palm Sunday	
All over Mexico	In the church atriums, palms in various forms are sold; the priest blesses them to commemorate triumphal entry of Jesus.
Holy Week	
Taxco (Gro.)	Reenactment of the Passion of Jesus Christ.
Tuesday of Holy Week	
Xochimilco (D.F.)	Flower Fair. Exhibition of flowers in the boats on all the canals.
Holy Friday	
Col. Roma (D.F.)	Procession of Silence.
San Luís Potosí (SLP)	Procession of Silence.
Saturday of Holy Week	
Plaza de Santo Domingo (D.F.)	Burning of cardboard Judases, representing famous people.
Corpus Christi Thursday	
D.F.	In the atrium of the cathedral and the basilica, the local speciality, *mulitas*, are sold. The children wear Indian dress and carry boxes of fruit.
April	
25 **Aguascalientes** (Ags.)	Saint Mark's Fair *(p 57)*.
May	
Morelia (Mich.)	International Organ Festival.
June	
Guadalajara (Jal.)	Parade of floats, dances and mariachis in honor of Saint Peter.
July	
17 **San Cristóbal de Las Casas** (Chis.)	Procession of San Cristóbal, Indian dances.
2nd & 3rd Mondays	
Oaxaca (Oax.)	*La Guelaguetza (p 148),* colorful festival of ethnic dances and costumes of the region.
August	
2nd Week	
Huamantla (Tlax.)	Assumption of the Virgin. Beautiful exhibit of small rugs made of flowers and sawdust – ancient pre-Hispanic tradition.
15 **Celaya** (Gto.)	Fair of the *Cajeta* (a local candy). Dances, fairs and fireworks.
27 **Zacatecas** (Zac.)	In the Pradera del Bracho (behind Cerro de la Bufa), the inhabitants reenact a battle between Moors and Christians, dressed in colorful costumes.
September	
14 **Zacatecas** (Zac.)	Our Lady of the Patronage. The *matachines* dance during ten days, coinciding with the National Fair and other events.
15 **D.F.**	From the National Palace, the president commemorates the Cry of Independence *(Grito de Independencia)*.
Dolores Hidalgo (Gto.)	Staging of the ceremony of the Cry of Independence.
October	
12 **Guadalajara** (Gto.)	Procession of the Virgin of Zapopan. Coincides with the October festivals and with a variety of events.
24 **Cuetzalan** (Pue.)	Coffee Fair, attended by the Indian groups of the region, who perform dances like the *Negritos* and the *Volador*.
Guanajuato (Gto.)	Cervantino Festival *(p 88)*.
November	
The 1st at midnight	
Janitzio (Mich.)	Festival of the Dead *(p 160)*.
December	
1 **Taxco** (Gro.)	The Silver Fair. Meeting and exhibit of the silversmiths' best work.
12 **D.F.**	Our Lady of Guadalupe. Pilgrimages; birthday songs *(mañanitas)* and dances in honor of the Virgin.
16-24 **Querétaro** (Qro.)	*Posadas*. Procession with images of Saint Joseph and the Virgin, going from church to church, asking for shelter. *Piñatas* (decorated clay pots filled with sweets and fruits) are broken.
31 **Villa Escalante Santa Clara del Cobre** (Mich.)	Procession of the Holy Sacrament; the participants carry images by candle and torchlight.

MEXICAN FOOD

The richness and variety of Mexican cuisine have made it one of the most appreciated in the world.

Its origins may be traced back to the pre-Hispanic period, to the so-called Corn Cultures, which developed varied recipies using corn, hot peppers *(chiles)*, rabbit, armadillo and turkey. Some dishes were specially prepared as offerings to the gods and to the dead. With the Conquest, New Spain's cuisine underwent enormous changes, owing to the introduction of fruits, cereals, spices, beef and lamb... The nuns took particular advantage of the fusion of the two gastronomic traditions to create some of the delicious dishes that can be enjoyed today.

During the rule of Maximilian (1860s), local cooking was further enriched by the influence of refined French cuisine.

Today, essential elements of Mexican cooking, offering a delicious gamut of flavors, smells and colors, are: the snacks, or **appetizers,** *(antojitos)* such as tacos and quesadillas; the soups, meats, fowl and fish, as varied as the regions of the country; the desserts, which mostly come from the colonial convent kitchens; the home-made sweets; the breads, of whimsical shapes and amusing names; and the drinks – tequila, mezcal, pulque, beer, tropical fruit juices and a drink made of cornflour called *atole*, which is sometimes mixed with chocolate *(champurrado)*.

STATE	TRADITIONAL DISHES AND DESSERTS
Aguascalientes	Barbecued steak wrapped in maguey leaves *(barbacoa de lomo)*
Baja California	Fish and shellfish *(pescados y mariscos)*: small fish *(cabrilla)*, lobster, abalone. Bread pudding *(capirotada)*
Campeche	Salted fish *(esmedregal)*, giant shrimp *(camarón gigante)*
Coahuila	Beef jerky with scrambled eggs *(machaca con huevo)*, tripe soup *(menudo norteño)*, beef jerky *(tasajo)*, milk sugar bars *(jamoncillos)*
Colima	Fish and shellfish
Chiapas	Spicy hotpot *(olla podrida)*, egg cakes bathed in syrup *(chimbo)*, roast pork spiced with garlic and chiles *(cochito al horno)*, beef jerky *(tasajo)*, tripe and liver with tomatoes *(putzaze)*
Chihuahua	Meats, fried jerky with scrambled eggs, *(machaca con huevo)*, tortillas with ham and cheese *(burritas)*, cheese *(queso)*
Durango	Tripe soup *(menudo)*
Guanajuato	Snacks: tacos, fried stuffed turnovers *(quesadillas)*, tortillas with chicken and beans *(chalupas)*, toffee twists *(charamuscas)*
Guerrero	Fish and shellfish: red snapper *(pescado a la talla)*, large oysters, clams. Green hominy soup *(pozole verde)*. tamarinds, coconut pudding *(cocadas)*
Hidalgo	Spicy stew *(tinga)*, marinated meat wrapped in maguey leaves and baked in a pit, *(barbacoa)*, spiced chicken wrapped in maguey leaves *(mixiotes de pollo)*, stuffed banana leaves *(zacahuiles)*, fried cactus worms *(gusanos de maguey)*, ant eggs *(escamoles)*, meat and potato turnovers *(pastes)*
Jalisco	Hominy soup *(pozole)*, chicken broth with avocado and chile *(caldo tlalpeño)*, meat broth with tomatoes *(birria)*, fried tortillas covered with meat, salad and sauce *(tostadas)*, steamed corn husks filled with meat *(tamales)*, custards *(dulces de leche)*, wine-flavored candies *(borrachos)*, fruit-flavored drops *(arrayanes)*
México and Valley of México	Red sausage *(chorizo)*, blood sausage *(moronga)*, spiced meats wrapped in maguey leaves *(mixiotes)*, cheese, butter, candied fruits grasshoppers *(chapulines)*, Oaxaca cheese, egg bread *(pan de huevo)*, chocolate. Broth of *indianilla*, meat and vegetable soup *(puchero mexicano)*, cactus paddle salad *(ensalada de nopales)*, pork cracklings *(chicharrón)*, rosemary cooked in chile sauce *(revoltijo)*, tamales, amaranth seed cakes *(alegrías)*, squash seeds in caramel *(pepitorias)*, round fritters with syrup *(muéganos)*, meringues *(merengues)*, grated cocount candies *(duquesas)*, paper-thin fritters *(buñuelos)*
Michoacán	White fish *(pescado blanco de Pátzcuaro)*, deep-fried freshwater fish *(charales)*, deep-fried pork *(carnitas)*, local varieties of tamales *(corundas and uchepos)*, fruit jellies *(ates)*, caramels *(morelianas)*
Morelos	Broth with tomato and chile *(clemole)*, cured pork ground with chile and spices *(longaniza en salsa verde)*, jerked beef *(cecina)*
Nayarit	White hominy soup *(pozole blanco)*, fish and shellfish, charcoal grilled fresh fish *(pescado zarandeado)*
Nuevo León	Roasted kid *(cabrito)*, custard tarts *(glorias)*

STATE	TRADITIONAL DISHES AND DESSERTS
Oaxaca	Numerous dishes with *mole,* the traditional thick sauce composed of chile, seeds, spices and chocolate *(mole negro and amarillo),* meat cooked with fruit *(manchamantel),* tamales, jerked meat, fried spiced rabbit wrapped in maguey leaves and steamed *(mixiotes de conejo)*
Puebla	*Mole,* with boiled poultry *(mole poblano),* peppers stuffed with meat in white walnut sauce *(chiles en nogada),* spicy pork stew *(tinga),* chapulas, tamales, boiled sweet potatoes (camotes)
Querétaro	Meatballs in chile sauce *(albóndigas en chipotle)*
Quintana Roo	Fish and shellfish: sea snails *(caracoles),* lobsters
San Luís Potosí	Mutton *(barbacoa),* banana leaves filled with meat *(patlache),* cheese tortillas with red sauce *(enchiladas potosinas),* cactus fruit candy *(queso de tuna)*
Sinaloa	Shredded pork with chile and spices *(chilorio)*
Sonora	Hare *(liebre)*
Tabasco	Sea turtle broth *(caldo de caguama),* turtle stew *(estofado de tortuga),* small turtle with herbs *(pochitoque en verde),* chocolate
Tamaulipas	Fish and shellfish: crabs *(jaibas)*
Tlaxcala	Chicken with green sauce and cheese *(pollo Tocatlán)*
Veracruz	Fish and shellfish, red snapper with tomato sauce, olives and chiles *(pescado a la veracruzana),* spicy shellfish soup *(chilpachole),* fish marinated in lime juice *(ceviche),* monkey meat *(carne de mono de Catemaco)* sausage *(embutido),* coffee
Yucatán	Chicken broth with fried tortilla *(sopa de lima),* suckling pig *(cochinita pibil),* stuffed tostadas *(panuchos),* tacos stuffed with hard boiled eggs in squash seed sauce *(papadzules),* stuffed cheese *(queso relleno),* almond figurines *(figurillas de almendra)*
Zacatecas	Meat broth with chile *(birria),* kid *(cabrito),* beef and vegetable stew *(puchero vaquero)*

(Photo Guillermo Aldana/Mexico)

ETHNOGRAPHY

Among the numerous ethnic groups that populated Mexico at the time of the arrival of the Spaniards in the early 16C, approximately fifty-six groups still exist.

The present-day lifestyles of the remaining groupes of pre-Hispanic Mexicans (i.e., economic activities – principally agriculture and poultry raising – habitat, clothing and the traditional crafts and customs that have survived the industrialization of the Mexican society) vary according to the climatic and topographical characteristics of the regions they inhabit.

GROUP	LOCATION	LANGUAGE
Amuzgos	Border of Guerrero & Oaxaca	Amuzgo
Cucapá, Kiliwa, Cochimí, Pai Pai, Kimiai	Baja California Norte	Yumana family
Cuicatecs	Northeast of Oaxaca	Cuicatec
Chichimecs	San Luis de la Paz, Guanajuato	Chichimec
Chinantecs	North of Oaxaca, at foothills of Eastern Sierra Madre	Chinantec
Chontals	Southwest of Oaxaca	Chontal or Tlequistlatec
Huastecs	San Luis Potosí & north of Veracruz	Huastec
Huichols	Jalisco, Nayarit & Durango	Huichol
Lacandons	Jungle of Chiapas	Lacandón
Mayas	Campeche, Yucatán & Quintana Roo	Maya
Mazahuas	México, Morelos, D.F., Michoacán	Mazahua
Mixes	Northwest of Oaxaca	Mixe or Ayook
Mixtecs	Northwest of Oaxaca, Guerrero & Puebla	Mixtec
Nahuas	San Luis Potosí, Hidalgo, Veracruz, Puebla, Guerrero, Morelos, Tlaxcala, D.F.	Náhuatl
Otomís	Puebla, Hidalgo, México, Guanajuato, San Luis Potosí	Otomí
Pimas	Southwest of Chihuahua & east of Sonora	Pima
Tarahumaras	Mountain knot of Sierra Madre Occidental	Tarahumara
Tepehuans	Durango & Nayarit	Tepehuan
Triques	Southwest of Oaxaca	Trique
Tzeltals	Center of Chiapas	Tzeltal
Tzotzils	San Juan Chamula, Chiapas	Tzotzil
Yaquis	Southeast of Sonora	Yaqui
Zapotecs	Valley of Oaxaca	Zapotec

Despite the fact that many of these groups adhere to modern legal structures, some groups still maintain a parallel traditional government based on customs passed down from father to son, and other groups remain autonomous, or unassimilated. Some of these Indian communities are integrated linguistically with the rest of the nation, while others are monolingual, speaking only a pre-Hispanic tongue.

Concerning religion, a process of **syncretism** has occurred; in spite of the predominance of the Catholic religion, there are nearly always present in their festivals and ceremonies, rites originated in the pre-Hispanic past, such as the deep-rooted cult for the dead, reflected in beautiful altars adorned with the most varied offerings. Their music and dances are also permeated with these religious feelings.

RELIGION	CRAFTS	DANCES & TRADITIONS
Catholic with pre-Hispanic elements	Textiles	Dances of the 12 Peers, the Conquest, Moors & Christians
No organized religious practices. Shamans	Weavings with beads, leather, istle, wood and palm fiber	
Catholic with pre-Hispanic elements	Textiles; Pottery	Male dancers dressed as women (Huehuetones)
Catholic	Jackets of istle; woolen blankets	La Checa game
Catholic with stewardships (Mayordomías) & pre-Hispanic elements	Textiles	
Catholic with stewardships & pre-Hispanic elements	Textiles; pottery	Dance of the Little Horse
Catholic with pre-Hispanic elements	Articles of palm & agave fibers	Dances of Huehues, Malinche, Negroes, Rebozos, Batons
Catholic with pre-Hispanic elements	Work in worsted wool; cups & textiles	
Offshoot of Maya cults	Bows and arrows	Renewal of the braziers
Catholic with pre-Hispanic elements	Embroidery; sisal work	Jaranas. Dance of the Pig's Head
Catholic with stewardships & pre-Hispanic elements	Rugs, bed-spreads & tablecloths	
Catholic with pre-Hispanic elements	Textiles; pottery	Dances: Negritos, Conquest and the Tiger
Catholic with animist elements	Palm articles	Dances: Los Charcos, Los Rubios and Los Chicholos
Catholic with pre-Hispanic elements	Textiles; figures of tin; bark paintings (amates)	Tlacoleros, the Snake, Ribbon Dance & agricultural rites
Catholic with pre-Hispanic elements	Textiles; embroidery; basket weaving	
	Basketry	Dance of the Matachines, the Pascola & the Deer
Catholic with animist elements	Simple ceramics; blanket weaving	Dance of the Matachines
Catholic with pre-Hispanic elements	Simple pottery	
Catholic with pre-Hispanic elements	Textiles	
Catholic with pre-Hispanic elements	Weavings; embroidery; wood-carvings; ceramics	
Catholic with pre-Hispanic elements	Textiles; embroidery; pottery	
Catholic with pre-Hispanic elements	Ceramics; basketry	Dances: the Deer, the Pascola & the Coyote
Catholic with pre-Hispanic elements	Textiles; pottery	Feather dances

HANDICRAFTS

Handicrafts constitute one of the deepest and most authentic expressions of the Mexican people. Their origins date back to pre-Hispanic times, and during the colonial period they evolved under the impact of new techniques and occupations, adopting the distinct features that characterize them today.
The enormous variety of Mexican handicrafts corresponds to the many different regions of the country, thus composing a multicolored spectrum of styles, symbols and traditions.

(Photo Antonio Mercado/Mexico)

Mexico. Handicraft market – waist loom

HANDICRAFT	CHARACTERISTICS	STATE
Ceramics	Pre-Hispanic features, without glazing	Guerrero, Chiapas, Yucatán
	Glazed	Jalisco, Michoacán, San Luis Potosí, México, Oaxaca, Puebla
	Burnished clay	Jalisco, Michoacán, Oaxaca
	Majolica	Puebla, Guanajuato
	Multicolored clay	México (Metepec)
	Ceremonial black pottery for the Day of the Dead	Michoacán, Puebla
Wood	White wooden furniture decorated with knife-carvings	Michoacán (Uruapan)
	Willow chairs with rush or leather seats *(equipales)*	Michoacán, Jalisco
	Furniture with shell and metal inlays	Jalisco, Zacatecas, Puebla
	Multicolored walking sticks	Tlaxcala
	Chocolate grinders	Michoacán
	Combs	Oaxaca
	Stringed musical instruments (guitars and violins)	Michoacán (Paracho)
	Percussion musical instruments (marimbas)	Chiapas
Textiles	Embroidery and openwork (blouses, sheets, tablecloths...)	Aguascalientes, Jalisco, Zacatecas, San Luis Potosí
	Embroidery and openwork with Indian influence	Michoacán, México, Oaxaca, Chiapas, Yucatán, Quintana Roo
	Women's tunics *(huipiles)*	Oaxaca, Hidalgo, México, Michoacán, Chiapas
	Embroidered shirts	Puebla, Oaxaca, Michoacán
	Ponchos *(tilmas)*	México, Puebla, Oaxaca, Guerrero, Hidalgo
	Belts, girdles and cords	Oaxaca, Michoacán, México
	Sarapes and woolen blankets	Tlaxcala, Oaxaca, México, Coahuila
	Plain rebozos	Guanajuato, San Luis Potosí, Jalisco, Morelos, Hidalgo, Sinaloa, Puebla, Oaxaca, México
	Fine rebozos	San Luis Potosí, México (Tenango)
	Knotted runners	México (Temoaya)

HANDICRAFT	CHARACTERISTICS	STATE
Leatherwork...	Articles for Mexican cowboys (charros)	D.F., Puebla, Guanajuato, Colima
	Articles for everyday use (wallets, handbags...)	Oaxaca, Guanajuato, Jalisco
Basketwork...	Willow (fruit baskets)	México, Michoacán, Oaxaca, Guerrero, Yucatán
	Rice and wheat straw	Michoacán (Pátzcuaro, Tzintzuntzan)
	Istle and henequen (rugs, runners...)	Michoacán, Yucatán
	Palm hats	Puebla, Guerrero, Oaxaca
	Jipijapa straw hats	Campeche
	Panama hats	Yucatán
	Rattan baskets and furniture	Jalisco, Michoacán, D.F., Guanajuato, Puebla
Metalwork....	Silver offerings	Puebla, Oaxaca, Querétaro Jalisco, Guanajuato
	Silver jewelry (necklaces, bracelets, rings...)	Guerrero (Taxco), Oaxaca México
	Religious jewelry	Oaxaca
	Gold jewelry (necklaces, bracelets, rings...)	Oaxaca, Yucatán, Chiapas. Michoacán
	Hammered copper	Michoacán (Villa Escalante)
	Laminated copper	Jalisco, Guanajuato, D.F.
	Wrought iron	D.F., Querétaro, Zacatecas
	Tin (frames, lamps...)	D.F., Puebla, Morelos, Chiapas, Oaxaca, Guanajuato (San Miguel de Allende)
	Steel (knives, machetes, daggers...)	Oaxaca, D.F., Zacatecas
Lacquerwork..	With gold leaf decorations	Michoacán (Pátzcuaro)
	Striped	Michoacán (Uruapan)
	Incrusted	Guerrero (Olinalá)
Glasswork....	Blown glass	Jalisco, México (Texcoco)
	Red-colored blown and cut lead cristal	Jalisco
	Nuggets (de pepita)	San Luis Potosí
Bark Paintings (Amates)....	White	Puebla
	Polichrome	Guerrero, Veracruz, Puebla, Oaxaca
Waxwork.....		Oaxaca, Chiapas
Toys.........	Polichrome cardboard	Guanajuato
	Cardboard Judas (p 132)	D.F.
	Papier mâché figures (Alebrijes)	D.F., México
	Clay (whistles, crèches)	Jalisco, Puebla, Oaxaca, Michoacán, México
	Wood (furniture, articulated dolls)	Guanajuato, Aguascalientes, Puebla, Hidalgo
	Multicolored reeds	Oaxaca, D.F.
	Ragdolls	México, Morelos, D.F., Michoacán
	Puppets	D.F.
	Piñatas	D.F.
Masks.......	Lacquered	Michoacán, Guerrero
	Cardboard	Guanajuato
	Paper	D.F.
	Colored wood	Oaxaca, Tlaxcala, Jalisco, Hidalgo
	Orangewood	Michoacán, Guerrero
	Wood combined with other materials (hair, hide, wire)	Puebla, Morelos
	Headdresses of tin flowers and ribbons	D.F., Puebla, Morelos, Chiapas, Oaxaca
	Topped with dried deer heads	Sonora

Key

Sights

★★★ Worth the trip
★★ Worth a detour
★ Interesting

Route description:

——————— Paved road

------- Unpaved road

⟹ Departure point

▭ Building

⛪ ⸸ Religious building

⛬ ⸪ Archeological site - Ruins

—+—|— Wall, gate

🔦 ✪ Lighthouse - Fort

◉ · Fountain - Statue

⌒ Grotto

🌟 ⋇ Panorama - View

Gardens, parks, woods

⸖ ⸖ Marsh

B Letter locating a sight

Other symbols

🛡160 Federal Highway   🛡150 Federal Toll Highway   🛡18 State Highway

▬▬▬ Divided highway Superhighway

▬■▬ Junction

▬▬▬ Major through road

⊞⊞⊞ ⟺ Street with stairs - Pedestrian street. Unsuitable for traffic

⊏⊐ --- Restricted street

🅴 Parking

2385 →← Pass - Altitude

🚆 🚌 Train Station - Bus station

Ⓜ ● Subway station

✈ Airport

⛴ Ferry: Car and Passenger service - Passenger service

++++ — Railroad

○•••••○ Cable car

▢ Public building

✉ Main post office

☎ ☏ Telegraph - Telephone

🛈 Tourist information

🛒 Shopping center

✉ Covered market

🥤 Cafeteria

⊞ ⸸⸸⸸ Hospital - Cemetery

🗼 ⚙ Water tank - Factory

⌣ ✕ Dam - Mine

∞∞∞ Athletic field

⬭ ⚑ Stadium - Golf course

≋ Outdoor swimming pool - Indoor swimming pool

Abbreviations

PG Government Palace

PM Municipal Palace, City Hall

J Palace of Justice

POL Police

M Museum

T Theater

U University

Michelin maps and town plans are north orientated.

Town plans: frequently used roads and those giving access to sights listed in this guide are fully drawn; lesser roads are indicated only at the junction with the above-mentioned roads. Area and local maps: only the primary and sightseeing routes are indicated.

Population

♦♦♦♦♦♦ over 1 000 000 inhabitants

♦♦♦♦♦ from 250 000 to 1 000 000 inhabitants

♦♦♦♦ from 100 000 to 250 000 inhabitants

♦♦♦ from 30 000 to 100 000 inhabitants

♦♦ from 15 000 to 30 000 inhabitants

♦ under 15 000 inhabitants

🕓 Opening Hours and Admission Charges: see explanations p 232.

SIGHTS

described in alphabetical order

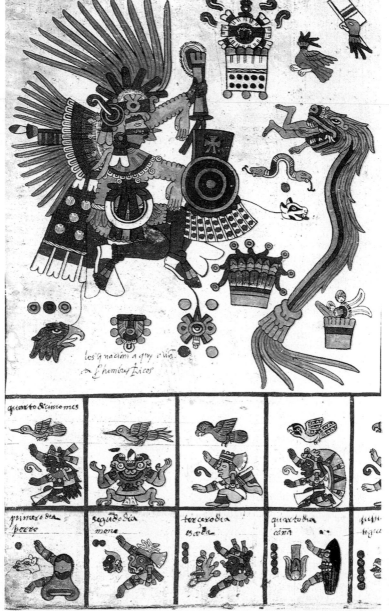

Codex Borbonicus (1490-1510). The god Xipe Totec and a feathered serpent
devouring a man. Bourbon Palace Library, Paris

Since ancient times considered by sailors and explorers a site of unequaled beauty, present-day Acapulco captivates the visitor with its natural attraction, which has earned it the epithet, the **Pearl of the Pacific.** In Acapulco, nature has shaped an enormous bay protected by mountains covered in tropical vegetation, making for a spectacular landscape of abrupt cliffs bathed by the sea and lovely beaches. All this, added to its year-round tropical climate, makes Acapulco one of the world's most fashionable resorts.

HISTORICAL NOTES

In their search for a route to the Orient, the Conquistadors arrived in Acapulco Bay in 1532, the year that the explorations of the Pacific coast began. In the middle of that same century, the route of the famous galleon, the *Nao China*, which sustained trade with the Far East for almost two centuries, was established in this port. Frequent pirate raids moved the Spanish crown to build **Fort San Diego** (Fuerte de San Diego), one of the most representative examples of Spanish military architecture on the Pacific coast of Mexico.

★★ ACAPULCO BAY (BAHÍA DE ACAPULCO)

Around the ample bay, which stretches for over 7 km – 4.3 miles, lies modern and sumptuous Acapulco with imposing hotel towers along the main boulevard, **Costera Miguel Alemán★**, where the main tourist activities are concentrated. After sunset, this artery is enlivened by the multicolored illumination of luxury hotels, restaurants and night clubs. At its western end, the spacious modern architecture of the **Convention Center** (Centro de Convenciones) stands out, surrounded by ample and well-tended gardens.

Beaches (Playas). – Parallel to the Costera, going from west to east at the foot of the high-rise hotels, there are numerous entrances to a string of beaches: Hornos, Hornitos, Condesa, Redonda and Guitarrón. The *palapas* (thatched palm sunshades) protect beachgoers from the burning sun, while they enjoy the lovely view of the bay, with its jutting formations – Farallón del Obispo – facing Redonda and Condesa beaches.

★★ **Fort San Diego** (Fuerte ⓥ **de San Diego).** – This is an important example of the Spanish architecture built in Mexico during the 18C. It was constructed to defend the site against marauding pirates. This pentagonal structure has been transformed into a Historical Museum, which includes exhibits on the conquest of the South Seas and trade with the Far East. Particularly noteworthy are the original model of the Manila galleon, the **Nao China,** and valuable objects, like Chinese porcelain vases of the 18C and delicately embroidered silks of the same era.

CLASSIC ACAPULCO

time: 1/2 day

The western part of the bay, following along Costera Miguel Alemán to the center of town and then Avenida Adolfo López Mateos (Gran Vía Tropical).

The Acapulco of the Forties remains in the constructions that appear to be suspended between the hills and the cliffs that gaze out to sea amidst tropical foliage.

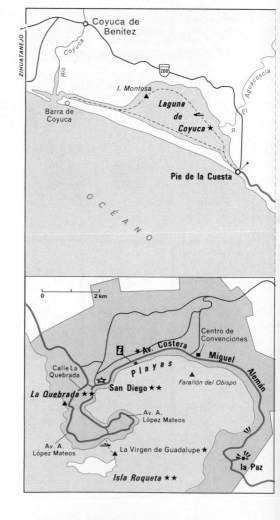

This same avenue that winds along the steep hillsides leads to the twin beaches, Caleta and Caletilla – the embarkation point for Roqueta Island.
Further along to the northwest, enchanting Angosta Beach appears, surrounded by two steep cliffs that defy the open sea from their vast heights.

★★**Roqueta Island.** – *1 km – 0.6 miles south of Playas Caleta and Caletilla.*
⏱ The fascinating crossing to this beautiful island in glass-bottom boats, provides an opportunity to observe the multicolored fish life and the rocks covered with many-hued sea fans, and to glimpse the image of the **Virgin of Guadalupe★** under 7 m – 23 ft – of water alongside the rocky islet called Yerbabuena. Skindivers find these beaches with crystal-clear water and varied undersea formations enticing.

★★**La Quebrada.** – *Following Avenida Adolfo López Mateos to the north, or from the Zócalo along Calle de Quebrada.*
⏱ This is an imposing gorge formed by cliffs more than 60 m – 197 ft – high, where the sea waves break furiously against the rocks. This is where the impressive **performance★** by daring local swimmers takes place. They dive from a height of approximately 45 m – 148 ft into the water at the bottom of the gorge. The location also affords fabulous panoramic views of the open sea and the spectacular sunsets.

COYUCA LAGOON (LAGUNA DE COYUCA) AND PIE DE LA CUESTA
13 km – 8 miles – to Pie de la Cuesta – time: 1/2 day

★**Coyuca Lagoon.** – *Embarkation points in front of the beaches of Pie de la Cuesta.*
⏱ This excursion is a true jungle safari – a fascinating tour around the lagoon in small boats through mangrove swamps and tidelands. Along the way, the rocky islet called El Presidio, the Isle of the Birds, inhabited by cranes and pelicans, and the exotic island, **La Montosa,** with its rustic *palapas*, will be seen. There the delicious shrimp, crab and a great variety of shellfish which are caught on the spot, can be tasted. The tour continues around the lagoon to the Coyuca Sandbar (Barra de Coyuca) beside the sea, and then turns back to the point of departure.

Pie de la Cuesta. – This site, at the exact point where the mountains join the coastal plain of the Coyuca Lagoon, consists of a large, straight stretch of beach, which is famous for its enormous waves, over 4 m – 13 ft – high. It is also a favorite spot for watching the **sunset★** over the ocean.

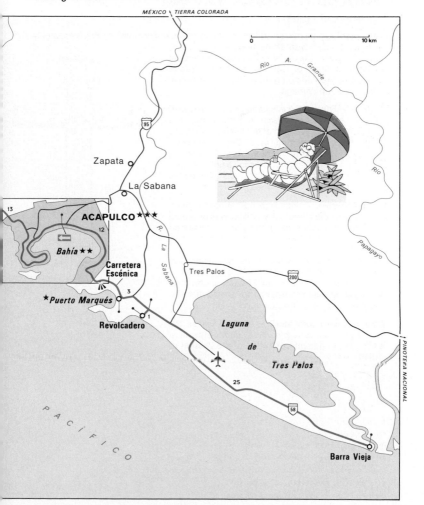

SCENIC HIGHWAY (CARRETERA ESCÉNICA)
16 km – 10 miles – 1/2 day

This road climbs through the hills to the southeast of the bay, on a route that offers breathtaking **panoramic views★** of the port, the bay, and Roqueta Island in the background. The road goes on to the other side of the mountains and unveils another lovely **panorama★** of the bay of Puerto Marqués. In the distance, almost out of view on the horizon, Tre Palos Lagoon (Laguna de Tres Palos) appears.

Chapel of La Paz. – *Access via Las Brisas residential area; follow the signs.*
There is a peaceful **lookout★★** here, next to a modern chapel with a tall cross, perched on the highest point southeast of the town; it commands a view of the entire bay of Acapulco and its sunsets.

★**Puerto Marqués.** – *Go southeast along the highway until you find the sign.*
This site used to be a natural pirate's hideout, consisting of a beautiful bay, similar to Acapulco's, although smaller, with quiet beaches of coarse sand and gentle waves, now enlivened by colorful little sailboats. Its crystalline and tranquil waters are ideal for skin diving or waterskiing. Along the beaches, local shellfish is served.

Revolcadero. – This long open beach fringed with palm trees has a very strong surf. Horseback riding along the beach is allowed. Nearby there is a beautiful spot at the foot of the mountains called La Encantada, formed by tidelands full of mangrove trees that give the place a special charm.

EXCURSIONS

Tre Palos Lagoon; Barra Vieja. – *(40 km – 25 miles to the southeast by highway n° 58 towards Barra Vieja.*
A straight road, parallel to the sea, leads through palm groves and fruit orchards to one of the arms of Tre Palos Lagoon, near the Barra Vieja beach in a marshy landscape covered by bulrushes, blooming lilies and green mangroves. The site is famous for its delicious fish *a la talla*, a specialty of the region.

★★ ACOLMAN MONASTERY México

Map of Principal Sights p 6

This notable Augustinian edifice is one of the few examples of Plateresque style in Mexico, blended with some features of the iconography and crafts of the Indian communities. Its layout is typical of 16C monasteries, despite having been rebuilt and remodeled various times, following flood damage.

Church. – The entrance is beautifully carved with regional plant and animal motifs. Inside the church, on the first stretch of the left hand wall, the tempera mural painting of a Churrigueresque altarpiece is noteworthy. The walls of the apse are decorated with beautiful fresco paintings representing saints, bishops, cardinals and popes seated on magnificent thrones.

Main Cloister. – Although contemporary with the facade of the church, the cloister was designed in the Renaissance style, with columns decorated in plant motifs that are interpreted in the Indian manner.
Both in the passageways of the **main cloister** and those of the smaller cloister, built later, there are lovely fresco paintings of the Passion of Christ, as well as ornamental borders and doorframes, no doubt copied from European engravings.

Atrium Cross (Cruz Atrial). – *Located across the road from the atrium's main door.* This is a fascinating Indian interpretation of the Passion of Christ.

(From photo by Luis Mariano Acévez/Mexico)

Acolman Monastery. Atrial cross

Map of Principal Sights p 6 – 54 km – 33.6 miles southeast of Palenque.

Access to the waterfalls is difficult in the rainy season.
To reach Agua Azul, meaning "blue water", the visitor must take a long and winding road across the tropical jungle of the Chiapas mountains.
High and low lands alternate, while the green hills blend into the distant blue sky. Suddenly the thread of a river seems to break out of the hills and pass through thick foliage where the fragrance of myriad flowers permeates the shadows.

(Photo Michelin)

Agua Azul Waterfalls

At the end, in a broad clearing, the Agua Azul Waterfalls pour forth – a complex of rapids, cascades and pools on a branch of the Tulijá River.
Surrounded by such dazzling vegetation, the beauty of the river is captivating, with its brilliant turquoise color, although its hues change on very rainy days. As the waters descend the different levels, they spread a white curtain over huge limestone rocks, turning golden in the sunlight. Numerous obstacles in this water course form singularly attractive pools.
The occasional chatter of parrots, macaws and toucans enhances the silence of this precious spot, far from civilization – a gem for nature lovers.

★ **AGUASCALIENTES** Aguascalientes   ◆◆◆◆◆

Map of Principal Sights p 5

Aguascalientes is a quiet city with clear skies, in a stark and rough semi-desert setting. Originally it was a manufacturing city, famous for its embroideries, weaving and openwork, as well as for its vast perfumed vineyards.
The notable work of the architect **Refugio Reyes Rivas** can be appreciated in many of the city's noble buildings. Since the 17C, during the months of April and May, the inhabitants of Aguascalientes celebrate **Saint Mark's Fair** (Feria de San Marcos), a very colorful festival noted for its fireworks, cock fights, bullfights, cultural events, gambling and business transactions.

CENTER OF THE CITY *time: 1 day*

⊙ **Cathedral Basilica of the Virgin of the Assumption** (Catedral Basílica de la Virgen de la Asunción). – This, the oldest church in the city, was elevated to parish church status in the 17C. It has a simple facade in the Baroque-Solomonic style. The frontispiece is decorated with a scene depicting four mitred saints, carved in gray stone by native craftsmen. This enormous basilica contains the tabernacle chapel (Capilla del Sagrario), with a beautiful 18C German-made altarpiece. The walls of the church are decorated with paintings by Miguel Cabrera.

Sacristy and Bishop's Offices (Sacristía y Oficinas del Obispo). – The paintings found here are a good sampling of colonial artistry; among them are works by well-known painters like Miguel Cabrera, José de Alcíbar and Manuel Osorio.

★ **Government Palace** (Palacio de Gobierno) (PG). – House of the Mayorazgo del Rincón (Casa del Mayorazgo del Rincón). This aristocratic mansion dates from the 18C. Its facade reveals a sharp contrast between the facing of dark *tezontle* (a porous local building stone varying in color from dark red to pink) and the carved stone of the balconies. The mansion was reconstructed during this century.
Inside, a large number of stone arches form two magnificent patios separated by a monumental staircase. On the walls, the painter Oswaldo Barra Cuningham reproduced the history of the people of Aguascalientes and scenes of Saint Mark's Fair.

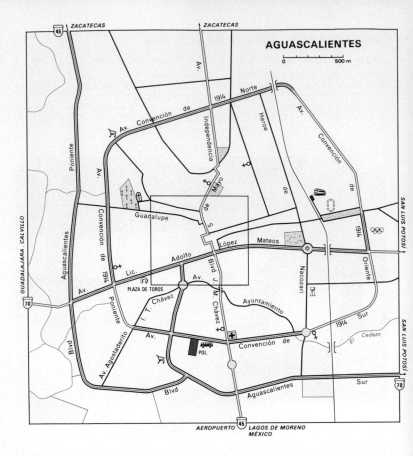

AGUASCALIENTES

○ **Saint Anthony's Church** (Templo de San Antonio). – This church (mid-19C), designed by Refugio Reyes Rivas in a peculiar yet graceful neoclassical style is one of the city's most striking monuments.

The design is a Latin cross, crowned at the crossing by a magnificent cupola with double stained glass windows. Beautiful, enormous medallions painted by Candelario Rivas, narrating the Life and Passion of Christ, adorn the walls.

★ **Aguascalientes Museum** (M¹). – **Former State Teachers' College** (Exescuela Normal del ○ Estado). This palace from the beginning of the 19C has a noble facade of pink stone framed in Greek-style columns – also the work of Refugio Reyes Rivas.

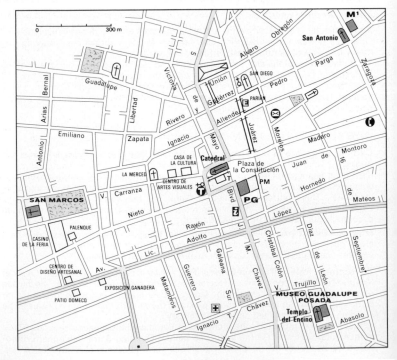

Museum. – This museum presents an enlightening overview of contemporary art, displaying pieces by renowned modern artists like Pedro and Rafael Coronel and works in charcoal, pencil, pastels and oils by Gabriel Fernández Ledezma. Particular attention should be given to the paintings of the extraordinary artist, **Saturnino Herrán** *(see p 41)*, who translated nationalist feeling in pictorial terms; his works *The Legend of the Volcanoes (La Leyenda de los Volcanes)* and *Our Gods (Nuestros Dioses)* are particularly distinguished.

⊙ **Church of the Oak Tree** (Templo del Encino). – Its 18C entrance was worked in the baroque style, with a profusion of curves and lines. It is located in one of the oldest neighborhoods of the city, Barrio Triana.
Inside the church, the miraculous Black Christ (Cristo Negro), called The Lord of the Oak Tree (El Señor del Encino) is venerated. The walls are decorated with twelve magnificent works by Andrés López (1768-1863), representing the Stations of the Cross and the Passion of Christ.

★★ **Guadalupe Posada Museum.** – **Former Priests' House** (Excasa Cural). – This collection
⊙ contains a good sampling of the work of J. Guadalupe Posada, who revolutionized the art of engraving, by introducing popular themes. Through his humorous criticism of the politics of his day, he strongly influenced mass opinion.
His noteworthy caricatures, **Skulls** *(Calaveras)*, encompass elements of life and death.

★ **Saint Mark's Garden** (Jardín de San Marcos). – Surrounded by a beautiful stone wall, with lovely arches at all four corners, this cool and shady oasis is a favorite spot for Sunday outings, and a source of inspiration for artists.

⊙ **Saint Mark's Church** (Templo de San Marcos). – Behind its humble 18C facade, this church houses a magnificent painting by José de Alcíbar (1751-1800), representing *The Adoration of the Magi (La Adoración de los Reyes Magos)*.

ADDITIONAL SIGHTS

⊙ **Plaza del Vestido.** – *10 km – 6.2 miles – to the south on highway n° 45, towards Lagos de Moreno.*
In this area, most of the clothing, household linens, embroidery and openwork manufactures are concentrated. Such articles can be purchased here.

⊙ **Viñedos de San Marcos.** – *13 km – 8 miles. Go north on Avenida Independencia towards Zacatecas.*
Since 1575, Aguascalientes has been famous for its vineyards. This industry reached a peak in 1936, when the first wine and spirits firm was established, producing liquor, brandy, and still and sparkling wines. The **cellars★** (bodegas) may be visited, to see the different procedures involved in the preparation of its delicious brews, whether distilled or fermented. At the end of the tour, the visitor is invited to sample some choice beverages.

★★ ÁLAMOS Sonora ♦

Map of Principal Sights p 4

Legends still circulate in the mines about Álamos, this noble city that sprang up in the 17C, in a warm valley at the foot of the Sierra Madre. The so-called Taxco of Sonora preserves elegant 18C and 19C constructions, built around flowery patios, embellished with ironwork, and protected by high walls steeped in history. **Church of the Immaculate Conception** (Iglesia de la Inmaculada Concepción), completed at the beginning of the 19C in a sober baroque style, dominates the main square. It is accompanied by the **City Hall** (Palacio Municipal), a building that recalls medieval Spanish fortresses. Álamos lights up with the tepid winter's arrival, when the present residents return to their sumptuous mansions, reconstructed in the original style, as befits a city considered a National Historical Monument.
One peculiarity of this region is the renowned jumping bean, a legume whose characteristic movement is caused by a small larva that develops in the bean.

Sonora Museum of Social Customs (Museo Costumbrista de Sonora). – *Guadalupe Victoria unnumbered, Plaza de Armas.*
This small museum exudes nostalgia for the 18C, the golden era of Sonora, when it was the richest city in the northwest region of the country. In its various rooms there are exhibits of Chinese porcelain, silverware and other objects that once were proudly used by the wealthy families of the city. Also displayed in the museum is an interesting collection of 19C coins from the mints of Álamos and Hermosillo.

The Michelin Green Tourist Guide New England
Picturesque scenery, buildings
Scenic routes
Geography, Economy
History, Art
Suggested automobile tours
Plans of towns and buildings
A guide for your travels

Map of Principal Sights p 4 – Map of Regional Tours p 7

The peninsula of Baja California, situated at the extreme northwest region of the country, is a narrow strip of land which runs from the United States border into the sea, parallel to the west coast of the continent, between the Pacific Ocean and the Gulf of California. It is linked to the rest of Mexico by a narrow desert corridor on its northeastern border.

The peninsula's coastline extends more than 3 000 km – 1 864 miles and is especially attractive to those who enjoy water sports. Its wide golden beaches seem undiscovered, and the magic charm of the desert contrasts with the bright blue sea. Under different names, a mountain chain runs the whole length of the peninsula, forming numerous valleys, some of which are under cultivation, such as the Valley of Guadalupe (vineyards and olive groves) northeast of Ensenada, or the Santo Domingo Valley (cotton and wheat) to the south. The highest peaks, such as the Sierra of San Pedro Mártir in the north, rise above 2 000 m – 6 562 ft. Their pine and oak forests provide a natural habitat for deer and hares.

Many caves have been formed in these mountains, which shelter one of the largest known concentrations of **prehistoric rupestrian paintings**, the precise date and cultural origins of which remain a mystery. This is a huge display of human and animal figures – vital, forceful and firmly drawn with ocre, red, white and black mineral-based pigments. The use of such materials has permitted the paintings to last for thousands of years so that they may still be admired, although unfortunately in most cases access requires specialized transportation and equipment or guidance.

In the northwest, the seacoast, with its cliffs and beaches, has cold waters and rough waves, while in the south, the waters are warm and tranquil in its numerous coves, like lovely **Concepción Bay** (Bahía de la Concepción). This area has high rocky coasts, beaches with fine sand and crystal-clear waters that reveal the rich sea life of this immense natural aquarium.

Very few of the islands along these coasts are inhabited or economically productive; the majority are only visited by seabirds and sea lions. From time immemorial, these coasts are host to a wondrous annual spectacle – the migration of the grey whale, seeking the lukewarm waters of the peninsula during the winter in order to give birth. Their main reproducing grounds are the **Ojo de Liebre Lagoon** (Laguna Ojo de Liebre) next to the largest salt flats in the world – las Salinas de Guerrero Negro –, and the **San Ignacio Lagoon** (Laguna San Ignacio) on the Pacific Ocean.

The peninsula's climate is extremely dry, except for the higher elevations of the northeastern part; consequently, the majority of the rivers and streams run dry during long periods. This favors desert vegetation like that found in **Vizcaíno Desert** (Desierto de Vizcaíno), where cereus plants, giant cacti, agaves and thorn bushes grow between wind-polished rocks that nature has distributed in a mysterious pattern.

HISTORICAL NOTES

The first European explorers arrived in the peninsula during the 16C, looking for a trade route to the Orient; however, the true conquest of these lands was carried out by Jesuit missionaries more than a century later.

For seventy years, they tirelessly made their way through this peninsula, planting vineyards and date palms, founding settlements around their missions, only a few of which remain in good condition. The Jesuits were followed by the Franciscans, and they, by the Dominicans until 1834, when the missionary period is considered to have ended.

⊙ **Access.** – Air links exist between Tijuana, Mexicali, La Paz and Los Cabos and various other Mexican, as well as foreign, destinations. There is also a ferry service, with a restaurant and a cafeteria, from Santa Rosalía to Guaymas, from La Paz to Mazatlán and to Topolobampo and from Cabo San Lucas to Puerto Vallarta.

FROM TIJUANA TO LOS CABOS *2 524 km – 1 568 miles – 10 days*

Tijuana. – *Description p 199.*

Mexicali. – *189 km – 117 miles east of Tijuana on highway n° 2.*
Mexicali, the present capital of the state of Baja California Norte, on the US border, developed at the end of the 19C, when the Colorado River waters were tapped to irrigate the Mexicali Valley, making it one of the most fertile cotton-growing regions of the country. Today it is the second most populated city in the state.

⊙ **Regional Museum of the Autonomous University of Baja California** (Museo Regional de la Universidad Autónoma de Baja California). – *Reforma and Calle L.* In this museum a brief overview of local geography and history is featured, along with an interesting display of regional fauna.

San Felipe. – *198 km – 123 miles south of Mexicali on highway n° 5.*
A fishing village, between sea and desert, with majestic rocky mountains all around, this is an ideal place for sport fishing and bathing on the attractive beaches of the Gulf of California.

Ensenada. – *108 km – 67 miles south of Tijuana on highway n° 1.*
This is the oldest deep-sea port on the peninsula. It was developed in the 19C as a consequence of the real estate boom in the southwestern region of the US. In the central city streets there are still California-style wooden structures reminiscent of that era.

(Photo Bob Schalkwijk/Mexico)

Beach at Cabo San Lucas

Social, Civic and Cultural Center of Ensenada. – Former Riviera del Pacifico Casino. – *Boulevard Costera Lázaro Cárdenas and Avenida Riviera.* This renowned hotel and casino of the Thirties, visited by the most famous movie stars of the period, was closed shortly after its inauguration when gambling was prohibited. The structure evokes southern Spanish architecture. It preserves part of its original decor, brought especially from many points of the globe. The section that contained the hotel rooms no longer exists.

La Bufadora. – *36 km – 22.4 miles. Go south from Ensenada on highway n° 1; 16 km – 10 miles to Maneadero and 20 km – 12.4 miles west by the road to Punta Banda.* In this spot where the mountains plunge straight into the sea, the ocean has formed a hole in the base of the cliff through which the waves penetrate with force, producing a peculiar snorting sound.

On the road between San Quintín and La Paz, fill your gas tank at every gas station along the way.

San Ignacio. – *751 km – 466.6 miles south of Ensenada on highway n° 1.* At the southern entrance to the Desierto de Vizcaíno, between lava rock hills, a crystal-clear stream springs out, watering vineyards as well as fig, pomegranate and palm groves. In 1728, this oasis was chosen by Reverend Juan B. de Luyando to found the Saint Ignatius Kadakaaman Mission.

Saint Ignatius of Loyola Church (Iglesia de San Ignacio de Loyola). – This construction was finished by Dominican missionaries, who continued the work begun by the Jesuits. Its baroque facade has a portal with a semicircular arch and paired columns. The layout is designed as a Latin cross with a single nave and contains imposing gilded altarpieces, including a baroque high altar.

Santa Rosalía. – *74 km – 46 miles east of San Ignacio on highway n° 1.* This town was founded in 1885, when a French company began to exploit the region's copper mines. The name given these fields, El Boleo, meaning ball game, was derived from the spherical shapes in which the copper was extracted. The wooden structures with pitched roofs in the center of town and on the top of the hill, seem to belong to a 19C town in the American West, despite a mixture of French-style buildings.

Saint Barbara Church (Iglesia de Santa Bárbara). – The prefabricated metallic structure of this church was designed by Gustave Eiffel, builder of the famous Parisian tower that bears his name. Parts of the two lateral sections have been replaced with concrete.

Mulegé. – *63 km – 39 miles south of Santa Rosalía on highway n° 1.* The view from the top of the hill embraces the whole sleepy town, lying in the shadow of the palm groves along the Mulegé River. On the summit stands the mission church, founded in 1705 by the Jesuit father, Juan Basaldúa. Its simple facade is flanked by attractive buttresses; the principal nave and the transversal annex form a square design, uncommon in this type of architecture. The bell tower rises between the nave and the annex.

Loreto. – *134 km – 83.3 miles south of Mulegé on highway n° 1.* In this place, where time seems to stand still, the first permanent settlement in Baja California was founded in 1697, as a base for the missionaries' work. Among the nearby beaches, Nopoló is worth visiting *(8 km – 5 miles to the south).*

The Mission of Our Lady of Loreto (Misión de Nuestra Señora de Loreto). – *14 Salvatierra.* This headquarters of the missions in colonial California had to be reconstructed as a consequence of damages caused by time and nature. It has a simple Renaissance style facade with a semicircular arch and a rectangular window; the finial and the bell tower are not part of the original design.

The interior consists of a nave divided into five sections and preserves its beamed roofing. The baroque-style high altar includes oils of Jesuit saints and the image of the Virgin of Our Lady of Loreto, patroness of Baja California.

Missions Museum (Museo de las Misiones). – *16 Salvatierra.* In the priests' house *(casa cural)* connected to the mission, this very simple museum was installed, where various objects and documents of the missionary period are exhibited.

Puerto Escondido. – *26 km – 16.2 miles. Go south from Loreto on highway nº 1; after 24 km – 14.9 miles, turn left and continue 2 km – 1.2 miles.*
At the foot of the impressive Sierra La Gigante, lies this enchanting bay of intense blues and greens. It is almost completely closed, with only a small opening to the sea. Its name means "hidden port", recalling the old galleons that sought protection in the bay, from storms or other dangers. At present an ambitious nautical and tourist center is being planned.

La Paz. – *351 km – 218 miles south of Loreto. Description p 163.*

★★ **Cabo San Lucas.** – *161 km – 100 miles. Go south from La Paz on highway nº 1, at km 29 – 18 miles turn off to the right and continue 132 km – 82 miles on highway nº 19. Description p 163.*

San José del Cabo. – *33 km – 20.5 miles northeast of Cabo San Lucas. Description p 163.*

CAMPECHE Campeche ◆

Map of Principal Sights p 6

The Spanish traders and seamen who in the 16C founded Campeche, converted it into the only deep-water port on the Yucatan Peninsula. Its success as a trading center attracted the much-dreaded pirates of the era: in 1685 the famous corsair, Lorencillo, sacked Campeche and took away even the doors and windows of the houses. For this reason, the village built a city wall for protection. The vestiges of the imposing hexagonal fortress today divide the old city from the modern quarters. While the large hotels and public buildings have been constructed on land recently reclaimed from the sea, the cobblestone streets around the cathedral are lined by old mansions with high roofs and large, sober facades sparsely decorated with geometric friezes. The warm atmosphere inside the walls evokes the first decades of the 19C, the period of the port's greatest development due to the exports of the *Palo de Tinte* plant, in great demand in Europe for the production of a red dye.

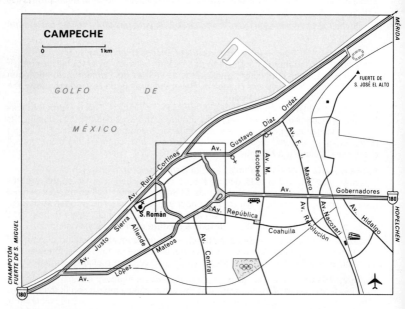

OLD CITY *time: 1 day*

★ **The Wall (La Muralla).** – In the 17C, construction of a strong belt of stone 2.5 km – 1.5 miles around, began. It had four gates, of which two remain, and eight bastions, of which seven have been preserved.

Sea Gate (Puerta de Mar). – This structure provides the only means of access to the city by water.

⊙ **Solitude Bastion** (Baluarte de la Soledad). – The **Museum of the Stelae** (Museo de las Estelas) is housed here; a dozen of these stones finely carved by the ancient Mayas, are displayed, as well as the curious sculpture of a man with a mask that resembles a nocturnal bird. Up the outside ramp along the 150 m – 492 ft of the sentry walk, there is a splendid **panoramic view** of the main park and the cathedral, on one side, and of the modern buildings with the Gulf of Mexico in the background, on the other.

Ⓥ **Santiago Bastion** (Baluarte de Santiago). – A small botanical garden has been created here.

Ⓥ **Saint Peter Bastion** (Baluarte de San Pedro). – Handicrafts are exhibited and sold in this bastion.

Land Gate (Puerta de Tierra). – In a stretch of the wall 400 m - 1312 ft long by 8 m – 26.3 ft high is found the ancient archway connecting the city to the suburbs. Looking through the arch, the sea gate can be seen at a short distance. This allows the visitor to appreciate the breadth of the city during colonial times.

Ⓥ **Saint Charles Bastion** (Baluarte de San Carlos). – Here the damp cellars where the powder was stored are open to visitors.

Ⓥ **Cathedral.** – The pale stone of this beautifully proportioned 18C building, seems to gain luminescence in the simple entrance, through the chiaroscuro effect produced by its five niches. These contain sculptures of saints and frame the great cedar door. At the sides there are two tall, elegant towers, ending in graceful little bulbular cupolas. Inside, to the left of the chancel, a prone Christ can be seen in the **Entombment** (Santo Entierro), finely carved in ebony with silver inlays, in the style of Sevillian images.

Ⓥ **Campeche Regional Museum** (M). – **House of the King's Lieutenant** (Casa del Teniente del Rey). In the seven halls on the first floor, there is an exhibit of Maya archeological objects.
Among those consecrated to religion, the jade mask and the **jewels★** discovered in the tomb of Calakmul are remarkable. The first floor presents an overview of the main historical events up to the 18C. There, a 17C tiller splendidly carved of African ebony in the form of a greyhound with a snake wound around it, catches the eye.

ADDITIONAL SIGHTS

Ⓥ **San Román Church** (Iglesia de San Román). – *Corner of Bravo and Calle 10. Plan p 00.* In this church, the faithful venerate the Black Christ (Cristo Negro), an image carved in wood and mounted on a filigree silver cross.

Ⓥ **Fort Saint Michael** (Fuerte de San Miguel). – *Leave Campeche by Avenida Ruiz Cortines and Avenida Justo Sierra and after 3 km – 1.9 miles, turn left and continue 300 m – 984 ft on the Camino Escénico.* In the 18C, this fortress was built on Buenavista Hill as a complement to the city's defense system. It still has its moat, ramp, drawbridge, and lookout posts; from this spot, a good **view** of the city and of the blazing sunsets can be enjoyed.

EXCURSION

Edzná Archeological Site. – *60 km – 37.3 miles. Go east from Campeche on highway nº 180 and at 41 km – 25.5 miles turn right. Description p 82.*

★★★ CANCÚN Quintana Roo ◆◆◆

Map of Principal Sights p 6

Cancún is internationally renowned for its magnificent location, its luxurious tourist facilities and the incomparable beauty of its setting, with an exciting seascape of turquoise waters and coconut palms. The quiet **Nichupté Lagoon★★**, enclosed by an old coral reef, delightfully contrasts with the nearby jungle. The daring, yet functional, Cancún architectural complex has fostered the rapid development of shops offering imported goods, tourist services and water sports.

SIGHTS

★★ **Beaches** (Playas). – The soft white sand sets off the strong blue-green tints of the warm waters that bathe the shore; at depths of a few meters, delicate coral formations mark the entrance to strange and fantastic worlds. The most popular beaches are: Langosta, Las Perlas and Linda, which are located on the north side of Avenida Kukulcán; and towards the south, Chac-Mool and Gaviota Azul.

(Photo Guillermo Aldana/Mexico)

Caribbean seascape

⊘**Regional Museum of Anthropology and History (Museo Regional de Antropología e Historia).** – *Avenida Kukulcán at one side of the Convention Center (Centro de Convenciones).* In this modern building, a simple exposition of the geography and history of the Yucatan Peninsula is displayed in two sections on the first floor; it illustrates the principal aspects of the Maya civilization with background information about the sites of the ancient empire, such as Cobá *(p 209),* Tulúm *(p 209)* and Kohunlich *(p 65).* On exhibit are precious, finely crafted objects, as well as some human bone remains such as skulls showing ritual deformations of children's heads.

⊘**El Rey Archeological Site (Zona Arqueológica el Rey).** – *20 km – 12.4 miles south on Boulevard Kukulcán.* Under the spell of the Nichupté Lagoon, this archeological site bears witness to the grandiose Maya past, which evolved amid palm trees and exuberant vegetation. The ruins are grouped around two small squares, where vestiges of walls and colonnades atop platforms remain. In one of these squares there is a two-level pyramidal structure with visible traces of superpositions and remains of a facade, all of which show the fine stylistic lines of the late post-Classic period in the region.

EXCURSIONS

★★ **Isla Mujeres.** – *Access by plane or launch. Description p 95.*

★★ **Cozumel Island (Isla Cozumel).** – *Access by ferry from Puerto Morelos and Playa del Carmen. Description p 75.*

From Playa del Carmen to Tulum. – *119 km – 73.9 miles. Estimate 1 day. Go southwest on highway n° 307 toward Felipe Carrillo Puerto (watch for the signs indicating the turn-off to the left, to reach the following places). All distances are calculated starting from Cancún.*

Playa del Carmen. – *66 km – 41 miles.* This is the beginning of a chain of attractive beaches, each with its own particular charm.

Xcaret. – *71 km – 44 miles.* Its small palm-fringed lagoon flows into the Caribbean through canals among limestone rocks. To be noted are the **cenotes** and caves, which connect with the lagoon, creating exotic settings with a peculiar, though wild, atmosphere. Among the ceibas and palms, small pre-Hispanic structures may be found; a dense vegetation has invaded them, as if to guard their secrets.

Akumal. – *101 km – 62.8 miles.* A broad cove with beaches full of small reef formations anchored in the depths. The location is ideal for skin diving. From Akumal excursions into the deep sea are available, to observe ancient pirate shipwrecks.

★★ **Xel-Ha.** – *108 km – 67 miles.* This **natural aquarium** of extraordinary beauty is situated over ⊘ a rocky cave connected to the sea. The translucent waters offer glimpses of fantastically colored, exotic fish. The surroundings combine a thick vegetation with palm-covered islets. The place has areas set aside for skin diving and canoe excursions to nooks seemingly untouched by man.

Archeological Site. – *Following highway n° 307 toward Felipe Carrillo Puerto, at 500 m – 0.3 miles from the junction to Xel-Ha.* To the right of the highway there is a simple pyramidal structure, with traces of paintings. At 1 km – 0.6 miles, along the unpaved road that leads' into the jungle, stands a group of buildings. The notable platforms, with the remnants of colonnades around a cenote, are hidden by the dense vegetation that frames the area in a bewitching combination of architecture and landscape.

★★ **Tulum Archeological Site.** – *119 km – 73.9 miles. Description p 209.*

★★★ **Chichén Itzá Archeological Site.** – *201 km – 124.9 miles to the west on highway n° 180. Description p 66.*

For telephone area codes of major Mexican cities consult the table pp 229-231.

CEMPOALA Veracruz

Map of Principal Sights p 5

Cempoala was the first great Mesoamerican city that was known to the Conquistadors. Furthermore, Hernán Cortés defeated the Narváez expedition here in 1520, thereby reasserting his hold over the campaign against Tenochtitlán.

This **archeological site** contains vestiges of the plazas, pyramids and shrines occupied by the **Totonac** Indians between the 9C and 16C.

Temple of the Chimneys (Templo de las Chimeneas). – *To the right.* It has been thus named for the stumps of clay columns which formerly had a wooden core. The crenellated circles in the front were probably the settings for rites and competitions.

Great Temple (Templo Mayor). – *In the background.* The broad stairway makes this temple the most imposing of all the shrines. The view at the top is wonderful.

> *Return to the highway (200 m – 656 ft) and continue 150 m – 492 ft on the unpaved road.*

Temple of the Air God (Templo del Dios del Aire). – Among the buildings of the present-day town, it is surprising to find this circular fort embedded in another of rectangular shape. It was crowned by cresting and its roof was cone-shaped.

CHETUMAL Quintana Roo   ◆◆◆

Map of Principal Sights p 6

This state capital is surrounded by impressive natural and archeological sites set deep in the jungle. Its location at the southeastern tip of the Republic gave it an important role to play as a strategic center of naval operations throughout the 18C and 19C. Today the city is an especially active trading center as a free port, thanks to its proximity to the northern shore of the Río Hondo mouth and to the Belize border.

SIGHTS

Calderitas Beach (Playa Calderitas). – *6 km – 3.7 miles north on Av. Héroes.* Located on the great Chetumal Bay, this beach reveals a characteristic Caribbean landscape, with calm waters, resembling a turquoise mirror, bathing its fine white sands. This spot is ideal for boating, and its natural jungle background highlights its overall beauty.

Milagros Lagoon (Laguna Milagros). – *12 km – 7.5 miles west on highway n° 186 towards Escárcega, turn left.* Very near the highway there is a beautiful lake formation along 4.5 km – 2.8 miles. Through its transparent blue-green waters the sandy bottom is visible.

EXCURSIONS

Bacalar. – *37 km – 23 miles. Go west from Chetumal on highway n° 186; at 18 km – 11.2 miles turn right on highway n° 307 and continue 19 km – 11.8 miles, to the entrance to the town of Bacalar.*

★★ **Blue Cenote** (Cenote Azul). – *At the entrance to Bacalar.* Circled by limestone rocks and exotic vegetation, in the stunning clarity of its waters, the twisted and buried tree roots are clearly perceptible. Myriad colorful fish swim around them, producing a radiant spectacle. Explorers maintain that no one has been able to find the bottom of this natural formation.

★★★ **Bacalar Lagoon.** – *To the eastern side of the town of Bacalar.* Along 55 km – 34.2 miles there are numerous entrances to the beautiful Bacalar Lagoon, which offers a spectacular sight. It is also known as "the seven color lagoon", owing to the gamut of different tones produced by the combination of coral formations and underwater flora on its smooth sandy bottom. It has a series of canals connecting with the Caribbean Sea, and its tranquil waters are surrounded by soft white sands that are intermittently shaded by mangrove trees and the intense green tones of the shoreline jungle.

★ **Fort San Felipe** (Fuerte San Felipe). – *To the east of Bacalar's Plaza Principal.* This fort, built in the early 18C, is a quadrangular structure punctuated with bastions at its corners. From its crenellated walls, where ancient guns still stand guard, the magnificent Bacalar Lagoon can be admired. During the 18C, the fort was the setting for bloody battles fought against the pirates and, later on, between the Spaniards and the Indians during the War of the Castes. The fort houses a museum that exhibits arms and utensils of the times, as well as some objects from the pre-Hispanic era.

Kohunlich Archeological Site. – *68 km – 42.3 miles. Go west from Chetumal on highway n° 186 towards Escárcega; after 59 km - 36.7 miles, turn left and continue for 9 km – 5.6 miles until reaching Kohunlich.*
Amidst ceibas and palm trees, rise a series of platforms and staircases, which are part of a ceremonial complex of the Early Classic period (3-6C AD). At the rear, in the dense foliage, the main pyramid appears, built on three levels, with beautiful **masks**★★ *(mascarones)* flanking its stairs. They are astonishing for their enormous size (more than 1.5 m – 4.8 ft) and their fine stucco decoration. They depict the solar gods, like the first figure on the left at the lower level which represents the god Kin, wearing a handsome headdress, eyes with incised hieroglyphs, nose ornaments, mustache cover and T-shaped teeth. The ensemble's delicate technique and style reveal the refinement of Maya art.

★ **Río Bec.** – *118 km – 73.3 miles to the west by highway n° 186. This zone includes the archeological sites of Xpuhil, Becan and Chicanná. Description p 177.*

Map of Principal Sights p 6

On the immense plain of the northern Yucatan Peninsula, with neither mountains nor rivers to disturb the uniformity of the landscape, among agaves, thorny bushes and short trees, stands monumental Chichén Itzá, one of the most spectacular ceremonial centers of all antiquity.

The vast **archeological zone** spreads over a peculiar type of soil: a permeable lime crust over a watertable. The natural sinking of this crust in ancient times revealed the existence of underground water, when two great cenotes were formed. Hence, the city's name is *Chi*, which means "mouth", and *Chen*, "cenote". *Itzá* corresponds to the name of one of the Indian groups that inhabited it, the Itzáes.

The fascination caused by the profiles of these enigmatic temples and pyramids is due not only to their balanced proportions, reflecting the purified Maya spirit, but also to the fact that the Toltecs – the dynamic and bellicose people of the Central Mexican Plateau *(p 35)* – also participated in their construction.

HISTORICAL NOTES

The combination of Maya and Toltec cultural values, different as they were, contributed to Chichén Itzá a monumentality that continued to inspire admiration in post-Conquest days. Various Maya accounts and Castillian chronicles created a legend about Chichén Itzá, full of fantasies and inconsistencies, which was gradually disproved in the 19C by the archeologists who studied the ruins. The first full-fledged scientific work, which was started in this century, has reconfirmed the magic and the fascination of this sacred city.

The earliest human settlements go back to 3C AD, when peasants in the region founded a simple economically self-sufficient agricultural community around the cenotes. A couple of centuries later, they were joined by a group of Yucatan Mayas, bearing the Classic culture of the great cities of Guatemala and Chiapas. The new leaders embraced the priestly ministry, and the art that they created was oriented almost exclusively to the worship of the rain god, Chac. Sumptuous temples were erected and at the beginning of the 7C, the ceremonial center reached the height of its splendor, which was interrupted by two invasions.

The first, carried out by Itzáe seamen and traders, occurred in the year 918. Almost immediately thereafter, warriors and craftsmen from the distant city of Tula, led by their ruler Kukulcán (a Maya translation of the word Quetzalcóatl) invaded Chichén Itzá. These Toltecs mixed with the natives, on whom they imposed a military theocracy, like those of the Plateau. They spread the worship of the feathered serpent, and the **Holy Cenote** (Cenote Sagrado) began to receive human sacrifices.

This flourishing period came to an end with a fateful event. At the beginning of the 13C, the Great Lord of the City, Chac Xib Chac, abducted the Governor of Izamal's betrothed during their wedding, which unleashed a war that Chichén lost. The majority of its inhabitants migrated to Petén in Guatemala where they remained until they were conquered by the Spaniards in 1697.

⊘ ARCHEOLOGICAL SITE *time: 1/2 day*

The civic and religious center extends over an area 3 km – 1.9 miles long and 1.5 km – 0.9 miles wide. Although the temples and pyramids are scattered over the site, each complex is artfully set in its surroundings, in which grand esplanades for public worship abound.

The Castle or Kukulcán's Pyramid (El Castillo o Pirámide de Kukulcán). – At the center of the great square stands this grandiose stepped structure, which reflects the military magnificence that surrounded Kukulcán, the god of creation, symbolized by the wind. It was built on a square plan with slightly rounded corners, and measures 55 m – 180 ft on each side. Its nine sloping levels bear a decoration based on protruding panels, which in the higher levels diminish in size, making the monument seem taller than it is (30 m – 98 ft). Its four sides are fitted with flights of steps; the main one stands out with its bordering ramps ending at ground level in ferocious serpents' heads.

During the equinoxes, a disturbing phenomenon occurs on the principal facade. When the rays of the rising sun hit the nine rounded corners of the pyramid's edge, the shadow they cast onto the ramp forms the body of the snake, which appears to be slithering to the ground. The mystery of this pyramid is further compounded by another puzzling fact: the steps of the four staircases, added to the one on the upper shrine, make a total of 365, which has led to speculation about its possible relation to our calendar.

Shrine. – Built on the top of the pyramid, its walls are so plain as to evoke the severity of the ruling castes that utilized it. The entrance columns are serpentine, with the head as the base, the body as the shaft and the rattles, the capitals. The jambs and columns have low reliefs representing various warriors who protect the sanctuary.

From the outer passageway, the stupendous **view★★★** embraces the enormous plain with the ruins in the foreground. Formerly the periphery was occupied by humble villages which, day after day, watched massive pilgrimages pass by, carrying jade, honey, feathers and salt.

⊙ **Inner Temple** (Templo Interior). – A recently excavated tunnel leads to the inner pyramid, over which the Castle was built. At the top, it has a shrine that preserves a stone sculpture depicting the messenger of the gods, the **Chac-Mool**, in front of a jaguar-shaped throne painted in bright red, with jade incrustations simulating his eyes and his spots.

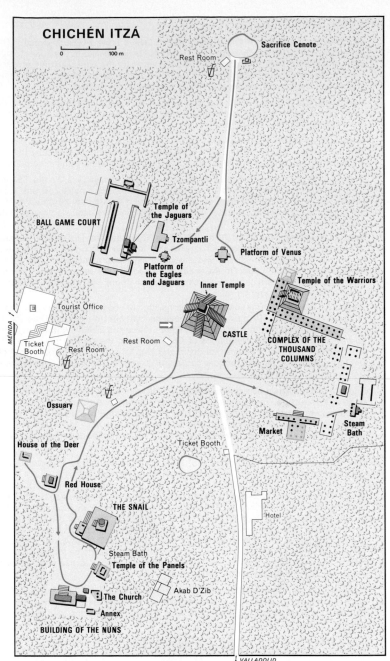

CHICHÉN ITZÁ

0   100 m

Sacrifice Cenote

Rest Room

BALL GAME COURT

Temple of
the Jaguars

Tzompantli

Platform of Venus

Platform of
the Eagles
and Jaguars

Temple of the Warriors

Inner Temple

MÉRIDA

Tourist Office

Rest Room

CASTLE

COMPLEX OF THE
THOUSAND
COLUMNS

Ticket
Booth

Rest Room

Ossuary

Market

Steam
Bath

House of the Deer

Ticket Booth

Red House

THE SNAIL

Hotel

Steam Bath

Temple of the Panels

The Church

Akab D'Zib

Annex

BUILDING OF THE NUNS

VALLADOLID

(Photo: J. M. Gabizon/Paris)

Chichén Itzá. The Castle, seen from the Temple of the Warriors

67

The Ossuary or Tomb of the High Priest (El Osario o Tumba del Gran Sacerdote). – This pyramid 10 m – 32.8 ft high was built in a natural hollow linked to the upper temple by a vertical shaft. At the end of the last century, seven tombs, with skeletons and jade, rock crystal, copper and gold offerings, were discovered in the underground room. The columns at the top are decorated with carved warrior figures.

Red House (Casa Colorada). – This spacious temple, named for the vestiges of red paint on its interior walls, rests on an elevated rectangular platform. The double roof combs are adorned with frets and masks.

House of the Deer (Casa del Venado). – According to popular legend, a deer was painted on one of its walls in the early 20C. Despite its ruinous condition, it is clear that the small shrine was built upon a high rectangular foundation with rounded corners.

Building of the Nuns (Edificio de las Monjas). – It was named thus by the Spanish conquerors because they associated its numerous rooms with a nuns' convent. There are several layers of construction, as can be observed through an enormous hole at the right side of the main staircase, where an 1868 dynamite explosion revealed the oldest foundation.

Annex. – *Connected to the left of the building*. This series of rooms is laid out in the form of a rectangle. The center was filled in, probably to build a second floor, which was never completed. The wealth and diversity of its exterior ornamentation sets off the mask of the rain god, Chac. On the main portal, where the entrance looks like the deity's mouth, on a cornice there is a seated human figure with a feather headdress that is thought to represent a ruler.

The Church (La Iglesia). – This small temple, consisting of one room, is a true gem of the Puuc style *(see p 172)*. The plain walls of the lower part effectively counterbalance the exuberant decoration of the upper zones, where the cornices show writhing serpents and the friezes have representations of Chac. Flanking the central mask, over the entrance bay, is a pair of panels that depict the four *bacabs*, or Maya gods, that held up the heavens and marked the four corners of the earth. The crest is adorned with frets in relief and complex lattices.

Temple of the Panels (Templo de los Tableros). – This rectangular edifice was built on top of an older structure. The spacious room at the entrance has a bench on three sides and two rows of columns that held up the roof. A staircase at the rear leads to the sanctuary, the side walls of which display, on their outside face, various warriors, gods and mythological animals in low relief. Its original multicolored stucco finish has been worn away by time.

The Snail (El Caracol). – This cylindrical structure, that served as an astronomical observatory, was erected on a broad terrace 6 m – 20 ft high.

After remodeling it, the Mayas connected a circular platform to the first level of the tower. This was later widened to a rectangle, with supports at the edges that were probably flag-holders. They also added a stairway at the front, divided in the center by a niche in which was found a broken stela with hieroglyphic inscriptions that have been dated to approximately 845 AD. Four doors lead to the observatory, located at the cardinal points. The interior consists of two circular passageways, one inside the other, with a massive column in the center, in which there used to be a spiral staircase (like a snail, whence the name of the building) leading to some narrow passages with small openings for observing the firmament.

Complex of the Thousand Columns (Grupo de las Mil Columnas). – This is a grandiose complex of buildings that were added over the years around a large quadrangle. The parallel lines of columns used to support roofs that formed spacious, well-lit galleries.

(Photo Michelin)

Chichén Itzá. Complex of the Thousand Columns

The Market (El Mercado). – On an elongated platform, an ample arcaded hall with pillars and painted columns, was built. Along the interior walls there was a bench with a slanted back, of which some vestiges can be seen. The central door connects to a rear patio surrounded by slim columns made of great stacked drums of stone with square capitals.

Steam Bath (Baño de Vapor). – Among the ruins of fallen buildings, there is a construction of three sections connected by a duct: the porch that perhaps served as a waiting room; the steam room, which was reached by a narrow passageway at floor level, containing a pair of benches and two ventilating holes; and an oven that was used to heat the stones over which the water was poured.

Temple of the Warriors (Templo de los Guerreros). – This is an imposing four-tier pyramid, which brings to mind the pyramid of Tlahuizcalpantecuhtli in Tula. It appears behind a row of columns with low reliefs of Indian warriors. Along the ample staircase, flanked by ramps that end in fierce serpents' heads, there are stunning panel reliefs of eagles and jaguars devouring human hearts – evidence of the war-like character of the Toltec priests. A statue of **Chac-Mool**, with his typical meditative gaze, rests at the summit, and behind him rises the sanctuary. On its walls are portrayed Kukulcán-Quetzalcóatl, surrounded by feathers, and masks of the rain god. Within the enclosure, attention is drawn to two superb **serpentine pillars** and several columns in the rear, with engravings of the earth monster at the base, warriors in the center, and *bacabs* holding up the heavens at the top. The small sculptures of men holding their arms up (atlases) served as a base for a large stone table.

(From photo Michelin)

Column from the Temple of the Warriors

Platform of Venus. – This square structure is barely 4 m – 13 ft high and has on its panels various reliefs in which serpents and feathered monsters with tiger's claws, symbolizing the planet Venus, can be seen. The edifice was used for rituals, according to the chronicles. The sculpture of Chac-Mool on exhibit in the National Anthropological in Mexico City was found here *(p 128)*.

Sacrifice Cenote (Cenote de los Sacrificios). – The pilgrimages organized by the military rulers entered Chichén Itzá by the sacred white road, or *sacbé (see p 37),* for the bloody rituals that were carried out in this impressive 60 m – 197 ft diameter well. Its vertically-cut walls measure more than 12 m - 39 ft down to the water level. The solemn sacrifices consisted in throwing clothed and bejeweled men, women and children into this cenote, the mouth of the netherworld, while the participants dropped lighted rubber figures and sumptuous objects of gold, jade and other materials into the water. If one of the victims survived several hours, he was taken out of the well, to impart to the priests the gods' message, particularly that of the rain god, Chac.

About ten exploration teams have managed to extract, from the depths of the cenote, part of this treasure, the bulk of which has found its way to foreign countries.

El Tzompantli. – The name means "stake", where the heads of the victims of human sacrifices hung, and it is related to the macabre Toltec ritual, which was used at the same time to intimidate the enemies of Chichén. This great rectangular platform supported the fence hung with skulls – a motif carved in its stone walls more than 500 times, alongside eagles devouring hearts and feathered serpents.

Platform of the Eagles and Jaguars (Plataforma de Águilas y Jaguares). – This small square structure has flights of steps on all four sides, flanked with ramps ending in serpents' heads. The recessed panels portray jaguars preparing to swallow human hearts, while the salient panels show eagles doing likewise.

Ball Game Court (Juego de Pelota). – This was the largest ball game court built in Mesoamerica, to serve this wide-spread ritual. Its colossal dimensions (168 m – 551 ft by 70 m – 230 ft), together with the rich ornamentation of the friezes, attest to the splendor achieved by Chichén Itzá around 11C AD.

The esplanade is laid out in the classic double T shape, and its whole length is bordered with benches that support the very high walls of platforms connected to the outside by wide stairways, while the end walls correspond to the respective temples. Three panels, at some distance from each other, are connected to the side walls of the court. The scene on each of them is the same: a dramatic representation of the decapitation ceremony associated with the game. The central motif is a ball with a skull on it towards which both seven-man teams run. The probable leader of the left-hand group carries a knife in one hand and in the other, the head of the leader of the opposing band. The latter is kneeling on one knee, while blood flows from his neck, in the form of six serpents and a bunch of flowers, the symbol of fertility.

The realism and the optimal balance between the figures can also be observed in the two serpent-decorated stone rings in the center of the great court, through which the ball should pass.

Due to a peculiarity of its construction, a curious acoustical phenomenon occurs in this court: a person at one end of the enclosure can hear clearly what is said by a person at the opposite end of the court, even if he speaks in a very low voice.

CHICHÉN ITZÁ★★★

⏱ **Temple of the Jaguars** (Templo de los Jaguares). – Two thick and impressive serpentine columns topped by feathers give a brutal appearance to the entrance of this sanctuary. The interior still has murals portraying a battle near the village.
On the courtyard level, a temple adjoins the foundations of the above structure. Its altar symbolizes the jaguar, and fine stone carvings of gods, warriors and Maya rulers cover its interior.

EXCURSION

⏱ **Balamcanché Grotto** (Gruta de Balamcanché). – *Guided tour : 40 minutes. 4 km – 2.5 miles to the east, on highway nº 180, turn left and follow the unpaved road 500 m – 0.3 miles.*
Set in nearly impenetrable undergrowth, where the iguanas remain motionless and the *chachalacas* squawk, lies this mysterious cave full of stalactites sculpted by the Mayas and grinding stones offered to the water gods.

★ CHIHUAHUA Chihuahua ◆◆◆◆◆

Map of Principal Sights p 5 – Local map p 72

An ancient legend placed the seven golden cities, which attracted the first explorers of the Conquest, in the north of the country. They did not find them, but their efforts bore fruit in various mining operations, the basis for Chihuahua's growth at the beginning of the 18C. This lively city, a state capital, is today an important livestock center. The town has also become world famous for the diminutive dogs named after the city, although their exact origin has not been definitively established.

HISTORICAL NOTES

The concentration of economic and political power in a small number of families at the end of the last century, caused tense situations that led to the emergence of local political chiefs, or *caudillos,* and, finally, to the Mexican Revolution of 1910.
One of the strongest revolutionary armies was organized in Chihuahua; it was the famous Northern Division (División del Norte) led by Francisco Villa *(see p 33)*, whose reputation as a great military leader has become legendary.

SIGHTS

Cathedral. – *Plaza Principal.* As a reflection of the mining bonanza, this magnificent 18C cathedral reveals notable coherence both in design and execution, although its construction spanned more than three decades. Its ample, richly-decorated facades were used as a model for the rest of the cathedrals in the north of the country. In the **main facade★★**, the figures of the twelve apostles in their niches, flanked by free-standing columns, are worth noting.
On the inside, under the left tower, is the Chapel of the Christ of Mapimí, with a fine 18C baroque altarpiece. The original high altar was made of stone, as can be seen from the side of the uninteresting present-day altar, built in 1930, which covers it.

★ **Museum of Popular Art** (Museo del Arte Popular). – *Reforma nº 5.* This small museum
⏱ allows a glimpse into the magic world of the Tarahumara Indians, through their woolen textiles, musical instruments and ceremonial and pastime artifacts of great ethnographic value.

⏱ **Miguel Hidalgo Prison** (Calabozo de Miguel Hidalgo). – *Libertad, between Venustiano Carranza and Vicente Guerrero.* At the back of the Federal Palace, adjoining the old Jesuit school of Chihuahua, a part of the church where Father Hidalgo resided from April to July 1811, has been preserved. Copies of documents pertaining to this era are on display here.

Government Palace (Palacio de Gobierno). – *Aldama, between Venustiano Carranza and Vicente Guerrero.* In this late 19C neoclassical building stands the Fatherland's Altar (Altar de la Patria), which has been erected on the spot where Father Hidalgo was shot on July 30, 1811. In the courtyard, murals by Piña Mora portray the main events of the nation's history and their relation to northern Mexico.

⏱ **Chihuahua Regional Museum.** – **Gameros Manor** (Quinta Gameros). *Bolívar and Calle 4.* This is one of the most beautiful examples of Art Nouveau architecture in Mexico. In it are exhibited lovely carved and many-colored wooden furniture designed for the Requena Mansion, belonging to the same style, in Mexico City. It also contains a sampling of ceramics from the Paquimé culture *(p 159)* and many elements illustrating the life and customs of the Mennonite groups *(p 71)* residing in the state of Chihuahua.

★ **Historical Museum of the Revolution in the State of Chihuahua.** – **Pancho Villa's**
⏱ **House.** *Calle 10 nº 304.* After Villa's death (1923), his widow, Luz Corral, turned their house into a museum, which she looked after until her death in 1981. The various rooms of the house radiate the atmosphere of the Revolution. Images and furniture, documents and arms recall the life of Francisco Villa and his legend, fueled by such daring feats as the attacking and burning of the town of Columbus, New Mexico (United States) in 1916. In the courtyard of the house, is the automobile in which General Villa was riding when he was assassinated in Parral (Chihuahua).

EXCURSIONS

★★★ **Chihuahua-Pacific Railroad** (Ferrocaril Chihuahua-Pacífico) **Barranca del Cobre.** – *Description below.*

★★ **Basaseachi Cascade.** – *265 km – 165 miles. Go southwest from Chihuahua on highway n° 16. In La Junta (139 km – 86.4 miles), take the road to the left towards Tomochic (205 km – 127.4 miles) and Basaseachi (262 km – 162.8 miles). At 3 km – 1.9 miles from Basaseachi, you find the parking area. From there you must walk to the cascade. It is recommended to get an early start, so as to spend the night back in Chihuahua.*

This is a very attractive excursion through meadows, fertile fields and apple orchards. The road goes into the mountains between pine and oak forests, winding streams and imposing rock formations. In the mountain woods, the waters of the Durazno de Tello and Basaseachi streams join, thence cutting a path through the rocks, subsequently to pour their

(Photo Lawrence Castañares/Bio imagen/Mexico)

Basaseachi Cascade

waters over this spectacular fall 310 m – 1017 ft high, in the Candameña Ravine (Barranca de Candameña) – a setting of stark, gigantic cliffs. It is the highest waterfall in Mexico and one of the largest in the world.

Mennonite Settlements (Campos Menonitas). – *99 km – 61.5 miles. Go southwest from Chihuahua on highway n° 16. 2 km – 1.2 miles before Cuauhtémoc City (93 km – 57.8 miles), take the right hand road towards Gómez Farías. 6 km – 3.7 miles farther along, an agricultural zone starts, together with the Mennonite settlements that can be reached by unpaved roads branching off the main highway.*

In this great agricultural region, Mennonite groups have settled. Most of them arrived in Mexico at the beginning of the century, coming from Canada in a pilgrimage to conserve their customs and religious principles. Their ideological roots lie in a pacifist group that developed within the Anabaptist movement during the Protestant Reformation. In the 16C, their leader was Menno Simon, hence their name. They are easily distinguishable from the local population by their typical dress, the features of their houses, and the organization and dynamism that they apply to their productive farms and cheese-making.

★★★ CHIHUAHUA-PACIFIC RAILROAD
(FERROCARRIL CHIHUAHUA-PACÍFICO) **Barranca del Cobre** Chihuahua-Sinaloa

Map of Principal Sights p 4

One of the most spectacular journeys in Mexico is through the **Barranca del Cobre** or **Copper Canyon**, on the railway from Chihuahua to the Pacific Ocean. The construction of this line was a daring enterprise, begun at the end of the 19C and only inaugurated in 1961, after overcoming enormous difficulties.

Barranca del Cobre is the name given to a series of deep gorges lying between imposing mountains that reach above 3 000 m – 9 843 ft.

This is the main homeland of the **Tarahumara Indians**. A community of 50 000 live off these lands by means of primitive agriculture and livestock raising.

As they are used to walking long distances, it is not unusual to see them covering great stretches on foot and reaching apparently inaccessible places by steep, rocky paths.

⊘ROUTE

653 km – 405.8 miles – 14 hours by train (cars also transported)

The tour begins in the city of Chihuahua *(p 70)*. From there the train proceeds at a leisurely pace, creating a friendly atmosphere that fosters conversation with other passengers – often local people traveling with the whole family down to Sinaloa.

Along the way, you can get off at Creel and at Bahuichivo to follow the unpaved roads through a marvelous mountain landscape, which will take at least two days.

CHIHUAHUA-PACIFIC RAILROAD★★★

The train climbs through wide meadows and farmland, until it enters the region of pine-covered mountains and winding streams.

At 297 km – 184.5 miles, the train stops at the former railway town of **Creel**, now mainly a lumber town.

Divisadero. – 58 km – 36 miles after Creel, the train stops at the Divisadero

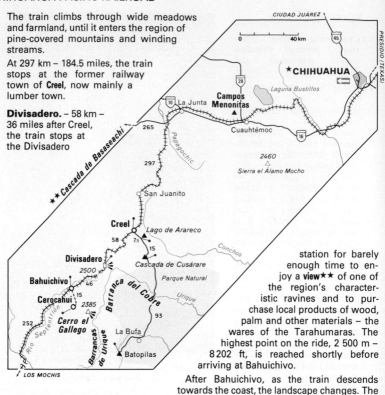

station for barely enough time to enjoy a **view**★★ of one of the region's characteristic ravines and to purchase local products of wood, palm and other materials – the wares of the Tarahumaras. The highest point on the ride, 2 500 m – 8 202 ft, is reached shortly before arriving at Bahuichivo.

After Bahuichivo, as the train descends towards the coast, the landscape changes. The vegetation becomes more abundant and ceibas, palms and hawthornes blanket the cliffs. At their base, the Septentrión River runs parallel to the train tracks. Before the end of the ride, in the city of Los Mochis, Sinaloa, there are numerous memorable **views**★★★ at different altitudes: mountains clad in various shades of green set aglow by the warm light of late afternoon.

EXCURSIONS

⊙ **Creel.** – Those who decide to leave the train at this point, will begin to discover the hidden treasures of the region: the **Arareco Lake** appears between pine and oak woods, that disappear under the winter snows; the **Cusárare Waterfall;** and the old **Batopilas** mines. These mines are located at an altitude of 500 m – 1 640 ft (116 km- 72.1 miles from Creel on a surfaced road), at the bottom of a canyon, hidden in exuberant tropical vegetation and lulled by the river of the same name.

⊙ **Bahuichivo.** – From this spot, situated at 401 km – 249.2 miles, the trip may be interrupted to visit the town of Cerocahui, the starting point for a fabulous climb through the mountain vegetation leading to the **Cerro el Gallego** lookout, which offers one of the best **views**★★ of the region. From there one of the **Urique Ravines** (Barrancas de Urique) is clearly visible, with its light and dark hues. The wind whistles and the river murmurs in the distance as it slowly winds along the bottom of the gorge, past the old mining town of Urique.

★ CHOLULA Puebla   ♦♦

Map of Principal Sights p 6 – Local map p 170

The city of Cholula spreads out at the foot of the ancient pre-Hispanic pyramid as though it were an enormous chessboard; its beautiful old colonial houses of different eras have severe facades. According to legend, Cholula has 365 churches - one for each saint of the year. In fact, at present there are only 39 churches in the city.

HISTORICAL NOTES

Cholula, one of the most important pre-Hispanic cities, is closely associated with the Toltecs, who took control of the city after fleeing from their capital, Tula, in the 12C. The city's name derives from the word *cholollan,* which means "the place of the flight".

During the Conquest of Mexico, Hernán Cortés visited the city and wrote that he had counted more than 400 towers and mosques, which should be understood as a reference to the pre-Hispanic temples found at the tops of the pyramids. During his stay, the frightful slaughter of the Indians took place, perpetrated by the Conquistadors on the pretext of forestalling an ambush against them. Alonso García Bravo designed the Spanish city, with a string and a square, laying it out in regular streets and blocks, like Santa Fe de Granada in Spain.

SIGHTS

Plaza Principal. – At the heart of the city is a large and handsome main square flanked by several important buildings: the city hall, with its enormous arcade that borders the west side; the parish church to the northeast; and the convent and open-air chapel to the east.

⏱ **Saint Gabriel Monastery (Convento de San Gabriel).** – *To the east of the Plaza Principal.* Founded by the Franciscans in 1529, it has a sober Renaissance facade and thick side buttresses, flanking a very lovely lateral portal. On the inside, the ribbed vault of the high altar is worth noting.

Cloister. – The cloister has remarkable mural paintings dating from the 16C: The Saint Sebastian and the Mass of Saint Gregory are noteworthy. In other parts of the cloister, there are fine oil paintings and ornamented sculptures from the 17C and 18C.

★★ **Open-Air Chapel (Capilla Abierta).** – **Royal Chapel** (Capilla Real). – *To the east of Saint* ⏱ *Gabriel Church.* This has an immense atrium where the Indians used to attend religious ceremonies. There are nine arches which are closed at present, but which were opened to show the interior with its great number of columns supporting **63 cupolas** – the only building of its type on the American continent.

⏱ARCHEOLOGICAL SITE *time: 1 hour*

From the Plaza Principal, follow the signs "Zona Arqueológica".

Museum. – *30 m – 98 ft before the ticket window (taquilla), across the highway.* This museum contains a **model**★ illustrating the different construction phases of the site's pyramid, as well as a collection of clay vessels found in the region.

Pyramid. – *At the side of the highway next to the ticket window, you will find the entrance.* Through 6 km – 3.7 miles of tunnels recently excavated by archeologists, four great structures were successively built over the small pyramid, from the beginning of the Classic period *(p 29)*, were discovered. One pyramid was constructed over the other with a view to correcting faults in the first structures and to demonstrate the power of the successive ruling groups. The latest phase of construction resembles a hill; each side is 400 m – 1 312 ft long at the base, which makes it one of the largest in Mesoamerica, although not the tallest. In the area already explored, various structures have been found, such as the traditional *talud-tablero* terrace *(see p 35)* and the **Plaza of the Stelae** (Plaza de las Estelas) – striking for its size and beauty. At the top of the pyramid, as a symbol of the imposition of the Spanish over the Indian culture, stands the Church of the Remedies (Templo de los Remedios). From this point, the **view**★ of the surroundings is splendid.

EXCURSIONS

★ **Tonantzintla.** – *4 km – 2.5 miles to the southwest.* This small church possesses the most important colonial work built by the Indians. The facade is covered with bricks and tiles; the sculptures are placed in small niches.

★★ **Interior.** – The interior of the church of Tonantzintla offers an unusual display of motley forms, where plant stems are combined with little angels, flower or fruit baskets with images of male and female saints – all rather rough forms, though lovely and touchingly simple. A canopy protects the Virgin of Tonantzin. The church's cupola is adorned with a *trompe l'œil* painting depicting Paradise. The decoration of this church interior requires close scrutiny, since in each stretch there are so many forms or scenes that some could be overlooked. This unusual work is complemented by a group of carved and gilded wooden altarpieces.

San Francisco Acatepec. – *5 km – 3.1 miles to the south.* This, the most beautiful and multicolored **facade**★★ of all the churches in Puebla state, is covered with Talavera style tiles of different colors and a larger size than those commonly used. The entrance arch is distinguished by the whitest mortar and the towers are covered with tiles and red brick; cornices and moldings seem to be in violent motion; and, at the top, the image of the Virgin is set in an eight-pointed star. This work dates from the 17C. Its interior is of recent vintage, because it was destroyed by fire in 1940, although some of the plasterwork decor has been repaired and some altars have been preserved.

Tlaxcalancingo. – *9 km – 5.6 miles. Go south from Cholula to Acatepec (5 km – 3.1 miles), turn left, 4 km – 2.5 miles on highway n° 190.* The beautiful **facade**★ of the church is ornamented with Talavera style tiles, brick and mortar. The rich colors make this parish church remarkable. In the atrium there is an 18C cross decorated with grape vines and clusters.

(Photo Michelin)

Tlaxcalancingo. Tiles from the church facade

CIUDAD HIDALGO Michoacán ◆◆◆

Map of Principal Sights p 5

This location was known as Taximaroa, which in the Tarascan language means "boundary", since it was possibly a border site between the Tarasc Kingdom and the Aztec empire. Today, Ciudad Hidalgo is a halfway point for trading industrial and agricultural goods in the state of Michoacán.

SIGHTS

Saint Joseph Parish Church (Parroquia de San José). – *Lerdo de Tejada and 5 de Mayo.* Founded at the end of the 16C and the early 17C, this parish church is noted for its solid construction, which resembles, like many other churches of this period, a great fortress. Its facade is simple, evoking Plateresque forms.
In the atrium there is a stone cross which reveals again the finesse and perceptiveness of the Indian craftsman. The baptismal font, inside the church, has impressive proportions and elegant ornamentation, from the same indigenous sources.

Parish Church of Perpetual Help (Parroquia del Perpetuo Socorro). – *12 Francisco I. Madero, between calles Nicolás Bravo and Allende.* This is a peculiar construction designed by the architect Carlos Mijares between 1969 and 1983. It was inspired by the project of an unfinished cathedral of five radial naves, created by Vasco de Quiroga in the 16C in Pátzcuaro *(p 160)*. Its attractive interior combines four chapels within tall towers dedicated to the sacraments. Branching out from them are four broad arches, one over the other, which open up like the fingers of a hand. The construction was made entirely of reddish brick, the ends of which form fans and produce very appealing light and perspective effects.

EXCURSIONS

⊙ **San José Purúa.** – *35 km – 21.7 miles. Go southeast from Ciudad Hidalgo on highway n° 15 towards Zitácuaro and at 28 km – 17.4 miles, turn right; continue 5 km – 3.1 miles until the entrance to the town. Keep on straight ahead 2 km – 1.2 miles, until reaching the lower part of the ravine.*
In the middle of a stunning natural cut in the rock, on a slope of more than 800 m – 2 625 ft, hot springs run through several pools, until reaching a rivulet that meanders through the bottom of this enchanting gorge. The heights opposite, with rough rocks and scant vegetation, resemble enormous walls and clash with the exuberant flora fed by the springs.

Angangueo. – *80 km – 49.7 miles. Go southeast from Ciudad Hidalgo on highway n° 15 towards Zitácuaro and at 56 km – 34.8 miles, turn left in San Felipe de los Alzate; 24 km – 14.9 miles to the town.*
Lying in a dramatic natural setting, Angangueo is noted for its characteristic white-washed constructions topped with pitched tile roofs. Once a prosperous mining center, the town is now a stopover for visitors interested in observing a marvelous natural phenomenon: the hibernation of the monarch butterfly.

★★ **Monarch Butterfly Sanctuary** (El Santuario de las mariposas monarca). – *From Angangueo* ⊙ *vehicles can be rented: estimate 1 1/2 hours from Angangueo to the sanctuary. Once arrived at the site, you must walk 1/4 hour to reach the sanctuary. A guide will accompany you during your visit.*
Hundreds of thousands of butterflies flutter about woods of silver firs on the border between Mexico and Michoacán states. After traveling enormous distances from southeastern Canada and the northeastern part of the United States, they remain in this region from November to March or April of the following year to ensure the survival of the species.

CIUDAD JUÁREZ Chihuahua ◆◆◆◆

Map of Principal Sights p 4

During the 16C, travelers who came through the north of the country by crossing the Río Grande used to stop at a ford called the Northern Pass (Paso del Norte). In the 17C, the Franciscan friars founded a mission on that spot, which later would become Ciudad Juárez. Today it is a busy border town, located in a fertile valley, unlike the desert vegetation of its surroundings and the **Dunes of Samalayuca** (Médanos de Samalayuca).
Large numbers of tourists visit Ciudad Juárez to watch the greyhound and horse races or bullfights and to enjoy the exciting night life of the city.

SIGHTS

Our Lady of Guadalupe Mission (Misión de Nuestra Señora de Guadalupe). – *Plaza Principal.* This 17C building has a simple facade, a stone portal and a baroque window. The round tower, shifted toward the atrium, consists of two very austere parts. The inside is noteworthy for its magnificent beamed roofs richly decorated with geometric figures. The triumphal arch is dressed in carved wood and the image of the Virgin shines in the apse from a golden frame.

⊙ **Art Museum.** – **PRONAF Commercial Center.** *Coyoacán and Av. Lincoln.* In this simple modern museum, various original pre-Hispanic ceramic pieces and sculptures from the western cultures of Mexico are noteworthy.

COLIMA Colima ◆◆◆◆

Map of Principal Sights p 5

This placid city at the foot of the imposing Nevado de Colima and Volcán de Fuego has a pleasant warm climate and a typical provincial air which make a stay in the city a very pleasant experience.

★★ **Museum of Western Cultures** (Museo de las Culturas Occidentales). – *Av. Paseo de la* ⏲ *Independencia and Niños Héroes.* This is one of the most complete museums devoted to the western civilizations of Mexico. Its modern and functional design features an inner garden flanked on all sides by the exhibit rooms. In these rooms explanations are offered concerning the western Mexican cultures and their relations with the rest of Mesoamerica. The importance of Colima in the region is underscored. Among the objects of particular archeological and anthropological value in the museum, the animal-shaped ceramics and the dancing puppies, called **ixcuincli,** that in the past were considered sacred animals, are to be mentioned. Another section of the museum is dedicated to two archeological sites near the city of Colima: Chanal and Cobano, still in the exploratory stages.

EXCURSIONS

★★ **Nevado de Colima and Volcán de Fuego.** – *21 km – 13 miles. Go north from Colima* ⏲ *on highway n° 16, towards the National Park, El Carrizal, and at 16 km – 9.9 miles, turn left and continue 5 km – 3.1 miles.* These two giants of the Mexican topography, situated at the western end of the Sierra Volcánica Transversal, a scant 5 km – 3.1 miles apart, are considered the most active volcanoes in Mexico. The **Nevado de Colima** (Iztlalcoliuhqui) 4240 m – 13911 ft high, has a sharp snow covered summit that seems to pierce the clouds brought by the Pacific winds, leaving in view only the green conifer forests that cover its flanks. The **Volcán de Fuego** (3820 m – 12533 ft) has a classic conic shape with a crater that occasionally emits spectacular fumaroles and small overflows of red-hot basaltic lava that run down its rough, barren slopes. This fabulous show can be seen on the way to the natural park, El Carrizal, where a winding road climbs through jungles and oak forests on its way to the volcano.

★★ **Pacific Coast.** – *60 km – 37.3 miles south. Description p 155.*

★★ COZUMEL Island Quintana Roo ◆◆

Map of Principal Sights p 6

Cozumel is one of the largest islands off the Mexican coast and is surrounded by warm seas of incomparable hues. The island is a natural limestone rock platform with an area of 490 km² – 190 square miles. The fine sands of its beaches contrast with the shallow underwater gardens, formed by extensive banks of coral inhabited by a variety of superbly colored fish.
Cozumel's setting combines dense island vegetation with a broad sea horizon, in an innumerable sequence of wondrous views.

Access. – Cozumel can be reached by air, since it has an international airport, as well as by ferry from Playa del Carmen (only passengers), and from Puerto Morelos (passengers and vehicles).

HISTORICAL NOTES

The Spaniards' first contact with these lands, according to some historians, took place in 1511, as the result of a shipwreck: the survivors reached the coast of Quintana Roo and were emprisoned on the island of Cozumel. One of these soldiers, **Gonzalo Guerrero**, integrated into the Indian community and married a chieftain's daughter, with whom he had several children, thus constituting the first recorded *mestizaje* in the New World.
In 1519, when Hernán Cortés *(see p 29)* reached Mexican territory, he commanded Guerrero to join his cause as a soldier and interpreter, which Guerrero refused. Instead, Guerrero taught the Indians many skills and participated on their side in numerous battles.

SIGHTS

★ **Chankanab.** – *10 km – 6.2 miles south on the main highway.*
This beautiful lagoon lying next to the sea and connected to it through natural caves, has been designated an ecological reserve. Its translucent waters mirror the slender palms, ceibas and ferns of the botanical garden that borders the lagoon. The nearby beaches abound in rock formations and coral reefs that complement the spectacle of underwater flora and fauna, in soft multishaded coloring – an unforgettable experience for divers.

Santa María Beach (Playa Santa Maria). – San Francisco. – *14 km – 8.7 miles south on the main highway.*
Santa María is a small cove fringed by coconut palms and thick jungle vegetation. The soft murmur of its blue-green waters as they moisten the smooth sands, unleashes the imagination as you rest under the shade of the *palapas*.

★ **Palancar.** – *21 km – 13 miles south on the main highway; at 19 km – 11.8 miles, turn right and continue on an unpaved road 2 km – 1.2 miles.*
This exceptionally beautiful site composed of the point and beach that belong to the **Palancar National Marine Park** (Parque Nacional Submarino de Palancar), is considered one of the best spots for skin diving and fishing in the world; it possesses the second largest reef on the planet with extraordinary coral formations in four precious varieties, including black coral. The enormous range of colored tropical fish complements the wondrous show.
The area has been the subject of scientific research by the renowned oceanographer, Jacques Yves Cousteau.
The main highway continues toward the south, leading to other lovely places, such as Laguna Colombia and Punta Celarain.

⊙ **San Gervasio Archeological Site.** – *14 km – 8.7 miles to the east on the transversal highway; at 8 km – 5 miles, turn left and continue 6 km – 3.7 miles on an unpaved road.*
In the heart of the island, these important ruins include a series of small temples with a main square in the center. On one of its sides there is a simple structure of columns atop a platform where traces of painting remain on the inside. Through the main entrance to the square, practically hidden by the tree trunks and dense foliage, a white road, or *sacbé (see p 37)* emerges; over this a curious false arch has been erected. The jungle's rapid growth overpowers the ruins of a glorious past.

EXCURSION

★★★ **Cancún.** *Description p 63*

The maps and plans are orientated with north at the top.

★ **CUERNAVACA** Morelos   ◆◆◆◆

Map of Principal Sights p 6

Known as the city of eternal springtime for its warm climate and exuberant vegetation, Cuernavaca was chosen by the pre-Hispanic emperors as a favorite summering place. Cortés followed this tradition and many other leading personalities have done likewise.
This city has a very irregular design; the gardens of its magnificent residences are guarded by high fences crowned by brightly colored bougainvilleas, creating pleasant nooks that evoke past splendor.
In the outskirts, there are important archeological sites, numerous colonial convents, old agricultural and livestock haciendas, converted into tourist centers, and lovely natural spots.

HISTORICAL NOTES

Cuernavaca was called Cuauhnahuac, which means "among the trees", and was inhabited during the pre-Hispanic era, like other nearby places, by Tlahuics and Nahuas.
In the colonial period it was the seat of the Marquisate of Oaxaca Valley, and in 1834 it was given the rank of a city. In 1855, it was the capital of the Republic, and at present is the capital of Morelos state.
This region was the birthplace of the Agrarian Revolution led by **Emiliano Zapata** *(see p 33)*. Today the country's sugar industry is concentrated in Cuernavaca.

CATHEDRAL COMPLEX AND SURROUNDINGS

time: 3 hours

⊙ **Cathedral Complex.** – **Franciscan Monastery** (Exconvento Franciscano). *23 Hidalgo, at the corner of Av. Morelos.* A large atrium with a crenellated wall encloses structures from different periods; among them, the **open-air chapel** *(capilla abierta)*, with a continuous half-barrel vaulted dome and original flying buttress arches.

Cathedral. – **Monastery Church** (Templo del Exconvento). Its construction was begun in 1529. Today it is an example of successful remodeling, carried out by Mathias Goeritz and Gabriel Chávez. The sober original elements of the building are harmoniously combined with the modern parts; thus the gilded altars blend with very plain architectural lines and simple stained glass windows in warm colors that give a pleasant atmosphere to the **interior★**.
The principal facade is devoid of ornamentation, but a Plateresque portal adorns, the **lateral entrance**. On the inside, the **mural paintings** depicting the crucifixion of the martyrs in Japan, are noteworthy.

Cloister (Exclaustro). – This plain 16C building consists of two floors in which mural paintings have been preserved. The corridors contain a series of valuable paintings and sculptures.

★ **Chapel of the Third Order** (Capilla de la Tercera Orden). – This chapel is a baroque construction of the 17C, with facades of a popular character, decorated in mortar. The most remarkable is the **lateral facade** with its splayed shape. Inside there is an admirable, baroque style gilded **altarpiece** with exquisite sculptures.

Cuauhnahuac Museum. – Cortés Palace (Palacio de Cortés). *Pacheco Garden (Jardín Pacheco)*. This is a stately **construction★** of civil architecture from the 16C, belonging to the illustrious conqueror, which was built upon a pre-Hispanic structure.

This greatly altered palace today houses a museum with interesting paleontologic material, documents, armor, furniture and other objects that illustrate the leading phases of Mexico's history. On the rear terrace there is a **mural★** by Diego Rivera (1930), which deals with Mexican history from the time of the Conquest to the Agrarian Revolution, including the War of Independence from Spain. The figures of Cortés, Emiliano Zapata and Morelos, the latter being the painter's self portrait, are prominent.

Handicraft Market (Tianguis Artesanal). – *Beside the museum*. Jewelry, leather, basketry, bark paintings, ceramics, textiles and other handicrafts are sold in this colorful market.

ADDITIONAL SIGHTS

⊘ **Ethnobotanical Garden and Traditional Medicine Museum (Jardín Etnobotánico y Museo de Medicina Tradicional). – Maximilian's House** (Casa de Maximiliano). *200 Matamoros, Col. Acapatzingo. In front of the Church of San Miguel Acapatzingo.* These institutions are located on Maximilian's former country estate, El Olvido. It is a rather modest building with an enormous garden, containing a great variety of plants and trees, classified by name and use.

House of the Pretty Indian (Casa de la India Bonita). – The emperor ordered this built for one of his paramours. Today it is a museum that exhibits different medicinal plants used by the Indians.

⊘ **Studio of David Alfaro Siqueiros.** – *7 Venus*. This famous Mexican muralist painted his last works here; some murals and artists' tools have been preserved, along with a small collection of photos and other documents illustrating his life. The visit to this house can be particularly moving, since it has not been changed since the artist's death.

⊘ **Shrine of Tlaltenango (Santuario de Tlaltenango).** – *2 Av. Emiliano Zapata*. This ensemble comprises two churches: Saint Joseph's (San José), built between 1521 and 1523, considered to be the first chapel on the American continent; and Our Lady of the Miracles (Nuestra Señora de los Milagros), a pleasant baroque church.

EXCURSIONS

★ **Ocotepec Cemetery (Cementerio de Ocotepec).** – *8 km – 5 miles to the northeast on the old highway n° 115 to Tepoztlán.*

⊘ In this picturesque site, death turns almost merry, because the majority of the tombs display different versions of miniature churches painted in cheerful colors and covered with multicolored mosaics – an example of popular funerary art.

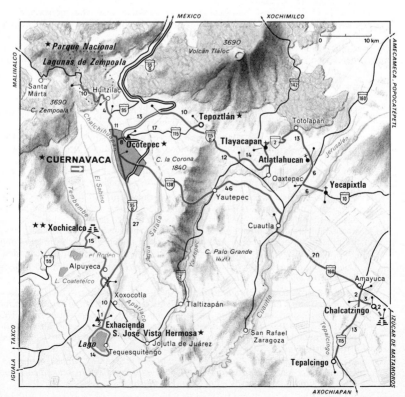

★**Zempoala Lagoons** (Lagunas de Zempoala). – *25 km – 15.5 miles. Go north from Cuernavaca on the free highway n° 95 towards Mexico City and at 11 km – 6.8 miles, turn left, 4 km – 2.5 miles to Huitzilac, go through the town; turn left, continue 10 km – 6.2 miles towards the west on the highway to Santa Marta, and you reach Zempoala Lagoons National Park (Parque Nacional Lagunas de Zempoala). Entrance to the left of the highway.*

Zempoala means "the place of many waters" *(Cempoall,* twenty; atl, water); in fact there are six lagoons – two of them permanent – constituted by closed basins which are flooded in the rainy season, thus depending on rainfall and surface drainage. They are set in the rough terrain of the Sierra of Zempoala at an altitude of 2 850 m – 9 350 ft. The **journey** by highway is well worthwhile, since it provides exciting, if partial, views of the Valley of Cuernavaca and charming sites for outings.

In this beautiful area, covered by the **Zempoala Lagoons National Park,** the majesty of the Sierra Chichinautzin, the turquoise colors of the lagoons and the shades of green of the surrounding woods provide fascinating landscapes. This is an ideal place for hiking around the nearby peaks, for camping and, above all, for boating and fishing in the lagoons.

★★**Xochicalco Archeological Site.** – *42 km – 26.1 miles to the southwest. Description p 220.*

★**Hacienda of San José Vista Hermosa; Lake** (Lago de) **Tequesquitengo.** – *55 km – 34.2 miles. Estimate 3 hours.*
Go south from Cuernavaca on highway n° 95 D until the toll booth fork to Alpuyeca (27 km – 16.8 miles), turn left, continue 6 km – 3.7 miles toward Xoxocotla, then turn right 4 km – 2.5 miles toward Tequesquitengo, turn right and continue 1 km – 0.6 miles, to reach the Hacienda of San José Vista Hermosa.

★**Hacienda of San José Vista Hermosa.** – This rich hacienda was built in 1529 by Hernán Cortés
Ⓥ as a sugar plantation, and was inherited by his son Martín, who spent long periods here. Later on, different owners enlarged and enriched it, until, finally, under the Revolution, Zapata distributed it among the peasants.

Structure. – It still has enormous fireplaces, dungeons, rooms with traces of mural paintings. In one of the rooms there is a permanent exhibit of carriages.
Today it is a hotel with pretty gardens, appealing nooks, a kind of rodeo ring called a *lienzo charro,* a golf course and various other attractions for the visitor.

Return to the highway, turn right, after 2 km – 1.2 miles you reach Lake Tequesquitengo.

Lake Tequesquitengo. – *14 km – 8.7 miles around the lake.* The lake is bordered by handsome houses and recreation centers where facilities for water sports like skiing, rowing, fishing, swimming and skin diving are available.
At the bottom of this lake lies the old town church – an added attraction for skin divers.

Monastery Route (Ruta de los Conventos). – *74 km – 46 miles. Estimate 3 hours.*
In a small area there is a concentration of a large number of fortress-type 16C monasteries that attest to the scope of the evangelizing work accomplished by the Spanish friars in this Indian country.
Among those of greatest historical and artistic significance, the monasteries of Tepoztlán, Tlayacapan, Yecapixtla, Atlatlahucan, Ocuituco, Oaxtepec, Tetela del Volcán and Totolapan should be noted.

Go east from Cuernavaca on highway n° 95 D, at 13 km – 8.1 miles, turn right on highway n° 115 D and   afterwards to the left, following the signs for Tepoztlán (10 km – 6.2 miles).

★**Tepoztlán.** – *Description p 199*
Return to highway n° 115 D and continue for 9 km – 5.6 miles to Cuautla; after the second toll booth, follow the road to Oaxtepec, 14 km – 8.7 miles on highway n° 142 towards Xochimilco, arriving at Tlayacapan.

Tlayacapan. – In this charming village surrounded by enormous hills, many of the 16C chapels, which were built by the Augustinians at the end of every road, have been preserved, such as those of Santiago, La Concepción and San Miguel. In the main square, in front of the monastery stand the remains of the famous Pantitlán sugar plantation. In the village examples of the region's varied pottery can be found.

Ⓥ **Monastery of Saint John the Baptist** (Exconvento de San Juan Bautista). – *Calle 5 de Mayo, unnumbered.* This is one of the largest Augustinian structures in Morelos state; the monastery is on the left side of the church. In what used to be the refectory, there is now an exhibit providing an overview of the region's history from pre-Hispanic times to the present, through photos and objects. Worth noting are the **mummies** of the 17C and early 18C, recently discovered when the church floor was being changed.

Continue to the east on highway n° 2 towards Totolapan and 13 km – 8.1 miles farther you will reach Atlatlahucan.

Monastery of Saint Matthew (Exconvento de San Mateo) **in Atlatlahucan.** – *Calle Independence, unnumbered. Enter by calle Misiones Culturales and turn left in Jardín Amador Salazar.* This Augustinian building preserves almost all the elements of the 16C fortress-type monastery, with a noteworthy processional passage and an open-air chapel of trapezoidal design, the entrance of which is marked by three arches topped by a small bell gable.

Continue on highway n° 2 towards the south and at 2 km – 1.2 miles, turn right, continue 4 km – 2.5 miles on highway n° 160 toward Cuautla, turn left and continue 6 km – 3.7 miles on highway n° 10 to reach Yecapixtla.

⊘ **Monastery of Saint John the Baptist in Yecapixtla** (Exconvento de San Juan Bautista). – *Calle No Reelección unnumbered.* This Augustinian edifice has an enchanting Plateresque **facade★** with Gothic traces. In addition, its unusual one-story cloister has ogee arches that lend it a medieval air.

Chalcatzingo; Tepalcingo. – *91 km – 56.5 miles. Estimate 3 hours. Go southeast from Cuernavaca on highway nº 138 towards Yautepec until Cuautla (46 km – 28.6 miles), go through the village; 20 km – 12.4 miles on highway nº 160 towards Izúcar de Matamoros, turn right at the sign Tepalcingo Microondas, continue 2 km – 1.2 miles to Tepalcingo, turn left 3 km – 1.9 miles to Chalcatzingo, in the town, along the right side of the plaza principal, continue 300 m – 984 ft on an unpaved road and turn right; continue 2 km – 1.2 miles to reach the archeological site.*

⊘ **Chalcatzingo Archeological Site.** – The ruins of Chalcatzingo, dating back to the year 1 000 BC, lie in the middle of a broad sun-scorched valley in the state of Morelos, enclosed by three imposing rock formations, which rise as the only sentinels on the plain. The visible archeological remains presumably occupied until the 16C AD, but the site's heyday was between 700 and 400 BC. In front of the guard house, next to a mound which must have been the site's main building, there are vestiges of a great square. Around this are scattered some remnants of shrines and foundations with excellent reliefs and a partially destroyed ball game court. To the right of the guard house, at the top of one of the hills, protected by a *palapa,* one of the site's most unusual reliefs may be seen. It is called **el Rey,** meaning "the King", and the towns-people still pay it tribute. On the other two rocky blocks, splendid stone carvings with human and animal motifs, worked in an excellent style, reveal a strong Olmec influence.

Return to the highway towards Tepalcingo, continue south 13 km – 8.1 miles to reach Tepalcingo.

Tepalcingo de Hidalgo. – This picturesque village is remarkable for its numerous religious constructions.

Jesus of Nazareth Church (Templo de Jesús de Nazaret). – *Plaza Hidalgo.* This is an attractive 18C baroque building with an elaborate mortarwork **facade★** on the theme of the life and crucifixion of Jesus. It includes many figures, symbols and decorative elements, perhaps inspired by medieval European engravings, but interpreted in a local popular manner. Inside the church, the attractive large **transept oil paintings** imitate baroque-style gilded altarpieces.

For historical notes on the country see pp 26-33.

★★ CUETZALAN Puebla ◆

Map of Principal Sights p 5

In the Náhuatl language, Cuetzalan means, "a place for *quetzales"* (a trogon that has brilliant red and green plumage and long tail feathers). Despite Cuetzalan's altitude (1 022 m - 3 353 ft), its weather is tropical with frequent fog or steady drizzle that produces many-colored plants, flowers and giant ferns over 4 m – 13 ft high, reminiscent of prehistoric times.

This lovely city stands between thickly vegetated mountain slopes. The climate requires tile-covered pitched roofs with eaves that sometimes hang more than halfway across the street, touching the neighboring houses and providing protection for the street vendors. Totonac or Nahua Indians enliven the town's routine – the men wearing their traditional cotton shirts and pants and the women, their crisp white gowns with many-colored **headdresses** over 0.45 m – 1.9 ft high. This sight is more frequent during the **festivals★★** on October 4th, dedicated to Saint Francis of Assisi and the Coffee Fair (Feria del Café) – the bean grown in Cuetzalan renowned for its excellent quality.

One of the leading attractions of the festivities is the pole flyers *(voladores)* – a symbolic Mexican ritual in which men swing on ropes round the top of a very high pole – wearing great feather headdresses resembling the bird for which the town is named. Noteworthy among their many dances is the one called *Los Negritos.*

During the festivities the normally narrow streets are thronged with people, making it difficult to get about. This adds to the confusion of smells and colors of the products that come in from the entire region for sale, especially the variety of fruits and regional handicrafts. Tobacco in the leaf and cigars made on the spot, by hand, may be bought.

SIGHTS

Parish Church (Parroquia). – *Plaza Principal.* The church is a 19C construction in the neo-Romanesque style with a basilica layout. Inside, the plaster decorations at the top of the transept should not be missed.

Los Jarritos Church (Templo de los Jarritos). – *Calz. Guadalupe, in the cemetery.* Strategically situated, this church has a superb view of the city and the surrounding hills. Its name comes from the fact that the spire is decorated along the edges with small baked clay jars or *jarritos.*

⊘ **Calmahuiztic Museum.** – *2 de Abril nº 1.* This museum features regional objects, such as dancers' costumes, musical instruments, ceremonial offerings to the dead, masks, fossils (which abound in the region), Indian costumes and some handicrafts.

Las Pozas. – *3 km – 1.9 miles to the east by the ravine path.* In several of these cold water pools, you can swim amidst the water-polished or moss-covered rocks.

Las Cascadas. – *5 km – 3.1 miles east by the ravine path.*
The most famous of these cascades is the one called Gloria, which can be seen from the highway; two others can be reached on foot. These cascades are formed by the falls of the Cuixiatl River, against a background of coffee bushes and wild flora.

Yohualinchan Archeological Site. – *7 km – 4.3 miles west by an unpaved road.* The monuments of this site, very similar to those of El Tajín, are set in exuberant vegetation. Three pyramids, with a square in front, were raised on terraces that correct the unevenness of the terrain. They are constructed of stone blocks from the area.

Libres. – *104 km – 64.6 miles by the highway to Puebla.*
Formerly called San Juan de los Llanos this town has preserved, in the nave and lateral aisles of its parish church, a group of magnificent altarpieces with paintings. The altarpieces are made of carved and gilded wood. The one on the **high altar★★** has decorated sculptures. The work is so fine that in certain parts it looks like filigree. Worthy of mention are the caryatids of the third section.

★★ CUITZEO MONASTERY Michoacán

Map of Principal Sights p 5

This striking religious complex was founded in 1550 by the Augustinian order. It is today part of a picturesque town.

Church. – This building's sober facade finely carved in stone, consists of three main sections in excellent Plateresque style. The entrance arch has abundant flower motifs, cherubs and Augustinian emblems; it is framed by baluster columns decorated with ribbons, grape clusters, and two-headed eagles, in the way of shields. The whole facade is the remarkable work of Indian craftsmanship, corroborated by an inscription in Latin to the right of the arch, which reads: "Francisco Juan Metl made me". The other two sections continue the sober decorative pattern, closing in the form of a bell gable. Its overall appearance is that of a fortress, so characteristic of the 16C.
The church's main door is magnificently carved, and the interior has a barrel-vaulted nave with thick columns. The ribbing in the apse has Gothic touches.

Monastery. – To the right of the church, there is a series of six arches ending in a crenellated wall. The archway performs three different functions: as an entrance to the cloister, as a gate house and as an open-air chapel. To the left of the cloister entrance there is a fresco painting on the wall, representing the Final Judgement.
The cloister possesses the same architectural richness as the church; its salient features are the monumental archways with powerful buttresses on the lower floor and the double arches on the second floor. Some paintings have been preserved in the corridor vaults. The cloister also contains a fascinating **Museum of Mexican Engravings★** (Museo del Grabado Mexicano), exhibiting reproductions of the leading engravers' work from the end of the 19C and first half of the 20C. Their motifs embrace popular themes, the Revolutionary period and the Cárdenas era.

DOLORES HIDALGO Guanajuato ♦♦

Map of Principal Sights p 5

Dolores Hidalgo, in the state of Guanajuato, is a quiet, semi-desert town on the left bank of the Dolores River. The fertility of this valley, has permitted the town to enjoy steady development since the 16C, despite the surrounding semi-arid conditions. The quality of its clay soil has fostered the progress of skillful potters. Father Hidalgo encouraged these craftsmen, creating home workshops that are still in operation today.
In this city on September 16th, 1810, Father Miguel Hidalgo y Costilla rang the church bell to arouse the populace against the Spaniards, thus starting a revolt that 11 years later would culminate in the Independence of Mexico *(p 30)*. This event is known as *El Grito de Dolores*, the Cry of Dolores.

PLAZA DEL GRAN HIDALGO AND ITS SURROUNDINGS
time: 1/2 day

In the tree-lined main square, there is a statue to Hidalgo, the leader. On the southwest side, stands the **Casa de Visitas**, with an elegant facade of lobulated arches. City Hall (Palacio Municipal), on the northeast side, is a fine example of colonial architecture; Mariano Abasolo was born there. On the north side lies the church atrium, where the president of the Republic celebrates Mexican Independence Day every five years in an impressive ceremony.

★ **Parish Church of Our Lady of Sorrows (Parroquia de Nuestra Señora de los Dolores).** – This is a magnificent example of 18C Mexican baroque architecture. Outstanding features are the shell that tops the entrance arch and the three pairs of *estípites* that adorn the facade, reflecting the regional style.

The towers add elegance to the ensemble; their shapes diminish in size as they rise and are crowned with small, stylized lanterns. Inside the church, of Latin cross layout, there are dramatic 18C Tenebrist paintings; the high altar is neoclassical and in the transept there are two enormous Churrigueresque altarpieces. The one dedicated to Saint Joseph is remarkable for its excellent wood carving, which, unlike most baroque altarpieces, has not been gilded and is, therefore, more clearly visible.

⊙ **Museum.** – **Tithe House – Hidalgo House** (Antigua Casa del Diezmo – Casa Hidalgo). *Calle Morelos n° 1.* This plain dwelling from the late 18C has a lovely, fragrant inner patio, bordered by modest rooms. Here are reconstructed the atmosphere, furniture and decorations that reveal Hidalgo's way of living.

EXCURSION

San Felipe Torres Mochas; Hacienda of the Marquis of Jaral de Berrio★★. – *91 km – 56.5 miles. Estimate one day. Go north from Dolores Hidalgo on highway n° 51 and at 51 km – 31.7 miles, turn right and you will reach San Felipe Torres Mochas.*

San Felipe Torres Mochas. – This picturesque colonial city owes its name to the fact that the towers of its 18C parish church have stood unfinished, blunted – *mochas* in popular parlance – during 243 years.

⊙ **Museum.** – The museum is located in the former home of Miguel Hidalgo. His furniture and personal objects are displayed there. The great variety and large number of locally made pottery pieces exhibited is notable as well.

Go through the town, continue 34 km – 21.1 miles on highway n° 37, turn right and go 4 km – 2.5 miles towards Carretón, on a stretch that is impassable during the rainy season, to reach the former hacienda.

★★ **Hacienda of the Marquis of Jaral de Berrio.** – In the midst of an arid terrain, stands an enormous
⊙ and attractive late 19C structure, with a monumental pink stone facade, framed by two towers at the front. Inside there is a grand neoclassical stairway; some of the rooms have conserved the period decor. The hacienda reached a population of 6 500 inhabitants. As a result of the Revolution and the land policy followed thereafter, the hacienda's population diminished considerably. Today 2 000 people live in the vicinity of the hacienda.

Avoid visiting a church during a service.

★ **DURANGO** Durango   ◆◆◆◆◆

Map of Principal Sights p 5

In the 16C, attracted by the lure of gold and silver, the founders of Durango crossed the Sierra Madre Occidental and chose the Guadiana Valley for the location of their city. Its buildings still reflect the 18C and 19C mining bonanza and related agricultural activities. The distinguishing features of the period's civil architecture were the facades' baroque finishings, the walls' ondulating cornices and the wrought-iron balconies.

CENTER OF THE CITY *time: 2 hours*

Cathedral. – *Plaza Principal.* This was the fourth church built on this site. At the end of the 17C, work was begun on the last reconstruction, to finish only seven decades later. Even though the cathedral displays a mixture of styles, the baroque predominates, as seen in the richly decorated lateral portals. On the **facade★★**, the notable left tower is made up of three sections, adorned with lovely, simple ironwork. The chancel's **choir-stalls★★**, with effigies of saints and apostles finely carved in ornamented wood, are admirable. In the high altar the image of the *Purísima* stands out. The sacristy has baroque-style carved furniture for storing the rich church ornaments, including magnificent silk chasubles embroidered in gold and silver. There are, in addition, four canvases by the painter Juan Correa of the 18C, which presumably belonged to the original high altarpiece.

★ **Government Palace (Palacio de Gobierno).** – *5 de Febrero, between Bruno Martínez and*
⊙ *Zaragoza.* This 18C baroque building originally belonged to the wealthy miner, José de Zambrano. It stands as a great palace on extraordinary arcades – the only colonial ones in the city. The exterior walls end in an ondulating cornice. Several patios have been conserved, as well as the former private family theater, now called Victoria Theater (Teatro Victoria).

⊙ **House of the Count of Valle de Súchil (Casa del Conde del Valle de Súchil).** – *5 de Febrero and Francisco I. Madero.* This residence is an authentic gem of the 18C, having belonged originally to the Conde del Campo y Valle de Súchil, a wealthy landowner of the region. It rises on a slope, with a two-part baroque **facade★** of carved stone. The first part is very sober and the second, richly decorated, with the Virgin in her niche as a prominent feature. It is crowned with large flower urns.
Beyond the entrance room with its baroque ceiling, an enormous and striking Moorish arch opens into the main patio. This is one of the richest parts of the ensemble, also worked in baroque style, with double arcades of semicircular arches on each side. The fluting of its columns creates a dizzying sensation of movement.

Archbishopric (Arzobispado). – *20 de Noviembre and Francisco I. Madero*. This late 19C work is distinctive for the neoclassical style of its facade finials, combined with some baroque and neo-Romanesque elements.

⊘**Museum of Anthropology and History. – Juarez University of the State of Durango.** *Francisco I. Madero and Aquiles Serdán*. This simple museum has a small collection of polychrome ceramics from the pre-Hispanic cultures of the region. It also exhibits examples of popular 19C painting and of oils by the Oaxacan painter, Miguel Cabrera (1695-1768), one of the most distinguished painters of the colonial period.

EXCURSIONS

Villa del Oeste. – Movie sets. *10 km – 6.2 miles north of the city on highway n° 45.* Amidst mountains with sparse and petrified vegetation stands a colorful cowboy town, which comes to life with each new film produced there.

El Tecuán Natural Park (Parque Natural El Tecuán). – *50 km – 31.1 miles to the southwest of the city on highway n° 40*. The winding road climbs through mountains with semi-desert flora to reach a thick pine and oak forest, filled with the sound of rushing streams, under an intensely blue sky.

Sombrerete. – *125 km – 77.7 miles to the southeast on highway n° 45. Description p 185.*

EDZNÁ Campeche

Map of Principal Sights p 6

In a broad valley surrounded by low mountains, the crenellation of the principal pyramid dominates this Maya **archeological site,** which brought together illustrious priests, merchants and craftsmen between the 3C BC and the 9C AD.

TOUR *time : 1 hour*

⊘ The excavated buildings are grouped around a small square which connects through a processional walk with another small complex, where the ticket booth is located.

Platform of the Knives (Plataforma de los Cuchillos). – *To the right*. The two central columns of this elongated structure mark the entrances to the interior chambers. It was named for the large collection of obsidian blades discovered there.

Turn right and walk to the other end of the platform

Annex of the Knives. – These are small mounds that surround on three sides an inner square. The one on the left has a vaulted arch leading from this chamber to the walk.

Return to the road and continue straight ahead until you reach a wide staircase.

Great Acropolis. – This is a symmetrical complex of residences and temples distributed around a patio that was formerly embellished with a stucco floor and a central altar.

★★★**Pyramid of the Five Stories** (Pirámide de los Cinco Pisos). – This majestic structure with 27 bays, rises elegantly to 31 m – 102 ft. The architectural solution for the staircase is unusual: it leads into the central chambers of the first and second floors through arches and, at the same time, has lateral steps to reach the terraces of the third and fourth floors.

On the way up, the first four steps are noteworthy because of the hieroglyphics inscribed on them, not yet deciphered. Note that all the interior walls are of rubblework in well-cut limestone, with a stucco finish and roofed in Maya style vaults. The lintels were wooden. The enormous openwork cresting at the top, reveals the cultural influences of Tikal in Guatemala and of Yaxchilán *(p 221)*. From the summit, there is an excellent **view** of the whole region.

★★ GUADALAJARA Jalisco ◆◆◆◆◆◆

Map of Principal Sights p 5

The city of Guadalajara is the capital of Jalisco state and the second-ranking city of the Mexican Republic. It is a mixture of the most varied cultures, which have meshed to form the present-day city: a metropolis rich in traditions and quick to assimilate the progress of modern times.

Dynamic on the whole, Guadalajara has generated symbols and products that are representative of the Mexican nation, such as the musical bands called **mariachis,** the **charrería** (Mexican rodeo), the dance known as **jarabe tapatío** and the liquor, **tequila.** A wealth of forms and colors enhance its numerous handicrafts, of which the pottery, openwork embroidery and leather goods are most striking. The variety of its regional drinks and dishes, like *pozole, birria* and *moles (see Mexican Food, p 46)* can be enjoyed all year round, but especially at the traditional October festivals. This mosaic of activities makes Guadalajara a showcase of natural beauty, history and art. In addition, Guadalajara is the birthplace of key personalities of contemporary Mexican culture, such as **Juan Rulfo, José Pablo Moncayo** and **Luís Barragán,** among others.

HISTORICAL NOTES

This region was originally populated by various groups of Indians (Nahuas, Otomís, Huichols, Coras, Tepehuans and Coyutccs), none of which succeeded in establishing a formal settlement because of the continuous attacks of the hostile Chichimec tribe. For this reason, the capital was moved several times, until its final foundation in the Valley of Atemajac in 1542.

During the Mexican War of Independence, Father Hidalgo proclaimed the abolition of slavery from the Government Palace of this city; and on December 20th, 1810, *El Despertador Americano*, the first newspaper of the region and also the first to espouse the ideas of Independence, began to be published in Guadalajara.

In the middle of the 19C, an important liberal and reformist movement began to spread, and it had considerable influence on the future of the country. During the coup d'etat of Comonfort, the Juárez Government sought refuge in Guadalajara, where Juárez, Degollado, Ocampo, Guzmán, Ruíz and Prieto arrived on February 14th, 1858. The Jalisco Division took part in fifteen of the important Reform War battles.

In the 20C, Guadalajara witnessed the events of the 1910 Revolution and, between 1926 and 1932, it was the center of the **Cristeros Rebellion.** Since 1940, Guadalajara has headed a vigorous industrial drive, coordinated with its mining, handicrafts, agriculture and livestock production and its commercial activities.

HISTORIC CENTER *time: 1 1/2 days – Plan of the center p 84*

★ **Las Cuatro Plazas** *time: 1/2 day*

These four squares form a Latin cross and constitute the main axis of the city's historic center.

Plaza de los Laureles. – This square owes its popular name to the laurels surrounding the large memorial fountain that commemorates the founding of the city of Guadalajara. The city's coat of arms in bronze rests on a marble cylinder.

⊘**Cathedral (A).** – This cathedral is the pride and symbol of Guadalajara. Its interior consists of three naves with ribbed vaults. In the sacristy hangs a painting of the *Immaculate Conception (Purísima Concepción)* attributed to the Spanish painter, Murillo (1618-82), and several Mexican oils signed by Cabrera, Alcíbar, Castro, Paez and others. The Chapter Hall has a canvas by Villalpando; the Altar of Our Lady of the Rose, located in one of the church naves, displays a beautiful sculpture that Charles V of Spain donated to the Diocese of Guadalajara at its inception in 1548.

Plaza de Armas. – This square is distinguished for its stateliness and for a handsome **bandstand★** *(kiosko)* wrought in Paris at the beginning of the century – an excellent example of Art Nouveau. It consists of eight *estípites* columns topped by feminine figures carrying different musical instruments.

★ **Government Palace (Palacio de Gobierno).** – This 18C building has witnessed key historical events, such as the abolition of slavery and the culmination of the Independence movement initiated in Dolores by Father Hidalgo. It still conserves its noble and austere baroque facade; its interior has been completely reconstructed leaving the original design unaltered.

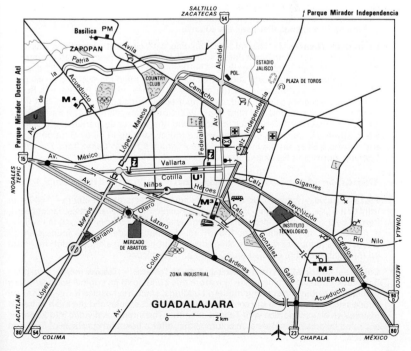

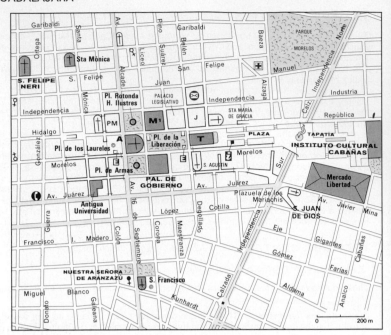

Murals by José Clemente Orozco. – In a stirring **mural★★** (1937-1939) on the side walls and the central vault of the main staircase, the artist treated the themes of militarism and the clergy, and the *Carnival of Ideologies (Carnaval de Ideologías)*. There the imposing central figure of **Hidalgo** is depicted, advancing towards the onlooker with a burning torch in his hand *(see illustration, p 41)*. Owing to its visual impact, vigorous design, and forceful and expressive use of color, this work is considered one of the most remarkable Mexican murals. In the former Chambers of Congress, located on the upper floor of the building, there is another mural that exalts Hidalgo, the priest of Dolores, as a legislator and liberator of slaves.

⊙**Regional Museum of Guadalajara** (M¹). – This 18C edifice, that was originally intended to be a seminary, is outstanding because its facade exemplifies the canons of baroque style. The building preserves a chapel of the period and a central patio, surrounded by ample cloisters with robust Tuscan arcades. It has been restored so as to better fulfill its functions as a museum.

It has various rooms with permanent exhibits, especially the collections of popular paintings from the 18C and 19C and fossils of a mammoth that was found in the region of Zacoalco.

Plaza de la Liberación. – This square is also known as Plaza de los Tres Poderes or Plaza de Dos Copas (in reference to the two fountains shaped like goblets, or *copas,* that adorn the square). This vast modern space provides a lovely setting for the public and religious buildings that flank the square.

★**Degollado Theater** (T). This mid-19C building with classical proportions was built ⊙under the direction of architect José Jacobo Chávez and has been named in honor of the Reform martyr, Santos Degollado. The front was faced in stone in 1961 and the mosaic of the frontispiece was substituted for a marble relief representing an allegory of the muses. In its portico, it has 16 Corinthian columns, like the Pantheon in Rome. The vestibule is elliptically shaped and supported by Doric columns on the first floor, continuing on the second and third floors with Corinthian columns. The **theater** (Salón de Espectáculos) itself, very much in accord with the style of the period, is shaped like a horseshoe. The **dome★** is decorated with a mural painting in oil by Gerardo Suárez and Jacobo Gálvez, on the theme of Dante Alighieri's *Fourth Canto* from *The Divine Comedy*, portraying Greek and Roman poets and writers in limbo.

Cabañas Hospice (Hospicio Cabañas) and Surroundings *time: 1/2 day*

Plaza Tapatía. – Inaugurated in 1982, this square covers almost 500 m – 1 640 ft in front of the beautiful building of the Cabañas Hospice. It is a broad pedestrian corridor, framed by a series of arcades that house shops and public offices. Around the square, a number of monuments are found: reliefs that allude to the foundation of Guadalajara to fountains, marble allegories and bronzes, and a huge sculptural group on the main fountain, entitled *Immolation of Quetzalcóatl.*

★★**Cabañas Cultural Institute** (Instituto Cultural Cabañas). – **Cabañas Hospice** (Hospicio ⊙Cabañas). Efforts are being made to restore this building to its original splendor, now diminished by the surrounding modern buildings, since the hospice is one of the few neoclassical landmarks in the country. Its layout is rectangular and the main entrance features an elegant portico with Tuscan columns. The interior is divided into 23 patios encircled by arches and Herreran columns that offer a beautiful spectacle of light and shadow.

History. – The Bishop of Guadalajara, Juan Ruíz de Cabañas y Crespo, founded in this building the House of Mercy (Casa de la Misericordia). The work was designed by Manuel Tolsá at the end of the 18C, largely built by José Gutiérrez, and finally completed around 1845 by Manuel Gómez Ibarra, with the construction of the chapel. Since 1983, the building has been used to host a variety of cultural activities, with a section set aside for the exhibition of some of José Clemente Orozco's original sketches for his murals.

Chapel. – It contains splendid **murals**★★ by Orozco, painted during 1938 and 1939. They embody a profound vision of Mexico's Conquest by the Spaniards; the work centers on the cupola where a **man aflame** disappears into infinity. Severe and grandiose, vibrantly colored, with a superb mastery of perspective and treatment of space, these frescoes are considered to be among the most important artistic expressions of the 20C.

San Juan de Dios District (Barrio de San Juan de Dios). – San Juan de Dios is a popular gathering point, with its church and small square, Plazuela de los Mariachis, enlivened by the larks' song, restaurants and street photographers. It is a fine spot for listening to popular music, drinking tequila and eating typical regional dishes. Both the architectural complex and the urban surroundings have undergone considerable modifications, becoming stereotypes of Mexican folklore.

⊙ **Libertad Market (Mercado Libertad).** – This interesting example of modern architecture – one of the largest and perhaps the most famous in the region – was built some 20 years ago. Here all sorts of products as well as tasty local food are sold.

San Francisco District (Barrio de San Francisco) *time: 2 hours*

Saint Francis' Garden (Jardín de San Francisco). – This charming shaded garden occupies what was the atrium of Saint Francis' Church, which was originally part of a vast architectural complex – the Province of the Minor Franciscan Friars.

⊙ **Saint Francis' Church (Templo de San Francisco).** – Built at the end of the 16C, altered during the 17C, and subjected to several recent modifications, this church survives as an example of Franciscan baroque elegance. Its interior is distinguished for its balanced proportions, which create a warm and inviting atmosphere.

★ **Chapel of Our Lady of Aranzazú (Capilla de Nuestra Señora de Aranzazú).** – This is an ⊙ exquisite example of the Mexican Churrigueresque style, notable for the gentleness of its forms and the grace of its proportions. Its enveloping interior conserves the splendor of its original **altarpieces** – a unique characteristic, since few have escaped the modifications and misfortunes due to modernist excesses.

Old University (Antigua Universidad). – **Telegraph Building** (Exedificio de Telégrafos). *In* ⊙ *Plaza de las Sombrillas.* A monumental early 19C facade of classical proportions stands as the only remnant of the church of Saint Thomas Aquinas, originally part of the university. Inside the former university building there are murals by David Alfaro Siqueiros and Amado de la Cueva, painted between 1924 and 1926. On the rear facade there is a solid wooden door carved with beautiful reliefs.

Santa Mónica *time: 2 hours*

⊙ **Santa Mónica's Church.** – This is one of the finest and most beautiful examples of a Solomonic baroque **facade** to be found in the city, although in fact it is a mere remnant of the former convent of Augustinian nuns, which once extended over a vast area, but after numerous vicissitudes, was demolished at the end of the 19C. The construction of the church was completed in 1773. Its preciousness is reflected in the delicate craftsmanship of its stone carving and in its **twin portals**★★. The latter are divided into two sections that are profusely decorated with lace-like vines, grape clusters, intertwined ribbons and curvilinear frets. This voluptuous ensemble contrasts with the severe monumental sculpture of Saint Christopher that replaces a column on the right-hand corner of the church front. This plain statue recalls a popular medieval carving and catches the eye of every passerby.

★ **Church of Saint Philip Neri (Templo de San Felipe Neri).** – Built by the Congregation of the Oratorians during the 18C, this church has a richly adorned facade and a beautiful large bell tower. On the inside, there is a neo-Gothic ceiling, which maintains a decorative and spatial balance with the rest of the building. Although adapted to the Churrigueresque models in fashion, this church has not lost its sober baroque character.

The following sights may be found on the area map p 83.

★★SAN PEDRO TLAQUEPAQUE *time: 1/2 day*

Pre-Hispanic in origin, and with a deep-rooted tradition in potterywork, San Pedro Tlaquepaque became a vacation spot for the aristocratic families of Guadalajara. At present it is an important handicraft center, producing works in ceramic, blown glass, *papier mâché*, weaving, embroidery, carved wood, jewelry, tin, leather, stone, gold, lead, candles and tiles, among others.

Recently, new measures have been taken to preserve the town's colonial character and to adapt it to commercial and tourist needs. Its most interesting buildings are the parish church of Saint Peter, the Church of the Solitude, the Hospital of the Refuge, the Hidalgo Garden, the Parián and various late 19C residences.

★ **Regional Ceramics Museum** (Museo Regional de Cerámica) (M^2). – **House of the Golden Donkey** (Casa del Burro de Oro). Upon entering this museum, inaugurated in 1954, the visitor discovers a wealth of objects. The delightful old-fashioned kitchen, Andalusian-style earthenware from Santa Cruz de las Flores, the Tlaquepaque figurines, the burnished pottery and palm-weavings *(petatillo)* of Tonalá, the gilded burnished Sayula pottery, the contemporary and highly-fired ceramics and the award-winning works of the National Ceramics Prize (instituted in 1977 and celebrated yearly in June) all contribute to an understanding of the city's cultural life, in a homey atmosphere without the formality of a conventional museum.

INDEPENDENCIA LOOKOUT PARK (PARQUE MIRADOR INDEPENDENCIA) AND SURROUNDINGS *time: 1/2 day*

Go north from Guadalajara on Calz. Independencia.

Independencia Lookout Park. – This park has broad, flowery terraces that seem on the verge of sliding into an awsome abyss. Their vantage points command the best possible views of the Oblatos Ravine (Barranca de Oblatos).

Science and Technology Center – Severo Díaz Galindo Planetarium (Centro de Ciencia y Tecnología – Planetario Severo,Díaz Galindo). – This modern building, constructed in 1980 – with some sections yet to be completed – has a magnificent planetarium, a didactic Physics section; several rooms featuring permanent exhibits will soon be open to the public.

UNIVERSITY AND ARCHEOLOGICAL MUSEUM
(UNIVERSIDAD Y MUSEO DE ARQUEOLOGÍA) *time: 3 hours*

University of Guadalajara (Universidad de Guadalajara) (U^1). – This building built in the beginning of this century, shows a French influence. In its main reception hall (Salón de Actos) it has important **murals★** painted by José Clemente Orozco between 1936 and 1939.
The stage wall displays a central theme: *The People and Its Leaders (El Pueblo y sus Líderes);* the cupola portrays an allegory, *Progress of Science (El Progeso de la Ciencia).* Both works are distinguished by clear lines, a skillful use of perspective and contrasting tones that make the paintings dramatic.

Archeological Museum of Western Mexico (Museo de Arqueología del Occidente de México) (M^3). – Built in 1960 and since remodeled, its function is to preserve, exhibit and restore the archeological objects found in the states of Jalisco, Colima and Nayarit. Despite its reduced dimensions, the museum contains a valuable collection of vessels and human- and animal-shaped figures that offer an overall view of pre-Hispanic cultures in the western region of Mexico *(p 35).*

ADDITIONAL SIGHTS

Albarrán Hunting Museum (Museo de Caza Albarrán) (M^4). – This is a private institution located in a well-furnished house, containing a collection of more than 200 hunting trophies, all exceedingly rare and handsome. An effort has been made to place them in their natural habitat.

Tonalá. – *To the east by Río Nilo.* In this ancient Indian village, traditional pottery techniques have merged with more sophisticated modern technologies. Trading in Tonalá has grown beyond the exhibition and sale of purely local products. However, one of the town's major attractions lies in the fact that not only the local handicrafts can be purchased but also the processes of their production can be observed in the specialized workshops.

Zapopan. – This is an important pilgrimage and religious worship center. Founded shortly after Guadalajara, it has a deep-rooted Indian tradition which survives, despite modern influence, principally in its Patron Saint festivals. These are celebrated in the atrium of the **Basilica of Our Lady of Zapopan** (Basílica de Neustra Señora de Zapopan) on October 12th, after a procession of the Virgin through various churches in the city of Guadalajara. Multitudes of communicants and dancing groups attend these festivities and spend the whole day performing Indian dances, dressed in rich, multicolored attire.
To one side of the main door of the basilica, there is a small **Cora-Huichol Museum** that exhibits objects of popular art, where elaborate handicrafts made by these Indian communities are sold.

Doctor Atl Lookout Park (Parque Mirador Doctor Atl). – *10 km – 6.2 miles from the junction with the highway to Tepic.* This is a strategic point for a view of part of the Oblatos Ravine, with its waterfall, popularly known as Cola de Caballo. In the rainy season the landscape is even more attractive.

EXCURSIONS

Tequila. – *57 km – 35.4 miles. Go northwest from Guadalajara on highway n° 15 towards Tepic and Nogales.*
Tequila is famous for its plantations of the *maguey tequilero,* the cactus from which tequila is made – the drink that has given Mexico international renown. Many of the tequila-producing enterprises may be visited by appointment.

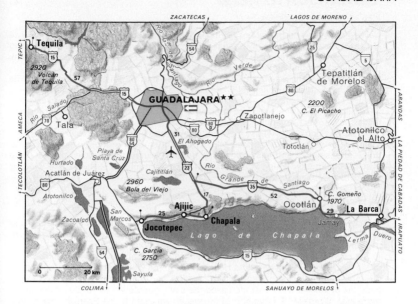

Chapala; Ajijic; Jocotepec. – *73 km – 45.4 miles. Go south from Guadalajara on highway n° 23 and after 48 km – 29.8 miles, you arrive in Chapala.*

Chapala. – Across a small mountain range, lies large and peaceful Lake Chapala. Its waters host a variety of fish, including the white fish of Pátzcuaro, and its birds still find it a hospitable habitat. The town of Chapala (Villa de Chapala), on the lakeshore, offers water sports, typical dishes of the region and boat trips to the Islands of Mexcala and Alacranes, as well as a visit to other picturesque villages in the vicinity. It is a good place to vacation.

Turn right, continue 10 km – 6.2 miles to reach Ajijic.

Ajijic. – The town features hotels with lovely gardens and a pretty view of the lake. Ajijic is also distinguished for its handicrafts and weavings.

Continue straight ahead 15 km – 9.3 miles to Jocotepec.

Jocotepec. – This town is famous for its excellent wool weavers.

La Barca. – *112 km – 69.6 miles. Go south from Guadalajara on highway n° 23 towards Chapala and at 31 km – 19.3 miles, turn left, continue 81 km – 50.3 miles to La Barca.*
La Barca, on the banks of the Lerma River, is one of the leading agricultural centers of Jalisco.

⊙ **House of La Moreña** (Casa de la Moreña). – **City Museum** (Museo de la Ciudad). – Built in the 19C, this structure has been recently restored. The most outstanding features of the building are its lovely **murals★★** located in the main patio, painted by Gerardo Suárez in the mid-19C.
These works from the Romantic period are done in a graceful style, and depict aspects of a society proud of its traditions and manners. The majority of the scenes seems to have been taken from lithographs by Casimiro Castro, edited in 1855 in the book entitled *Mexico and its Environs (México y sus Alrededores)*. However, on amplifying them to mural dimensions, Suárez modified the features, refined the figures, subdued the attire and embellished the forms, revealing his technical mastery and academic training.

MICHELIN GUIDES

The Red Guides (hotels and restaurants)
 Benelux – Deutschland – España Portugal – Main Cities Europe –
 France – Great Britain and Ireland – Italia.

The Green Guides (beautiful scenery, buildings and scenics routes)
 Austria – Canada – England: the West Country – Germany – Greece –
 Italy – London – New England – New York City – Portugal – Rome –
 Scotland – Spain – Switzerland

 ... and 9 French regional guides in English.

Nestled between arid mountains within a deep, narrow gorge, lies the Royal City of Mines. It resembles a lovely stage setting of clustered houses, with flowering balconies and slim lampposts that shed a pale light over the city. Its old riverbed is now an underground highway, **La Belauzarán.**

Guanajuato owes its wealth to silver, and a good part of it has been invested in its many baroque structures and its French-style palaces of the Porfirismo era.

It is one of the most attractive colonial cities in Mexico, rich in history as well as in art. In addition, it has a lively student population that lends it a youthful, boisterous and restless air. In its Cervantino Festival, **entremeses** (short plays) are performed in the squares by young actors whose great enthusiasm and love for the theater compensate their lack of experience. The **estudiantinas** (musical student groups) wearing colonial dress and singing and playing merry popular songs that sound all the more mischievous in their young voices, can often be encountered in the narrow winding streets of the town.

HISTORICAL NOTES

The city was founded in 1552 thanks to the discovery of rich mineral deposits by Juan de Jaso. Five years later the Mines of **Santa Fe** and the **Royal Mines of Guanajuato** (which, in the Tarascan language, means "Frog Hill") were established.

At the end of the 16C, Guanajuato experienced a spurt of growth with the discovery of the **Veta Madre de Plata**, one of the richest veins in the world, and the development of the mines: Cata, Mellado, Tepeyac, **La Valenciana** and many others. These led to the outbreak of a silver fever that increased the city's population to 78 000 inhabitants – more than at present. A large part of the wealth was sent to the Spanish crown, until 1810, when Mexico became independent. Guanajuato participated in the struggle for Independence, and on the 28th of September of that year, the **Alhóndiga de Granaditas** was captured in bloody battle. This was achieved by the heroic action of a miner known as the **Pípila**, who reached the door of the grain-storage fortress to set it afire, carrying a stone slab on his back in order to deflect the bullets raining down on him.

The Reform War (Guerra de Reforma) provided Guanajuato an opportunity to affirm its commitment to the Federal Republic. Furthermore, it had the honor of sheltering Benito Juárez and of serving as provisional capital of the Republic, from January 17th to February 13th, 1858.

Under Porfirio Díaz's regime, when foreign companies explored the mines afresh, Guanajuato enjoyed a new boom period, evidence of which may be seen in the opulent buildings of the epoch. At present, Guanajuato is the capital of the state of the same name, the seat of the state powers and of the university.

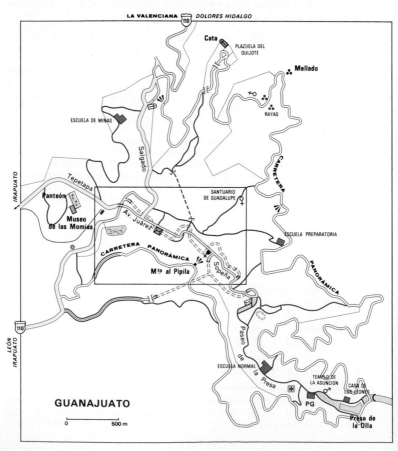

★★★ HISTORIC CENTER *time: 1 day*

A stroll through Guanajuato's labyrinthine center, sometimes on stairs or cobblestone ramps, will reveal the geometric shapes of the houses that cling to the cliffs, the broad pink church, and the terraced retention walls, that have conserved the magic of period stage settings.

From Unión Garden to Hidalgo Market
(Del Jardín Unión al Mercado Hidalgo) *time: 1/2 day*

Unión Garden. – This is a center where intellectuals, politicians and students gather, attracted by the pleasant shade of its old laurel trees – an ideal place to take the pulse of the city.

★★ **Juárez Theater** (Teatro Juárez). – In the 20C, architect José Noriega built this elegant theater with a European air, that has long been the principal center of Guanajuato's cultural life. The Hellenic-style facade is guarded by solemn lions and graceful Art Nouveau lanterns flank the entrance.

Church of San Diego de Alcala (Templo de San Diego de Alcala). – This church has an impressive Churrigueresque **facade★**, a work of the 18C Guanajuato school, and massive lateral towers. Under the intense sunlight, the moldings' capricious curves, and the ornamented niches that shelter placid sculptures, combine to create a chiaroscuro effect.

Plaza de la Paz. – At this busy and lively juncture of avenues, Guanajuato families gather under the shadow of the imposing parish church and the presence of *La Mona*, as the populace commonly calls the **sculpture** of *Peace* created by Jesús Contreras in the 19C.

⊙ **Minor Basilica of Our Lady of Guanajuato** (Basilica Menor de Nuestra Señora de Guanajuato) **(B)**. – This is a severe 17C construction in baroque style. On the high altar of its remodeled neoclassical interior still stands the medieval-looking image of Our Lady of Santa Fe de Guanajuato, resting on an enormous silver pedestal.
The parish church was elevated to the category of minor basilica in 1957.

City Hall (Palacio Municipal) **(PM)**. – **Early Royal Houses** (Primitivas Casas Reales). Juárez stayed in this mansion and from it sent out to all the Mexicans his famous proclamation, *The Reestablishment of the Supreme Power*, making Guanajuato the provisional capital of the Republic.

Superior Court of Justice (Tribunal Superior de Justicia) **(J)**. – **Mansion of Coronel Diego Rul** (Casa del Colonel Diego Rul). This is a magnificent neoclassical palace made of pink stone, a work of the notable architect, Francisco Eduardo Tresguerras. In 1810, the mansion hosted Baron Alexander von Humboldt, one of the first natural scientists of the 19C, who studied and admired the varied Mexican geography *(see p 19)*.

⊙ **Legislative Palace** (Palacio Legislativo). – The illustrious historian and chronicler of Mexico City, Luís González Obregón, was born in this *Belle Epoque* palace – the work of architect Luis Long. Its grey-green facade is one of the most notable of the stone structures created by the great architects of Guanajuato. The **interior** shows a clear French neoclassical influence, especially in the Assembly Hall (Sala de Sesiones), which is adorned with fine anonymous 19C and 20C paintings, as well as period furniture, fashioned by the cabinet-maker, Jorge Luna. In the **library**, there is an enormous **clothes rack★**, carved in precious woods in the shape of a ship's helm topped by an urn, which symbolizes the control and balance of the state powers.

Royal Assay House (Casa Real de Ensaye) **(D)**. – **Administrative Offices of Bancomer** (Oficinas de Bancomer). On the frontispiece of this stately mansion's baroque-style facade, the coat of arms of the Marquis of San Clemente, the first noble title of Guanajuato, is displayed. There is also an unusual round window, or oculus, as well as artistic ironwork on the windows and balconies.

★ **Callejón del Beso.** – This renowned and popular spot is famous for the narrowness of the street, which is reached by a stairway flanked with flowering balconies. **Legend** has it that a romance flourished there between a young suitor and a beautiful, wealthy girl, who courted from balcony to balcony, against her father's will. When the latter caught them, he sent her to a convent and the young man in exile.

★ **Plaza de San Roque.** – Under the shadow of the 17C Jesuit church dedicated to Saint Roque, the work of José Sopeña y Cervera, the square comes alive twice a year with the performances by the university students of Cervantes' *Entremeses* and other **old Spanish plays.**

Morelos Garden (Jardín Morelos). – Lined by 17C to 19C structures, and amidst thick laurel trees, this garden is a favorite meeting place for the art and engineering students. It is enclosed by a plain portico and the surviving columns of the Reforma Market – a work by the architect José Noriega.

★ **Hidalgo Market** (Mercado Hidalgo). – Created at the end of the 19C by the engineer ⊙ Ernesto Brunel, this building retains in its polished stone walls the European elegance of its original design. The structure is made of iron, as was the style in the era of Porfirismo. Its **interior** contains all sorts of merchandise, making the place a festival of oranges, tomatoes, chiles of different colors and many other products that alternate with the regional handicrafts: basketry, weaving and leatherwork.

GUANAJUATO★★★

From the Alhóndiga de Granaditas to Plaza del Baratillo
time: 1/2 day

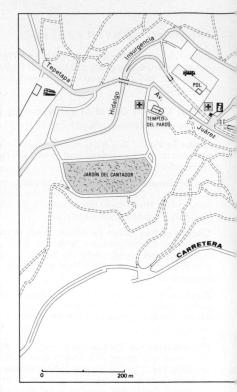

The city was formerly divided into neighborhoods, which today retain their flavor, full of life and folklore. Some of these neighborhoods were founded by craftsmen, like San Luisito; another peculiar neighborhood, called *Terremoto*, is known for its brave population of potters and miners. One of the oldest city quarters sits on top of the hill known as Cerro Cuatro, where the university is located. The development of the 17C city was begun here, under the protection of the fort, and the neighborhood still has some colonial buildings.

★ **Regional Museum** (**Museo Regional**) (**M¹**). – **Alhóndiga de Granaditas.** This superb building resembles a fortress and was called the Corn Palace because grain was stored there as a Spanish government measure to avoid shortages in case of poor harvests.
Its stately facade, designed with sobriety and elegance, is the work of José del Manzo y Avilés. At the beginning of the War of Independence, the building was captured by the rebels in a fierce battle. Once the rebel leaders were shot in Chihuahua, their heads were brought to Guanajuato and hung from the four corners of the building.
The museum offers an interesting overview of the history and art of Guanajuato, as well as examples of its handicraft production.

Ground Floor. – One of the rooms is dedicated to the memory of the Independence heroes, with a perpetual flame that is renewed every year on September 28th, as a symbol of Mexican Independence. The walls flanking the stairs are decorated with mural paintings by José Chávez Morado, entitled *The Abolition of Slavery (La Abolición de la Esclavitad)* and *The Song of Guanajuato (El Canto de Guanajuato)*.

Upper Floor. – A survey of Guanajuato's history, from pre-historic times to the 20C, is presented through such varied objects as paintings, ceramic pieces and mining tools. The collection of pre-Hispanic seals *(rooms 4 and 5)* and paintings by Hermenegildo Bustos and Romualdo García are particularly noteworthy.

Diego Rivera Museum (**Museo Casa Diego Rivera**) (**M²**). – In this house, built at the end of the 19C, the muralist Diego Rivera was born and lived part of his childhood. The museum offers a glimpse of everyday life in 19C Guanajuato, as well as a general view of the artist's work.

Ground Floor. – A reconstruction of the atmosphere, furnishings and decorations of Diego Rivera's modest house is displayed here.

Upper Floor. – Some of Rivera's works, which include those belonging to the Academy period, the Spanish school and his contacts with Pablo Picasso, are to be seen here. Of particular interest are Rivera's sketches for murals painted in other buildings.

Museum of Guanajuato (**Museo del Pueblo de Guanajuato**) (**M³**). – This museum occupies the manor house that was the residence of the Marquis of San Juan de Rayas in the 17C. The museum presents a panorama of the pictorial arts and handicrafts of Guanajuato from the 17C to 19C and some works by Hermenegildo Bustos.

Upper Floor. – This has an elegant Churrigueresque exterior and, inside, fresco murals by José Chávez Morado, which express in vivid colors the birth and the history of the city of Guanajuato.

University (**Universidad**) (**U**). – The present building of this 17C educational establishment, with its austere, somewhat over powering facade, is the work of the architect, Vicente Urquiaga, who built it in 1955. Under its roof is the original **16C chapel**, representing the evangelic design of Father Vasco de Quiroga.

★ **Jesuit Church** (**Templo de la Compañía**). – The construction of this Churrigueresque jewel began in the middle of the 17C, thanks to José Sardaneta y Legazpi, and was completed in 1765. The church, which occupies a prominent hilltop site, features a noble facade in pink stone. Standing under the 19C cupola, the visitor can best appreciate the church's impressive dimensions. The vast stark neoclassical interior is divided into three naves and contains some paintings by Miguel Cabrera.

Plaza del Baratillo. – This lively area is frequented primarily by Guanajuato's student population. In the center of the square there is a fountain, from which came, in 1852, the first running water supply to the city. Its source was the La Olla Dam *(p 91)*.

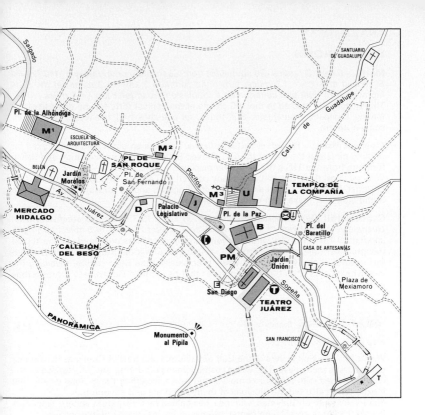

★ PANORAMIC HIGHWAY (CARRETERA PANORÁMICA)

22 km – 13.7 miles – 1/2 day by car – Map p 88

The 17 km – 10.6 mile circuit around the mines that gave life to Guanajuato, from the Caliche to the San Miguel Hills, is a pleasant and interesting ride. There is a good **view** of the city from here, with its many buildings, streets, gorges, and squares, large and small. Various lookout points provide a chance to stop and enjoy the landscape, visit a mining center like Cata or Mellado, walk around the gardens of the La Olla Dam or buy some handicrafts at the foot of the Pípila Monument, where the tour ends.

Mummy Museum (Museo de las Momias). – Municipal Pantheon. In a broad passageway that looks like a catacomb are more than fifty mummified bodies – of men, women and children – most of which were buried last century. The mummification was due to chemical components in the soil, which preserved the bodies intact.

La Valenciana Church and Mine (Templo y Mina de la Valenciana). – On a small hill near the Valenciana Mine stands the **church★★** that was built by the Count of Valenciana in gratitude for the wealth he had obtained.

Church. – This 18C building, dedicated to Saint Cayetano of Siena, has a Churrigue-resque facade, crowded with saints and baroque ornamentation. The interior has several splendid altarpieces, worked in gilded wood, with fine ornamented sculptures. In addition, there are two elegant academic paintings and the original mortarwork decoration. One of its treasures is the **pulpit★** inlaid in wood and bone, with a marvelous sounding-board that resembles the finial of a Chinese pagoda.

Mine. – Seen from a distance, the 18C entrance pavilion called San Cayetano resembles a crown, which the people of Guanajuato say is that of the King of Spain. On the inside, a shaft over 530 m – 1 739 ft deep, that is still in operation, can be seen.

Cata Church (Templo de Cata). – Facing the charming little Quijote Square, this church is a good example of Mexican baroque, with a facade as rich as that of the Valenciana. Inside, the image of Christ of Villaseco, brought from Spain in 1618, is worshipped.

At one end of the square, there is a small **museum of the Pedro Domecq firm** describing the wine industry, in which the machinery used for wine-making is displayed, including the old barrels and bottles.

Rayas Mine (Mina de Rayas). – This 16C mine was abandoned as a result of the mining slump in the late 18C. Today some of the old structures remain, including the square with its bygone atmosphere and the lovely 18C baroque church. In its baptistry and sacristy, significant mural paintings of the same era have been preserved. On the south side stands a massive construction, today partially destroyed, which was probably the old cloister.

La Olla Dam (Presa de La Olla). – This dam was built at the beginning of the 17C and today is surrounded by trees, gardens and paths, which make it an ideal spot for Sunday outings. The Basin of San Renovato opens its gates the first Monday of July to fill the dam, and this event is celebrated with a lively popular fiesta. Around the dam there are numerous beautiful structures from the era of Porfirismo.

Pípila Monument. – This monument stands atop San Miguel Hill, with Guanajuato in all its splendor at its feet.

GUANAJUATO★★★

EXCURSIONS

Marfil. – *6 km – 3.7 miles. Go southwest from Guanajuato on highway n° 110 toward Silao and at 3 km – 1.9 miles, turn right, continue 2 km – 1.2 miles on the state highway, turn right and continue on a cobblestone road for 1 km – 0.6 miles.*
This village was erected in the 16C as one of the earliest forts for the defense of the Mining Camp of Guanajuato. Still today, its churches and haciendas retain their colonial charm.

🕐 **Museum (Museo).** – **Hacienda of San Gabriel Barrera.** This was an old manor house used for refining metals at the end of the 17C. Carved Spanish, Chinese, Victorian and Italian furniture from the 17C and 18C are on display.
In its **old chapel** there is a valuable many-colored 17C altarpiece depicting the Passion of Christ. Its service patios are colorful and fragrant, and its nooks, under the shade of the old trees, make for a peaceful oasis.

Cubilete Hill (Cerro del Cubilete). – **Cristo Rey.** *31 km – 19.3 miles. Go southwest from Guanajuato on highway n° 110 toward Silao and after 23 km – 14.3 miles, turn right, continue 8 km – 5 miles after the junction, up a cobblestone road.* At the top of this prominent hill, stands a colossal sculpture of *Christ the King (Cristo Rey).* From this lookout, there is a splendid **view★** over much of the Bajío region, revealing the vast wheat fields and strawberry patches that have made Guanajuato a prosperous state.

GUAYMAS Sonora ♦♦♦

Map of Principal Sights p 4

Washed by the blue waters of the Gulf of California, the port of Guaymas lies on one of the coast's many bays. This was a cosmopolitan port during the 19C, dazzled by the riches it traded with the four corners of the world, including the mineral wealth that it exported. It also fed the illusions of many explorers and adventurers.
The modern city of Guaymas, with beaches bathed by transparent waters, is today a leading business and fishing center, renowned for the quality of its shellfish.

San Carlos Bay (Bahía de San Carlos). – *18 km – 11.2 miles. Go northwest from Guaymas on highway n° 15, after 6 km – 3.7 miles turn right, continue 12 km – 7.5 miles, crossing the highway on the overpass.*
Many coves cut into the steep cliffs of this region, where the sea is rich with fish and sea birds. Among the fossilized vegetation lie stunning stretches of beach.

HERMOSILLO Sonora ♦♦♦♦♦

Map of Principal Sights p 4

Wedged between sea and mountains, as though to temper the desert harshness of the Pacific coast, lies Hermosillo, the lively and modern capital of Sonora. Its 19C neoclassical buildings retain the characteristic charm of a Mexican province. Today it is an important business center, particularly for agriculture and livestock.

HISTORICAL NOTES

The colonization of Mexico's northwest was carried out by Jesuit missionaries during the 17C. They were indefatigable, riding over the rough terrain, sowing in the desert and founding towns near their beautiful missions such as Tubutama and Caborca, which – modified and renovated – still exist today.

SIGHTS

🕐 **Sonora Museum (Museo de Sonora).** – **Hermosillo Penitentiary.** *At the end of Jesús García at the crossing with California.* A visit to this modern museum, installed in an early 20C remodeled penitentiary, provides an overview of local history through photographs, silk prints and diverse objects, covering periods from the early settlements to today, including the Conquest and the 1910 Revolution. It also contains a small collection of notes and coins from the 16C to the 19C.

★ **Sonora Ecological Center (Centro Ecológico de Sonora).** – *2 km - 1.2 miles south of the*
🕐 *city on highway n° 15 towards Guaymas.* This modern center displays the flora, fauna and different ecosystems of the region, in an area of 1 000 hectares – 2 470 acres. This center extends over abrupt mountains, rich meadows, deserts, and part of the warm Gulf of California. A quick survey of the regional fauna includes eagles and snakes, pheasants and *berrendos* (American antelopes), sharks and tortoises.

EXCURSION

Bahía Kino. – *98 km – 60.9 miles to the southwest on highway n° 16.*
The road along the desertic coast of Hermosillo, now transformed into one of the most productive agricultural regions in the country, leads to a fishing village named Kino Viejo (in honor of the tireless Jesuit evangelist Francisco Eusebio Kino), where the peaceful surroundings accompany golden beaches and the murmur of the sea.

Map of Principal Sights p 5

This, one of the oldest mining cities of Chihuahua, was founded in 1631, in the timber-rich foothills of the Sierra Madre Occidental. During the 17C, mining made Hidalgo del Parral the most important admininstrative and commercial center of Nueva Vizcaya. Francisco Villa, the legendary leader *(caudillo)* of the Mexican Revolution, was ambushed and killed here in 1923 *(p 33)*.

SIGHTS

Plaza Guillermo Baca. – *Av. Gral. Maclovio Herrera and Pedro T. Gómez*. This square is a meeting place, where people gather to relax. The statue, *The Illusion Seeker (El Buscador de Ilusiones)*, by the Durango sculptor Ignacio Asúnsolo (1890-1965), stands prominently in the square.

Church of Our Lady of Guadalupe (Templo de Nuestra Señora de Guadalupe). – *East of Plaza Guillermo Baca*. This church was built in the 17C and modified in this century. It is important to note its tall neo-Romanesque towers. Inside there are stained glass windows depicting the discovery of America and the conversion of the Indians, in addition to scenes recalling the relations between Christopher Columbus and the Franciscans of the La Rábida Convent in Spain.

Saint John of God Church (Templo de San Juan de Dios). – *West of Plaza Guillermo Baca*. This 17C building, formerly called the Church of La Soledad, has preserved its original appearance, except for the neoclassical tower on the facade. On the inside, there is a gilded altarpiece dedicated to the Virgin of Solitude (Virgen de la Soledad) and to the Passion of Christ, in an 18C baroque style.

Alvarado Palace (Palacio de Alvarado). – *12 Riva Palacio*. This surprising structure belonged to Pedro de Alvarado, one of the richest miners of the region. Built of stone in the 19C neoclassical style, it is reminiscent of Italian Renaissance palaces. It has two levels, with a rich neo-baroque facade★ topped by a lovely balustrade.
Unfortunately, the stone of the facade foundation has been replaced with cement.

Church of Saint Nicholas (Templo de San Nicolás). – *Juan Rangel de Viezma*. In this small church, there are two vast 18C paintings. One represents San Salvador de Orta and the other, the investiture of the chasuble on San Ildefonso, both good paintings by an unknown artist.

★ **HUASCA** Hidalgo ◆

Map of Principal Sights p 6

Huasca is a picturesque town of large rustic estates with bramble covered walls and pretty white houses with pitched metal roofs that offer shade to the pedestrian walking along the cobblestone streets. The main square is surrounded by arcades with a provincial atmosphere. At the center of the town, rises the sober Plateresque **Church of Saint John the Baptist** (San Juan Bautista).

SIGHTS

Hacienda of San Miguel Regla. – *2 km – 1.2 miles to the northeast*. The magnificent hacienda for metal refining was built by the first Count of Regla in the 18C. In what was its main dwelling, there is now a hotel set in a park with lovely woods and transparent ponds. The arches that surrounded the patios and the furnaces used for refining silver are still standing. In addition there are facilities for horseback riding and fishing.

Basalt Prisms of Santa María Regla (Prismas Basálticos de Santa María Regla). – *8 km – 5 miles northeast*. This impressive gorge reaches a depth of 50 m – 164 ft and is noteworthy for its basaltic formations which resemble symmetrically arranged hexagonal columns covered with surfaces that appear to have been paved by man. The odd prism formations are a result of the retraction of the basalt's crystaline components which occurs when the volanic lava, upon contact with the air, undergoes rapid cooling. At one end of the gorge, is a waterfall fed by the San Antonio Dam and at the other end, the visitor can admire the summit of the **Hacienda of Santa María Regla,** *(not open to the public)* built by the Count of Regla. This complex was formerly Mexico's oldest and largest metal-processing hacienda.

EXCURSIONS

El Chico National Park (Parque Nacional El Chico). – *37 km – 23 miles. Go west from Huasca and at 7 km – 4.3 miles turn left, 19 km – 11.8 miles to the south on highway n° 105, turn right, 11 km – 6.8 miles to El Chico.*
This is one of the most beautiful parks in the country, set in a mountain area densely covered with pines, oaks and firs, with unusual rock formations like Las Ventanas and Las Monjas, where mountain-climbing and fishing are popular sports. It also has impressive landscapes, pleasant walks, horseback-riding and camping sites as well as a tourist center.

Atotonilco el Grande; Metztitlán. – *66 km – 41 miles. Estimate 3 hours. Go west from Huasca and after 7 km – 4.3 miles, turn right; after 11 km – 6.8 miles to the north on highway n° 105, you reach Atotonilco.*

⊘ Atotonilco el Grande. – In the town's main square stands the 16C **Convent of Saint Augustine,** with enormous buttresses and battlements. Its **open-air chapel** is placed at the left side of the church on a level with the choir and is, in fact, a balcony between two buttresses.

Follow highway n° 105 and after 28 km – 17.4 miles turn left for 20 km – 12.4 miles to reach Metztitlán.

Metztitlán. – This picturesque town with steep cobblestone streets is located in a lovely region of abundant vegetation composed of fertile valley lands irrigated by a river and surrounded by imposing mountains.

★ **Monastery of the Holy Kings** (Exconvento de los Santos Reyes). – Built by the Augustinians in the higher part of the town, from which there is a splendid **view★** of the valley, this is an example of the monastery-fortress architectural prototype. Although it has the characteristic features of the 16C religious complexes of New Spain, they are interpreted in a rather unusual way, since the **open-air chapel** is double and one of the **posas** or corner chapels is directly across from the church portal.

The church has a rich Plateresque **facade,** finished off by a pretty bell gable with seven bays. Within the church, there are valuable gilded **altarpieces★** of different eras with splendid sculptures and paintings and striking mural **frescoes** made by Indian artists. The former monastery is decorated with paintings devoted to didactic themes, presented in a simple manner, when addressed to the populace, and in a complex fashion, when addressed to the friars, as is the case in the **stairwell.**

★★ HUEJOTZINGO Puebla ◆

Map of Principal Sights p 6 – Local map p 170

This is a small town set in the center of cider-producing apple orchards, to which it owes its fame.

Franciscan monastery (Convento Franciscano). – This massive building was constructed by Fray Juan de Alameda and it is believed that it was finished in 1570. It was probably built on a pyramid's foundation, since it rises above the town. Its main facade is a mixture of styles – the low entrance arch is Gothic, the choir window embrasure is Mudejar, and the rest belongs to the Renaissance style. The lateral entrance is one of the most beautiful parts of the building. The **gilded wooden altarpiece★★** is one of the few such 16C pieces preserved. Its sculptures are attributed to Luis de Arciniega and the paintings were signed in 1586 by the Flemish artist Simón Pereyns. There are traces of mural paintings on the walls. The main gate is a noteworthy work, with two semicircular arches, decorated in different motifs, and supported by a central column in two parts, separated by a band in braided, or *petatillo*, design.

(From photo Michelin)

Huejotzingo. Corner chapel

Cloister . – Note the remnants of mural paintings that it conserves, especially the *De Profundis* Prayer Hall, with the portraits of the first Twelve Friars and passages from the life of Saint Francis of Assisi.

Museum. – In this museum a number of sculptures that had been scattered throughout the monastery have been brought together, and photographic murals of other monastic complexes have been added, so as to establish a comparison with Huejotzingo.

★★ **Posas** (Capillas Posas). – Together with the chapels of Calpan, these are the most beautiful corner chapels for their rich decoration depicting angels, each one carrying a symbol of the Passion of Christ.

⊘ Church of San Diego de Alcalá (Templo de San Diego de Alcalá). – The sacristy has a beautiful coffered ceiling with gilded stars. In the nave there is a well of miraculous water, in addition to 17C baroque paintings and a fine high altarpiece.

EXCURSION

Calpan. – *10 km – 6.2 miles southwest of Huejotzingo by an unpaved road.*
This is a small village at the feet of the Popocatépetl and Iztaccíhuatl volcanoes, with a splendid view of both.

⊘ Monastery of San Andrés Calpan (Convento de San Andrés Calpan). – Built in 1548, its facade is one of the most beautiful in the state of Puebla. To be noted are two angels holding the Franciscan shield, the mullioned window and the column capitals finished in cactus flower *(maguey)* designs. But more important still are the *posas* decorated with different themes: among others, the Virgin of Sorrows, the Annunciation and Christ the Judge amidst the dead who abandon their tombs at the angels' trumpet call.

⊘ Parish Church (Parroquia). – A few meters farther on, stands the parish church, with a fine 16C San Andrés worked in feathers *(at the top of the high altar).*

Map of Principal Sights p 5

This town, originally named San Marcos de Iriguato (in the Tarascan language Iriguato means "place of water vendors"), was founded in 1547 by the Spaniards as a livestock ranch. In Irapuato, traditional colonial architecture mingles with the town's modern buildings. It is at present a great agricultural and trading center, famous for the strawberries and asparagus that it exports to various countries.

HISTORIC CENTER *time: 1 day*

Hidalgo Garden (Jardín Hidalgo). – This is the very heart of the town, full of light and color. Around it stand the **City Hall** (Palacio Municipal), with a very large patio; and the 17C **Saint Francis' Church** (Templo de San Francisco), commonly called the Convent. Within its traditional Latin cross layout, this church conserves two valuable paintings: *The Virgin of Guadalupe* by Miguel Cabrera, and *The Apocalypse* by Eduardo Tresguerras.

Hospitalito Church (Templo del Hospitalito). – *Libertad, to the northeast of Jardín Hidalgo.* This church has a beautiful baroque facade from the 18C, carved by Crispín Lorenzo, who expressed the popular imagination and creativity. The fine sculpture of the *Purísima*, with her attributes, the moon and sun, stands out in the center of the finial, surrounded by a border made of curly waves.

Plaza Hidalgo. – *Southeast of the town center.* This large, reddish esplanade is bordered by religious structures of the 18C. To the west stands the **parish church,** with its baroque facade profusely decorated in plant motifs. To the south, **Saint Joseph's Church** (Templo de San José) displays a frontispiece of popular craftsmanship, *estípites* and stone canopies carved to resemble fabric. During the popular and religious festivals, this square becomes an explosion of color and merriment.

★★ ISLA MUJERES Quintana Roo ◆

Map of Principal Sights p 6

This island is surrounded by such transparent waters that the intense colors of the coral reefs on the ocean bottom can be clearly seen. It is said that, in one of his expeditions at the beginning of the 16C, Francisco Hernández de Córdoba found on the island a large number of clay female figurines or *mujeres* and that is why he named it thus.

Access. – From Cancún by plane or launch *(embarkation point at Av. Kukulcán)* and from Puerto Juárez by launch or ferry. You can drive around the island *(see section on Practical Information at the end of the guide).*

SIGHTS

Los Cocos Beach (Playa de los Cocos). – *At the north end of the island.* This is an ideal place to learn how to swim, because the water is shallow for several hundred meters.

★ **Makax Lagoon (Laguna Makax).** – The lagoon is a stunning combination of underwater limestone formations and thick mangroves that spread their shifting shadows over the lagoon's waters.

Lancheros Beach (Playa Lancheros). – *To the north of Playa Garrafón.* It is especially attractive for the giant sea turtles on its shores. Also, 200 m – 656 ft inland lie the ruins of what was the hacienda of the 18C pirate, Fermín Mundaca.

Los Manchones. – *Across from Playa Garrafón.* This is a magnificent site for underwater fishing. The many, rich species that swim amidst the coral formations of its shallow waters are a major attraction.

El Garrafón National Marine Park (Parque Nacional Submarino El Garrafón). – *To the south of the island.* The transparency of this park's waters, full of multicolored fish, provides the amateur or professional diver with a marvelous adventure and an unforgettable spectacle.

Maya Observatory (Observatorio Maya). – *On the high point at the southern end of the island.* On a small limestone cliff, carved by the sea, there is a simple structure with a solid roof that popular usage has designated as an observatory, owing to its lovely setting. From there the view of sea and sky is limited only by the distant horizon.

The symbol ⊘ placed in the left margin beside a sight description indicates that specific visitor information can be found in the Opening Hours and Admission Charges section at the end of this guide.

The sights are listed alphabetically in this section either under the place – town, village or area – in which they are situated or under their proper name.

At the edge of the highway rise the sumptuous temples and residences of the old Maya city of Kabah, famous for its profusely ornamented facades. These structures are immersed in rich and thick savannah vegetation. The most important section consists of three groups of structures standing close together.

ARCHEOLOGICAL SITE *time: 1 hour*

Third House (Tercera Casa). – *300 m – 984 ft to the rear.* The elegance of this residential area is comparable to the House of the Turtles at Uxmal *(p 214).* At the front it originally had a terrace that was used to collect the rainfall that was stored in a cistern with two outlets 15 m – 49 ft from the edifice.

The Palace (El Palacio). – *First building on the left as you return to the highway.* This two-level structure standing on a hill is notable because its roof slopes towards the interior, perhaps recalling the straw roofing of early Maya houses.

Palace of the Large Masks (Palacio de los Mascarones, or Codz-pop). – *Facing the highway.* On a high and broad terrace stands one of the most extraordinary Maya structures. It is remarkable for the quality as well as the profusion of the stone mosaics on its ample facade★★★, where the rain god **Chac** is represented with his typical elongated nose, symbolizing lightning. This rich ornamentation embodies the highest degree of exuberance reached in the Puuc style *(see p 172).* The insistent repetition of the rain prayer, creates a mesmerizing litany. In front of this building, a repaired cistern still in use and a small square platform with undeciphered hieroglyphics are found.

Cross the highway.

The largest part of the ceremonial center on this side of the highway has been destroyed, and it is impossible to visualize how it looked in its prime. However, some 200 m – 656 ft down the white road, or *sacbé*, which probably connected Kabah with Uxmal, still stands a majestic **arch**★ 10 m – 33 ft high.

EXCURSION

★**Xtacumbilxunán Grottos (Grutas).** – *Guided tour: 40 minutes. 33 km – 20.5 miles south on highway n° 261 toward Hopelchén, turn right, 750 m – 2 461 ft on an unpaved road.*

⊘Just inside the cave, there is a green wooden cross which the local residents put up as a memorial to a young girl who was lost there in the 19C – an event that gave the grottos the name Xtacumbilxunán, which means "lost girl" in the Maya language. The road penetrates this fantastic underground world to a lookout point in an imposing amphitheater adorned with curiously shaped stalactites and stalagmites. To the right, there is a well which leads to another cave with pools, where the Indians used to come for water in the summer.

★ **LAGOS DE MORENO** Jalisco   ◆◆◆

Located in a beautiful and fertile valley called los Altos de Jalisco, the old town of Santa María de los Lagos was founded by Hernando de Martel on March 31st, 1563. He built it in order to protect the travelers coming from Mexico City or Nueva Galicia to the Zacatecas mines, against attacks by the Xiconaqui and Custique Indians. In 1829, by Congressional Decree of the Mexican Union, its name was changed to honor the rebel martyr, Pedro Moreno – a native of this town. From 1831 to 1915, the city was the capital of Jalisco state.

Lagos de Moreno is full of surprises, seemingly untouched by time. A noble *mestizo* elegance pervades this provincial town, which is the birthplace of important men such as the musician Juventino Rosas, the poet Juan de Dios Peza and the writer Mariano Azuela. Its squares, gardens, mansions and churches constitute a charming ensemble.

SIGHTS

Parish Church (Iglesia Parroquial). – *Av. Hidalgo facing Plaza Principal.* This church was built in the 18C and stands out from the surrounding buildings.

The principal facade is a lovely Churrigueresque-style filigree of finely carved pink stone. Inside is conserved the Relic San Hermión Mártir, removed from Santa Ciriaca Cemetery in Rome and donated in 1790 to be exhibited and worshipped in this church. Its lateral altars have beautiful sculptures by the artist Perusquía, from Querétaro.

Rinconada de Capuchinas. – *Calles Miguel Leandro Guerra and Pedro Moreno.* This is an elegantly proportioned architectural complex, comprising the house where Dr. Agustín Rivera lived (1824-1916), the church and convent of the Capuchin Nuns and the Miguel Leandro Guerra School of Arts and Trades.

⊘**Rosas Moreno Theater (Teatro Rosas Moreno).** – *Calle Doctor Salvador Camarena.* This 19C theater has been recently restored. The neoclassical structure reflects the tastes of the local social elite of the last century.

Rivera Drive (Paseo de la Rivera). – *Behind the Rinconada de Capuchinas.* This tree-lined drive circles the city. It reaches the legendary Puente Grande, the Renaissance-style bridge that affords a wonderful view of the city.

LEÓN Guanajuato   ◆◆◆◆◆

Map of Principal Sights p 5

This city was established in the 16C, amidst the drums of war and the bloodshed of the Spanish and Chichimec battles. Today León is a progressive city that, on account of its economic and industrial performance, is ranked among the ten most important urban centers of the country, and first in footwear production. In its unusual urban profile, the 19C **Triumphal Arch** (Arco Triunfal) is prominent; it symbolizes a city where old architectural jewels stand beside modern edifices. It has a great bullfighting tradition, as the birthplace of the famous bullfighter, Rodolfo Gaona, called Gaona el Califa, who captivated the world during the Forties.

HISTORIC CENTER*time: 1/2 day*

Martyrs' Square (Plaza de los Mártires). – This square is bordered by outstanding 18C buildings: **Los Portales** form a harmonious arcade; the **León Casino** has a neo-Mudejar facade; the **City Hall** (Palacio Municipal) conserves in its interior two large historical murals; and the Church of the Tabernacle (Templo del Sagrario) with its typical baroque facade.

★★ **Cathedral of the Most Holy Mother of Light (Catedral de la Madre Santísima de la Luz).** – ⏱This is a beautifully proportioned 17C building with elaborate ornamentation. Laid out according to the Latin cross, the stylistically homogenous interior houses paintings by disciples of Miguel Cabrera.

Doblado Theater (Teatro Doblado). – *Diagonally across from the corner of calles Pedro Moreno and Hermanos Aldama.* Built in the 19C, this structure has a noble appearance, with its neo-Mudejar facade designed by the architect José Noriega.

★ MALINALCO México   ◆

Map of Principal Sights p 6

This attractive town is set among the vegetation and rock formations of the Valley of Mexico. It retains part of its old design and some chapels of its former districts. The name Malinalco comes from the word *malinalli*, which means "twisted grass" in Náhuatl, referring to a plant of fibrous texture used for rope-making. The region was inhabited from the first years of our era by the Matlatzincs, an ethnic group belonging to the Otomí branch. The Matlatzines were conquered by the Aztecs in 1476, and the region was annexed as a subject province of the Aztec empire until the time of the Conquest, when the Spaniards arrived in 1521 and destroyed a large part of the ceremonial center, following the orders of Andrés de Tapia.

⏱ ARCHEOLOGICAL SITE *time: 3 hours*

Take the street along the south side of the square and follow the signs to the chapel of the Santa Mónica district. Pass by the left side of the chapel and go through the narrow corridor to arrive at the site entrance.
The site is located in the central part of the hill called Cerro de los Idolos. A long ramp-like flight of 423 steps skirts the mountain and offers at every resting place lovely views, such as the bottom of the ravine *(on the left of the stairs)*. There, are ruins of small temples made of rubblework, with a stairway cut into the rock, that climbs to a small cave hidden in the foliage. In the rock formation facing the site, cave-like transversal striations can also be seen. These were used by the early inhabitants both as vantage points and as places to worship the principal Matlatzinc god, Oxtoctéotl, or Lord of the Cave, with offerings and ceremonies.

Principal Temple (Templo Principal). – This is one of the most important examples of Aztec art. Its structural characteristics and sculptural style make it unique. Totally carved out of the mountain rock, it forms a monolithic structure with a central staircase bordered by ramps and flanked by two partially destroyed sculptures of seated jaguars. At the center sits a much deteriorated human figure, which served as a standard bearer. To the right of the latter, a staircase (also carved into the rock) leads to the upper part of the building. On the last step, an interesting construction technique can be observed: small holes were carved into the rock and filled with wooden wedges. When these wedges were soaked in water, their swelling cracked the rock.
The temple was dedicated to the **eagle warriors** *(cuauhtli)* and **tigers** *(ocelotl)*, divinities in the Aztec society, distinguished for their readiness and ferocity in combat and their deeply rooted code of nobility and valor. In this temple, religious ceremonies were held to honor the sun.

Facade. – The portal features an unusual **relief** in the shape of a serpent's head, with open jaws and very protruding eyes and fangs. The forked tongue of this enormous snake spreads out on the floor like a carpet at the entrance of the temple. On either side, a complex sculpture can be seen: a serpent's head and a drum, on which are found, respectively, the remains of what may have been an eagle warrior and a tiger.

★★ **Interior.** – The interior houses one the most extraordinary examples of **stone carving;** it consists of a circular shrine 3 m – 10 ft in diameter. The back wall has a semicircular bench on which there are three sculptures: in the center, the stretched out skin of a jaguar with its head, claws and tail; beside the jaguar, the skins of eagles; and on the floor, the relief sculpture of another eagle, facing the door.

Behind the eagle, also on the floor, there is a small basin carved in the rock, which was used to receive the hearts of sacrificial victims. All these figures were carved in high relief directly on the rock face and, like many pre-Hispanic sculptures, they were painted with dyes, probably derived from minerals.

In the rest of the site, some temples of simple construction can be noted. Of special interest are the one to the right of the Principal Temple, which is also circular, and the enormous rectangular-shaped one at the end of the site, which was carved into the hillside. Along the edge of the path facing this temple, retaining walls can be observed. These were constructed to make the artificial terraces which support the buildings. From this point there is the best **view★** of the fertile valley of Malinalco.

ADDITIONAL SIGHT

Return to the city.

Malinalco Monastery (Convento de Malinalco). – *Plaza Principal.* This convent, founded by the Augustinians in 1540, has a Renaissance-style cloister. It is decorated with beautiful and masterfully drawn **paintings★** representing grotesques and religious figures. In the lower cloister, the paintings in the tympanums retain some of their colors.

MANZANILLO Colima   ◆

Map of Principal Sights p 5

Manzanillo has an ample bay, where large cargo ships are often seen, and a complex port infrastructure, coexisting with a modern tourist zone, installed on the northwestern shore. To the southeast, there are pleasant beaches and lovely areas in the surroundings of Cuyutlán Lagoon.

Beaches (Playas). – *At the northwest end on highway n° 200, toward the tourist complex called Las Hadas, you will find Playa Audiencia.* It is a small cove of fine sand, flanked by high cliffs covered in vegetation. The white facades of hotels and Greek Mediterranean-style residential complexes stand out against the rich green foliage. *To the northwest of this beach, at 2 km – 1.2 miles, is Playa Santiago on the bay of the same name (Bahía Santiago).* Enclosed by the mountains of Punta Juluapan and Punta Santiago, the soft pink sand and the gentle waves make this an enchanting place.

EXCURSIONS

Cuyutlán Lagoon; El Paraíso; Cuyutlán. – *52 km – 32.3 miles. Estimate 1/2 a day. Go southeast from Manzanillo on highway n° 200 towards Tecomán and after 45 km – 28 miles, turn right to reach Paraíso.*

Cuyutlán Lagoon (Laguna Cuyutlán). – During the drive through the hills that rim this large lagoon, beautiful views of the landscape, including the salt marshes and the ocean on the horizon, can be appreciated. **El Paraíso,** on the Armería River's right bank, consists of a landscape that blends lagoons, jungles, and palm groves. The natural beauty of the tidelands, densely covered with mangroves and bullrushes, where the transparent waters are adorned with water lilies, adds an exotic touch to the setting.

Return to the highway and continue 7 km – 4.3 miles to Cuyutlán.

Cuyutlán. – This town is located on a narrow strip of land between the lagoon and the sea, with long open beaches of very fine, dark-colored sand. In this area the visitor can observe the impressive **Green Wave★** (Ola Verde), an ocean swell that produces enormous waves, called Tsunami by the specialists, related to the volcanic activity in the region, as well as to the sea currents in this part of the Pacific. The phenomenon is particularly noticeable in the springtime, late in the afternoon, and is almost imperceptible during the rest of the year.

★★ MAZATLÁN Sinaloa   ◆◆◆◆

Map of Principal Sights p 4

A city of beautiful sunsets, bathed by the sea, encircled by cliffs, islands and beaches, Mazatlán radiates a resort atmosphere under the shade of jacarandas and poincianas. A tourist center *par excellence*, it figures as one of the leading Mexican ports on the Pacific, with a sunny climate and pleasant temperatures throughout the year. Besides its tourist resources, Mazatlán hosts a number of recreational activities, like the famous Mardi Gras (Carnaval) and the Marlin and Sailfishing Tournaments.

SIGHTS

Beaches (Playas). – To the north of the port, near Avenida Camarón Sábalo, there are beaches in front of the hotel zone such as: **Sábalo, Gaviotas** and **Cerritos,** with soft pink sand and medium surf. From them, the pleasant seascape of **Venados Island** (Isla de Venados) and **Pájaros Island** (Isla Pájaros), inhabited by seals, can be enjoyed.

Paseo del Malecón. – *Avenida Del Mar and Paseo Claussen.* South of Punta Camarón, on Paseo del Malecón, one of the longest drives on the Mexican coast, there are views of the sunset from the cliffs and monuments to be admired. Among these, monuments to the fisherman and to the women of Mazatlán are to be noted.

⊙**Sea Shell City.** – **Museum** (Museo del Caracol). *Calle Rodolfo T. Loaiza n° 407*. This curious museum has an interesting collection of corals and sea shells typical of the Mexican coasts as well as exotic specimens from other parts of the world. Handsome handicrafts fashioned from these materials are on sale in the museum.

⊙**Aquarium (Acuario).** – *111 Avenida de los Deportes near Avenida Del Mar*. The aquarium is a hexagonal-shaped modern building, with an immense fish tank in its center, that holds several varieties of sharks. Around the walls there are also various sections with smaller fish tanks, containing more than 250 classified marine species. A pleasant botanical garden is located outside the aquarium. It is also a museum of marine art, presenting the methods and equipment used for the different types of fishing in the region.

★**Panoramic Circuit** (Circuito Panorámico). – **Paseo Claussen**. *3 km – 1.9 miles by car*. From the seacliffs between the rocky points of Nevería and **Vigía Hill** (Cerro del Vigía), there are beautiful views of old and new Mazatlán. On Vigía Hill *(continue on Paseo del Centenario)*, is located the **Angela Peralta Pergola,** in memory of the great singer who lived in this city. This lookout point was strategic to the defense of Mazatlán port; today it offers views of the main wharf and of **Crestón Hill** (Cerro del Crestón) – a natural hill that rises 150 m – 492 ft above the sea and is crowned by the second-highest lighthouse in the world.

EXCURSIONS

★**Concordia; Copala.** – *48 km – 29.8 miles. Estimate 1 day. Go southeast from Mazatlán on highway n° 15 until Villa Unión (28 km – 17.4 miles), turn left and continue 20 km – 12.4 miles on highway n° 40 to Concordia.*

Concordia. – Its 18C parish church is noteworthy for the harmonious simplicity of its architecture, featuring geometric forms and elegant moldings. Concordia's local handicrafts are also worth mentioning: particularly its fine cabinetry in richly carved cedar wood, basketry and crackled pottery.

Continue on highway n° 40, 24 km – 14.9 miles until the signs for Copala, from there, 1 km – 0.6 miles on an unpaved road.

★**Copala.** – This picturesque old mining town, at the foothills of the Sierra Madre Occidental, clings precariously to the mountain slopes. It offers a delightful spectacle to lovers of old Mexico with its narrow cobblestone streets, multicolored facades, and ironwork balconies and windows. Added to this rustic atmosphere is the charm of exuberant palms and poincianas, that temper the effects of its warm semi-tropical climate. The small central square is particularly lovely, for its mixture of 17C and 18C popular architecture. In an effort to retain the period atmosphere, the restaurants and inns of the locality reflect Mexican tradition, offering typical cuisine, music and customs.

La Paz. – *Access by air or ferry. Description p 163.*

Respect the environment
Drive carefully on country roads
Protect wildlife, plants and trees.

★ # MÉRIDA Yucatán   ♦♦♦♦♦

Map of Principal Sights p 6

Mérida, also called the White City, was founded in 1542 on the ruins of old Ichcanzihó. The Spanish Conquistadors called it Mérida, because the buildings they found there reminded them of the Roman ruins in the city of the same name in Extremadura, Spain. Today Mérida has developed as an important industrial, business and tourist center, although its population has maintained its deep-rooted, graceful and colorful traditions.

Some of its palm fiber, rattan, stone, wood and clay **handicrafts** date back to the Maya era. Others were added in the colonial period , such as silversmithing, embroidery and leatherwork. Attractive **dances** are also part of these traditions.

The **Yucatan cuisine** is one of the richest and most varied of the Republic: suckling pig *(cochinita pibil),* lime soup, stuffed cheese *(queso relleno),* egg-stuffed tacos in squash seed sauce *(papadzules),* small fried stuffed tortillas *(panuchos),* and many other dishes compose a delicious mosaic of flavors, usually accompanied with beer or a cold rice drink *(horchatas de arroz).*

CENTER OF THE CITY *time: 1/2 day – Plan p 101*

⊙**Convent of the Conceptionist Nuns** (Exconvento de las Monjas Concepcionistas). – This former convent was originally intended to house the young daughters of the Conquistadors who were unable to adjust to life on the remote country estates. Today the Church of Our Lady of Consolation still stands. Worthy of mention in its interior are the lower choir and, on the outside, the balcony over the chancel, with its Mudejar-style arches, from which a panoramic **view★** of the city can be enjoyed. *Access to the balcony is located across the patio.*

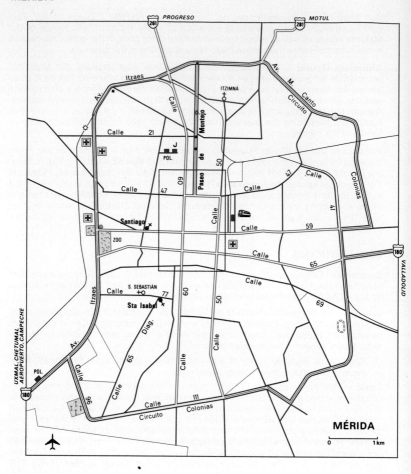

Montejo House (Casa de Montejo). – Banamex Offices. This building was constructed for the highest authority (El Adelantado) designated by the Spanish Crown in America at the time of the Conquest.

Only its beautiful **facade★★**, a unique example of Mexican Plateresque civil architecture, has been preserved. It consists of two sections; the lower part has stylized lines framing an architraved door topped by a bracket in the form of children's heads that supports the central balcony. The upper section of the edifice is less refined but equally ornate.

On the outer corners there are savages dressed in lamb pelts; at the center hangs the Montejo family coat of arms, flanked by warriors who are stepping on Indians' heads. The busts on the upper frieze presumably represented the Adelantado, his wife and his son.

Cathedral. – This is the oldest cathedral in Mexico. It was built by Miguel Agüero on the site occupied by the original church (Iglesia Mayor). The **facade★** consists of five sections: the side ones end in slender towers and the central ones have Renaissance-style portals.

On the main portal, the figures of Saint Peter and Saint Paul are prominent. Above are placed the choir window and a handsome shield framed by an arch that surmounts the central section.

The chapels on the south side were destroyed at the beginning of the 20C, when the Revolution Passageway (Pasaje Revolución) was built. Of the remaining chapels, the most noteworthy one is devoted to the Christ of the Blisters (Cristo de las Ampollas). Its name harks back to a fire in the church of Ichmul, which this effigy survived with only blisters. Following this episode, the statue was transferred to Mérida's cathedral.

Government Palace (Palacio de Gobierno). – This elegant palace was built on the site of the Royal Houses at the end of the 19C. The interior is arranged around a graceful patio.

The walls of the staircase are covered with paintings by Fernando Castro Pacheco: *The Maya Cosmology (La Cosmología Maya); The Symbology of the Four Cardinal Points (La Simbología de los Cuatro Puntos Cardinales)* and *The Creation of Man (La Creación del Hombre).*

In the History Room are exhibited other works by the same Yucatan painter, showing scenes from the state's history, such as the Indian Rebellion led by Canek in the 18C and the War of the Castes, caused by the political and social instability prevailing in Yucatan during the 19C.

⊘**Santiago Parish Church (Parroquia de Santiago).** – *Map p 100.* This slendor 17C church rises in the heart of the old Indian district. It is surrounded by a spacious atrium, which provides a good angle for viewing the building's most attractive features including the elegant facade, the rounded-off buttresses and the graceful parapet that circles the roof.

On the inside, the vault covered with arches and round beams, as well as the high altarpiece at the rear of the chancel, make for a lovely composition.

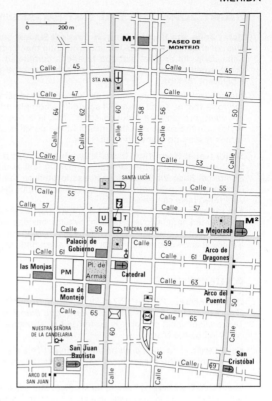

★PASEO DE MONTEJO

time: 3 hours

The prosperity enjoyed by the region, thanks to the sisal boom, is reflected along this attractive thoroughfare. Its construction began in 1888 and was concluded for Porfirio Díaz's visit in 1906. Handsome residences were erected along this beautiful promenade, with its wide, shaded sidewalks and venerable tamarind trees. Today some of the mansions have been converted into tourist agencies or banks and others were replaced by modern buildings, hotels, boutiques and cafeterias. Along its route (nearly 1 km – 0.6 miles), there are three monuments *(map p 100)*: the first on the south, in honor of Carrillo Puerto; the second one, dedicated to Justo Sierra, created by Jesús Contreras; and, to the north, the monument to the Fatherland by Rómulo Rozo.

⊘ **Regional Museum of Anthropology (Museo Regional de Antropología) (M¹).** – **Cantón Palace.** This beautiful **building★** was constructed along Italian Renaissance lines by General Cantón, following a design by Enrique Deserti. Especially noteworthy are the stairway to the second floor and the spacious north terrace. The collection pieces and the corresponding explanations are arranged according to themes referring to the Maya culture: its environment, its social evolution and its economic, religious and cultural activities.

LA MEJORADA *time: 2 hours*

⊘ **La Mejorada Monastery (Exconvento de La Mejorada).** – This plain 17C construction dedicated to the Death of the Virgin, housed Franciscan monks who wished to practice a rigid and strict observance of their rule.

Today the remains of the convent are occupied by the School of Architecture. The single-nave church has a domed transept; the original altarpiece disappeared during the Revolution. At present it has a fragment of a Churrigueresque altarpiece of unknown origin.

⊘ **Museum of Popular Art (Museo de Arte Popular) (M²).** – This pleasant museum houses an admirable collection of popular arts and crafts including embroidered women's tunics, straw hats and multicolored ceramics from various parts of the Yucatan Peninsula. A selection of characteristic handicrafts from other regions of Mexico are also on display.

The Bridge Arch and the Dragons' Arch (El Arco del Puente y el Arco de Dragones). – These simple and slendor Moorish-style arches were built in the last decade of the 18C. Opinions differ as to whether they were erected to mark the city limits, or as the first step of a plan to build a wall around Mérida.

⊘ **Saint Christopher's Parish Church (Parroquia de San Cristóbal).** – The church was built in the center of the district of the same name. It is a good example of 18C Yucatan architecture.

The facade is made up of three sections. The two lateral sections are crowned by towers; and the central section is composed of a porch topped by a great shell which encompasses the simple baroque portal, with its portico and choir window framed by a lovely trefoil arch.

SAINT JOHN THE BAPTIST (SAN JUAN BAUTISTA) *time: 2 hours*

⊘**Saint John the Baptist Church (Templo de San Juan Bautista).** – This beautiful church was constructed in the mid-18C in the building that formerly housed the Hermitage of Saint John. Its original baroque facade is completed by two towers, linked by an ornamented pediment. The half-columns that flank the entrance give the composition a pleasant rhythm.

Interior. – Inside this church, there are well-preserved samples of the **round beams★** called *rollizos* – that is, small beams of sapodilla wood placed across the arches that divide the vault, producing a Moorish effect. This is a decorative custom peculiar to the region. On the south side the priest's house portal is notable, with its Mudejar-style arches resting on stone Doric pilasters.

⊘**Santa Isabel Hermitage (Ermita de Santa Isabel).** – *Map p 100.* In the old city quarter of San Sebastián stands the hermitage known at first as the **Hermitage of the Safe Journey** (La Ermita del Buen Viaje), because it was located on the Royal Road (Camino Real) to Campeche. From the atrium entrance, the graceful facade crowned by a bell gable with three bays can be seen.

The old cemetery situated in the southern part of the hermitage has been recently transformed into a lovely garden, where, besides enjoying the Yucatan tropical flowers, visitors can admire some Maya archeological remains. Within the enclosure a cascade and an open-air theater (where a serenade is performed on Fridays at 9 PM) have been built.

EXCURSIONS

⊘**Dzibilchaltún.** – *22 km – 13.7 miles. Go north from Mérida on highway nº 261 toward Progreso and at 15 km – 9.3 miles, turn right, then 7 km – 4.3 miles to Dzibilchaltún.* This archeological complex is composed of structures discovered in the vast zone occupied by the Maya.

Xlacah Cenote. – *To the south of the complex.* This well is 40 m – 131 ft deep. In it, several interesting pieces have been found; they are on display in the small site museum.

Temple of the Seven Dolls (El Templo de las Siete Muñecas). – *To the east at the end of the main street.* This temple contains a chamber where seven rustically crafted clay dolls were discovered. These dolls are associated with illnesses, because of the physical deformations they bear.

Open-air Chapel (Capilla abierta). – *In the center of the main square.* This chapel was built toward the end of the 16C and consists of a short nave covered with a barrel vault and a small sacristy against the north wall.

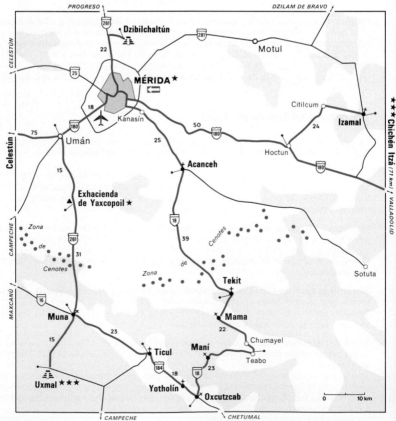

★ Hacienda of Yaxcopoil (Exhacienda de Yaxcopoil). – *33 km – 20.5 miles. Go southwest from Mérida on highway nº 180 and at Uman, turn left on highway nº 261 toward Uxmal; 15 km – 9.3 miles to the hacienda.*

This former hacienda exemplifies the economic progress achieved in the late 19C and early 20C in Yucatan. During this period, the haciendas that had engaged almost exclusively in livestock raising in colonial times, converted to sisal cultivation. The life of the workers and the owners revolved around a central plaza bordered by the main components necessary for the autonomous operation of the hacienda: the main house, chapel, orchard, corrals, stables, machine house – with all the equipment needed for sisal processing – storerooms, workshops, hacienda store, school and infirmary.

Izamal. – *74 km – 46 miles. Go east from Mérida on highway nº 180 towards Valladolid; go through Hoctum (50 km – 31.1 miles) and through Citilcum (14 km – 8.7 miles) and continue 10 km – 6.2 miles on to Izamal.*
At the center of this city there are two parks: Cinco de Mayo Park, where city hall is located; and the Diego de Landa, or Zammá, Park, in which an arch similar to those in Mérida stands at the southeast corner. Some 200 m – 656 ft north of this square is the **archeological site of Izamal.** From its summit a wonderful panoramic view embraces the city and several mounds that conceal other unexcavated buildings.

Izamal Monastery (Convento de Izamal). – Founded by Fray Diego de Landa in the middle of the 16C, this complex stands between the two plazas and on the foundations of a pyramid from the old city established by Zammá. Three ramps lead to the vast **atrium★★**, a splendid ensemble with arched galleries. In the atrium *posas* or corner chapels have been set up. Inside the church there is an altarpiece to the Virgin of Izamal, Patroness of Yucatan. The cloister, with its sundial and the Virgin's dressing room *(camarín)* should also be seen.

★★★ Archeological Site of Uxmal. – *79 km – 49.1 miles south on highways nº 180 and 261. Description p 213.*

Celestún. – *93 km – 57.8 miles. Go west from Mérida on highway nº 180 through Umán (18 km – 11.2 miles) and Kinchil (26 km – 16.2 miles) and continue 49 km – 30.4 miles on highway nº 281 to Celestún.*
This picturesque fishing village is located between the coast of the Gulf of Mexico and the tideland that extends from Punta Nimún for more than 30 km – 18.6 miles. In the early morning hours, flocks of flamingos that nest in the Lagartos River come to the tidelands to feed on seaweed. Weather permitting, the breathtaking **spectacle★** of these birds may be seen, turning the horizon into a pink ribbon and the sky into an immense, ondulating cloud of fire.

★★★ Archeological Site of Chichén Itzá. – *121 km – 75.2 miles east on highway nº 180. Description p 66.*

Monastery Route (Ruta de los Conventos). – *Circuit of 214 km – 126.8 miles. Estimate 1 day. Due to the fording area and to the road conditions, it is recommended to begin the tour in the morning in a southeasterly direction on highway nº18 toward Kanasín, and continue through Oxcutzcab on highway nº 184 until Muna and then on highway nº 261 to Mérida.*
Concrete evidence of the work of evangelization carried out by the Franciscans beginning in the 16C can be seen in the churches and monasteries that remain along this route. Their stylistic unity is apparent, with its prevailing strength and simplicity, in the manner of medieval forts: thick walls topped by battlements and crenellations; buttresses; and a single external ornamentation – the **bell gable.** Some bell gables are single and ornamented like those of **Tekit;** others are double and ornamented like those of **Muna;** still others are connected by complicated pediments like those at **Ticul;** they may be small, like the ones in the Guadalupe Chapel at **Acanceh,** or large, like the one at **Yohtolín.**
This model of religious architecture is peculiar to Yucatan, because the Spanish element assimilated the Puuc-style *(see p 172)* crestings of the Maya structures developed in this region.

Mama. – The rich ornamentation of the facade exemplifies the modifications that the monasteries underwent in colonial times. There is a lovely fountain in what used to be the orchard.

Maní. – When Diego de Landa founded this monastery, he destroyed the Maya structures that were there. In the present building, the main altarpiece and the multicolored Plateresque altars deserve attention.

Oxcutzcab. – On the façade, the simple decorations and the bell gables are interesting, while, on the inside, the vault arches and the high altarpiece should not be overlooked.

Join us in our never ending task of keeping our guides up to date.

Please send us your comments and suggestions.

Michelin Travel Publications
Michelin Tire Corporation.

One Parkway South
Greenville, South Carolina 29615 – USA.

Magnificent Mexico City, which astonished the Spanish Conquistadors with its size and splendor, was comparable then only to Seville or Beirut. In the 19C, Alexander von Humboldt described this, the largest metropolis on the American continent, as the City of Palaces. The remnants of the city's rich past and its enormous size continue to impress visitors.

Today Mexico City is the largest and most populous city in the world (17 000 000 inhabitants), taking into account the metropolitan area. The quick pace of its growth over the last 40 years has stimulated the building of skyscrapers which are dwarfed only by the scope of the city itself and the height of the mountains surrounding the valley in which the city lies.

The city's vivid contrasts in layout and architecture are reflected in its social fabric. This has led to the coexistence of a great variety of social types who have turned many streets of the city into their workplace, much to the entertainment of drivers and pedestrians. On a street corner there might be a chewing gum peddler alongside a singer, whose fleeting melody lasts only as long as the red traffic light. For the traveler arriving at night by plane, the city offers a fabulous spectacle with a stunning **view★★★**, resembling a magic and luminescent carpet, especially when the night is clear.

GEOGRAPHICAL NOTES

Mexico City is located in a broad valley at the southern end of the Mexican plateau, also called Meseta del Anáhuac (alt 2 240 m – 7 349 ft), in the basin of what was formerly a great lake, surrounded by volcanos and mountain ranges. Towards the south, rises the imposing Ajusco range, and towards the east the two colossal volcanoes, Popocatépetl and Iztaccíhuatl, unveil their snow-capped majesty on clear days.

HISTORICAL NOTES

The foundation and fall of México-Tenochtitlán. – After a long march from the mythical city of Aztlán, the Mexicas arrived in the Valley of Mexico, led by their main god, Huitzilopochtli, and guided by the priest Tenoch. In 1299, they settled in Chapultepec, whence they were later expelled by groups already established in the area. Once the alliance they had concluded with Cocoxtli, Lord of Culhuacán, broke up, the Mexicas were forced to seek refuge in the reed grasses beside Lake Texcoco. According to legend, while searching for food one day, a group of Mexicas witnessed the fulfillment of Huitzilopochtli's prophecy: on a small island an eagle appeared, devouring a serpent while standing on a prickly pear tree that was rooted in a rock. It was 1325, the founding date of the great city of **México-Tenochtitlán.** It took the Mexicas less than two hundred years to build the large urban complex that appeared to the Spaniards as one of the Wonders of the World, with its lofty temples atop magnificent pyramids, burnished with stucco that gleamed like silver in the rising sun. Straight, well-laid streets and canals accommodated a population estimated to have reached 200 000 at the time of the Conquest. The once subjected and scorned Mexicas became warlike, overwhelming not only neighboring peoples but also those in far-off Central America. The heavy taxes they imposed provided the means to erect this sumptuous metropolis, which ruled over a large number of cities and villages.

This expansion should also be attributed to the wisdom and cunning of its rulers. Outstanding among them were Tlacaelel, Ahuizotl, Cuauhtémoc, Moctezuma I and Moctezuma II. The latter witnessed the decline of his city at the setting of the Fifth Sun, with the arrival of the Spaniards in 1519.

The Spaniards led by **Hernán Cortés** ran into countless difficulties in their drive to reach México-Tenochtitlán, since they had to conquer and convert Totonacs, Maxcaltecs and Cholutecs before confronting Moctezuma II and occupying the city. After the **Sad Night** (La Noche Triste, June 1520), when the Spaniards were beaten by the Mexicas and were compelled to retreat, the reduced army of Hernán Cortés took refuge in Tlaxcala, strengthening its ranks with more than 450 000 Indians. On May 30th, 1521 the siege of the city began with intense fighting on both sides; landings were attempted but the invaders were repeatedly driven back. As time passed, the Mexica army grew short of arms, food and men; their courage alone kept them fighting. Cortés ordered that the city be leveled and the canals and ditches be filled with the rubble, to facilitate his army's entry. The Spaniards began to despair because the Mexicas would not capitulate; fighting intensified and, finally, Tlatelolco, the marvelous trading city, fell. On the 13th of August, 1521, after a heroic and bloody defense, México-Tenochtitlán surrendered.

Colonial Period and Independence. – Hernán Cortés never imagined the problems Mexico City would face as a result of his decision to rebuild it on the same site as Tenochtitlán, surrounded by lakes as it was. In 1626, 1627 and 1629 there were great floods. The last one continued for three years, and in fact the city remained under water until 1637. The Indians' adobe houses collapsed, and the great mansions of the Spaniards crumbled as well. By October 1629, 30 000 Indians had died and of the 20 000 families which inhabited the city, only 400 remained. Transportation was only possible by canoe since streets and roads lay under water. When the water level subsided in 1637, they had to construct a city that differed greatly from the one dreamed of by the Spanish conquerors, echoing the Renaissance and baroque styles in fashion in Europe at that time. The Spanish King Philip V brought a pervasive French influence into Spain and her colonies.

The baroque forms that had fashioned such beautiful temples and palaces, were supplanted by the neoclassical style, which the recently established Academy of San Carlos imposed during the last third of the 18C. In time the Mexicans became familiar with pre-Revolutionary democratic French thought. The Bourbon reforms introduced into Spain by Charles III restored the state's role in economic and administrative matters, but other measures, such as banning of the Jesuits and high taxes, aroused grave discontent.

The War of Independence and, subsequently, various civil conflicts put an end to this French influence. Later on, during the Second Empire (1864-67), deep-rooted nationalist feelings in Mexico disavowed this trend. However, in the last third of the 19C, the state and the aristocracy accepted the French pattern as their style of life, which is reflected in the architecture of Mexico City's western sector.

Revolutionary Period. – On February 9th, 1913 the so-called Ten Tragic Days (la Decena Trágica) began in the city, when Generals Bernardo Reyes, Manuel Mondragón and Félix Díaz rebelled against President Francisco I. Madero. During the attack on the National Palace, Reyes was killed and the other two generals, faced with defeat, retreated to la Ciudadela. General Victoriano Huerta, a leading figure in the Federal Army, resentful of Madero, was appointed by him to combat the rebels. Huerta made a deal with the rebels, while pretending to remain loyal to the president. In agreement with the United States ambassador, Henry Lane Wilson, Huerta betrayed Madero and seized power for himself. Madero was arrested, together with Vice President Pino Suarez, and was taken to the penitentiary, where both were assassinated. After a farcical episode, whereby a president was instituted for 45 minutes, Huerta was made president of the Mexican Republic. In the course of the Ten Days, the city became a battlefield, many civilians fell and hunger appeared anew. In the north of the country, Venustiano Carranza refused to recognize an illegal president and, in accord with the Guadalupe Plan, launched an operation to reinstate constitutional government. Carranza was supported by military leaders such as Alvaro Obregón, Plutarco Elías Calles, Pablo González and Francisco Villa. The Ten Tragic Days were decisive in unleashing the genuine revolution, which changed the social, economic and political structures of the country, culminating in the establishment of the constitutional government in Mexico City.

Mexico City Today. – The administration of Plutarco Elías Calles, in 1924, set the country on the path of institutionalization. It laid the foundations which ended chaos and brought economic and political stability, based principally on the establishment of the National Revolutionary Party (today called the PRI, Partido Revolutionario Institucional, and of the Bank of Mexico, as well as on land distribution to the peasants. Since 1940, Mexico City has undergone major changes, breaking out of the historical city limits in all directions. With this expansion, the old city is being gradually surrounded by skyscrapers.

The opening of broad avenues and expressways served to link the suburban areas of Mexico state to the city proper. These now belong to the megalopolis which makes Mexico City the most populated urban center in the world. The city's profile has changed considerably as a result of its expansion. Nevertheless, buildings of different eras stand side by side in gracious harmony, making for part of its charm. The dizzying rhythm of city life does not prevent visitors from enjoying the shows, concerts, exhibitions that the city has to offer or an excursion to the popular Zona Rosa by night. For **shopping,** there are numerous department stores in the center and exclusive boutiques on Insurgentes Sur, Paseo de la Reforma and Polanco. At lunchtime, a wide gamut of restaurants offers different sorts of menus, ranging from the varied Mexican cuisine to the international bill of fare.

★★★HISTORIC CENTER *time: 5 1/2 days*

The following eight tours should be made on foot.

★★★ ① Plaza de la Constitución and Surroundings
time: one day – (see plan pp 110-111)

★★★ **Plaza de la Constitución.** – **Zócalo.** In this extraordinary square lies the heart of Mexico. The superb **buildings** which delimit its unusual proportions seem dwarfed by this immense expanse, where time appears to have stopped. In fact, the echo of fantastic legends and thundering gods, the drums of the powerful **Aztec empire** and the clamor of the **Conquest,** still seem to reverberate through it. The glorious historic events that the site has witnessed over the centuries have endowed the square with a majesty that transcends the physical beauty of its architectural components.

Its local name, **Zócalo,** comes from an unfinished work, the Monument to Independence, planned in 1843, of which only the base, or *zócalo,* was built. By analogy, the word *zócalo* is frequently used to designate the main square of any city or town in Mexico.

Day and night the Zócalo is intensely alive with crowds of people and the cheerful lights of its **night-time illumination** *(on weekends and during the Christmas season).* It is especially animated during the Independence Day celebrations, which culminate in the **Mexican Night** (Noche Mexicana - *September 15th),* when the president of the Republic, speaking from the balcony of the National Palace, commemorates Mexico's Independence.

Where once stood palaces and temples of prosperous **Tenochtitlán,** today there are sober structures of different tonalities derived from the stone and *tezontle* employed in the facades of the buildings that now house the main national institutions.

★★★ **Metropolitan Cathedral** (Catedral Metropolitana). – This is an enormous and imposing ⊘ edifice, constructed in grey stone that sets off the white marble used in the reliefs, producing different chiaroscuro effects, according to the time of day. Today's cathedral is not the first built on this site; the original was a rather small structure, erected on the ruins of a wing of the Great Temple (Templo Mayor - *p 110*), largely using materials from the pre-Hispanic structure.

The present cathedral was begun in 1573, according to a design by the architect **Claudio de Arciniega**, who was inspired by the cathedral of Salamanca in Spain, completed in 1560. Construction proceeded very slowly; by 1629 only the rear section – the sacristy, the apse and the chapter house (sala capitular) – was finished. Since services could be held in the sacristy, demolition of the first cathedral was initiated in that year. Subsequent work carried out over the centuries, involved certain stylistic modifications of the original design to reflect changing trends.

Facade. – Built in 1681 in the baroque style, the facade's ornamental reliefs were inspired by **Rubens'** engravings. The centerpiece represents *The Assumption (La Asunción),* to which the cathedral was dedicated. To the left is depicted *The Presentation of the Keys (La Entrega de las Llaves)* and to the right, *The Ship of the Church (La Barca de la Iglesia).* The clock and the sculptures *Faith, Hope and Charity (Fe, Esperanza y Caridad)* at its crowning point are the work of **Manuel Tolsá** *(see p 40).* The bell-shaped tower finials, built in 1788, are an innovation by **José Damián Ortíz de Castro.**

Interior. – The cathedral's interior projects an air of solemnity. It has five naves: the side aisles contain fourteen chapels, the sacristy and the chapter house; the adjoining two naves are used for processions; and the central nave is outstanding for its greater height and breadth.

Among the **chapels** on the right, note the one dedicated to **San Isidro** *(2nd chapel),* with a beautiful baroque door the Tabernacle *(Sagrario)* and a **Black Christ** (Cristo Negro), known to his devotees as the Lord of the Poison (El Señor del Veneno). This stems from the legend about an archbishop, owner of the originally light-colored image, who used to kiss the feet of the statue every day. His servant tried to kill him by rubbing poison on the feet of the crucifix, but the image absorbed it, turning black in the process, thereby saving the archbishop's life. The **Chapel of the Relics** (Capilla de Las Reliquias) *(7th chapel)* has a magnificent altarpiece with paintings by Juan de Herrera and elaborate relics.

★★ **Sacristy.** – *To the right of the chancel.* ⊘ The sacristy displays intricately ribbed vaults and a **painting** attributed to the Spanish artist **Bartolomé Esteban Murillo** (1618-82). It is also outstanding for the work of two of the greatest artists of the Golden Century of Mexican painting, **Cristóbal de Villalpando** (17-18C) and **Juan Correa** (17C). The prolific output of these gifted masters is found throughout Mexico and as far away as Guatemala. The works here exhibited are *The Triumph of the Church (El Triunfo de la Iglesia)* and *The Apparition of Saint Michael (La Aparición de San Miguel)* by Villalpando, and *The Death of the Virgin (El tránsito de la Virgen)* and *Christ's Entrance into Jerusalem (La Entrada de Cristo en Jerusalen)* by Correa.

The unusual **Chapel of the Kings** (Capilla de los Reyes), built in the old chancel of the cathedral, possesses the first baroque **altarpiece★★★** (retablo) in which *estípites (see p 40)* were used. This was the work of **Jerónimo de Balbás**, who devoted seven years to its construction, starting in 1718. It is a composition of sculptures of saints, kings, queens and two very large paintings by Juan Rodríguez Juárez (1675-1728) depicting *The Adoration of the Kings (La Adoración de los Reyes)* and *The Assumption of the Virgin (La Asunción de la Virgen).*

Among the **chapels★** on the left side, two should be highlighted: the one dedicated to **San Felipe de Jesús** – so far the only Mexican saint – which contains the remains of the first emperor of Mexico, **Agustín de Iturbide** *(see p 30)*; and the last chapel, dedicated to the **Archangel Michael** (San Miguel Arcángel), with outstanding 17C retables and excellent painted and gilded carvings *(estofadas).* One part of the central nave is taken up by the **choir,** fashioned in the style of the Spanish Renaissance cathedrals. In the rear stands

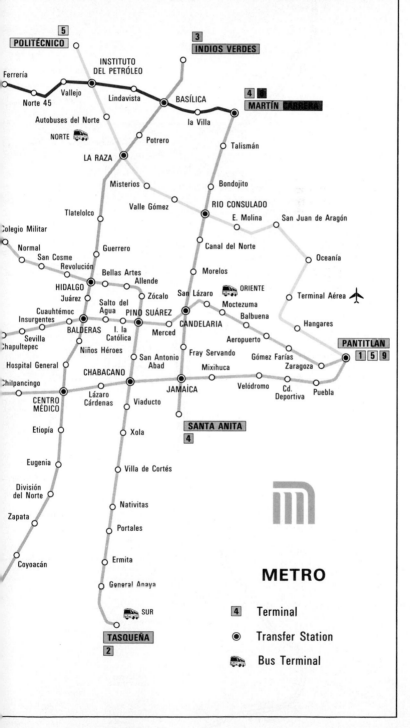

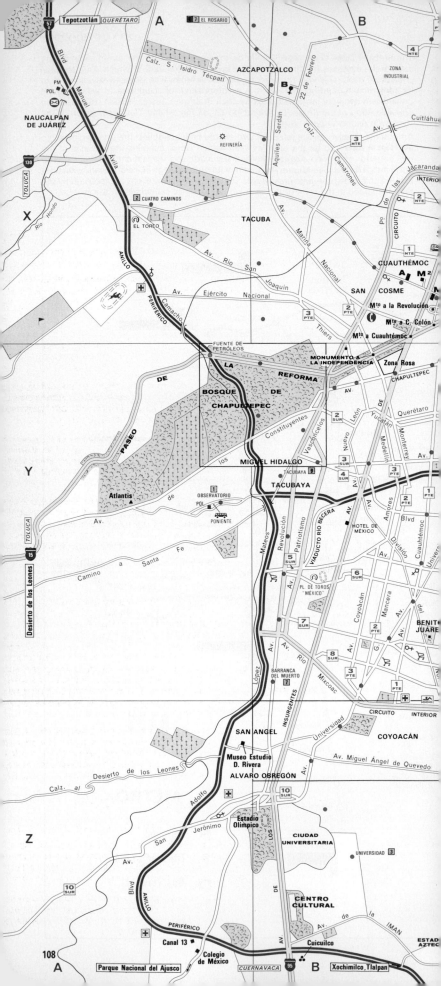

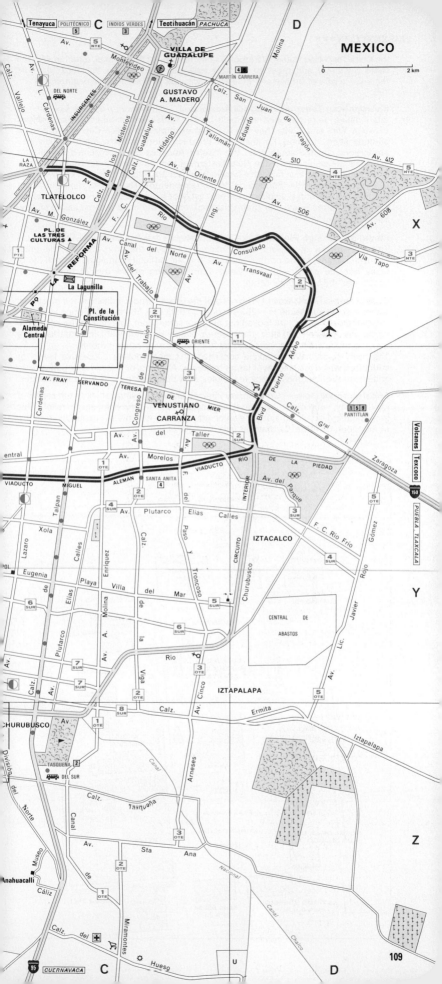

the **Altar of Forgiveness** (Altar del Perdón), a faithful copy of the original, together with the **organs** (restored) and most of the **choir stalls** damaged during the 1967 fire. The remarkable **grille** of bronze and gold alloy was cast in Macao at the beginning of the 18C.

Metropolitan Tabernacle (Sagrario Metropolitano). – *Illustration, p 39.* The **facades★★** of this building were designed and built by the Andalusian architect **Lorenzo Rodríguez** between 1749 and 1760. They are the best example in Mexico City of the *estípite* baroque style, not only for their rich ornamentation but also for their balanced proportions. On the south side, the Twelve Apostles are represented on pilaster pedestals, hence its name, the New Testament Facade (Portada del Nuevo Testamento); while on the east face, the Twelve Prophets are depicted, so it is known as the Old Testament Facade (Portada del Viejo Testamento). The interior, laid out in the shape of a Greek cross, displays over the east door a monumental anonymous **painting** portraying Saint Christopher (San Cristóbal), one of the most revered saints of New Spain.

Model of the High Plateau Lake Region (Maqueta de la Zona Lacustre del Altiplano) (A). – This fine model of ancient Lake Texcoco portrays the twin cities – the great Tenochtitlán and, to the north, Tlatelolco. It is not difficult to imagine the rich life of these lakeside cities, with the Great Temple rising above the 72 temples that constituted the ceremonial center.

Great Temple (Templo Mayor). – The ruins of the Great Temple indicate that it measured 100 m – 328 ft across, 80 m – 262.5 ft deep and 33 m – 108 ft high. Facing west, the twin temples at its summit looked out onto the setting sun. The one on the left, to the north, was dedicated to Tlaloc; the southern one, to Huitzilopochtli. In front there were two enormous staircases, bordered by four ramps with serpent motifs.
The basic construction principle consisted of superimposing successive layers of structures, which made for ever larger buildings. At times, only facades or patios were added, but at other times complete temples were built on top of the ancient structures.

A Bit of History and Legend. – On February 28th, 1978, while laying cables in the center of Mexico City, workmen discovered an ancient stone carved in sharp relief. This important find set off a major excavation effort, which brought the beautiful sculpture of the moon goddess, **Coyolxauhqui,** into the light of the 20C.

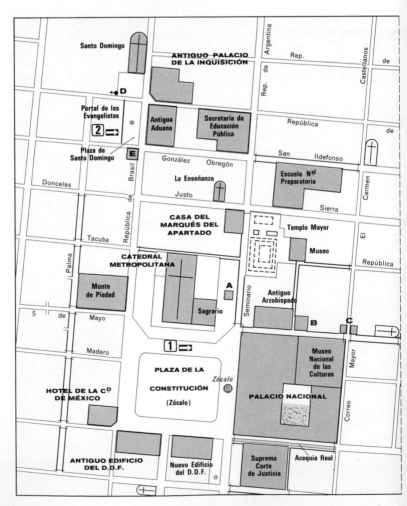

Legend relates that she was the daughter of **Coatlicue,** mother of heaven and earth, life and death. One day, so continues the legend, while Coatlicue was sweeping the temple on Coatepec Hill, she found some precious feathers which she kept in her bosom, as a result of which she became pregnant. Coyolxauhqui and her brothers, the stars – the 400 Surianos –, jealous and indignant, came to kill her. At that very moment, **Huitzilopochtli** was born, dressed as a warrior, with a serpent afire in his hand. He decapitated the moon and sent it rolling down the mountain, where it disintegrated; then he expelled the stars, which scattered over the firmament.

⊙ **Archeological Site.** – The lower walk, where part of the drainage canal built at the turn of the century can be seen, explains the construction principle described above. In Stage IV b the reproduction of Coyolxauhqui *(see below)* has been placed on the site where it was found, together with multicolored serpents and incrusted skulls. In the previous stage, eight standard bearers were found, since the custom was to leave the completed old temple to be used as the foundations for the new building. In the center of the area, the major discovery of the two temples confirms the stories told by Spanish chroniclers. In front of the Temple of Tláloc stands a polychrome **Chac Mool,** the messenger of the gods of Chichén Itzá; and before the Temple of **Huitzilopochtli,** a **sacrificial stone** embellishes the platform. The date of each construction era is carved in stone.

The Temple of the Frogs (Templo de las Ranas), which is linked with Tláloc, can be seen on the lower level to the left. In the north courtyards, eagles crown two ramps, and the bases of the columns and benches are reminiscent of the Toltec palaces. To the east, the Red Temple, in Teotihuacan style, is to be noted; and, near the exit, a beautiful sculpture in green stone, representing a **snail.**

Museum of the Great Temple (Museo del Templo Mayor) (**M**). – This modern building, situated next to the archeological site, was especially designed to house the extraordinary collection of artifacts found during the excavation of the Great Temple (1978-1982). An innovative museographical feature of the exhibit is the attractive presentation of explanatory texts and illustrations on thick glass plates illuminated laterally. The displays are exhibited in rooms designed to resemble temple ruins thereby creating a solemn atmosphere and giving the visitor the impression of observing the objects as they were discovered in the excavations.

The visit begins on the right and proceeds to the upper floors. The exhibit traces the history of the Aztecs from their departure from legendary Aztlán to the Spanish Conquest and underlines the economic and commercial evolution of the region as well as México-Tenochtitlán's military prowess.

The collection includes numerous finely carved stones of various dimensions as well as objects in obsidian, gold, rock crystal, bone, jade and alabaster. Also noteworthy are the beautiful Teotihuacan style masks, the offerings depicting Mezcalan figures from the state of Guerrero, terra cotta eagle warriors and an elegantly carved stone shell. A large-scale model of the ceremonial center, displayed in the center of the first floor, gives a general overview of the site's remarkable urban design.

★★★ **Coyolxauhqui.** *On the second floor, in front of the window.* This is one of the finest pieces found during excavation. It is a monolithic, roughly oval object of 3.05 m – 9 ft by 3.25 m – 10.8 ft in diameter, which weighs eight tons. This magnificent archeological piece, that evokes the tragic legend of the goddess *(see above),* used to lie at the bottom of the staircase of Huiztilopochtli's Temple as a monument to an ancient battle. The relief and the proportions are faultless. In the center the static torso shows the scars of dismemberment, and the limbs seem to swirl around at a surprising pace. The graceful droop of the head is prolonged in its feather and the belt is adorned with a skull.

Old Juan Pablos Printing Press (Antigua Imprenta Juan Pablos) (B). – This old printing press is in a dilapidated 19C house, on the spot where the first printing press on the American continent went into operation in 1536. The press was brought to New Spain by the first Viceroy, Antonio de Mendoza. The master printers were Esteban Martín and Juan Pabli, popularly known as Juan Pablos.

⊙ **Houses of the Mayorazgo de Guerrero (Casas del Mayorazgo de Guerrero) (C).** – These twin houses stand on either side of the same street. They were built in 1713 by the architect Francisco Guerrero y Torres, who crowned them with towers to make them more imposing.

111

The one closer to the Zócalo is better preserved and still has fine patios. Over its main staircase, a mural painted in 1933 by Rufino Tamayo, entitled *Music (La Música)*, can be admired. Its theme alludes to the previous use of the house as the National School of Music.

The other house is important because **José Guadalupe Posada,** the outstanding engraver, had his workshop on the premises *(see p 59).*

Ⓥ **Church of the Most Holy** (Templo de la Santísima). – This church has one of the most beautiful baroque (18C) **facades★** in the city, comparable to those of the Metropolitan Tabernacle. Its construction is attributed to the architect Lorenzo Rodríguez. Its slendor *estípites* and the central bas relief of the Holy Trinity are particularly noteworthy. The reliefs on the lateral facade should also be noted.

Ⓥ **Cloister.** – This is a lovely patio surrounded by low arches where the present owners have endeavored to preserve the atmosphere of the past. In the 19C this cloister served to house the Congregation of Saint Peter (Congregación de San Pedro) and to provide accommodation for both traveling priests and the sick.

Ⓥ **National School of Fine Arts** (Escuela Nacional de Artes Plásticas). – Formerly the Academy of San Carlos (Antigua Academia de San Carlos). In the locale of the old Hospital del Amor de Dios, the renowned Royal Academy of San Carlos *(see p 40)* was established in 1791. As time passed, it became the controversial National School of Fine Arts. During the second half of the 19C, a new facade more directly related to its functions was erected. Among the reliefs of this facade there is one of King Charles III of Spain in acknowledgement for founding the Academy in New Spain in 1785. Under the interior courtyard arcades, there are still the plaster reproductions of Classical and Renaissance sculptures brought from Europe for the students to copy. At present the building is used for cultural events and temporary exhibits of the students' work.

Ⓥ **National Museum of Cultures** (Museo Nacional de las Culturas). – This didactic museum was set up in the former Mint, which until 1964 housed the collection now on display in the National Anthropological Museum. It contains original pieces and reproductions belonging to many different civilizations of the world. The masks and the utensils of daily life exhibited in the rooms reserved for African countries are especially interesting. In the vestibule there is a mural by Rufino Tamayo (1899) entitled *Revolution (Revolución),* done in fresco technique, on the theme of the Mexican Revolution of 1910.

Old Archbishopric (Antiguo Arzobispado). – This building has a striking baroque facade dating back to 1743 and composed solely of two severe *estípites*. The construction date coincided with the period when Jerónimo de Balbás was working on his altarpiece in the Chapel of the Kings *(p 107)* in the cathedral. It has a simple courtyard with four passageways on two levels, supported by pilasters.

★★ **National Palace** (Palacio Nacional). – On the site of the New Houses of **Moctezuma,** which Ⓥ fell to the hands of **Hernán Cortés** after the Conquest, a building was erected to house the Viceroys. In 1562 the King of Spain bought it from Martín Cortés to convert it into the Palace of the Viceroys. In 1692 a mob partially destroyed it. A year later, Viceroy Gaspar de la Cerda rebuilt it almost entirely. During Viceroy **Revillagigedo's** rule it was remodeled. The north gate was opened at the time of President Mariano Arista's government; hence the name, **Puerta Mariana.** In 1927 a third floor was added to the structure.

The palace has various courtyards; the south gate leads to the President's offices *(not open to the public)* and the central gate opens onto the main courtyard where a replica of the original colonial **fountain** stands.

(Photo Guillermo Aldana/Mexico)

Mexico City. Detail of the mural *Epic of Mexico* by Rivera in the National Palace

Main Staircase. – To the left of the main courtyard. The staircase is decorated with murals★★★ by the renowned artist, **Diego Rivera** (1886-1957). These present a synthesis of Mexican history, from pre-Hispanic times to 1929.

North Wall. – This mural portrays pre-Hispanic life in Mexico: work, the arts, agriculture, warmaking and myths.

West Wall. – The story recorded on this mural begins in the lower part with scenes of the **War of Conquest;** Spanish soldiers on foot and on horseback fight against the indigenous warriors, attired in their colorful garments. The second panel shows **scenes of everyday life in colonial society:** slavery, the Inquisition, the evangelizing friars are among the themes represented. Within the five upper arches Diego Rivera depicted the two so-called **international wars** (19C) at the far ends: the French intervention to the left and the North American one to the right. In the intermediate arches, the **Porfirismo** era is on the right, with its leading men and inventions; to the left, the era of Santa Anna and the **Reform,** leaving for the central arch **Independence** in the lower part and the **Mexican Empire** and the **1910 Revolution** in the upper part. The numerous personalities portrayed in the mural are intended to offer a great history lesson.

South Wall. – This mural illustrates various aspects of modern life: labor, strikes, police repression, society and its vices, the Church and its exploitation of the people, the proletariat, workers unions and a large portrait of Karl Marx, the great hope for a better future, according to Diego Rivera.

North Corridor. – This area is decorated with eleven paintings, starting with two grisailles, *What the World Owes to Mexico (Lo que el Mundo debe a México)* and *The Culture of Ancient Mexico (La Cultura de México Antiguo)*.
Most of the **panels** treat themes exalting ancient Mexican cultures. Salient among them are the first panel, showing the **Tlatelolco Market** *(see p 127),* the fourth, which is a tribute to the **Culture of El Tajín** *(p 186),* and the ninth, which portrays the **Conquest** with the portrait of Hernán Cortés repeatedly reproduced.

⊙ A few meters further on, stands the original **House of Representatives** (Cámara de Diputados) of Mexico, a horseshoe-shaped hall encircled by the legislators' benches, with a section corresponding to the Speaker of the House (Presidente de la Cámara). In the entrance hall, there is an exhibit of the various constitutions under which Mexico has been governed.

The First Floor. – The left corridor on the first floor, after the staircase, leads to the Federal Treasury Office and, immediately beyond, there is the cantilevered Staircase of the Empress, because it was commissioned by Carlota Amalia, the wife of Emperor Maximilian of Habsburg *(see p 31)*.
Further along may be found the **Marianos courtyards** (patios Marianos), which today are occupied by the Secretary of Economy and Public Credit. In the first courtyard there is a sculpture of President **Benito Juárez,** cast in the metal of the guns captured from the French army, which imposed Maximilian of Habsburg as Emperor of Mexico. On the ⊙ left side is the **Juárez Wing** (El Recinto a Juárez) containing a library devoted to his life and works, and rooms he occupied during his regime, including the bedroom where he died. The rear of the main patio gives onto another very beautiful courtyard, designed by the Empress Carlota Amalia; on the left is a former chapel, transformed into the Mint and presently used as a conference room.

The Royal Canal (La Acequia Real). – In the colonial period this was the most important waterway that crossed the city. It began in the town of Tláhuac (to the south of the capital) and from there hundreds of canoes traditional vessels called *chalupas* and *trajineras* carried the city's supply of fruit, vegetables and flowers.
This canal was closed around the end of the 17C and was forgotten until 1970, when some stretches of it were restored.

⊙ **Supreme Court (Suprema Corte de Justicia)**. – This building was constructed at the initiative of President Cárdenas *(see p 33)* between 1935 and 1941. The interior is of particular interest: in the central hall at the top of the staircase is a **mural**, entitled *Justice (La Justicia),* painted in 1941 by **J. Clemente Orozco** *(see p 41);* and on either side of the entrance to the library there is another mural named *War (La Guerra),* painted by George Biddle in 1945. In front of this building stands the monument commemorating the **foundation of México-Tenochtitlán** (1970).

New Federal District Building (Nuevo Edificio del Departamento del Distrito Federal). – This edifice was constructed in 1935, imitating the facades of the old building so as to preserve the architectural harmony on the south side of Plaza de la Constitución.

★ **Old Federal District Building (Antiguo Edificio del Departamento del Distrito Federal)**. – From ⊙ the 16C this building had been the seat of municipal government. It was refurbished in 1789 by one of the most renowned architects of the 18C, Ignacio Castera. The carved stone **facade** has windowed balconies jutting out at either end. Its coats of arms, made of Puebla tiles, portray the men and the sites that were crucial in the discovery, conquest and consolidation of New Spain. Inside the building, the staircase and the **courtyards,** surrounded by arcades, are noteworthy.

★ **Hotel de la Ciudad de México**. – This former department store, El Centro Mercantil is one of the most representative examples of the French architectural style (1900) that prevailed during the Porfirista era *(p 31).* On the exterior it has two-story stone columns. Inside are some Art Nouveau elements, such as the elevator, the staircase and the balustrades on the upper floors; the **leaded** roof in the hallway is ornamented with plant motifs in vivid color. A similar stained glass window can be seen in the nearby department store, El Palacio de Hierro, one of the earliest of such establishments in the city (1868).

⊙ **Monte de Piedad.** – Built in the first half of the 19C and reconstructed in the 20C, this edifice imitates the style of colonial houses. The Monte de Piedad is a kind of pawnshop run by the government for lending money to the poor. It was founded in 1775 by Pedro Romero de Terreros and was permanently settled in this locale in 1836, where it continues to operate today.

On this site, towards the north, in pre-Hispanic times, stood the house of **Axayácatl**, where Hernán Cortés and his army stayed in 1519. Once the Conquest was accomplished, Hernán Cortés chose to erect one of his palaces on the south side site formerly occupied by Moctezuma's residence.

★★ ② **Santo Domingo and Surroundings**
time: one day – Plan pp 110-111

Plaza de Santo Domingo. – This popular square has preserved a special charm, together with its surrounding buildings, the arcades, the fountain, the monument to La Corregidora, pigeons and street vendors. In pre-Hispanic times, this site was part of the Palace of the Emperor Cuauhtémoc. In 1526, Dominican friars chose land in this area for their monastery and began building. In 1900, it was embellished with the central fountain which supports the monument to **Josefa Ortiz de Dominguez,** Corregidora of Querétaro *(see p 173)*.

Portal of the Evangelists (Portal de los Evangelistas). – *On the west side of the plaza.* These arcades serve as a workplace for the "evangelists" – the traditional and popular name for the **scribes,** who have operated on this spot since the last century. As a rule, these are older men, who sit at a table cluttered with all sorts of pens, inks, pen-knives, paper and typewriters. They transcribe the thoughts of the illiterate and poor people who come to them to have their loves, business transactions or messages put into writing. In the same area, a number of small shops perform low cost printing jobs, such as invitations, Christmas greetings and calling cards.

Church of Santo Domingo (Templo de Santo Domingo). – This was the first convent founded by the Dominican order in New Spain. At the outset, the friars settled on the site of the Inquisition Palace *(see below)*. The building that housed them was consecrated in 1590, but they were subsequently obliged to abandon it, due to serious damage caused by the humidity of the terrain. For their new establishment, they were assigned land located north of Plaza de Santo Domingo, and there they built the convent and the church, consecrated in 1736.

This religious complex was preserved intact until 1861, when the Reform Laws were enacted *(see p 31)*, leading to the demolition of most of the buildings. Only the church and the Chapel of the Lord of Expiration (Capilla del Señor de la Expiración) *(see below)* were spared. The portals on the west side were added in the present century.

Facade. – This facade belongs to the transitional baroque of the 17C, evidenced in the treatment of the columns, which are adorned with plant decorations and wavy fluting. It is made up of two parts, a finial and a tower. In the niches between the columns of the first part, are the effigies of Saint Augustine (San Agustín) and Saint Francis (San Francisco). In the second part, the relief representing *The Protection of Saint Dominic by Saint Peter and Saint Paul (La Protección Otorgada a San Pedro y San Pablo por Santo Domingo)* is remarkable.

Lateral Facade. – The central relief is noteworthy because of the candid manner in which Saint Dominic and Saint Francis are depicted: facing away with their hands outstretched, attempting to prevent the collapse of the church which appears behind them. This symbolizes Pope Innocent III's dream about the fall of the Christian Church.

Interior. – Inside the church, baroque features were introduced, which would influence the design of the majority of the churches built from the 17C onward. These are: the layout based on the Latin cross, with side naves that become chapels, and the use of a dome over the crossing. In the decoration, which has been since modified, the 18C baroque altarpiece dedicated to the Passion of Christ in the right transept should be noted, as well as paintings by Fray Alonso López de Herrera, el Divino Herrera, (second half of the 16C), and Saint Dominic's Chapel (Capilla de Santo Domingo), with its small colonial sculpture of Our Lady of the Revelation (Nuestra Señora de la Bien Aparecida), who carries the viceroyal scepter as patroness of Mexico City at that time.

Chapel of the Lord of Expiration (Señor de la Expiración) **(D)**. – This chapel of limited artistic merit was the only one left standing in what had been the portico of the Church of Santo Domingo, when the Reform Laws of 1861 were enforced.

★★ **Old Palace of the Inquisition (Antiguo Palacio de la Inquisición). – Museum of Medecine**
⊙ (Museo de la Medicina). The Inquisition functioned in Mexico from 1571 to 1820. It was founded fifty years after the Conquest was completed, as a result of the conspiracy led by Martín Cortés, who wanted to make New Spain an independent state. Therefore its founding was prompted more by political repression than by the supression of heresy. The location of the Old Palace in Plaza de Santo Domingo was not fortuitous, as from its inception in Spain, the Inquisition was entrusted to the Dominican order.

The present **building** was constructed in the first third of the 18C, the work of architect **Pedro de Arrieta**, who introduced such innovations as the octagonal entrance and, in the corners of the extraordinary **courtyard**, the use of interlaced arches with unsupported junctures, which creates the impression that they are hanging freely. In 1854, the building was turned into a National Medical School (Escuela Nacional de Medicina). Today it houses a small museum devoted to the history of medicine in Mexico. A replica of a 17C pharmacy is on display. In the amphitheater, some of the old stalls can still be seen.

⊙ **Old Custom House** (Antigua Aduana). – Offices of the Department of Public Education (Oficinas de la Secretaría de Educación Pública). Due to the humidity of its site, this 18C building also had to be modified and restored. However, its original appearance was not changed. Inside the building, there are two outstanding ample courtyards, and on the walls of the baroque staircase that separates them are the notable **painting Patricians and Patricides** *(Patricios y Patricidas)*, by **David Alfaro Siqueiros**, on which he worked from 1945 to 1971.

⊙ **House of Diego y Pedraza** (Casa de Diego y Pedraza) (E). – In 1525, the house of Master Diego y Pedraza, the first surgeon in the capital of New Spain, stood at what is now the corner of calles Brazil and Cuba. The architectural features of the present building, dating from the 18C, contribute to the harmony of the square. Inside there is a small remodeled courtyard, which retains a certain air of times gone by.

La Enseñanza. – This is a small church that belonged to the convent of the same name. Although it was built in the second half of the 18C, its facade does not have the typical baroque features. Outstanding for their wealth of embellishments are the central niche and the choral window, in front of which is placed the graceful figure of the Virgin of the Pillar (Virgen del Pilar), patroness of the church.

★★ **Interior.** – This church has only one nave and all of its magnificent original gilded **altarpieces** have been preserved; the one on the high altar is most remarkable. Nuns' **choirs** stand on either side and, above it hang two paintings by Andrés López (18C).

★ **House of the Marquis del Apartado** (Casa del Marqués del Apartado). – This is one of the most beautiful neoclassical houses of Mexico City. The sober facade is worked in stone and not in *tezontle,* which was then the fashionable material. It has three levels and is framed by four Doric columns which support a triangular pediment. A balustrade similar to that of the Cathedral and the Minería Palace (Palacio de Minería), the work of Tolsá, finishes off this ensemble.

Interior. – Although the house has been altered at different periods, it retains its aristocratic allure. At one end of the ample courtyard, below the flagstones, some remains of the Great Temple (Templo Mayor) have been preserved *(p 110)*. According to legend, this residence was built by the Marquis del Apartado, to offer it to Ferdinand VII of Spain after he was dethroned by Napoleon. One section of the house has been used to set up a simple site museum, which illustrates, through photographs and drawings, the process of construction and restoration of the building. It also contains a library and a cafeteria.

⊙ **Department of Public Education** (Secretaría de Educación Pública). – Between 1921 and 1922, this building was constructed on the original site of the Convent of the Incarnation (Convento de la Encarnación). When the work was nearing completion (1923), several painters began the **decoration★★** of the walls surrounding both courtyards, based on scenes suggested by the philosopher, writer and Minister of Education, José Vasconcelos *(see p 44)*.

Diego Rivera painted these murals shortly after returning from Europe, where he had studied and worked, hence the influence of Cézanne, Picasso and Paolo Uccello (15C) in his works.

Jean Charlot left several frescoes, but only one has been preserved: *The Washerwomen (Las Lavanderas),* in which Rivera's influence can be detected. The same is true of *The Small Bull (El Torito)* by **Amado de la Cueva.**

First Floor. – Murals by Diego Rivera, Jean Charlot and Amado de la Cueva are found here; their themes are inspired by life and work in the countryside, merry-making and local customs, as well as industrial labor. A great deal of attention is focused on one particular region of Oaxaca state, Tehuantepec, where Diego Rivera had sojourned a mere two years previously and which had impressed him deeply with its landscape, people and customs.

Second Floor. – On this floor are found the grisailles by **Rivera,** together with paintings in very vivid colors by Charlot representing the states of the Mexican Republic. The grisailles portray themes such as science, chemistry and medicine.

Third Floor. – Both the grisailles and the paintings are by Rivera, and the subjects evoke the arts, the trades and the national heroes of this century, all aimed at promoting social change.

Staircase. – *Left side.* These outstanding paintings were designed to be seen in motion. The three levels are covered with aquatic themes, such as *The Goddess of the Ocean (La Diosa del Agua Marina),* which is clearly a version of *The Birth of Venus* by Botticelli with a Mexican background and characters. On the second level, there are two landscapes of Tehuantepec and a fine allegory of the pre-Hispanic god of spring, Xoohipilli, which ends on the third floor with four frescoes devoted to farm labor and a magnificent self-portrait.

Elevators. – *First floor on the north side.* Rivera took advantage of the dim light in the elevator shaft to create a vision of the **Yucatan cenotes,** thus displaying his technical prowess in finding such an artful solution to the decoration of this difficult space.

⊙ **Escuela Nacional Preparatoria.** – Formerly San Ildefonso College (Excolegio de San Ildefonso). This sober baroque building (18C) which today houses a public school has a stone and *tezontle* facade with a relief of San Ildefonso of Toledo (the college patron) receiving the chasuble from the hands of the Virgin.

Interior. – The interior is important because the great contemporary muralists, along with other artists, have contributed to its **mural paintings★★★.** Here the artists develop themes and notable figures seldom portrayed in Mexican painting *(see p 41)*.

Main Courtyard. – In this part of the building, **José Clemente Orozco** offers a very personal interpretation of the Mexican Revolution. On the first floor, he criticizes the regime of Porfirio Díaz. On the second floor he treats themes and ideals underlying the Revolution. Particularly admirable are **Motherhood** *(La Maternidad),* **The Trinity** *(La Trinidad),* **Christ Destroying the Cross** *(El Cristo Destruyendo la Cruz)* and **The Trench** *(La Trinchera).* On the staircase the excellent nude portraits of Hernán Cortés and La Malinche *(see p 29),* symbolizing the birth of a new nation, are compelling.

El Generalito. – *Second floor of the main courtyard, on the left.* This endearing nickname is given to a small reception hall in which are found the **choirstalls** from Saint Augustine's Church. These important examples of Mexican colonial woodcarving were executed by Salvador Ocampo.

Staircase of the Smaller Courtyard. – **David Alfaro Siqueiros** was entrusted with its decoration. In this unfinished painting, the worker's burial is to be noted.

Bolívar Amphitheater (Anfiteatro Bolívar). – *Entrance on Justo Sierra n° 14.* **Fernando Leal** (1896-1964) painted scenes from Simon Bolívar's life in the vestibule, and on the stage **Diego Rivera** in 1922 painted his first mural, entitled *The Creation (La Creación),* utilizing the encaustic technique. Female figures representing science, the virtues and the arts stand out in what would appear as a third dimension, an optical illusion created by incised lines.

Loreto Church (Templo de Loreto). – This is the best example of religious architecture in the neoclassical style to be found in the city. It's facade preserves a fine relief depicting the angels transporting the house of the Virgin and Saint Joseph from the Holy Land to the village of Loreto in Italy.

Interior. – It has an uncommon design consisting of a single nave, leading to an enormous circular structure, surrounded by several chapels. This layout, rare in Mexican churches, creates an unusual atmosphere, enhanced by a large **dome.** In the sacristy there are various good paintings, especially *The Assumption of the Virgin (La Asunción de la Virgen)* by Miguel Cabrera (18-19C).

Abelardo Rodríguez Market (Mercado Abelardo Rodríguez). – This market is part of an architectural complex built in 1933 on the land formerly occupied by Jesuit schools. Like the Department of Public Education *(p 115),* its walls were decorated with large **murals★** by different artists (**Angel Bracho, Pablo O'Higgins** and **Antonio Pujol,** among others). The excellent murals at the southeast entrance show an idealization of farm labor, dawn and dusk.

③ Mexico City Museum (Museo de la Ciudad de México) and Surroundings
time: 1/2 day – Plan below

Mexico City Museum. – **Palace of the Counts of Santiago de Calimaya** (Palacio de los Condes de Santiago de Calimaya). This lovely aristocratic **house★** dating from the latter part of the 18C has a noble facade framed by classical columns. The handsome door carved with scenes referring to the Counts of Santiago de Calimaya and the triple-arched balcony crowned with the coat of arms, are particularly beautiful. On the corner, as part of the foundations of the building, a large **serpent's head** that probably came from the Great Temple (Templo Mayor) can be seen.

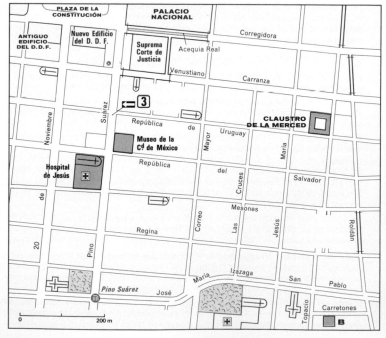

Interior. – In the first courtyard, a fountain adorned with a double tailed mermaid playing a Spanish lute is striking. A majestic staircase, covered by a cantilevered triple arch, divides at the landing leading to the upper floor. On the roof, the **studio★** of Mexico's only Impressionist painter, **Joaquín Clausell** (1866-1935), has been preserved. There he has left an interesting mural composed of curious scenes unrelated to each other. It is believed that such paintings were made as a way of cleaning his brushes.

Museum. – The museum provides an attractive panoramic version of the city's history. On the lower floor the evolution of Mexico's Valley and its development until the Conquest is depicted. Particular mention should be made of the **Model of the Great Temple** (room 6) and the mural by Manuel Capdevilla, *The Return of Quetzalcóatl (El Regreso de Quetzalcóatl – room 7)*.
The Library and the Map Collection, as well as models of the city and the Valley of Mexico, are located in the second courtyard.
On the upper floor, restored furnishings help to recreate the atmosphere and decor of the mansions of the period, which convey an idea of life in the 19C and early 20C.

⊙ **Jesus Hospital** (Hospital de Jesús). – This small, peaceful hospital was founded in the 16C by Hernán Cortés on the spot where he allegedly met Moctezuma.

★ **Courtyards.** – Two lovely courtyards remain from the original construction; they are surrounded by nicely proportioned arcades and separated by a staircase adorned with pre-Hispanic sculptures found on the site. The high **corridors** covered with woodwork are especially attractive. On the south wall there is a long frieze of grotesques in which symbols of the Passion of Christ are alternated and repeated; between the beams there are decorations of roses and human faces, among which can be spotted the Conquistador and his family, accompanied by the soldiers and priests who followed his miltary campaign.

⊙ **Main Office** (Dirección). – *In the second courtyard, in the north wing of the lower floor.* This hall, which was the church's sacristy, posseses one of the most beautiful 16C **coffered ceilings★** in the country. Here the fine wood carvings and two interesting portraits of the hospital's founder can be admired.

⊙ **Church** (Templo). – The interior of this church is of particular note. To the left of the chancel, the **remains of Hernán Cortés** are preserved in a small urn, since it was his wish to remain the loyal warden of the good works that he had initiated. In the choir and the following section, the **mural★**, *Apocalypse (Apocalipsis)* (1942-44), by the renowned painter, José Clemente Orozco, depicting the horrors of the Second World War, should not be missed.

★★ **Cloister of the Monastery of the Merced** (Claustro del Exconvento de la Merced). – This ⊙ two-story structure, erected in the early 18C by the famous preacher, Friar Juan de Herrara, is reputedly the most beautiful cloister ever built in New Spain. The exquisite archways on the upper floor are covered by a network of vines with exuberant foliage, and the arches are emphasized with diamond points. There are rich baroque ornamentations between the panels and sculptures of saints of the order of Mercy (Orden de la Merced) in the spandrels, or triangular spaces between the arch and the enclosing right angle.
To the left side of the entrance there is a carved **door** from the 1920s, containing panels sculpted in motifs reminiscent of those used by the muralists.

⊙ **Carretones Glass Factory** (Fábrica de Vidrio de Carretones) (B). – In operation since 1889, this is the oldest blown-glass factory in the city. It is possible to watch the artisans at work making different multicolored objects, like decanters, glasses and plates in the rustic traditional fashion.

4 **Residence of the Counts of San Mateo Valparaíso**
(Antigua Casa de los Condes de San Mateo Valparaíso) **and Surroundings**
time: 1/2 day – Plan p 118

★ **Residence of the Counts of San Mateo Valparaíso.** – Offices of the National Bank of ⊙ Mexico. This elegant baroque palace (18C) is the work of **Francisco Guerrero y Torres**. The *tezontle* and stone facade is adorned with delicate carvings on doors and windows as well as on the niche of the corner balcony. Above the entrance arch the old family coat of arms has been preserved; the **gate** is also an excellent example of wood carving. Inside, at the rear of the courtyard stands the distinctive helicoidal **staircase★** with a double ramp and domed roof. The patio is often used for temporary exhibits.

⊙ **Saint Augustine's Church** (Templo de San Agustín). – **Old National Library** (Antigua Biblioteca Nacional). The lovely baroque facade of this church is noteworthy above all for the unique **relief★** showing Saint Augustine protecting the friars of his order while treading on the heads of a group of heretics. The edifice dates back to 1691 and, together with the monastery, made up an impressive architectural group, which was destroyed in 1859 when the Reform Laws were applied *(see p 31)*. The nave, although substantially altered, retains its beauty and distinction. Frequently it is used for temporary exhibits, as well as for cultural events.

⊙ **Church of Saint Philip Neri** (Extemplo de San Felipe Neri). – Its delicate baroque **facade★** (18C) is reminiscent of the work of architect Lorenzo Rodríguez because of the *estípites* framing the sculptures and the beautiful central relief.
At present the building houses a library. In 1974, the artist Vlady painted, in explosive colors, 2 000 square meters of its walls with themes referring to revolutions and the elements.

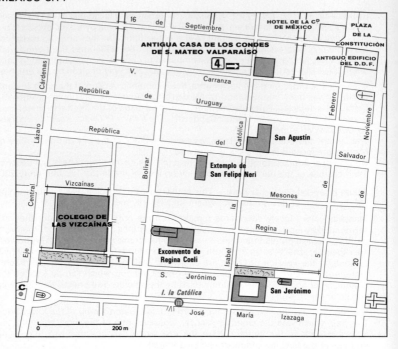

⊘**Church and Convent of Saint Jerome** (Templo y Exconvento de San Jerónimo). – This religious architectural group from the early 17C is of great significance because **Sor Juana Inés de la Cruz** lived there as a nun. She was the best-known Mexican poetess and has been called the "Tenth Muse" *(see p 43)*. The church is unusual since it has only a lateral entrance, above which stands the naive sculpture of Saint Jerome. From the size of the **cloister★** it is estimated that this might have been the largest church in the city. In 1977 restoration was begun to bring back its original splendor. Today it houses a school of Humanities.

Regina Coeli Convent (Exconvento de Regina Coeli). This was the second convent founded in New Spain (1573). As is the case with the majority of these buildings, the church of this former convent has two simple lateral entrances.

Interior. – Among the baroque **altarpieces★**, or *retablos,* found inside this church, the one on the right side, dedicated to the Virgin of the Fountain (Virgen de la Fuente) (a devotion of Basque origin), flanked by elegant sculptures of archangels, and the central altar devoted to the Virgin as Queen of Heaven (Regina Coeli), are outstanding. In the lower choir a mystical atmosphere has been preserved, which is underscored by Francisco Antonio Vallejo's paintings (18C).

★ **Chapel of the Medina Picasso** (Capilla de los Medina Picasso). – The altars in this side chapel, which display paintings by **Juan Rodríguez Juárez** (18C), are of astonishing quality. The chapel floors and baseboards are covered with delicate Talavera style tiles, which make it particularly colorful.

★ **Colegio de las Vizcaínas.** – This building was erected between 1734 and ⊘1757 thanks to the efforts of three Basques, members of the Brotherhood of Aranzazú (Cofradía de Aranzazú), from the Saint Francis Monastery of Mexico City, to be used as a hospice and school for poor Spanish girls and widows. Some relief is provided to the otherwise austere *tezontle* facade by round windows, or oculi, and a pinnacled crowning. The three entrances are decorated with reliefs of Jesuit saints, the Virgin of Aranzazú (Virgen de Aranzazú) and Saint Rose of Lima (Santa Rosa de Lima). The building's central courtyard is graced with a monumental staircase leading to the second level, where the chapel containing original altars (18C), furniture and rich gold objects of the period is located.

Fuente del Salto del Agua (C). – This is a replica of the original fountain which served to mark the end of one of the aqueducts that supplied the capital from the springs at Santa Fe and Chapultepec.

★★★ ⑤ **Madero and its Surroundings**
time: 1/2 day – Plan p 119

⊘**Latin-American Tower** (Torre Latinoamericana). – This is the second tallest building in Mexico; it has 47 stories and is approximately 162 m – 531.50 ft high. On the top floor there is an observation deck from which, on clear days, there are breathtaking **views★★★** of the gigantic city and the Valley of Mexico.

★ **House of Tiles** (Casa de los Azulejos). – **Palace of the Counts of Valle de Orizaba** (Antiguo Palacio ⊘de los Condes del Valle de Orizaba). *Today occupied by a store and a restaurant.* This house constitutes a unique example of an aristocratic 18C mansion and was a fashionable meeting place during the first decades of the present century.

The facade was covered with tiles reputedly brought from China. It is further enhanced by the carved stone doorframes and balconies, while the wavy finial adds a touch of movement. The **courtyard** retains the atmosphere of bygone days, with its impressive columns and baseboards also covered with tiles. On the landing of the staircase, there is a **mural** by José Clemente Orozco, called *Omniscience (Omnisciencia),* painted in 1925.

Monastery of Saint Francis (Exconvento de San Francisco). – This was one of the largest and most opulent religious complexes in Latin America. In 1856, when a conspiracy was discovered among the Franciscans, their punishment was to have their architectural complex cut up, running streets through it and selling the parcels of land to private buyers. As a result, many of its components are now scattered: the **porter's lodge** (la Portería) in the Pasaje Savoy (Eje Central), **Saint Anthony's Chapel** (Capilla de San Antonio) in Venustiano Carranza and the cloister in calle Gante.

★ **Saint Francis' Church** (Templo de San Francisco). – Access to this church is gained through the chapel originally dedicated to Our Lady of Aranzazú (Nuestra Señora de Aranzazú). Although its reliefs and sculptures are missing, the 18C baroque **facade★** remains one of the most beautiful in the capital.

★ **Cloister.** – Now an Adventist church, this beautiful structure consists of fine baroque arches topped by two high stories.

★★ **Iturbide Palace (Palacio de Iturbide).** – **Offices of the National Bank of Mexico** (Banco Nacional de México). One of the most exquisite 18C houses in Mexico City, this was the official residence of the Marquis of Jaral de Berrio and was occupied by the first emperor of Mexico, **Agustín de Iturbide,** from 1821 to 1823. The construction, attributed to **Francisco Guerrero y Torres,** has three levels and a mezzanine – an unusual design in colonial civil architecture. The facade is richly worked in stone, with a tower at either end and a gallery in between.

The **courtyard** is the most imposing in the civil architecture of the city. It was modified in 1890 by the architect, **Emilio Dondé,** to make it into a hotel. It originally had three galleries of arches, which he changed into four so skillfully that it is hardly noticeable. In each corner, carvings of cameo-like human heads suggest the Plateresque style.

La Profesa Church (Templo de la Profesa). – This stately edifice built in 1720 of stone and *tezontle* is typical of the starkness the Jesuits generally displayed on the exteriors of their buildings. Nevertheless, inside, a definite taste for monumentality can be seen both in the vast scale of the basilica plan, consisting of three naves, and in the richly decorated neoclassical altars.

To the right of the chancel are the sacristy and a vestibule, where a **sculpture** of the *King of Mockeries (Rey de Burlas)* is on display in a glass case. It is considered a good example of the **bleeding Christs** (Cristos sangrantes) made in Mexico during the 18C.

★ **Painting Collection** (Pinacoteca). – *Access to this collection is gained by a staircase located beyond the entrance hall.* This gallery contains a splendid **collection** of colonial paintings by **José de Páez, Cristóbal de Villalpando** and **Miguel Cabrera,** among others.

Spanish Casino (Casino Español). – This building has a handsome **facade** made in rose-colored stone reminiscent of a Renaissance palace. Built at the beginning of the 19C, it has served since its opening as a meeting place for the Spanish colony. The flamboyant interior decoration includes a palatial **staircase.** On its landing are exhibited: the coat of arms of the Spanish King Charles V; and, on the lower part, a painting of Christopher Colombus on his death bed. The **Hall of the Kings** (Salón de los Reyes) on the first floor displays leaded decorations with floral allegories.

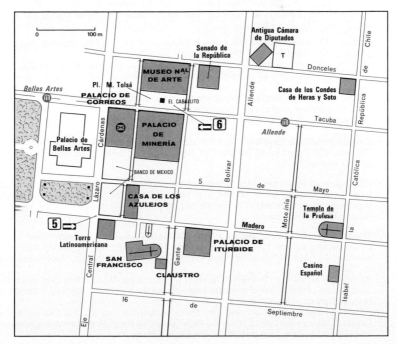

★★ ⑥ Plaza Manuel Tolsá and Surroundings

time: 1/2 day. Plan p 119

Plaza Manuel Tolsá. – Surrounded by impressive buildings, this square was selected in 1982 to honor the renowned Valencian architect and sculptor because of its proximity to one of his masterpieces: the Minería Palace. At the same time, his equestrian statue of Charles IV of Spain, *El Caballito (see below),* was moved to the square.

★ **El Caballito.** – **Equestrian Statue of Charles IV.** This statue, whose popular name means "little horse", is the best example of neoclassical equestrian sculpture in Mexico, and it has been compared to that of Marcus Aurelius on the Capitoline Hill in Rome. Manuel Tolsá first made a version in plaster in 1796, but the statue was not cast until 1802, because the funds needed to purchase the necessary amount of metal were not immediately available.

El Caballito has been successively placed in the Plaza Mayor, in the courtyard of the old university and in the traffic circle where Paseo de la Reforma and Bucareli meet.

★★ **Minería Palace** (Palacio de Minería). – *Illustration, p 40.* This magnificent gray stone edifice is one of the best examples of neoclassical architecture in Mexico City. The facade's central section consists of three arches separated by Doric columns and topped by a pedimented structure that used to be an observatory.

Main Courtyard. – This exceptional courtyard is surrounded by arcades which, on the first floor, are supported by pillars of square hewn cushion-shaped stones and, on the second floor, by tall shapely pairs of Ionic columns. The stately staircase topped by balustrades adds to the elegance of the building.

Among the various rooms, the most prominent are the reception room and the chapel, with its original decoration of murals (19C) depicting themes related to the Virgin of Guadalupe by the Spanish artist **Rafael Ximeno y Planes.**

★ **Central Post Office** (Palacio de Correos). – This refined two-story building was constructed with carved white stone and contains elements of the Italian Renaissance blended with Elizabethan Gothic, such as the Venetian openwork and the ornamentation in which plant and animal motifs are combined with figures of little angels. Designed by the Italian architect, **Adamo Boari,** this eclectic building was constructed between 1902 and 1907.

Interior. – The combination of materials, the metallic structures and the use of marble make a visit worthwhile. Especially noteworthy are the main staircase, the banisters, the screens and the door and window frames, made, along with the structures, at the Pignone Foundry in Florence, Italy.

On the second floor the **stamp collection** (Museo Filatélico) is displayed and collectors can frequently be seen there buying, selling or exchanging stamps.

★ **National Art Museum** (Museo Nacional de Arte-MUNAL). – The splendid proportions of this grey stone edifice recall the Renaissance palaces. Built between 1904 and 1911 to house the Palace of Communications and Public Works, it was planned by the Italian architect **Silvio Contri.**

A handsome **staircase** leads to the museum proper (the lower floor is occupied by the Central Telegraph Office). The ironwork and the **ceilings** decorated with plaster moldings and paintings are striking. The use of metal structures makes for these astonishingly spacious rooms.

Museum. – The museum contains some religious paintings from the colonial period as well as a fine **collection**★ of 19C and 20C art.

The first floor houses a good sampling of works from the first half of the 20C with examples of the Open-Air school (Escuela al Aire Libre) and the Mexican school of painting.

On the second floor works of the Academy of San Carlos are exhibited. The works of the distinguished painter who recreated the landscapes of the Valley of Mexico, **José María Velasco** (1840-1914), are especially noteworthy.

Senate (Senado de la República). – The Senate stairwell has **mural paintings** by **Jorge González Camarena** (1908) portraying freedom of expression and treason, as well as national heroes and symbols.

Old House of Representatives (Antigua Cámara de Diputados). – This is a sober building with a neoclassical stone facade and Ionic columns; on the frontispiece reliefs depicting the administration of justice can be seen. In the last century the building housed the Iturbide Theater.

House of the Counts of Heras y Soto (Casa de los Condes de Heras y Soto). – This is one of the leading palatial residences of the late 18C. The last heir of the viscountship, owner of the house, Manuel de Heras y Soto, was a signer of the Act of Independence in 1821.

Particularly noteworthy is the rich **facade**★, with stone carvings so fine they resemble lace. On the corner it has a baroque **relief** representing a cherub holding a basket of fruit, all framed in authentic filigree.

At present the house is occupied by the Superintendent of Mexico City's Historic Center (Dirección del Centro Histórico de la Ciudad de México), and contains valuable archives and a library specializing in the city's history.

⑦ Alameda Central and Surroundings

time: 1/2 day

★ **Alameda Central.** – This is the oldest promenade in the city. It was created in the 16C, once the marshes were drained and poplars *(alamos)* were planted – hence the name.

During colonial times, it was the popular meeting place for the New-Spanish society. It was the stage on which duels were fought for love and honor. During that period it was also surrounded by a wrought-iron fence in order to keep out the populace. After Independence, the promenade became a popular meeting place for diverse social groups. The traditional character of these old grounds has inspired great artists. The numerous monuments and sculptures created for the Alameda, such as the **Hemiciclo a Juárez** and the monument to **Beethoven**, as well as the surrounding buildings, contribute to its charm. At present, especially on holidays, the Alameda shelters a noisy, colorful multitude of all sorts of people, in search of amusement.

⊙ **Palace of Fine Arts (Palacio de Bellas Artes).** – This majestic **edifice★**, made almost entirely of Carrara marble, was constructed on the site formerly occupied by the Convent of Saint Isabel (Convento de Santa Isabel) to provide a locale for the National Theater.

At present the palace is the center for the most important cultural events and is also used for temporary exhibits of renowned artists' works.

The difference between the styles perceptible in this building, both outside and inside, is striking. This may be explained by the fact that thirty years were required for its construction. The exterior, which has some elements of Art Nouveau, is part of the original design (1904) by **Adamo Boari**. The interior, the work of **Federico Mariscal** (1932), was fashioned with Art Deco forms. What is remarkable is that both architects used ornamental figures of pre-Hispanic tradition, such as masks of warriors, tigers, eagles, Maya deities and serpents, for the decoration of the building.

★ **Murals.** – On the second floor there are works by **Rufino Tamayo** (1952-53). On the third floor there are works by **Rivera,** *Man at the Crossroads (El Hombre en el Cruce de los Caminos,* 1934); by **Siqueiros** *The New Democracy (La Nueva Democracia,* 1945) and *Tribute to Cuauhtémoc (Homenaje a Cuauhtémoc,* 1950); and *Catharsis (Catarsis,* 1934) by **J. Clemente Orozco.**

★ **The Crystal Curtain** (Cortina de Cristal). – *This front drop curtain is located on the stage*
⊙ *in the theater.* The crystal curtain was made by **Tiffany** according to a design by **Dr. Atl.** The curtain depicts the two volcanoes Popocatéptl and Iztaccíhuatl and recreates dawn and dusk through a skillful play of lights before each performance of the **Mexican Folkloric Ballet** (Ballet Folclórico de México).

⊙ **Arts and Crafts Museum (Museo de Artes e Industrias Populares).** – It was installed in the 17C building which had been the Corpus Christi Convent Church (Templo del Convento de Corpus Cristi). In this colorful place, a wide gamut of **crafts★** from all over Mexico is displayed for sale. Among them are beautiful silver pieces, fabrics from different regions, baskets, bright ceramics, tin-work and simple wooden toys.

★★ **Alameda Museum (Museo de la Alameda).** – A special building was constructed to house
⊙ the famous mural by Diego Rivera that was moved from the Hotel Del Prado. He painted it in 1947 and called it **Dream of a Sunday Afternoon on the Alameda★★** *(Sueño de una Tarde de Domingo en la Alameda Central).* In this work, the painter recreated the festive multicolored atmosphere of the Alameda at the beginning of the 20C, portraying some leading figures from Mexican history.

⊙ **Viceroyal Painting Collection (Pinacoteca Virreinal).** – In order to become familiar with colonial painting, a visit to this museum is indispensable. The collection is housed in the church that was the Monastery of San Diego (Convento de San Diego), which was built facing the Inquisition burning stake. It includes the principal masters of the 16C,

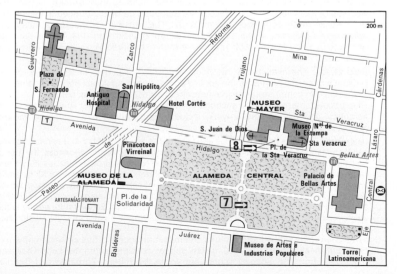

17C and 18C, such as **Simón Pereyns, Baltazar de Echave Orio,** the Maestro of Santa Cecilia, Luis Juárez, the exceptional miniaturist **Luis Lagarto** and **Sebastián López de Arteaga,** who introduced the chiaroscuro made fashionable in Spain by Zurbarán. Also represented is José Juárez, who in *The Martyrdom of Saint Lorenzo (El Martirio de San Lorenzo)* expertly combines the Tenebrist and Mannerist styles. Other painters present in this collection are **Cristóbal de Villalpando** and the brothers **Juan** and **Nicolás Rodríguez Juárez.** These two painters, although working already in the 18C, preserved the outstanding qualities of the painters of the previous century, known as the Golden Century of Mexican Painting. The Rodríguez Juárez brothers were grandsons of the master Luis Juárez and children of Antonia Juárez and Antonio Rodríguez, a reputed 18C painter.

Plaza de San Fernando. – Surrounded by historic buildings, the square has in its center the **monument★** in honor of **Vicente Guerrero** *(see p 30)* by Miguel Noreña. On the north side stands **San Fernandós Church** (18C), which displays a relief of the saint fighting the Moors. Inside the church, the following elements are worth noting: the pulpit, the sacristy door and the chancel stalls, as well as the exquisite rostrum on the left. The altarpiece is a replica of an 18C engraving.

⊙ The **Pantheon of Famous Men** (Pantéon de Hombres Ilustres), known as the **Pantheon of San Fernando** (Panteón de San Fernando), adjoining the church, is a cemetery-museum in which heroes and leaders *(caudillos),* most of whom participated in the Reform War are buried. Prominent among them is the tomb of President Benito Juárez *(see p 30).*

⑧ Plaza de la Santa Veracruz and Surroundings

time: 1/2 day – Plan p 121

Plaza de Santa Veracruz. – This small square has a popular atmosphere, and the surrounding churches are remarkable.

Santa Veracruz Church (Templo de la Santa Veracruz). – Built in 1730, this church has a beautiful stone facade in baroque style. The handsome lateral facade is dedicated to San Blas. Inside are found a Christ donated by King Charles V of Spain and the remains of the architect **Manuel Tolsá** *(see p 40).*

⊙ **National Museum of Engravings (Museo Nacional de la Estampa).** – On the first floor of this rather simple museum, the various tools and materials employed in the different engraving techniques are exhibited.

The second floor presents the evolution of engraving in Mexico, starting from pre-Hispanic times, with the **pintaderas,** or fired clay seals, which were used to print fabrics, paper, hides, ceramics and other materials.

From the colonial period have come generally coherent works, principally on religious themes, employing engraving techniques on wood in the 16C and 17C and on copper in the 18C.

The 19C is represented by the works of teachers and students of the Academy of San Carlos and distinguished artists such as **Manilla** (1830-90) and **José Guadalupe Posada** (1852-1913).

Contemporary engravings are represented by the work of **Jean Charlot** – who is credited with the revival of engraving in Mexico – and by the Popular Engraving Workshop (Taller de la Gráfica Popular). Other works to be found here are by **Siqueiros, Rivera, Leopoldo Méndez** and **Federico Cantú** among others.

Saint John of God (Templo de San Juan de Dios). – This church has the only splayed facade in the city. It was built in the 17C and during colonial times religious plays were performed in front of its facade, taking advantage of the excellent acoustics of this space.

★★★ **Franz Mayer Museum (Museo Franz Mayer).** – **Applied Arts Museum** (Museo de Artes ⊙ Aplicadas). This unusual museum occupies the building that formerly housed the Hospital of Saint John of God (Hospital de San Juan de Dios), founded in the 18C for the care of mestizos, blacks and mulattos. The museum possesses an exquisite **collection** of European, Asiatic and American art objects from the 15C to the 19C, gathered by Franz Mayer (1882-1975), a German naturalized Mexican, who willed it to his adopted country.

Lower Level. – The exhibits on this floor, which are displayed in four large rooms, present a general overview of the applied arts during the colonial period and the 19C. The collection comprises attractive household objects from those periods.

Of particular interest are the sections devoted to European and American **sculpture,** ceramics, and religious silver-work, including the collection of monstrances and processional crosses.

Upper Level. – On this floor paintings and sculptures are on display in a series of seven rooms arranged chronologically. The 16C room contains the **ejecutorías,** the hand-painted books that testified to the bloodlines of New Spain's nobles, as they were ratified by the King. In the 17C rooms, a series of delicately made **desks,** with splendid work in lacquer and marquetry, as well as a partial replica of an 18C **pharmacy,** can be admired. Among the remarkable religious images of Puebla alabaster (18C), a **relief** of the Virgin of the Rosary (Virgen del Rosario) is outstanding. Equally noteworthy is the section devoted to the **Talavera ceramics** of Puebla, where a colonial-style kitchen has been reconstructed.

In addition to its applied arts exhibits, the museum houses a fine collection of works from European artists: the 17C Italian school is represented by Luca Giordano *(Lucrecia);* from the Spanish school are works by Ribera, Zurbarán and Sorolla;

among the Flemish paintings are *The Legend of Saint Mary Magdalene (La Leyenda de Santa María Magdalena)* and *The Embroidered Leaves (Las Hojas Bordadas* - 16C). The Mexican section consists primarily of works by artists from the colonial period, including Correa, Villalpando, Arellano and the great landscape painter, **José María Velasco,** with a few paintings from the 19C and 20C.

The museum has an exceptional library, specializing in art, which is open to specialists.

Cortés Hotel. – This building, which was used as a guest house for membres of the Augustinian order, is a good example of 18C Mexican architecture. In a niche situated in the center of the building's baroque facade, stands a statue of Saint Thomas of Villanueva (Santo Tomás) to whom the Augustinians dedicated the house. The **patio,** brimming with brightly-colored flowers, has a pleasant atmosphere.

Church of San Hipólito (Templo de San Hipólito). – The slender towers somewhat protruding from its baroque facade (18C) give a certain sense of movement to the building. On the exterior, the relief of San Hipólito above the main entrance and the cupola covered with ceramic tiles are noteworthy.

Originally the church was a simple chapel built in the 16C in memory of Hernán Cortés' soldiers who died on this spot in the most disastrous battle fought by the conquering Spanish army. Later it was dedicated to San Hipólito in remembrance of the capture of México-Tenochtitlán.

At the corner of calles Hidalgo and Zarco, on part of the atrium wall, there is a **relief** which portrays an Indian being lifted by an eagle and carried through the air, symbolizing one of Moctezuma II's premonitory dreams of the fall of México-Tenochtitlán.

⏱**Hospital of San Hipólito (Antiguo Hospital de San Hipólito).** – *Next to the church on the left side.* This austere *tezontle* and stone building was inaugurated in 1777. The hospital formerly housed here was founded in 1566 by Fray Bernardino Alvarez who wished to establish a charitable institution to care for the needy, especially the mentally ill.

San Cosme *time: 2 hours – tour by automobile – Plan p 108 –* BCX

Monument to the Revolution (Monumento a la Revolución) (BX). – This work has gigantic dimensions and massive lines. Originally, during the Porfirio Díaz regime, construction was begun on a building that was to be the Legislative Palace (Palacio Legislativo). However, the structure was never finished on account of the 1910 Revolution. In 1933, the architect, Obregón Santacilia, using the structure intended for the dome, designed the present Monument to the Revolution.

The sculptured groups in the upper corners are by Oliverio Martínez. Each of the four pillars contains the remains of outstanding figures of the Revolution: Francisco I. Madero, Venustiano Carranza, Plutarco Elías Calles, Francisco Villa and Lázaro Cárdenas.

⏱**National Museum of the Mexican Revolution** (Museo Nacional de la Revolución Mexicana). – *Located in the basement of the Monument to the Revolution.* The museum has a permanent exhibit, explaining the many stages involved in the construction of the monument itself, based on the original plans. In addition, the museum has halls for temporary shows depicting the different phases of the Revolution, seen from economic, political and social perspectives.

⏱**San Carlos Museum (Museo de San Carlos)** (BX M¹). – This museum occupies a lovely neoclassical **mansion★★,** which was designed as the residence of the Count of Buenavista. The building's architect, **Manuel Tolsá,** was inspired by the Palace of Charles V of Spain, in the Alhambra, Granada.

Part of the painting collections exhibited in this museum belonged to the **Academy of San Carlos:** *The Adoration of the Magi (La Adoración de los Magos)* by **Berruguete,** *The Holy Family (La Sagrada Familia)* by **Botticelli,** the portrait of Frederick of Saxony by **Lucas Cranach the Elder** (1472-1563) and some works by **Goya** as well as several by the English painters, **Thomas Lawrence** and **Joshua Reynolds.**

⏱**University Museum of the Chopo (Museo Universitario del Chopo)** (BX M²), – This is a curious building from the late 19C in which part of the metal structure was left exposed. It has gone by different names: the Crystal Palace, the Japanese Pavilion and most recently, Museum of the Chopo.

This museum has become a forum for presenting young artists through temporary exhibits of painting, engraving, and photography. It has even been used for rock concerts. The museum also organizes shows of works by established artists.

House of Masks (Casa de los Mascarones) (BX A). – The construction of this house was begun in the 18C. Commissioned by the Count del Valle de Orizaba, as a country house, the building was never finished. Its facade is adorned with *estipites* and crowned by caryatids, which frame the richly ornamented windows.

★★ PASEO DE LA REFORMA

time: 1/2 day – tour by automobile – Plan p 108

This beautiful and bustling avenue, 12 km – 7 1/2 miles in length and shaded by age-old trees, is one of the main thoroughfares of Mexico City. The oldest stretch goes from Bucareli Circle to the entrance to Chapultepec Park. It was constructed by order of Emperor Maximilian of Habsburg, so as to have a direct link between Chapultepec Castle, where he resided, and the National Palace – hence its name, the **Emperor's Promenade** (Paseo del Emperador).

Over the years, Paseo de la Reforma has been further embellished. Besides its modern buildings, many circles have been constructed, some of them adorned with fountains and important monuments. The nearby **Zona Rosa** (**BY**), where art galleries, elegant boutiques, lively restaurants and sidewalk cafes are concentrated, adds to the animation of the great Mexican capital, particularly at night.

The second stretch, running from the Chapultepec entrance to the Petroleum Fountain, is bordered by part of the woods and by the great museums. The last stretch of Paseo de la Reforma ends at the Toluca exit near **Chapultepec Hills** (Lomas de Chapultepec), one of the most exclusive residential areas in the city, with fine examples of modern architecture.

Christopher Colombus Monument (Monumento a Cristóbal Colón) (**BX**). – Made in France by **Carlos Cordier** in the 19C, this sculpture shows Colombus at the top, accompanied by priests symbolizing the evangelization of the New World.

Cuauhtémoc Monument (Monumento a Cuauhtémoc) (**BX**). – This bronze monument by the sculptor **M. Noreña** (1883) portrays Cuauhtémoc shooting an arrow into the air. On its base there are **reliefs** depicting the capture and tortures suffered by this Mexican chief at the hands of Hernán Cortés.

★★**Independence Monument** (Monumento a la Independencia) (**BY**). – Symbolizing Mexico City, this monument consists of a great column 36 m – 118 ft high, crowned by a winged victory commonly known as **El Angel.** This impressive work by the architect **Rivas Mercado** was inaugurated the 16th of September, 1910, to commemorate the Centennial of Mexican Independence and to pay tribute to its leaders, whose sculptures appear on the column.

(Photo Pablo Gómez Gallardo/Paco Macías/Mexico,

Mexico City. Independence Monument

⊙ **Center for Contemporary Art** (Centro Cultural Arte Contemporáneo). – *At the corner of Campos Elíseos and calle Jorge Eliot – plan p 125.* This is a modern edifice of ochre-colored concrete. Inside, four levels of terraces overlook the busy lobby, which is the setting for temporary exhibits of popular or contemporary art from Mexico and abroad.

★★★**CHAPULTEPEC** *time: 3 days*

Located in a vast zone comprising 223 hectares – 551 acres, this old forest is planted with ancient cypress trees, which stand as silent witnesses to the events that have occurred there since pre-Hispanic times.

Here was the first settlement of the Mexica people in the Valley of Mexico, ending their long pilgrimage from mystic **Aztlán.** For many years, Chapultepec's rich springs supplied the city with water. On the top of its Chapulín Hill, the legendary **Castle** (Castillo) was built and a **monument** to the **Niños Héroes** (Young Heroes) who defended it in 1847 was erected.

Two sections have been added to the park, making it the most important ecological area of the city.

Furthermore, it serves as a recreational and cultural center, containing the leading museums and amusement areas of the city, such as lakes, parks and a zoo.

★★**Chapultepec Forest** (Bosque de Chapultepec) *time: 1/2 day*

⊙ The **first section,** situated to the east, is the oldest part of the forest with romantic paths and pleasant shady nooks enlivened by the colorful balloon vendors and the cheerful splash of the Fountain of Nezahualcóyotl. This festive atmosphere has made Cahapultepec a favorite spot for Sunday outings.

Automobiles are forbidden in this zone, so the tour must be made on foot.

⊙ **Zoo** (Zoológico). – It comprises a rich sampling of captive animals from the fauna of the Americas and other continents.

⊙ **Little Train** (Trenecito). – This miniature train provides an amusing tour of the zoo and part of the lakeshore.

Lake (Lago). – A popular spot where rowboats can be rented to explore the farthest corners of the lake, with its many springs and abundant water fowl.

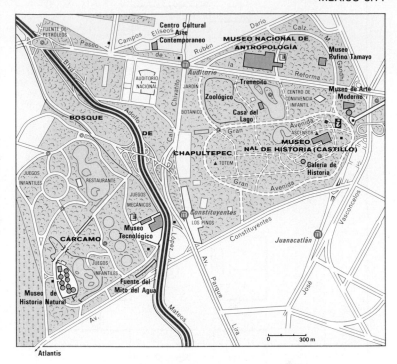

Atlantis

⊙ **Lake House** (Casa del Lago). – In the pleasant surroundings of this lakeside house, built at the beginning of the century, every day except Monday – and especially on weekends – varied shows are presented: experimental plays, poetry readings, movies and – during March and April – open-air evening performances of the **ballet**, *Swan Lake.*

Rufino Tamayo Museum (Museo Rufino Tamayo). – This modern **edifice★**, located in the northeastern corner of Chapultepec Park and inaugurated in 1981, was built especially for the contemporary international art collection donated by the painter, Rufino Tamayo. Besides the artist's own works, it includes paintings by Picasso, De Chirico, Magritte, Vassarely and by Mexican painters or painters residing in Mexico, such as Cuevas, Gerzo and Goeritz.
Cultural events organized by the museum include temporary painting exhibits, concerts and plays.

★★★National Anthropological Museum (Museo Nacional de Antropología)

time: 1 day

⊙ Amidst the dense vegetation of Chapultepec Forest stands the majestic and well-proportioned building that houses Mexico City's most renowned museum. The principal treasures of Mexico's indigenous cultures, both ancient and modern, are exhibited here.

Historical Notes. – The dazzling collection of pre-Hispanic material exhibited in the museum was begun by Viceroy Antonio María de Bucareli in the Royal Pontifical University of Mexico at the end of the 18C. Discoveries continually enlarged this collection, to such an extent that in 1865 Archduke Ferdinand Maximilian of Habsburg transferred it to the Mint building (Casa de Moneda), in the architectural complex of the National Palace *(p 112).*
New findings and the reappraisal of the indigenous cultures during the current century required the construction of the present-day building, inaugurated in 1964.

The Building. – **Pedro Ramírez Vázquez** was the architect in charge of the project and numerous specialists, technicians, and craftsmen collaborated in the work. The result amounts to a formal break with traditional museum architecture. The Mexican architects created a functional space, reflecting contemporary cultural life, while applying some basic principles of pre-Hispanic architecture, such as harmony with the landscape and the preservation of the building materials' natural textures and colors.
Inspiration for the project came from the **Quadrangle of the Nuns at Uxmal** *(p 213),* a prominent Maya ruin, with facades composed of stark walls topped by rich ornamental friezes. The friezes adorning the museum's facade consist of a grandiose sequence of stylized aluminum serpents.
The museum is designed in such a way that, on the lower level, no more than two rooms can be visited without stepping out into the central courtyard, so as to make a restful pause and admire the imposing and refreshing **Umbrella** (El Paragúas). This structure has a dramatically high waterfall through which a sculptured column cast in bronze that narrates the history of Mexico can be seen.

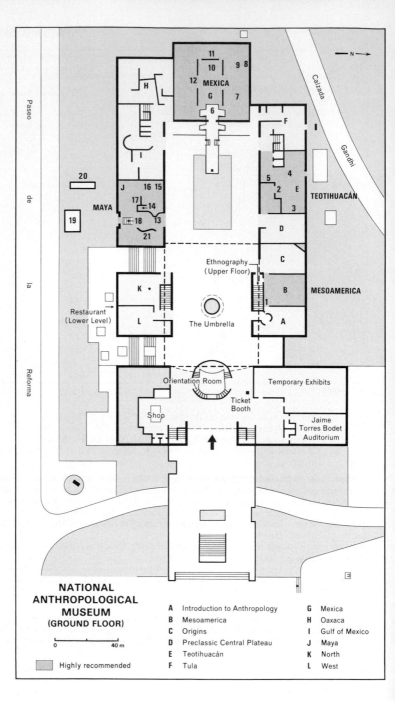

**NATIONAL
ANTHROPOLOGICAL
MUSEUM
(GROUND FLOOR)**

0 _____ 40 m

▨ Highly recommended

A	Introduction to Anthropology	**G**	Mexica
B	Mesoamerica	**H**	Oaxaca
C	Origins	**I**	Gulf of Mexico
D	Preclassic Central Plateau	**J**	Maya
E	Teotihuacán	**K**	North
F	Tula	**L**	West

Museum. – It has twenty-three permanent exhibition rooms: twelve on the ground floor devoted to archeology, spanning the period from the settlement of the American continent to the flowering of pre-Hispanic civilizations; and eleven rooms on the upper floor dedicated to ethnography, showing the most salient features of the present-day indigenous population. It also contains an **Orientation Room** *(in the vestibule)* which provides a survey of Mesoamerican culture by means of models and films.

It is suggested to follow the itinerary described below, so as to find, in this exceptionally rich museum, a selection of the most important works.

Mesoamerica. – The **Map (1)** points out the location of some of the material remains of this great culture, which encompassed part of Mexico, Belize, Guatemala, Honduras and El Salvador, between the 18C BC and the arrival of the Spanish in the 16C AD.
The rest of the exhibit identifies the different pre-Hispanic civilizations, while highlighting their common features.

Teotihuacán. – The copy of the vivid **Tlalocan Mural (2)** clearly illustrates life after death in the Paradise assigned to those who perished in floods and other water-associated disasters.
The life-size reproduction of the first three units of the **Temple of Quetzalcóatl (3)**, a deity represented by snake heads, conveys an impression of the sheer immensity of the Central Plateau's main ceremonial site. The series of grotesque masks is associated with Tláloc.

In front of this facade stands the 57-ton **monolithic sculpture** (**4**) symbolizing Chalchiuh-tlicue, the goddess of earthly water. She wears earrings, a necklace, a blouse or *quechquémetl,* a feathered skirt and sandals. The practice of elevating the gods' images above common mortals was solemnly followed in Teotihuacán.

Among the **funeral masks** (**5**) in the showcase, the most remarkable is the one incrusted with turquoise, shell and coral. These masks were placed over the faces of the dead in order to protect them on their voyage to the netherworld.

Mexica. – The museum's main hall is devoted to the Aztec or Mexica culture, which ruled Mesoame-rica by means of a strong military government from 1325 until the 13th of August 1521. On that date, the Spanish soldiers, led by Her-nán Cortés, forced the indigenous army and its last ruler, Cuauh-témoc, to surrender, after two years of bloody battle. At the entrance, stands the stunning **sculpture of a ferocious ocelot** (**6**) carry-ing on its back a basin, or Cuauh-xicalli, containing an offering of human hearts which, according to Aztec beliefs, served to nourish the sun.

The Tizoc Stone (Piedra de Tizoc) (**7**) records the conquests of this se-venth ruler, who is portrayed de-feating his enemies with great force.

An enormous **mural** (**8**) shows the islet where the Aztecs con-structed their capital, México-Tenochtitlán. This, the principal religious, administrative and cul-tural center in pre-Hispanic

(Photo Pablo Gómez Gallardo/Paco Macías/Mexico)

Aztec calendar

America, extended over 13 km² – 8 square miles and housed 300 000 inhabitants.

The heart of the metropolis is recreated in a large **model** (**9**) in which the Templo Mayor *(p 110)* is prominent, with a blue worship room for Tláloc, the water god, and a red one for Huitzilopochtli, the god of the sun and of war. In the 16C, the complex was destroyed and over it was erected today's Plaza de la Constitución *(p 105).*

On a copper altar, against a great white marble wall, is set the **Sun Stone or Aztec Calendar** (Piedra del Sol o Calendario Azteca) (**10**). The solemn and magical forces which the Nahua priests instilled in this stone pervade the atmosphere of the hall. It weighs 24 tons and measures 3.60 m – 11.8 ft in diameter. To the right of the calendar is a version done in its original colors, featuring the face of Tonatiuh, the sun, in the center, with his tongue hanging out as an obsidian knife, symbolizing the need to eat human hearts and blood. He is surrounded by symbols of the four eras which, according to

the Mexicas, preceded them. The next circle is formed by hieroglyphics representing the days of the month in their 260-day religious calendar, from which radiate forceful sun rays. The perimeter of this famous relief is circled by two fire serpents or Xiuh-cóatl, deities that guided the sun across the heavens. In the lower part, the gods Xiutecuhtli and Tonatiuh emerge from the enormous jaws of the serpents. The small upper square records the date on which this tribute to the sun was consecrated.

The unusual diorama of the **Tlatelolco Market** (Mercado de Tlatelolco) (**11**) shows the great variety of items traded either by barter or using cocoa grains or quills filled with gold dust as currency. At the right end the slave market was located and at the rear, the judges who maintained order in all transactions.

The power, vitality and maturity of Aztec sculpture are particularly appar-ent in the piece protraying Huitzilo-pochtli's mother, the earth goddess, **Coatlicue** (**12**). This impressive statue 2.57 m – 8.43 ft tall was dedicated to the principle of duality – a basic tenet of Mexica philosophy.

(Photo Pablo Gómez Gallardo/Paco Macías/Mexico)

Goddess Coatlicue

Maya. – The **relief map** (13) shows the south of Mesoamerica, a vast territory occupied by this remarkable civilization from the 12C BC to the end of the 17C AD. The lights on the map indicate the location of its numerous archeological sites.

Despite rudimentary Maya technology, in which metals were not processed, on the 8C AD **lintel of Yaxchilán** (dintel de Yaxchilán) (14) they exhibited great artistic ingenuity in depicting the ruler of the Jaguar Shield (Escudo Jaguar). Dressed as a warrior, he carries a knife in his right hand and, with his left, receives a feline headdress presented by a woman with ritual scars adorning her face.

The reproduction of the **Dresden Codex** (códice Dresden) (15) contains astronomical calculations. These codices, which were fashioned from agave fibers, hides or bark, treated with calcium carbonate, were written testimonies reserved for intellectuals' use. The majority of these documents was destroyed during the Spanish Conquest.

The **Jaina figurines** (figurillas de Jaina) (16) reveal fascinating aspects of the life and customs of the governing class, such as the skull deformation which they achieved by tying boards at the front and back of the babies' heads throughout their infancy.

In the **Panels of the Foliated Cross from Palenque** (Tableros de la Cruz Foliada de Palenque) (17), two persons may be seen standing on either side of a corn plant, represented by a cross. An astonishing degree of calligraphic detail was achieved in the hieroglyphics at either end of these panels, which have only been partially deciphered. Beauty of
ⓥ design and profound death symbolism are combined in the **Tomb of the Temple of the Inscriptions** (Tumba del Templo de las Inscripciones), also from Palenque (18). A life-size replica of this tomb can be admired part way down the stairs in the center of the hall. A mystic atmosphere, which emanates from the copy of the **Hochob Temple** (19) in the garden, is greatly enhanced by the **Bonampak Temple** (20), hidden in the background among trees and vines.

The glittering **Chac-Mool** (21), or messenger of the gods of Chichén Itzá, opens the section devoted to post-Classic Maya, when militarist governments took over the Yucatan peninsula.

Upper Floor. – The rooms on this floor illustrate the clothing, physical characteristics, political organization, family life, religious practices and means of subsistence of the main ethnic minorities of Mexico.

The exhibits offer insight into the multicultural makeup of Mexico, revealing the society's complexity as well as its achievements.

More than 8% of the Mexican population belongs to purely Indian communities, which have preserved their distinct identity through their traditions, customs and languages.

Chapultepec Castle (Castillo de Chapultepec) and other Museums
time: 1 day

★★ **National Historical Museum** (Museo Nacional de Historia). – **Chapultepec Castle** (Castillo de
ⓥ Chapultepec). On the summit of Chapulín Hill, stands this impressive neoclassical edifice which resembles a fortress and was designed by the Catalonian **Agustín Mascaró** in 1786, to serve as a residence for the viceroys – an aim that was never fulfilled.

Historical Notes. – In the 19C, once independence was achieved, the castle became a military academy. Its teachers and students, who came to be known as the **Niños Héroes** or Young Heroes, gallantly defended it in 1847 during the invasion by the North American army. It is said that one of the youngsters jumped to his death wrapped in the national flag to avoid its capture. Later on, during the short-lived empire of Maximilian of Habsburg, the fortress where the emperor resided (el Alcázar) was added. After his fall, the castle was inhabited by various rulers until 1939, when Lázaro Cárdenas decided it should be used to house the National Historical Museum (Museo Nacional de Historia).

Museum. – The two floors of this museum contain exhibits of paintings, sculptures, tools and objects for daily use that illustrate the country's evolution between the Conquest and 1917. This evolution can thus be appreciated in the economic organization, the social structure and the cultural achievements of Mexico.

On the lower level, in **Room VI** is the **mural by Orozco**, which illustrates the triumph of the Reform and the fall of the empire, including a large head of Benito Juárez.

Room XIII has been reserved for a **mural by Siquieros**, in various panels, pointing to the decadence of Porfirio Diáz's regime as an immediate cause for the Revolution.

Fortress (Alcázar). – As an example of a historical mansion, the rooms used by Emperor Maximilian and Empress Carlota have been preserved.

ⓥ **History Gallery** (Galería de Historia). – Also known as the **Snail** (El Caracol) because of its circular plan that exploits the steepness of the terrain; it spirals downward, facilitating the display of the museum pieces. Historical and didactic in character, this museum offers – through dioramas, models, portraits, chronological charts and maps – a view of the important events and personalities of the country from the end of the Viceroyal Era (18C) to the adoption of the 1917 Constitution. At the end of the visit, one is moved by the mystical aura of the **Sanctuary of the Nation** (Recinto a la Patria).

Museum of Modern Art (Museo de Arte Moderno). – This museum consists of two modern circular and independent glass-enclosed modules. In the larger *(room II)*, there is a permanent exhibit of contemporary art with paintings by Orozco, Rivera, Siqueiros and Tamayo, as well as other artists, such as Frida Kahlo, Cuevas, Mérida, Corzas, the Coronel brothers and Leonora Carrington. These represent the many different trends that Mexican painting has followed during this century.

The other rooms, like the gallery *(the smaller module)*, are used for temporary exhibits, and sculptures are on view in the pleasant gardens around the museum.

Second and Third Sections of Chapultepec Forest
(Segunda y Tercera Sección del Bosque)

time: 1/2 day – tour by automobile

The **second section** of the forest is characterized by spacious and modern thoroughfares ornamented with fountains and modern sculptures, which lead to the museums, lakes, restaurants and amusement parks that provide for family weekend diversion.

★ **Cárcamo.** – This small building, surmounted by a cupola, gathers the waters from the springs of Lake Lerma (Laguna del Lerma), which was once the principal water source for much of Mexico City. The interior was decorated by Diego Rivera, who also created the nearby **Fountain of the Water Myth** (Fuente del Mito del Agua).

⊙ **Natural History Museum (Museo de Historia Natural).** – This museum is composed of nine connecting circular modules which depict the evolution of the planet and the different species that inhabit it. In addition it contains a large collection of stuffed animals placed in dioramas of their natural habitats.

⊙ **Technological Museum (Museo Tecnológico).** – In the four rooms that make up this museum, different means of transportation devised by man from antiquity to the present day are reproduced in miniature. Furthermore, small instruments are provided on which the laws of physics and chemistry may be tested or applied; in this way, the museum performs a didactic role.

Lakes (Lagos). – At the Chapultepec Forest's two artificial lakes, facilities are provided for boating in rowboats or pedal craft.

⊙ **Amusement Park** (Parque de Diversiones). – There are in fact two amusement parks in the forest: one where the rides are geared to children under ten years of age; and another for adults, where the main attraction is the roller coaster.

⊙ **Third Section of Chapultepec Forest.** – Here the **Atlantis** Marine Park (Parque marino Atlantis) offers dolphin and trained bird shows, as well as fountain spectacles.

TLATELOLCO AND LA VILLA
time: 1/2 day – tour by automobile – Plan p 109

Tlatelolco (CX). – In this ancient and noble pre-Hispanic village, the richest **market** of all Mesoamerica was located. Tlatelolco was the last bastion where the Mexicas defended their sovereignty.

★ **Plaza of the Three Cultures** (Plaza de las Tres Culturas). – This is a spacious square where vestiges of pre-Hispanic architecture blend with religious buildings of colonial times as well as with the **modern edifices** of the housing development by architect **Mario Pani.**

Church of Santiago (Templo de Santiago). – A mystical atmosphere permeates the church's well-restored **interior**★ owing partially to the cool colors in the modern **stained glass windows,** which admit filtered light. The rather plain altar contains a 16C **relief** depicting the saint treading on the Indians. In the upper part of the side door, note the monumental **mural painting** of **Saint Christopher** (San Cristobal).
The remodeled building adjoining the church formerly housed the **School of the Holy Cross** (Colegio de la Santa Cruz), founded in the 16C by Fray Pedro de Gante for Indian children.

⊙ **Tecpan.** – *Behind the Church of Santiago, some 200 m – 656 ft to the east on the pedestrian street, Almacenes.* This 16C edifice was a courthouse in which Indians from the Tlatelolco district were tried for their crimes. In the north room, there is a **mural by Siqueiros** depicting the fall of the Mexica empire, symbolized in the figure of Cuauhtémoc. This work provides an example of Siqueiros's technique for foreshortening a figure in perspective.

★ **Villa de Guadalupe** (CX). – This is the most important place of worship in Mexico, since, according to tradition, it was here that the **Virgin of Guadalupe** appeared four times to the Indian, **Juan Diego,** in 1531.
Each year, on December 12th, thousands of pilgrims come from every corner of the country to sing a birthday song *(las mañanitas)* to the Virgin.

⊙ **Old Basilica** (Antigua Basilica). – Built by Pedro de Arrieta between 1695 and 1709, this imposing structure has an Italian Renaissance layout with a huge central dome and two towers. Its facade was the richest that had been constructed until then in New Spain, with a central relief depicting one of the four apparitions of the Virgin.

New Basilica (Nueva Basilica). – This is a good example of contemporary religious architecture, designed by **Pedro Ramírez Vázquez.** He devised an innovative round plan that can accommodate 40 000 people while permitting all of them to view the original statue of the Virgin of Guadalupe *(located on the high altar).* There is a passageway beside the altar on a lower level, allowing a closer view of the statue.

⊙ **Guadalupe Museum** (Museo Guadalupano). – *Adjoining the basilica.* The walls of the entrance passage are covered with **votive offerings**★, largely made of thin metal plaques, dating from different epochs, whereby the faithful thanked the Virgin for the blessings bestowed on them. Those of a more handmade appearance are eye-catching. On display there is also a fine **collection**★ of works by famous artists of the colonial period, such as Juan Correa, Nicolás Rodríguez Juárez, Cristóbal de Villalpando, Baltazar de Echave Ibia. Among the furniture on exhibit, two banks of choirstalls and a wardrobe with polychrome decorations are noteworthy. So are the hammered silver **altar** – a likeness of the Church of Saint Augustine Acolman (Templo de San Agustín Acolman) *(p 56)* –, the **balustrade** and the **screen** – all to be seen in the chapel (18C) of the baptistery.

★★ **Chapel of the Little Well** (Capilla del Pocito). – This is one of the few structures in Mexico that is baroque not only in its decoration but also in its **layout.** It was built by the famous architect **Guerrero y Torres** (18C), who designed six separate sections around a central oval: four chapels in honor of the Virgin's apparitions, one as the high altar and another to cover the well. The outside walls are an interplay of straight and curved lines, faced in a variety of rich materials: *tezontle,* stone and tiles.

Chapel of the Roses (Capilla de las Rosas). – This chapel sits on the crest of a hill, which offers a stunning **view** of Mexico City on a clear day. According to tradition, this is where the Indian Juan Diego gathered the wild roses that he was to take to the Bishop, Fray Juan de Zumárraga, as a proof of the apparitions of the Virgin.

SOUTHERN DISTRICTS (BARRIOS DEL SUR)

time: 3 days – tour by automobile – Plan below

Churubusco *time: 2 1/2 hours*

A pleasant little square serves as an entrance to the 17C **Monastery of San Diego** (Convento de San Diego) which housed the Mexican Forces of **General Anaya** in 1847, when he defended the city from an attack by the invading American army. On the square, there stands today a statue of the general.

⊙ **Museum of Foreign Interventions** (Museo de las Intervenciones). – This museum – installed in the Convent of San Diego – contains maps, documents, models, uniforms and arms illustrating the American and French invasions.

⊙ **Church of San Diego** (Templo de San Diego). – Adjoining the convent, this church has a small chapel at the entrance, crowned by two cupolas covered in vivid tiles. Inside the church there is a sampling of baroque **altarpieces** from the 17C Church of the Piedad (Templo de la Piedad).

Anahuacalli *(Plan p 109 – CZ).* – **Diego Rivera Museum.** *Calle Museo nº 4.* – This strange and imposing building is constructed entirely of grey stone, which further accentuates its massiveness. It was planned and financed by the artist Diego Rivera, who used it as a studio and as a museum to exhibit his excellent **collection of pre-Hispanic objects** from the different Mexican civilizations. Also to be admired are the sketches subsequently used for some of his murals.

★★**Coyoacán** *time: 1 day – Plan below*

This old suburb arouses speculation about the legends and secrets concealed in its ancient houses and squares. The flavor of the area's mysterious past is enhanced by a stroll along its cobblestone streets, dotted with pleasant squares and restaurants, as well as fascinating art galleries and bookstores. On weekend afternoons, Coyoacán comes to life with children's games and popular festivities. Coyoacán possesses great historical importance as the homeland of a sizeable Indian population before the arrival of the Spaniards. Here history and legend intertwine, since **Hernán Cortés** took up residence here along with some of his collaborators, including Captains Ordaz and Alvarado, as well as **la Malinche** *(see p 29).* At the outset the Conquistador considered Coyoacán as the site for a new city which would be the center of Spanish power. Indeed the second city government *(ayuntamiento)* was founded here and functioned as such until 1532. The most appealing entrance to this traditional suburb is through calle de Francisco Sosa, which starts at the small 18C **Panzacola Chapel** (Capilla de Panzacola) and the romantic **bridge** of the same name.

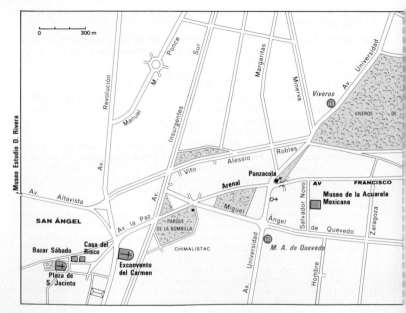

★ **Avenida Francisco Sosa.** – This is one of the most typical avenues of Coyoacán, lined by ancient structures and restful nooks, like the **Plaza of Saint Catherine** (Plaza de Santa Catarina). Shaded by towering ash trees, this square owes its name to the simple **chapel**. At the end of this avenue there is an 18C **structure** known as the **Ordaz House** (Casa de Ordaz) – named for a captain in Cortés' army. On the corner it has a graceful niche with a statue of Saint Joseph (San José).

Mexican Watercolor Museum (Museo de la Acuarela Mexicana). – *88 Salvador Novo.* This former private residence now houses beautiful works by more than forty Mexican artists who have excelled in watercolor technique. Outstanding among these are the **works** by Saturnino Herrán and Leandro Izaguirre of the late 19C, who early on in their careers gained renown as watercolorists. The Contemporary Room displays very expressive modern works in this technique.

Centennial Garden (Jardín Centenario). – This distinguished square, surrounded by historic **buildings,** served as the atrium of the ancient Dominican convent.

Church of Saint John the Baptist (Templo de San Juan Bautista). – The present building is a recent reconstruction of the church that originally belonged to the 16C Monastery of Saint John the Baptist. In the **Chapel of the Most Holy** (Capilla del Santísimo) *(to the left of the high altar)*, there remains an excellent **altarpiece★** (18C), adorned with exquisite paintings portraying scenes from the lives of Christ and the Virgin.

Coyoacán Municipal Hall (Delegación Coyoacán). – House of Cortés, Old City Hall (Casa de Cortés, Antiguo Ayuntamiento). This house was rebuilt in the 18C by the Dukes of Terranova, descendents of Hernán Cortés. It also served as the Conquistador's official residence and as the second seat of city government in New Spain.

Museum of Popular Cultures (Museo de las Culturas Populares). – Established in an old mansion, this museum comprises three rooms in which temporary exhibits are held, illustrating the activities and life of rural and urban social groups.

Plaza de la Conchita. – Protected by lofty ash trees, the graceful **Chapel of the Conception** (Capilla de la Concepción, or la Conchita) stands in the center of this square, its baroque facade covered with decorations resembling ribbons and arabesques. Inside the chapel several fine paintings from the colonial period are on exhibit. The **House of la Malinche** (Casa de la Malinche), where the renowned Maya woman *(p 29)* is believed to have lived with Cortés, and the **House of the Camilos** are two of the outstanding edifices on the square.

★ **Frida Kahlo Museum (Museo de Frida Kahlo).** – In this house the extraordinary painter, Frida Kahlo (1910-54), was born and later lived with her husband, Diego Rivera. Many works by Kahlo and Rivera as well as by their contemporaries can be seen. The numerous personal effects displayed bring the visitor closer to the daily life of the couple. This vast collection of paintings reflects Frida Kahlo's interests in popular traditions, surrealism and the Communist Party.

★ **San Ángel** *time: 1/2 day – Plan p 130*

The development of this peaceful and typical suburb stems from the establishment in this location of the Carmelite convent in the 17C. The region's abundant rivers facilitated the establishment of workshops and mills during the colonial period. Their wealthy owners were the first important residents in the area. Moreover, its mild climate and many orchards turned San Angel into a favorite spot for the well-to-do city dwellers who could afford to build country houses there.

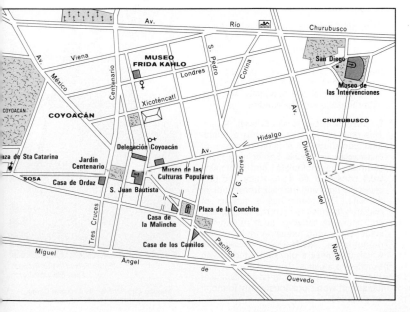

Strolling down **calle del Arenal**, the neighborhood's romantic atmosphere is immediately felt. The town's cobblestone streets, squares and alleys evoke charming scenes from the past.

Carmelite Convent (Exconvento del Carmen). – This former conventual compound was founded by the Carmelites (17C). Most remarkable in the church are the bright polychrome tiles covering its **cupolas** and altars. In the old convent adjoining the church, there is a small **museum** of colonial art, with outstanding works by **Villalpando** and **Correa**, as well as numerous rooms with tiled floors and baseboards, decorated with vivid geometric designs.

Plaza de San Jacinto. – This square, surrounded by a simple **church** (17C) and old **buildings,** comes to life, especially on Saturdays, when craftsmen and budding artists gather there to offer their works for sale. Also on that day only, the 18C mansion holds its **Saturday Bazaar** (Bazar Sábado) with an assorted display of fine crafts.

⊙ **Casa del Risco.** – This 18C house is noteworthy because of the beautiful and intricate tile-covered **fountain**★ that embellishes the courtyard. It also has a fine collection of colonial painting.

⊙ **Diego Rivera Studio Museum (Museo Estudio Diego Rivera)** *(Plan p 108 – **AZ***). – Calle Diego Rivera nº 2 (formerly called Palma), corner of Altavista Col. San Ángel Inn. **Diego Rivera** entrusted the construction of this house to **Juan O'Gorman** in 1931, as he wished to install his studio there. The design was based on the principles of functionalist architecture, and the plans are on exhibit.

The museum displays some **works** by Rivera, but above all its aim is to preserve the atmosphere in which the artist ordinarily worked, amid his brushes, pigments, pre-Hispanic figures, letters and photographs of friends like André Breton. A striking feature of the museum is the magnificent collection of multicolored **Judases** which particularly intrigued Diego. These large human figures with demoniacal features are made of a hardened paste *(cartón piedra)* – a mixture of paper, plaster and blotting oil. Until recently it was a popular tradition to burn these effigies in the streets on Easter Saturday in remembrance of Judas.

★**University Campus (Ciudad Universitaria)**
time: 1/2 day – Plan p 108 – **ABZ**

The university campus was built in the 1950s on a sprawling tract of land. The project was a combined effort of architects and artists designed to blend the buildings with the complicated terrain, largely covered with lava rock from the Xitle Volcano.

Offices of the President (Rectoría). – Three sides of the **exterior** are covered with the **mural work** by Siqueiros, *The People to the University and the University to the People (El Pueblo a la Universidad y la Universidad al Pueblo),* where the artist makes ample use of the *escorzo* technique – a special method for foreshortening the figure in perspective. In this case, he employed figures covered in bits of colored glass that protrude as much as one yard from the wall.

Central Library (Biblioteca Central). – This building is a veritable explosion of color on its four **outside walls,** where architect **Juan O'Gorman** sought to represent the cultural history of the nation by portraying the leading events and figures that contributed to the making of Mexico. These **murals**★★ were made of bits of tile in natural colors.

Former Faculty of Science (Antigua Facultad de Ciencias). – This structure has several thought-provoking **murals** by **José Chávez Morado** showing the progress of mankind through work and science.

Olympic Stadium (Estadio Olímpico) (ABZ). – On the central section of the stadium's exterior wall, an unfinished **mural**★ by **Diego Rivera** appears to emerge from the lava that covers the terrain. With multicolored bits of stone, the artist fashioned his interpretation of the university emblem, with the eagle and the condor.

★★ **Cultural Center (Centro Cultural) (BZ).** – This recently completed group of buildings constitutes a striking example of **contemporary architecture.** For its successful completion, geologists and botanists were consulted, so as to study and preserve the flora and the rock formations of the site. The center has a number of research facilities (a map room, a library) and sponsors activities such as movies, stage plays and concerts held in the ⊙ monumental **Nezahualcóyotl Concert Hall,** which combines a pleasant interior with ⊙ excellent acoustics. The **sculpture area** (espacio escultórico) is an open air display of the sort of works previously only found in art galleries.

(Photo Pablo Gómez Gallardo/ Paco Macías/Mexico)

Mexico City. University Cultural Center – sculpture by M. Felguérez

⊘ **Cuicuilco Archeological Site** (Zona Arqueológica Cuicuilco). – *time: 1 hour – Plan p 108* (BZ). – *Av. Insurgentes and Periférico Sur.* This interesting site belonged to the upper strata of the pre-Classic period of central Mexico. The culture flourished between 1 500 and 200 BC, when Xitle, a small volcano in the Ajusco Range, erupted and thus cut short its development.

The remains discovered in 1922 after an arduous excavation through the rock, uncovered a cone-shaped pyramid with four layers from different construction eras and an entrance ramp facing west. On the top there is an interior altar. At the beginning of the walk leading to the museum, note the crypt constructed of stone slabs that still show traces of red paint.

Site Museum (Museo de Sitio). – This museum houses a sampling of Preclassic art and a series of drawings and explanations related to the evolution of this important Mesoamerican ceremonial center. The beautiful mural by González Camarena depicts the eruption of the Xitle Volcano. Nearby, there is an attractive ecological park with interesting botanical walks.

Tlalpan

time: 1 1/2 hours – also see plan p 108 (BZ)

This town, owing to its location on the slopes of the Ajusco Mountains, enjoys a pleasant climate and was selected in past centuries by prosperous families as a site for their country houses, surrounded by orchards. Some of Tlalpan's past charm still permeates the **Plaza de la Constitución,** which is flanked by the 17C **parish church** (parroquia) with its baroque facade, the arcades, the market and several **old mansions.**

⊘ **Casa Chata.** – *At the corner of Matamoros and Hidalgo.* This is a beautiful example of the typical country residences built in Tlalpan. The stately building has a harmonious 18C pink stone facade as well as lovely gardens and a colorful terrace.

Xochimilco

time: 1/2 day – also see plan p 108 (BZ)

★★ **Canal Tour** (Paseo por los Canales). – The Xochimilco Canal Tour goes around this ancient lake on charming cruise barges, popularly called **trajineras,** which bear girls' names written in flowers of many colors. Since pre-Hispanic times, it has been invaded by *chinampas,* a sort of artificial island, made of tree trunks covered with earth to make vegetable and flower gardens. The picturesque *chinampas* are interspersed among the canals that are pleasant to tour.

This popular amusement area attracts so many visitors on weekends that the entrance and canal traffic are often jammed.

(Photo Pablo Gómez Gallardo/Paco Macías/Mexico)

Xochimilco. A *trajinera* on the canal

133

San Bernardino Parish Church (Parroquia de San Bernardino). – Note the interesting **lateral facade** dating from the 16C when the parish was in the hands of the Franciscans. Inside, a gigantic **mural painting** (16C) representing **Saint Christopher** (San Cristóbal) is worthy of note, as is the good sampling of **altarpieces,** especially the **high altar★** in the Plateresque style (16C).

Rosary Chapel (Capilla del Rosario). – This chapel's 18C facade is covered with lovely stucco decorations that resembles lacework.

Market (Mercado). – The main attraction of this, one of the liveliest markets in the Federal District, is the variety of plants for sale.

ADDITIONAL SIGHTS   Plan pp 108-109

Lagunilla Market (Mercado de la Lagunilla) **(CX)**. – On Sundays this flea market is set up in one of the oldest and most populous neighborhoods in the city. It is similar to the Rastro Market in Madrid or the Marché aux Puces in Paris. Antiques, paintings, furniture, sculptures, books, or simply old used objects are sold here.

Azcapotzalco Monastery (Exconvento de Azcapotzalco) **(BX B)**. – This ancient town was the leading settlement when the Mexicas arrived in the Valley of Mexico. On the base of a pre-Hispanic pyramid, a Dominican monastery was built around 1540, under the orders of **Fray Lorenzo de la Asunción.** Remaining from this period are the *posa* or corner chapel on the right side of the atrium, the traces of a mural painting (representing Dominican saints) in the entrance room and the cloister, which has retained vestiges of its coffered ceiling.
The church's interior, although significantly remodeled in the 18C, still has a 17C altarpiece in the chancel, dedicated to Saint Rose of Lima (Santa Rosa de Lima), with **paintings** by Villalpando.

⊙ **Rosary Chapel** (Capilla del Rosario). – This chapel is richly decorated with a series of altarpieces dating from the 18C. The most striking are the one on the right transept, dedicated to the Virgin with **paintings** by Juan Correa (1674-1739) and the one on the high altar, consecrated in 1779 to the Virgin of the Rosary (Virgen del Rosario), with fine gilded sculptures.

Ajusco National Park (Parque Nacional del Ajusco). – *20 km – 12.4 miles south.* **(AZ)**. *Take the Periférico and follow the signs.*
At the turn-off to the park, there are excellent examples of modern architecture in the
⊙ buildings for Channel 13 and the **College of Mexico★** (Colegio de México). Further on lies
⊙ the children's amusement park, **Reino Aventura,** that has rides and a dolphin show. On the slope of the inactive Ajusco volcano – also called **Eagle's Peak** (Pico del Aguila) because its curved summit resembles the head of an eagle – there is an extensive park, one of the main wildlife reserves near the great city.

Tenayuca. – *12 km – 7.5 miles. Head north out of Mexico City on Av. Lázaro Cárdenas.*
⊙ **Tenayuca Archeological Site** (Zona Arqueológica Tenayuca). – This is an important pre-Aztec site founded in 1224. It was probably inhabited by the Chichimecs for over 200 years.
Reconstruction work on this impressive pyramid revealed that it is composed of superimposed structures, which are clearly visible in the passageways. The stairways are divided by narrow ramps ending in cubes. At the top of the pyramid, twin temples were erected and dedicated to Huitzilopochtli, the god of war, and to Tlaloc, the god of rain (which served as a pattern for the Great Temple of Tenochtitlán) *(p 110).*
A beautiful wall, adorned with serpents carved in stone, called **coatepantli,** surrounds the temple. It is said that the north serpent points to the sunset during the summer solstice and that the south serpent indicates the sunset during the winter solstice.

EXCURSIONS

Desierto de los Leones. – 20 km – *12.4 miles west on highway n° 15 (Plan p 108 –* **AY***) towards Toluca.*
This thick forest near Mexico City is a favorite spot for weekend outings. In the midst of this romantic pine and oak forest, where imaginations take flight, stands the ancient
⊙ **Carmelite Monastery** (Convento Carmelita). It was built in the 17C as a place where the friars could fulfill their vows of isolation and dedicate themselves to prayer and meditation. In the large, severe stone building, the sections are arranged around a series of patios forming a labyrinth of sorts. The dank cellars may also be visited *(bring a flashlight);* they not only serve as foundations, but also contain the monastery's water system.

Chapel of the Secrets (Capilla de los Secretos). – Located outside the monastery, this chapel produces a strange acoustical effect: a whisper from one corner can be clearly heard in the other three.

★★★ **Seminary of Tepotzotlán** (Excolegio de Tepotzotlán). – *38 km – 23.6 miles north on highway n° 57 D. Description p 198.*

★★ **Acolman and Teotihuacán Archeological Site★★★** (Acolman y Zona Arqueológica **Teotihuacán**). – *Allow one whole day. 53 km – 33 miles to the northeast on highway n° 85 D. Description p 56 and 193.*

From the Autonomous University of Chapingo to Papalotla (De la Universidad Autónoma de Chapingo a Papalotla). – *54.5 km – 33.9 miles. Allow one whole day. Go east from Mexico City on highway n° 150 (Plan p 108 –DY), turn left toward Texcoco and 39 km – 24.2 miles farther, turn left again, continuing 0.5 km – 0.3 miles to Chapingo.*

⊘ **Autonomous University of Chapingo** (Universidad Autónoma de Chapingo). – Between 1926 and 1927 Diego Rivera decorated the Renaissance-style **Reception Hall** (Salón de Actos), the Chapel of the Chapingo Hacienda, with a series of splendid **mural paintings★★★**, complemented by the lunettes of the dome, where he painted foreshortened male nudes representing human labor.

On the right side is *The Natural Evolution of Man (La Evolución Natural del Hombre),* the second panel, *Germination (La Germinación),* being the most remarkable. On the left is *The Social Transformation of the Mexican Man in the 20C (La Transformación del Hombre en el Siglo Veinte Mexicano).* The force displayed in the stylized figures in its third panel, *The Flowering (La Floración),* is noteworthy.

The back wall synthesizes the work with a nude, Mother Earth, protecting man in his constant conflict with Nature.

At the chapel exit, in the arch over the choir, there is an extraordinary female nude, the sleeping mother, with a seed flowering in her hand. This is one of Rivera's finest works.

> *Continue 0.5 km – 0.3 miles until reaching highway n° 136, cross it and take the turn-off to Huexotla; 3.5 km – 2.2 miles further on, turn right and continue 1 km – 0.6 miles on an unpaved road.*

Huexotla. – In this humble village, the church of the old Franciscan monastery (16C) has a delicate 18C facade made of mortar adorned with popular-style sculptures. The enchanting miniature cloister radiates an appealing atmosphere. It is said that here **Fray Gerónimo de Mendieta** wrote his *Indian Ecclesiastical History (Historia Eclesiástica Indiana),* a chronicle of the 16C. The building was erected on top of the main foundations of the old pyramid belonging to the pre-Hispanic ceremonial center. Some vestiges of the great **wall** *(southern axis of the atrium wall)* have been preserved.

> *Return to highway n° 136 and continue 2 km – 1.2 miles to Texcoco.*

Texcoco. – During pre-Hispanic times, Texcoco was an important city located on the shores of the former lake. It reached the height of its development under King **Nezahualcóyotl** (1481), who increased production by grouping the workers in communities and gave the people more equitable laws. According to tradition, he also enjoyed writing poetry. At the time of the Conquest, the brigantines, which played a crucial role in the fall México-Tenochtitlán, were armed in Texcoco.

A visit to Texcoco and its surroundings provides an introduction to the Texcocan baroque style, with its characteristic enchanting **mortarwork,** combining ingenuity and delicacy, on the buildings' exteriors.

Texcoco Cathedral (Catedral de Texcoco). – *Southeastern side of Plaza de la Constitución.* This cathedral complex is composed of three churches that were part of the ancient Franciscan monastery, in which Fray Pedro de Gante founded the first European-style school in America (1523). The Church of the Third Order (Templo de la Tercera Orden) has a remarkable facade and fine 17C altarpieces.

> *Go north from Texcoco toward Tepexpan; after 4 km – 2.5 miles, turn left and continue 1.5 km – 0.9 miles to Chiconcuac.*

Chiconcuac. – This is a traditional textile center, famed for its woolen clothing, especially sweaters, sarapes and small rugs, which can be purchased in the many shops scattered throughout the town.

> *Go back 1.5 km – 0.9 miles to the road junction, cross the highway and take the road to Papalotla, continue 2 km – 1.2 miles straight ahead and turn left, continue 1 km – 0.6 miles to Papalotla.*

Papalotla. – In this simple town, the graceful 18C **facades** of the atrium of its **church** are covered with intricate plant forms made of mortar and topped by sculptures of rampant lions.

★★★ **Popocatépetl and Iztaccíhuatl Volcanoes** (Volcanes Popocatépetl – Iztaccíhuatl). – 89 km – 55.3 miles. Go east from Mexico City on highway n° 150 towards Puebla (Plan p 109 –DY) and at 33 km – 19.9 miles take the turn-off to the right towards Chalco, continue 4 km – 2.5 miles until the sign Amecameca-Chalco, continue 22 km – 13.7 miles on highway n° 115 until Amecameca. 30 km – 18.6 miles to Tlamacas. Description p 164.

Other Michelin Green Guides available in English are:

Austria	London	Brittany
Canada	New York City	Châteaux of the Loire
England: The West Country	Paris	Dordogne
Germany	Rome	French Riviera
Greece		Normandy Cotentin
Italy		Normandy Seine Valley
New England		Provence
Portugal		
Scotland		
Spain		
Switzerland		

The name Mitla comes from the Náhuatl word *mictlan,* meaning "place of the dead". It refers to a location for the burial of important persons. Established around the year 100 AD, Mitla became one of the leading power centers of the Zapotec region. This preeminence lasted until the Spaniards arrived to found a new city in 1528. Sharing the location with the present town, the archeological site is unique, on account of the simplicity of its architecture, which could be described as delicate rather than monumental. The decorative forms in **frets** *(grecas)* of multiple motifs are composed of thousands of small pieces of stone, masterfully cut and set in clay, arranged in incomparable geometric patterns. The site architecture is characterized by its distinctive layout: a series of patios with small temples in the center surrounded by rectangular rooms.

(From photo by Revault/PIX/Paris)

Mitla. Frets

Entrance to these patios is gained by steps on the only open side. The main rooms of each group have a curious construction at the rear – a sort of annex, consisting of a small patio enclosed by chambers. A door in the main room leads to this courtyard.

⊙ ARCHEOLOGICAL SITE *time: 2 hours*

This important site comprises five groups of pre-Hispanic structures. At present, only the two complexes described below have been fully explored.

Church Complex (Grupo de la Iglesia). – Part of the construction material of this intriguing structure was used in the 16C to erect the small church that can be seen today on top of it.

The richly decorated upper levels of the buildings and the use of the *tablero escapulario (see p 37)* as a decorative feature make this otherwise simple group of buildings memorable.

(Photo J.M.Gabizon/Paris)

Mitla. The church complex

Column Complex (Grupo de las Columnas). – This complex is arranged around two broad courtyards that connect at one corner; both are surrounded by rooms lending the ensemble a fine balance and scale.

First Courtyard. – *First building on the right.* It has splendid decorative panels, and, on the upper level, the **Temple of the Columns.** This structure possesses an entrance portico consisting of a door with three openings divided by two thick columns. Notice the strong, monolithic lintels and, inside, the spacious rectangular hall divided down the middle by six monolithic columns. In the right corner of this chamber, a small passage connects with a diminutive patio enclosed by rooms.

Known as the **Fret Patio** (Patio de las Grecas) because of the elaborate geometric ornamentation in stone that adorns its walls, this patio is the site's most outstanding feature.

Second Courtyard. – *To the left of the first building.* This architectural group is similar to the previous one. To the left and to the right under two of the buildings in the courtyard, are the entrances to two simple cross-shaped tombs, decorated with frets on large slabs. The building to the right has a roof supported by a thick monolithic column, called the **Column of Life** (Columna de la Vida). Many visitors embrace this column because it is believed that the distance left between their fingertips indicates how many more years they will live.

ADDITIONAL SIGHT

⊙ Frisell Museum (Museo Frisell). – *On the way out of town, on the road leading to the highway, on the main square.* This museum is located in a small 18C house and exhibits an unusual **collection★** of more than 2 000 pre-Hispanic pieces from the Mixtec-Zapotec periods in the Oaxaca Valley. Through a small window in one of the rooms facing the patio, the laboratory where restoration and research on ceramics is in progress, can be observed.

EXCURSIONS

From Yagul to the Tule Tree (Arbol de Tule). – *48 km – 29.8 miles. Estimate 1 day. Go northwest from Mitla on highway n° 190 to Oaxaca and at 10 km – 6.2 miles, turn right, 2 km – 1.2 miles on a paved road.*

⊙ Yagul Archeological Site. – In the Zapotec language, Yagul means "old hill". The city is strategically set on the slope of a hill and, together with Mitla, belongs to the group of the last Zapotec capitals in the valley. Admirably situated, the site conserves the remains of some structures, among which the salient ones are: the entrance plaza, which provides access to a **triple tomb;** the tombs themselves are all cruciform in design, and one of them has beautiful decorations and Mitla-style frets; the **ball game court,** one of the largest and best proportioned discovered in the Oaxaca Valley; and the **Palace of the Six Courtyards** (Palacio de los Seis Patios), a building with square patios surrounded by rooms with an intricate system of passageways interconnecting the whole complex. On the top of the hill some vestiges of tombs remain, as well as an old lookout post affording a good view of the valley.

Return to highway n° 190 towards Oaxaca and continue 3 km – 1.9 miles, turn left and follow straight ahead on the main street until the church.

Tlacolula de Matamoros. – In this traditional trading town, the splendid **Chapel of the Lord of Tlacolula** (Capilla del Señor de Tlacolula) stands next to the Convent of Saint Jerome (Exconvento de San Jerónimo). Its **interior★★★** contains excellent works of colonial art. The entrance grille, the small choir, and the pulpit are among the most beautiful wrought-iron works from the beginning of the 17C. There are also exquisite plasterwork and sculpted and painted religious figures. Similarly, the chancel railing, two magnificent processional candlesticks and two lamps hanging from the ceiling are to be noted – all masterfully wrought in silver. Scattered around the chapel are mirrors with gilded frames, symbolizing the purity of the soul.

Return to highway n° 190 and continue 2 km – 1.2 miles, and then turn left.

⊙ Lambityeco Archeological Site. – This was a great Zapotec regional trading center, as well as the residence of important religious and administrative personalities. It was active from the 7C BC, reaching periods of splendor between the 7C and 8C AD. Notable among structural remains, at the top of the main building, is a small complex of two courtyards surrounded by chambers. In the center of the main patio stands a shrine with panels on its sides that portray reclining human figures, identified as important leaders. Under the shrine, through the entrance to a tomb, two magnificent and realistic masks are to be admired. Across a small walk to the right of the main building, there are two temples; one of them has panels with spectacular **masks** of the rain god, Cocijo, who wears a headdress bearing the stylized face of a jaguar and carries the symbols of air and fire in his hands.

Return to highway n° 190 and continue 4 km – 2.5 miles, then turn right and continue 4 km – 2.5 miles further.

Teotitlán del Valle. – The name of this small town means "the land of the gods". Its church, built in the middle of the 17C at the top of a hill overlooking the town, has a facade with floral decorations. To the right, in the **posas** or corner chapels *(see p 39)* and in the small cloister, there is a series of pre-Hispanic sculptures and stone slabs with Mitla-style fret decorations. The church interior contains paintings and the remains of good altarpieces and sculptures. The townspeople make small **woolen rugs** on home looms, colored with natural dyes, copying designs by internationally renowned artists like Miró, Picasso and Escher, or with the traditional fret designs and the typical Moxican sonso of color.

Return to highway n° 190 and continue 3 km – 1.9 miles, turn left and drive on 1 km – 0.6 miles on an unpaved road.

⊙ Dainzú Archeological Site. – This name means "hill of the organs". Chronologically it belonged to a group of cities contemporary with Monte Albán, and it was inhabited over a period running from 750 BC to 1 000 AD. Its architecture was adapted to the topography of the terrain; and the buildings are distributed over a slope. To the left of the entrance, lie the remains of a pyramid with a simple staircase flanked by ramps; to the right of these are tombstones carved with figures of ball game players posed for action, whose attire demonstrates the complexity of this rite. The ruins of the other structures are scattered over the slope; among them the Tomb of the Jaguar and a simple ball game court are preeminent.

Return to highway nº 190 and after 10 km – 6.2 miles turn right.

★ **The Tule Tree** (Arbol del Tule). – The enormous iron fence that surrounds the church atrium also encloses the impressive *savin* or juniper tree. The veins of the wood turn in capriciously shaped knots, evoking fantastic forms and providing shelter for birds. This ancient tree is approximately 2000 years old and is still growing. It is 40 m – 131 ft high, with a perimeter of about 42 m – 138 ft. Its volume has been calculated at 705 m³ – 919 cubic yards and its weight at 550 tons.

This great green mass contrasts with the diminutive Saint Mary's Church (Templo de Santa María) that stands next to it. The lively facade of this engaging church features vivid colors – yellows, ochres and reds – that lend it a popular character.

(Photo BOTTIN/Paris)

Santa María del Tulé

★★★ MONTE ALBÁN Oaxaca

Map of Principal Sights p 5

From its formidable location, the majestic ceremonial center of Monte Albán watches over the broad valley where the city of Oaxaca is situated. Full of mysterious nooks and hidden surprises, the harmony and majesty of this massive complex provoke vivid emotions. In the late afternoon, the sun plays an enigmatic game of chiaroscuro in which the entire site takes on a magical appearance. The changing seasons contribute rich nuances of color and light. The warm gold color and brilliant light in the dry season, and the soft greens and pale haze of winter speak the silent language of the pre-Hispanic gods.

HISTORICAL NOTES

The history of Monte Albán covers five periods, of which three are particularly important: Periods I and II correspond to the years of its foundation, from 600 BC to 350 AD. Period III, the richest of all, spans 400 years (350 to 750 AD). The population peaked at 25000 inhabitants, occupying some 6.5 square kilometers – 2.5 square miles. Use of the *tablero escapulario (see p 37)* for large-scale symmetrical constructions became widespread. The majority of the buildings that can be seen today in Monte Albán belong to this era. The subsequent periods witnessed the arrival and hegemony of the Mixtecs, a group with cultural features similar to those of the Zapotecs, with whom they gradually mixed, to such an extent that they took over part of the city and the burial grounds on the outskirts. The foundation of the Mixtec-Zapotec capitals in the valley brought about the gradual abandonment of the ceremonial center. This period ended with the arrival of the Spaniards.

⏱ ARCHEOLOGICAL SITE *time: 3 hours*

Entrance on Calzada Valerio Trujano, to one side of the 2nd class bus terminal

Cultural Services Unit (Unidad de Servicios Culturales). – This modern structure houses a small museum, which features a general survey of this archeological site. It shows aspects of the geography and chronology of the archeological area, as well as lovely pieces of sculpture and architecture, some of which are originals.

Ceremonial Center (Centro Ceremonial). – This vast rectangular plaza, flanked by the remains of imposing structures, constitutes the nucleus of the archeological site. On either end of the plaza rise massive platform structures. From the top of these monuments, beautiful **views★★★** of the valley can be enjoyed.

It is suggested to tour the area in a counterclockwise direction. In this visit, surprise follows surprise, as the unusual architectural lines and forms unfold. At the entrance there is a **monument to Doctor Alfonso Caso**, the renowned archeologist of this site.

North Platform (Plataforma Norte). – A broad stairway flanked by impressive ramps leads to the summit, which accommodates a group of small temples, divided into squares. In the central part, the sunken patio *(patio hundido),* which constitutes an independent space with very peculiar designs in the corners, is outstanding.

System IV (Sistema IV). – The visitor enters the monument via a raised platform that leads to an enclosed patio with a temple at its center. Behind the patio rises a tiered structure whose upper level contains the vestiges (four rubble columns) of a **temple-patio-sanctuary,** a characteristic feature of Zapotec architecture.

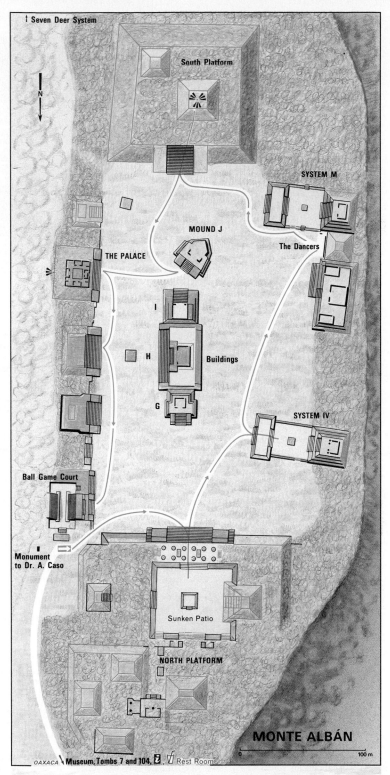

† Seven Deer System

N

South Platform

SYSTEM M

MOUND J

THE PALACE

The Dancers

I

H

Buildings

G

SYSTEM IV

Ball Game Court

Monument
to Dr. A. Caso

Sunken Patio

NORTH PLATFORM

MONTE ALBÁN

0   100 m

OAXACA ⭢ Museum, Tombs 7 and 104, 🅩 🚻 Rest Room

(Photo Michelin)

Monte Albán. System IV

The Dancers (Los Danzantes). – At one side of this simple temple, there is a set of stone slabs in vertical position that decorate the foundation with a series of **reliefs** of human figures in strange dance-like positions, hence the name. A strong Olmec *(see p 37)* influence is apparent in the physical features of these figures. Some researchers believe that these reliefs represent sacrificial victims.

System M (Sistema M). – This building presents the same characteristics as System IV. Both compounds were designed to complete the architectural balance of this section of the plaza.

South Platform (Plataforma Sur). – This platform includes a central stairway with wide ramps. It has only been partially explored. From its summit there is a marvelous **view** of the site and its surroundings.

Mound J (Montículo J). – This is one of the oldest and most complex constructions of the archeological site. Its arrowhead shape, that accounts for its unusual proportions, combined with its southwestern exposure, make this mound the key element of the asymmetric layout that distinguishes Monte Albán.
The foundation is pierced by two narrow tunnels of peculiar design, thought to have been used for astronomical observations. Both passages contain a series of stone slabs with linear drawings of symbols and persons, similar to those decorating the exterior – hieroglyphs depicting the peoples conquered by Monte Albán. The carvings on the building are excellent reproductions; the originals can be seen in the site museum.

The Palace (El Palacio). – Through a simple door, over which the original lintel has been preserved, a passageway leads to a marvelous patio, suggesting that the chambers were designed to house high-ranking persons. The intriguing interior is divided into various rooms, some of which were laid out utilizing the patio corners to create private quarters.

Buildings G, H, I (Edificios G, H, I). – This complex of buildings constitutes the central core around which the plaza was built. It is believed that they were constructed around a large rocky promontory. The design allows for access to their upper sections from three sides of the plaza.

Ball Game Court (Juego de Pelota). – This court has very sloping sides and raised platforms for spectators. On its field there is a round stone that was part of the game. Around the site, on the slopes of the hill, other fascinating details can be explored, such as the **Seven Deer System** or the surprising **tombs** with beautiful offerings inside, especially Tombs 7 *(see p 150)* and 104. These show rich mural paintings that recall the Teotihuacán style, which have been masterfully reproduced for the National Anthropological Museum in Mexico City.

Sights described in this guide are rated:

★★★ *Worth the trip*
  ★★ *Worth a detour*
   ★ *Interesting*

Map of Principal Sights p 6

On the border with Guatemala, the folds of the Sierra de Chiapas embrace these spectacular multicolor lakes which go from turquoise blue to leaden tones, passing through an ample spectrum of brilliant greens and metallic grays. The water reflects the surrounding peaks, blanketed with pines and oak woods laden with orchids.

Panoramic Highway (Carretera Panorámica). – *4 km – 2.5 miles.* This road through the park (6 022 hectares – 13 674 acres) provides beautiful views of the Agua Tinta, Ensueño, Esmeralda and Bosque Azul Lakes. Since this region remains unvisited most of the year, its silence is broken only at dawn and at dusk by the musical songs of the goldfinches and mockingbirds and the din of flocks of parakeets.

Stone Arch (Arco de Piedra). – *At the end of the panoramic highway, continue 600 m – 1 969 ft on an unpaved road; then walk 500 m – 1 640 ft down the path at the left.* Through a dense forest, amid striking flowers and unusual butterflies, the path leads to a strange river: its swift flow suddenly disappears into the opening of a monumental arch carved into the rock by the rivers' waters next to some unexplored grottos. This surprising phenomenon is due to the force of the water which eroded the limestone riverbank, forcing the torrent to go underground.

Camino de Terracería. – *14 km – 8.7 miles. The road begins after the sentry house (caseta de vigilancia).* This unpaved road leads to a ranch beside **Lake Tziscao,** the largest in the area. On the way, hikes can be taken to other nearby lakes, through forests so dense that the sun's rays do not reach the ground.

EXCURSION

Comitán. – *56 km – 34.8 miles to the west on highway n° 190 towards San Cristóbal de Las Casas.* This bucolic and traditional town stands on the top of a hill overlooking a lovely valley. Along its steep streets, flanked by low mansions with double pitched roofs, there are numerous small parks that face sanctuaries.

⊘ **San Caralampio Church** (Templo de San Caralampio). – *3a Oriente Norte at the corner of Benito Juárez Oriente.* The image of San Caralampio, the old martyr with the tired beard, was first venerated after an epidemic of smallpox and cholera decimated the population in the 19C. Today people come to worship this popular saint from many distant places, as can be seen in the showcases full of cards, photographs and votive offerings in the chapel.

⊘ **Dr. Belisario Domínguez Museum House** (Casa Museo). – *Av. Belisario Domínguez n° 29.* In the house of this Revolutionary hero (1863-1913) a magnificent replica of his pharmacy and dispensary has been installed, and in many rooms important documents relating to his public life are on exhibit.

Except where otherwise stated,
all recommended itineraries in towns,
are designed as walks.

The main parking facilities are indicated on the town plans.

MONTERREY Nuevo León   ◆◆◆◆◆◆

Map of Principal Sights p 5

Set in a large valley at the foot of the Sierra Madre Oriental, Monterrey, capital of Nuevo Leon state, is surrounded by imposing mountain formations like **Cerro de la Silla,** the symbol of the city. Known as the **Sultana of the North** (La Sultana del Norte), Monterrey has developed into the country's second largest industrial center, with a privileged location as a major center for communication and transportation. Its remarkable modern urban development is reflected in its expressways and buildings, which make for a striking contrast with the quiet pedestrian streets found in the center of the city. Although its climate is extremely dry, the higher parts of the mountains that lie to the south are endowed with abundant vegetation and temperate climate and serve as a refuge from the summer heat.

HISTORICAL NOTES

The Metropolitan City of Our Lady of Monterrey (Ciudad Metropolitana de Nuestra Señora de Monterrey) was founded the 20th of September of 1596 by Diego de Montemayor, in honor of the then Viceroy of New Spain, Gaspar de Zúñiga Acevedo, Count of Monterrey. In the ensuing years, the town underwent a long period of stagnation, which came to an end with the North American invasion in 1846. The signature of the Treaty of Guadalupe liberated Monterrey in 1848. Later on, during the French Intervention *(see p 165),* the city was again under attack. Mariano Escobedo, leading Mexican troops, finally expelled the invaders, thereby showing support for President Juárez's regime.

The industrialization of Monterrey began in the final years of the 19C, with the establishment of many private enterprises, among which the smelters and the internationally famous brewery were outstanding. This has been the basis for the economic growth and power of present-day Monterrey.

★ **GRAN PLAZA** *time: 3 hours*

This spacious modern square has particular features that set it apart from the majority of Mexican plazas. Mention must be made not only of its unusual size, for which it has been popularly called the **Macroplaza,** but also of the surprising mixture of architectural and decorative components that make up its contradictory unity. Sculptures of different styles and periods, from Greek mythology to the local state heroes, ultramodern concrete, steel and glass buildings – like the city hall (Palacio Municipal) – or neoclassical – like the cathedral – unite amid fountains and gardens, as a living symbol of the boundless activity of Monterrey.

Beacon of Trade (Faro del Comercio). – This is a monumental prism built by the local chamber of commerce to celebrate the centennial of the foundation of that institution. It is a work by the architect, Luis Barragán. This novel symbol, which at night emits a powerful laser ray, illuminates the principal points of the city (Cerro de la Silla and the Bishop's Palace, among others).

Cathedral. – *Calles Abasolo and Zazua.* In this notable construction, various 17C to 19C styles have been harmoniously combined. Of particular importance is the three-part facade, richly worked in baroque style with paired neoclassical columns in the lower part and two Plateresque medallions on the portal.
Above this stands a slendor tower crowned by a lantern. Inside the cathedral there are beautiful **murals★** behind the altar.

Government Palace (Palacio de Gobierno). – *Calles Zaragoza and Cinco de Mayo.* This lovely palace, built at the beginning of Porfirio Díaz's era, was called the Palace of Playing Cards (Palacio de los Naipes), because it was financed with gambling money. It is a lordly edifice with a portico lined in neoclassical columns and remarkable stained glass windows.

ADDITIONAL SIGHTS

★ **Church of La Purísima (Templo de la Purísima).** – *Calles Padre Mier and Zarco.* This is one
⊙ of the most important modern religious buildings in the country, a work by the architect Enrique de la Mora.

Facade. – The slender bell tower, with an admirable terra cotta sculpture of the Immaculate Conception and, on the frontispiece, a 4.5 m – 15 ft bronze statue of Christ with the stylized sculptures of the twelve apostles, can all be appreciated on the facade of this church.

Interior. – The brilliant light coming through the stained glass windows surrounding the high altar, frames an impressive seemingly three-dimensional Christ. On a pedestal in the center, the Little Virgin (La Virgen Chiquita) is worshipped. She was named after a legend involving a Tlascaltec woman called the Shoemaker (La Zapatera), who, during the inundation of the city in the 17C, took a small effigy of the Virgin to the edge of the flood, causing the waters to recede. To commemorate this miracle, the population erected a chapel, which has been rebuilt on two occasions.

★ **Bishop's Palace (Obispado).** – *Calle Rafael J. Verger, unnumbered.* This imposing construction dating back to the second half of the 18C resembles a fort, due to its strategic location at the top of a hill and did, in fact, serve to defend the city during the North American invasion in 1846.
This building complex, the Palace of Our Lady of Guadalupe (antiguo Palacio de Nuestra Señora de Guadalupe), was the residence of Bishop Fray Rafael José Verger. Note the attractive central chapel and in particular, its noble facade with splendid baroque decoration, its superb cupola, and its elegant door with an ogee arch framed by *estípites (see p 40),* a wide frieze and a pediment with medallions.

Nuevo León Regional Museum (Museo Regional de Nuevo León). – The collections exhibited in this museum present, in chronological sequence, the history of the region, through diverse materials ranging from mammoth bones to the personal effects of heroes and leaders of Nuevo León. The Prayer Room (Sala del Oratorio) devoted to religious art, with paintings by Cabrera and Vallejo, is noteworthy.

⊙ **Monterrey Museum (Museo de Monterrey).** - *Av. Universidad 2202.* This recently established museum was installed in the former Cuauhtémoc Brewery.
It offers a select exhibit of works by contemporary masters – painters, muralists and sculptors – like Orozco, Mérida, Siqueiros, Rivera and Tamayo.

★ **Alfa Cultural Center (Centro Cultural Alfa).** – *Roberto Garza Sada 1000.* This building is
⊙ an example of simple contemporary architecture. With its slanted profile, it looks like a telescope pointing to the sky, encircled by large, beautiful gardens.

Science and Technology Museum (Museo de Ciencia y Tecnología). – This museum was conceived for didactic exhibits geared to students, presenting temporary and permanent shows on astronomy and physics. The visitor is allowed to operate various machines or instruments that reproduce physical phenomena. It is equally entertaining for adults and for children.

Planetarium (Planetario). – Located in the center of the complex, it offers interesting hemispheric projections on astronomy and other related themes.

★ **Huastec Canyon (Cañon Huasteco).** – *Go west on Boulevard Díaz Ordaz and turn left following the signs for the road to Catarina.* The arid landscape of the canyon is suddenly embellished by the enormous, slender stone slabs that nature has placed at random in vertical display.

EXCURSIONS

Mesa de Chipinque. – *20 km – 12.4 miles to the south on the State Highway.*
This plateau is a pleasant recreation spot, reached by a steep road that winds through cool natural oak and pine forests. There are also several charming landscaped areas. From the lookout at the end of the road, there is a splendid view of the city of Monterrey.

★ **Cola de Caballo; La Boca Dam (Presa de la Boca).** – *44 km – 27.3 miles. Estimate 3 hours. Go south from Monterrey on highway n° 85 towards Linares, and 36 km – 22.4 miles to Santiago, turn right for 8 km – 5 miles to Cola de Caballo.*

★ **Cola de Caballo.** – Through a picturesque ravine, following the stream bordered by poplars and oaks, the footpath reaches the base of the breathtaking waterfall, approximately 35 m – 115 ft high. The lookouts are set deep in this natural garden.

Return to Santiago and facing it you will find Boca Dam.

Boca Dam (Presa de la Boca). – Back in the city, artificial lake formed by the Boca Dam, offers facilities for water sports like skiing and sailing; there is a fully equipped tourist center as well.

★★ **García Grottos (Grutas de García).** – *45 km – 28 miles. Go west from Monterrey on highway n° 40 and at km 21 – 13 miles, turn right for 15 km – 9.3 miles, until reaching Villa García and continue 9 km – 5.6 miles.*
Along the route, the contrast of arid plains and imposing mountains is striking. To reach the grottos, there is an exciting 80 m – 236 ft funicular ride up the mountain, that is topped by the profile known as **Indian Head** (La Cabeza del Indio).
Inside the grottos, a very well-lit gallery leads to a world of fantasy through 16 scenarios on an intricate tour. Capricious forms of stalactites and stalagmites may be seen on all sides. In the **Theater** the heavy folds of the curtain may be clearly perceived. The 34 m – 112 ft balconies permit a complete view of the gallery. The impressive **Hand of the Dead** (Mano del Muerto) seems to grow larger in the shadow it casts. This mysterious and intriguing tour leads to the **Glory Hall** (Salón de la Gloria), with a monumental dome in which a skylight lets a shaft of sunlight penetrate the gloom. Next comes the small chapel delicately adorned with coral that resembles fine lace.

★★ **MORELIA** Michoacán   ◆◆◆◆◆

Map of Principal Sights p 5

On a gently sloping hill, in the old valley of Guayangareo, stands Morelia, the capital of Michoacán state. Encircled by great stone banks that give it a regal appearance, including palatial and viceroyal features, this is a city of splendid architecture and fine living.
As the cultural center of the state, Morelia's student activity pervades it with color and bustle. The colonial traits of the aging buildings transform their silhouettes in the late afternoon into an extraordinary golden play of light and shade. Amid soft landscapes, handicrafts of varied forms and materials can be found in the nearby towns. Also the traditions, dress and Purépecha language, which are still used by the local Indians, should be noted.

HISTORICAL NOTES

The vast territory of Michoacán was occupied in about 15C BC by agrarian groups that spread throughout the western regions. Little is known about the origins of the Tarascs and the different historical periods of the area, but it is believed that they belonged to an ethno-linguistic branch of the Nahua family who migrated from the lowlands to Pátzcuaro *(p 160)* and to Tzintzuntzan *(p 211)* in the post-Classic period. In 1542, the first Viceroy of New Spain, Antonio de Mendoza, decided that the capital of the province of Michoacán should be erected on a hill occupied by a Tarascan village, giving it the name of Valladolid, to honor the favorite Spanish city of King Charles V. The first to arrive were estate holders, who had settled in neighboring regions, friars and some Indians. Morelia obtained the title of city and a coat of arms in 1546, the year in which the political offices and ecclesiastical administration were established under the control of **Vasco de Quiroga** *(see p 160)*. The evangelization of the region was completed by the Augustinians in the second half of the 16C.
Agriculture and livestock raising expanded rapidly during the colonial period, due to the quality of the soil and climate.
The 19C brought important changes to the political life of the city. Morelia became a main stage for the struggle for independence from Spain. Valladolid changed its name to Morelia in 1828 by a decree of Congress, in honor of the renowned leader, José María Morelos y Pavón *(see p 30)* who was born there in 1765. The Revolutionary period was intense and the various factions fought vigorously throughout the territory, even though during the regime of Porfirio Díaz, the city continued to progress. With the victory of the Mexican Revolution, administrations of various political tendencies succeeded one another, all of them trying to solve the economic and social problems of the Mexican people. Among these national rulers, the prominent figure was Lázaro Cárdenas *(see p 33)*, a brilliant military man born in Jiquilpan *(p 225)*, whose political achievements were instrumental in the creation of modern Mexico.

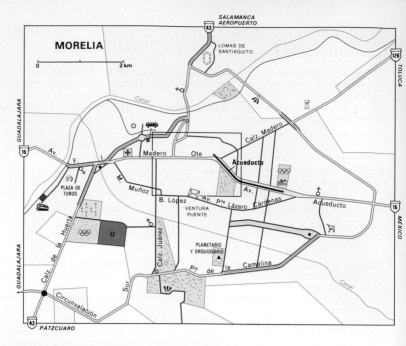

★★CENTER OF THE CITY *time: 2 days*

★★★Cathedral and Surroundings *time: 1 day*

★★Cathedral. – The construction of Morelia's cathedral was begun in 1660 according to a design by Vicente Barroso de la Escayola and was only finished in 1744. Built in a simple baroque style, the ensemble is graced with stately proportions that lend a solid appearance to the construction.

Facade. – The cathedral facade is composed of three portals in the manner of a triptych, each one corresponding to an interior nave of the church. They are flanked by high towers 62 m – 203 ft, which contribute unity and verticality to the ensemble. The rigorous style makes frequent use of panels with moldings and pilasters. The profusion of valances causes a play of chiaroscuro, which appears as a formal decorative element in other Morelia monuments. In the three portals, the vertical sense dominates, and the reliefs depicting themes from the Life of Christ stand out: at the center, *The Transfiguration (La Transfiguración)*; to the left, *The Adoration of the Shepherds (La Adoración de los Pastores)*; and to the right, *The Adoration of the Magi (La Adoración de los Reyes Magos)*.

⊙ **Interior.** – The **doors★** of the cathedral are covered with leather tooled in the Cordovan style. On either side of the entrance, there are chapels, the interior arches of which support the towers' weight with an impressive display of architectural mastery. The church's interior, consisting of a central nave flanked on each side by an aisle, is enlivened by unusual light effects created from the profusion of elliptical windows in the nave. The decoration is neoclassical and among its treasures are the German **organ,** installed in 1905, and the extra-ordinary 18C wrought-silver **manifestador.** This is a temple-shaped holder where the Holy Sacrament is displayed to the faithful, on the free-standing high altar – a reminder of the old baroque riches that adorned this church in its era of splendor.

⊙ **Baptistry** (Baptisterio). – On the left side of the cathedral, next to the portal devoted to the Virgin of Guadalupe, lies the baptistry. During religious ceremonies, the unique wrought-silver **font★**, made in the 17C by an anonymous artist, is displayed there. The patriots José María Morelos y Pavón and Agustín de Iturbide *(see p 30)* were christened at this font.

Government Palace (Palacio de Gobierno). – **Tridentine Seminary** (Exseminario Tridentino). This former seminary, which dates back to the 18C, has educated distinguished heroes of the War of Independence, such as José María Morelos, Ignacio López Rayón and Agustín de Iturbide.

Facade. – This architecturally balanced and symmetrical structure stands at the corner of the street. The main portal is aligned with the second level balcony, and ends in a great frontispiece with a curved and stepped ornamental edging, containing a bell – the replica of the one at Dolores *(p 80)*.

Expression is added to this massive architecture by the gargoyles and pinnacles that finish off the upper level. The delightful Oriental-style towers that top the corners of the structure also contribute to this effect.

Interior. – The interior contains a series of three patios, which should be noted for their arcades adorned with intricately carved moldings. On the walls of the second floor there are murals illustrating aspects of the history of Michoacán and of Independent Mexico. The handsome staircase leading to the second floor divides, without a landing, into curved steps that terminates beneath a cupola.

Plaza de Armas. – This square is also called Martyrs' Square (Plaza de los Mártires), because the pro-Independence leaders, José Guadalupe Salto (1812) and Mariano Matamoros (1814), were shot there, the latter in the portal facing the square that now carries his name.

In the center of the well-shaded garden, a lovely French-style bandstand, erected on a stone foundation, displays its iron structure. The plaza is bordered by sober arcades that convey a peaceful atmosphere.

Palace of Justice (Palacio de Justicia) (J). – The site where this building stands had previously been the locale for the town meeting house (Casas de Cabildo). After Mexico gained its independence, it housed first the city hall, then the Government Palace and, later, a school. In 1883 the present building was reconstructed by the engineer Woddon de Sorinne, who gave it a new facade while maintaining the original interior.

Facade. – The style of the facade is a combination of neoclassical and Art Nouveau decorative elements. Specifically, it meshes mixed-style arches with handsome *estípites* on the first level and semicircular balcony windows with cast-iron banisters on the second.

Interior. – There are strong baroque elements in the arcades of the main patio, where the corner columns have been eliminated. The elegant staircase leading to the second floor is aligned with the entrance and finishes in a double ramp with a banister, under a double arch without a column.

★ **Michoacán Museum (Museo Michoacano).** – Constructed in the 18C, this prominent building has been used as the residence of members of the Morelia social elite. In the last third of that century, the second floor was added, and during the 19C, the upper finials were installed. Although the building is not on the main square, its architectural style blends effectively with its urban surroundings, particularly the second-floor corner balcony. On the facade, as well as on the side section of the ensemble, a very forceful ornamental style predominates. There are fine moldings on doors and windows, while those of the cornices and eaves are more robust so as to support the gargoyles and finials.

Interior. – A massive door of joined wood leads to the lovely vestibule, where an imposing arch with moldings and a lantern as its keystone frames an iron grille. The approach to the main patio reveals exceptional arcades with austere columns; at the rear, aligned with the entrance, lies the stairway to the second floor, which starts from

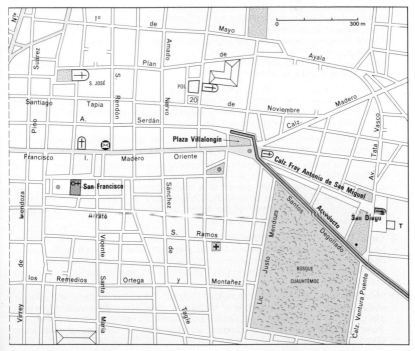

a double arch devoid of a central support, with a sculpture of Saint Anthony (San Antonio) held up by a winged cherub forming the keystone. The stairway ends on the second level in a double ramp with handsome banisters. There are two more inner patios, similar in style.

Museum (Museo). – Its collections are displayed in six rooms and present an overview of ecological and archeological aspects, as well as the history of the Michoacán territory from colonial to modern times.

San Nicolás de Hidalgo School (Colegio de San Nicolás de Hidalgo) **(A)**. – Founded originally by Vasco de Quiroga (1540), it was given the name of San Nicolás Obispo, or bishop. When the ecclesiastical power was moved to Valladolid in 1580, it was joined with the Franciscan school of San Miguel. The priest **Miguel Hidalgo y Costilla** *(see p 30)* was the school's principal in 1780, a period in which school reached great artistic and scientific heights.
Despite numerous reconstructions, its architectural harmony with the rest of the city has been preserved.

Clavijero Palace (Palacio Clavijero) **(B)**. – **Jesuit Church and School** (Extemplo y Colegio de la Compañía de Jesús). Built in the late 16C and early 17C, this monumental architectural complex bears the name of one of the most brilliant teachers of the Jesuit order.

Church (Templo). – The church has a simple facade, framed by modest towers, that is surmounted by a triangular pediment decorated with graceful curvilinear forms. Its sober architecture is highlighted by a profusion of moldings and panelled in pilasters and cornices.
The building houses the state public library (Biblioteca Pública del Estado), which conserves a valuable collection of books.

Facade. – Forming an angle with the church, the facade is baroque in style with beautiful moldings and flutings.

Interior. – The principal patio is bordered by great arcades of simple and forceful proportions, which become, on the second floor, elegant windows aligned with the arches and flanked by pilasters that strengthen the vertical lines. To the left of the entrance, the enormous stairway to the second floor rises from a shell-shaped arch and ends in a double ramp with a beautifully molded triple arch. The stairwell is covered by an imposing cupola that has a spherical crowning with eight oval windows.

Church and Convent of the Roses (Templo y Exconvento de las Rosas) **(D)**. – This was the first convent for Domincan nuns in Morelia, founded in 1590. In the 18C, the convent was in such a state of decay that it was decided to build a new one on the main boulevard of the city, to which the nuns moved in 1738. A large painting in the Regional Museum of Michoacán (Museo Regional Michoacano) depicts this event. The School of Santa Rosa María was established here in 1743 in order to shelter and educate poor children. It was repaired in 1757, when its portal was constructed, and dedicated to Saint Rose of Lima (Santa Rosa de Lima).

★ **Facade.** – A sloping little street leads to the magnificent entrance of this church. It is the best architectural example in Morelia of the sober baroque style. There is a double portal, connected by a solid buttress as though it were a pilaster. In the frieze there are outstanding reliefs of the Holy Family and Saint Rose of Lima (Santa Rosa de Lima) between two friars; in the finials, to the left, San Firmín and Saint Francis Xavier (San Francisco Javier), and to the right, Saint Martin (San Martín) and Saint Teresa of Jesus (Santa Teresa de Jesús). The gargoyles are shaped like crocodiles, reminiscent of medieval architecture.
To the left of the facade, stands the small tower of the former convent, which contrasts with the rest of the ensemble.

Interior. – The church has a single nave and has preserved the lower choir grille. In the chancel there are three altarpieces of gilded wood in the Churrigueresque baroque style. Among them, the high altarpiece is outstanding. It resembles a rich filigree with diminutive angels decorating the *estípites*.

Convent (Exconvento). – *Access through the door to the right of the church facade.* Note the handsome arcade that finishes the upper part of the cloister.

Interior. – The interior has only one level with strong columns that increase the garden's contemplative atmosphere. To the rear there is another small patio containing the convent wash basins, finely carved in a demonstration of baroque fantasy and inventiveness. The cloister is now the Conservatory of Music (Conservatorio de Música) and the headquarters of the famed choral group, the Young Singers of Morelia (Los Niños Cantores de Morelia).

⊘ **State Museum** (Museo del Estado) **(M¹)**. – The first room of this 18C stone mansion houses the complete collection of a Morelia **pharmacy★** founded in 1868. In the section on archeology, there are admirable jewels by Tarascan master craftsmen made of rock crystal, turquoise and other semi-precious stones, as well as jewels of gold and obsidian.

★★ **Ethnological Section** (Sección de Etnología). – Upper Floor. The ecologic and cultural characteristics of the eight regions of Michoacán state, where the *mestizos* live with groups of Purépecha, Mazahua, Otomí and Matlatzinc Indians, are exhibited in a didactic fashion by means of models, clothing and the products of their main economic activities.

Cultural Center (Casa de la Cultura) and Surroundings *time: 1/2 day*

⊘ **Cultural Center.** – **Carmelite Convent** (Exconvento del Carmen). The construction of the convent began at the end of the 16C and continued during the 17C and 18C. The building is huge, occupying almost a complete block, and preserves remnants of its architectural grandeur. It has been put to varied uses and has undergone frequent restorations that have substantially altered the balance of its original spaces. Noteworthy are the broad main patio and, before the stairs to the second floor, the space to the right – formerly the convent refectory – that contains a valuable pulpit attached to the wall with a wooden support dating back to the 16C. On the rear wall's tympanum a beautiful fresco representing the Holy Family can be found. The monumental staircase leading to the second floor has three flights covered by cloister vaulting, and connects with passageways lined with the former cells now used as offices.

⊘ **Museum of Colonial Art** (Museo de Arte Colonial) (M²). – This museum is housed in a modest 18C building, in which a diminutive and unusual patio is to be noted. In the five rooms around this patio, going from right to left, there is an extraordinary collection of Christs made of corn and sugarcane paste (16-19C), a variety of old books and some fine anonymous paintings. In the center of the courtyard there is a painting by the renowned Oaxaca artist, Miguel Cabrera *(p 40)* dedicated to Juan Palafox y Mendoza, and two other expressive paintings by the same artist are displayed in one of the rooms: an *Ecce Homo* and a *Saint Joseph with Child (San José con el Niño)*.

Saint Francis' Church and Convent (Templo y Exconvento de San Francisco). – The foundation of this convent (1525-1536) preceded that of Morelia itself. Fray Juan de San Miguel began the construction of the cloister; the church was finished in 1610 and restored in 1948.

Facade. – Though modest and austere, the facade has strong Plateresque overtones, expressed in the slendor columns that flank the arch and the choir window, as well as in the carved decorations on the entrance arch and the left side facade.

Convent (Exconvento). – This structure stands elegantly to the right of the church in a noble arcade with five semicircular arches that shelter the gate house. The columns between the arches are fluted and finish in a cornice that supports the second floor, where the ogee arches of the small cell windows are lined up with the arches of the first floor.

Cloister. – The large powerful buttresses around the courtyard resemble a fortress that harmoniously combines the high cloister arches with the small ones on the second floor. In the passageways, the ceilings have vaults with lunettes, separated in sections by the arches. Today the cloister houses the handicraft museum and has the most extensive **collection**★ of the state's production, as well as representative samples from other states of the Republic.

Plaza Villalongín and Surroundings *time: 1/2 day*

Plaza Villalongín. – This pleasantly shaded square owes its name to the pro-Independence leader, Manuel Villalongín. It blends well with its surroundings, particularly with the famous **Fountain of Tarascan Women** (Fuente de las Tarascas) – a symbol of Michoacán tradition and sensitivity.

Aqueduct (Acueducto). – This massive structure borders part of Plaza Villalongín, then continues with its 253 arches over 1 700 m – 5 577 ft, along the Cuauhtémos Woods (Bosque Cuauhtémos) ending in the city reservoir.

★ **Calzada Fray Antonio de San Miguel.** – This ancient route, in front of the Fountain of Tarascan Women, has preserved its old cobblestones and thick, bench-lined walls on either side. The residences that appear amidst the shadows and foliage of robust trees, have retained a distinctly provincial air. It would hardly be surprising to find an elegant ancient carriage standing at their gates.

San Diego Church (Templo de San Diego). – This church has a simple baroque facade from the second half of the 18C.

★ **Interior.** – The interior is exquisitely decorated in fired and colored clay with plant and geometric motifs that recall the parish church of Tlalpujahua (Parroquia de Tlalpujahua) *(p 206)*.
To the south of the city, up a winding road, is situated the district of Santa María de Guido. From the top of the hill, there is a breathtaking **view**★ of Morelia.

EXCURSIONS

Quiroga and Tzintzuntzan. – *46 km – 28.6 miles to the west on highway n° 15. Description p 211.*

★★ **Cuitzeo and Yuriria Monasteries** (Conventos de Cuitzeo y Yuriria). – *59 km – 36.7 miles to the north on highway n° 43. Description p 80 and p 222.*

For telephone numbers of Mexican tourist offices in your country and in major Mexican cities see pp 226-231.

In the heart of a broad valley, closed by a densely forested mountain range, lies this state capital. Oaxaca preserves its colonial charms with prominent baroque monuments and examples of aristocratic architecture. The numerous tourists and bustling youth of the city contrast with the deep-rooted Indian presence.

A provincial atmosphere permeates its small plazas and gardens. The ample arcades of the main plaza bask in the shadows of the ancient dove-filled trees. Many of Oaxaca's lovely churches have had to be reconstructed time and again on account of the frequent earthquakes in the region.

Around the city there are significant archeological sites; some reveal their secrets while others remain hidden. In the nearby towns, local traditions have been preserved, as can be seen, for example, in the original and colorful Oaxacan handicrafts.

★ **Guelaguetza.** – This was originally a ceremony that brought together the Zapotec population in times of need.

At present this ancient tradition, which has remained in the spirit of the people despite the passing of time, has become a brilliant high-colored festival (p 45), in which the inhabitants of the seven ethnic regions of the state congregate in their traditional costumes.

HISTORICAL NOTES

The pre-Hispanic past of Oaxaca dates from the 7C BC to the 16C AD. During this long period a large number of Indian settlements – each with a distinct ethnic identity – have flourished there. Mixtecs and Zapotecs were the salient groups, having developed an advanced culture that found expression in such magnificent cities as Monte Albán and Mitla, as well as in the unusual architectural solemnity of Yagul, Dianzú and Lambityeco.

In the second half of the 15C, during their thrust to expand, the Aztecs established a garrison in the valley where the city now stands, in an effort to collect the tributes imposed on some neighboring towns. In 1521 this military post was taken over by the Spaniards who founded the Villa de Antequera on the site. Under colonial control, the military expansion advanced to the rest of the Indian communities, with the religious activity of the Dominican friars contributing to this endeavor.

The pro-Independence movement gained great momentum in Oaxaca, and in the following years the state became a breeding ground for ideas, feats and men of great courage, who played most important roles in consolidating the Republic. One of these was **Benito Juárez** (see p 30), born in an isolated mountain region, who became state governor and president of the Republic. Other personalities from the region were Porfirio Díaz (p 31) and, in the literary world, José Vasconcelos (p 44).

In 1910, during Madero's times, Oaxaca joined the struggle against the tyrannical regime of Porfirio Díaz and in favor of the revolutionary ideals. When these triumphed, the new regimes gradually managed to consolidate and pacify the Republic.

Today Oaxaca still reverberates with greatness through its culture and its arts, under the shadow of its splendid archeological past, and its bewitching colonial baroque monuments.

★★ ZÓCALO AND SURROUNDINGS time: 1 day – Plan p 149

Zócalo. – This beautiful square is lined by unassuming buildings that blend with its serene atmosphere.

During the afternoon, on the elegant French-style bandstand at the center of the square, the state band plays pleasant melodies for all to enjoy.

⊙ **Cathedral.** – Set in front of a small square that accentuates its volume, this squat construction (17-18C) has massive proportions that give an impression of great solidity.

Facade. – The facade rises in three harmonious sections. The pale green stone is adorned with capricious ornamental forms in sculptures and reliefs. The central section has a high relief of the Virgin of the Assumption, to whom the church was dedicated, crowned by the Holy Trinity. This exquisite example of the stonecarver's art, worthy of a goldsmith is a replica of a painting by the Italian artist, Titian (1477-1570).

Interior. – It was designed as a spacious basilica with five naves. On either side of the threshold, hang very large paintings: to the left is *Saint Christopher (San Cristóbal)*, dated 1726; and to the right, *The Seven Archangels in Glory (Los Siete Arcángeles en Gloria)*, both works painted by Marcial de Santaella. In the rear of the central nave, an austere neoclassical altar (19C) made of bronze by the Italian sculptor, Tadollini, can be admired.

Government Palace (Palacio de Gobierno) (PG). – This palace is a large neoclassical construction (19C) that blends well with the other buildings around the square. The building encloses three large courtyards. The central one displays a modern mural narrating the history of the state of Oaxaca.

Jesuit Church (Iglesia de la Compañía de Jesús). – The Jesuit order was the second to arrive in Oaxaca in the 16C. They built a school, no longer used for religious purposes, adjoining the church. The church facade has handsome balustraded columns in the Plateresque style, which stand out discreetly from the ensemble, in contrast with the 17C pilasters on the second floor.

Church of Saint John of God (Iglesia de San Juan de Dios). – This modest construction, which dates back to the early 16C, was the first church built in Oaxaca. The church served as a provisional cathedral and See of the Bishopric until 1536. Inside, to the left there are two stone medallions built into the wall; one shows the Zapotec arms encircling the head of Princess Donají; and the other has religious symbols. On the ceiling of the nave are oval portraits of the bishops that served in the Diocese of Oaxaca.

Benito Juárez Market (Mercado Benito Juárez). – This gigantic market represents an exciting polychromy of fruits and vegetables, amid the vendors' cries and the bustle of the crowds. The large variety of dishes and typical delicacies, including many types of **moles** sold on the premises, are a temptation to the palate. Along the aisles, **typical dresses** from different regions of the state are on sale, together with textiles, ceramics, leathergoods, hides and myriad forms of handicrafts.

CHURCH OF SANTO DOMINGO
AND SURROUNDINGS *time: 1 day*

Santo Domingo Monastery (Iglesia y Exconvento de Santo Domingo). – This architectural complex stands on a broad and handsome plaza, which gives it a refined air. The enormous construction, carried out from the end of the 16C to the beginning of the 17C, displays a very simple balance, combining the vertical lines of the church's baroque facade with the horizontal profile of the stately Renaissance-style complex.

Church Interior. – The dazzling abundance of late 17C **plasterwork**★★ is overwhelming. One of the most outstanding pieces is the genealogical tree of the Guzmán family in the lower part of the choir, with its impressive profusion of images. It was restored in the 19C.
Also striking is the **main altarpiece,** a lovely replica of the original, replaced in 1959. The present altarpiece was inspired by one from the church of Yanhuitlán, Oaxaca. It is

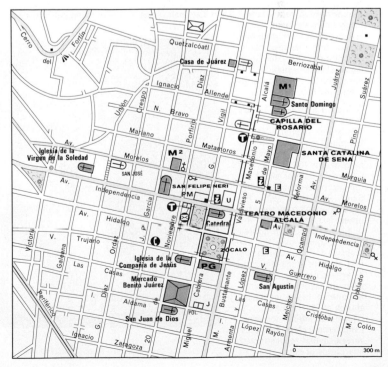

composed of three parts and is adorned with pierced Solomonic columns. Except for two contemporary pieces, the statues and paintings are all from the 17C or 18C.

★★ **Rosary Chapel** (Capilla del Rosario). – Located on the right side of the church, this chapel displays the same ornamental plasterwork as the main church. It possesses images of popular devotion, and prominent among them is the Virgin of the Rosary in the cupola, surrounded by the Apostles – all the figures executed in rounded volumes and beautiful colors.

Monastery (Exconvento de Santo Domingo). – Inside this relatively plain building, valuable paintings are preserved on the cloister walls. However, the staircase adorned with plasterwork is the most impressive feature. Today the building houses the **Regional State Museum** (Museo Regional del Estado) (**M¹**), with notable collections of archeological objects of the Zapotec and Mixtec cul-

(Photo BOTTIN/Paris)

Oaxaca. Church of Santo Domingo

tures, as well as religious sculptures from the colonial period, and a room dedicated to the ethnography of the Oaxaca region. In room II of the upper cloister there is an extraordinary **collection**★★ of artifacts found in Tomb 7 of Monte Albán, with finely crafted objects in gold, shell, alabaster, obsidian and rock crystal.

⊘ **Juárez House (Casa de Juárez).** – This is a small museum of domestic objects, documents and photographs from the house where Benito Juárez *(p 30)* lived during his youth.

★★ **Convent of Saint Catherine of Siena (Exconvento de Santa Catalina de Sena).** – Hotel **Presidente.** This structure was built in the 16C to house the nuns of the Conceptionist order. Its excellent adaptation to its present function as a hotel has preserved some original features of the convent architecture. To the rear of the building, in one of its gardens, is found a unique construction, consisting of beautiful **laundry basins**★★ grouped under a cupola around a central fountain.

★★ **Macedonio Alcalá Theater (Teatro Macedonio Alcalá).** – This building, initially a casino, today bears the name of the famous composer and musician from Oaxaca. Its architecture reflects the neoclassical style popular in 19C Paris. The theater was inaugurated in 1909.

Saint Augustine's Church (Iglesia de San Agustín). – This handsome church, with a baroque facade was built at the end of the 17C and beginning of the 18C. Inside, the admirable central **relief**★ of the second section, showing Saint Augustine with his cape extended to protect his order, is remarkable. In the relief, the robes of the figures seem to move over the expressive faces placed at the feet of Saint Augustine. For its artistic excellence and realism, this work rivals a similar one in the Augustinian church of Mexico City.

The church interior follows a Latin cross plan and conserves several reconstructed altarpieces of note.

(Photo GIRAUDON/Paris)

Oaxaca. Gold pectoral – Regional State Museum

SAINT PHILIP NERI CHURCH (IGLESIA DE SAN FELIPE NERI) AND SURROUNDINGS

time: 1/2 day – Plan p 149

★ **Saint Philip Neri Church.** – Its lovely facade (18C) recalls the Plateresque style with its elegant balustraded columns that give the impression of a stone altarpiece. A prominent detail is the yellow stone carving of Saint Philip Neri in a magnificent molded frame that stands out against the green stone of the ensemble.

Interior. – It contains a rich group of nine **altarpieces** – the most striking in the city – typical of the 18C Mexican Churrigueresque style, which fit admirably into the church space. Worth mentioning are the excellent carved sculptures on the main altarpiece and the popular paintings of religious images in the other altarpieces, by Agustín Santaella and José de Páez (18C).

⊙ **Mexican Pre-Hispanic Art Museum – Rufino Tamayo (Museo de Arte Prehispánico de México Rufino Tamayo) (M²).** – This museum, housed in a simple 17C building, has a select collection of more than one thousand pre-Hispanic objects, donated by the famous painter Rufino Tamayo *(see p 41)*. In its five rooms are works by the Maya, Zapotec, Mixtec, Teotihuacán, Toltec, Aztec, Olmec, Totonac and Huastec cultures, as well as objects from Michoacán, Jalisco, Colima and Nayarit. The exhibit follows a chronological order and emphasizes the expressive character of the Indians' artwork.

Church of the Virgin of Solitude (Iglesia de la Virgen de la Soledad). – In this 17C church, the patroness of the city, the Virgin of Solitude, is worshipped. It was connected to a convent for Capuchin nuns that was abandoned in the 19C.

★ **Facade.** – The facade of this church is another leading example of Mexican baroque. Its unusual architectural design evokes a large screen, richly ornamented in a combination of decorative styles, with columns, niches and very realistic sculptures. Most beautiful is the central relief of the Virgin of Solitude in prayer, framed in rich molding. The statue's unaffected attitude is extremely moving.

EXCURSIONS

Tlalixtac de Cabrera. – *7 km – 4.3 miles. Go east from Oaxaca on highway n° 190 towards the Isthmus and after 5 km – 3.1 miles, turn left and continue for 2 km – 1.2 miles.*
This unassuming village has a small church founded by the Dominicans in the 16C, which was dedicated to the Archangel Michael. Inside, on the left side of the chancel, there is an altar to the Virgen of Solitude, executed in a sober baroque style.
The village bears the name of one of the most important and prolific painters of New Spain: **Miguel Cabrera** *(see p 40)*, who was born there in 1695 and whose artistic talent flourished in the 18C.

★ **Monastery of Cuilapan de Guerrero (Exconvento).** – *9 km – 5.6 miles south on the highway to Xoxocotlán.*
⊙ This monastery, begun during the second half of the 16C, was an ambitious and impressive project. It preserves the majesty of its enormous **open-air chapel,** with three naves and large open arches on the side walls. Its grandiose interior, no longer roofed, reveals lines of columns running parallel to the walls. To the right of the chapel, connected to the modest present-day church, stand the silent remains of the enormous unfinished church. These still show the bases of the powerful Gothic-style ribs for what was to be the dome, in a colossal display of lines carved in stone.

Interior. – To the rear of the very large atrium, the gate house arches are visible. Inside, the walls of the cloister retain some traces of painting; its moderate proportions contrast with the exterior of the complex. Especially attractive are the kitchen with its enormous hearth, the refectory, and, on the upper floor, the small cell that served as a prison for General Vicente Guerrero *(see p 00)* before he was shot behind the complex. For this reason, the former convent bears this illustrious soldier's name.

San Andrés Huayapan. – *9 km – 5.6 miles. Head east from Oaxaca on highway n° 190 towards the isthmus and at 3 km – 1.9 miles, turn left on highway n° 175 towards Tuxtepec, continue 4 km – 2.5 miles and turn left 2 km – 1.2 miles on a stretch of unpaved road following the sign: Parque Brígida García.*
This is a small town with a little parish church dedicated to San Andrés. The church's interior still has a magnificent baroque altarpiece in the chancel; its beautiful Solomonic columns have elegant openwork resembling rich filigree. It also possesses some fine paintings.

★★★ **Monte Albán Archeological Site.** – *10 km – 6.2 miles to the southwest. Description p 138.*

San Bartolo Coyotepec. – *10 km – 6.2 miles south on highway n° 175 towards Puerto Angel.*
Coyotepec means "hill of the coyote". The town is famous for its rich production of **black clay** handicrafts. The beautiful and varied shapes, which are more ornamental than utilitarian, are in great demand abroad.

⊙ **Zaachila Archeological Site.** – *14 km – 8.7 miles to the southwest on the highway to Xoxocotlán. To the right of the church, a modern stairway takes you up to the small path leading to the site.*
This site was one of the last capitals of the Zapotecs (12C AD); the ruins consist of a small section of the patio, surrounded by vestiges of rooms. During excavations two magnificent tombs were discovered. They were particularly significant for their rich

adornments and inner lintels. In one of them, figures of persons and animals made of stucco were found, among which a man with a skull head and a priest with a serpent mask and a turtle shell covering his body are most striking. In these same tombs simple gold and jade objects were also found.

San Pedro Apóstol Etla. – *16 km – 9.9 miles. Go northwest from Oaxaca on highway nº 190 towards Huajuapan de León and after 15 km – 9.3 miles, turn left, 1 km – 0.6 miles on a paved road.*
The name Etla means "a fertile and productive place" in Náhautl and Zapotec. For this reason, the Etla Valley was given to Hernán Cortés, who introduced wheat cultivation and set up flour mills. The town has a church built in the 16C and a monastery constructed in the following century. The surprisingly spacious church has enormous arches on the right side of the nave, leading to the cloister. There it can be noted that the building's walls are more than 2 m – 6.6 ft thick. The cloister is simple and welcoming, with large buttresses inside. It also has some traces of mural paintings, and in the corridors there are fine ornamented sculptures. In the rear, the structure is embellished with simply landscaped gardens.

★★**Mitla Archeological Site.** – *41 km – 25.5 miles to the southeast on highway nº 190. Description p 136.*

★**Monastery of Yanhuitlán** (Exconvento). – *110 km – 68.4 miles to the northwest on*
⊘ *highway nº 190 towards Huajuapan de León.*
Built in the 16C on top of an enormous ceremonial platform, both the church and the monastery of Yanhuitlán gained monumental proportions. On this height, an imposing yet simple facade was erected, featuring a lovely relief in the center with the Virgin of the Rosary. The church's side portal reveals a distinct Gothic influence, with balustraded columns and a finial in a mullioned window crowned by a rosette.

Cloister. – To the right of the church, lies the simple cloister. In the entrance room, and in some other parts of the interior, there is a small exhibit of religious sculptures, maps and photographs of different churches and monastic complexes of the region.
Lovely samples of stone carving can be seen in the corridor niches, in the lintels of the cells and in the fine banister of the staircase. On the wall of the stairwell, there is a colossal painting representing Saint Christopher (San Cristóbal). Through the cell windows, the monastery's past seems to return to the old ruin.

★★**Teposcolula.** – *135 km – 83.9 miles. Go northwest from Oaxaca on highway nº 190 towards Huajuapan de León and at 123 km – 76.4 miles, turn left, 12 km – 7.5 miles on highway nº 125 towards Tlaxiaco and Pinotepa.*
⊘ The **open-air chapel**★ *(see p 39)* in the atrium is a unique monument with colossal dimensions. Its Renaissance style contrasts with the great artistic vigor apparent in its naves, that open to the atrium through a sturdy arcade. The remains of the dome synthesize the force of its great Gothic star, the ribbing of which runs down into powerful fluted columns that, in their turn, become two handsome buttresses to carry the weight of the structure.
The church, to the right of the chapel, dates back to the 17C, and its facade is distinctly stark. To the church's right is the entrance to the cloister; before entering, a visit should be made to the small basilica plan chapel with an interesting interior architecture of thick columns that carry the vaults. The one-story cloister is also simple in design, and in its corridors, there are paintings on exhibit.

ORIZABA Veracruz ◆◆◆◆◆

Map of Principal Sights p 5

Populated in ancient times by the **Totonacs** *(see p 37),* Orizaba paid tribute to the Aztecs in the 15C. The original name of the region was Ahuilizapan, a term that means "in the pleasant water", alluding to the numerous springs that originated in filtrations and melting snows of the Citlaltépetl volcano, or Pico de Orizaba, that still provide water for the region. Over the centuries, the term has been distorted until acquiring its present form. The winding descent from the Sierra Madre Oriental offers a great variety of vegetation. When the dense fog lifts, the city appears, spread out over the foothills. Its pleasant warm climate favors the thriving coffee and sugar plantations. The first railway lines intensified the trading activities of the city.

SIGHTS

City Hall (Palacio Municipal). – *Francisco I. Madero and Av. 4 Poniente.*
This building stands out because of its peculiar French-style architecture; the structure was made of wrought iron forged and laminated in Belgium and transported in sections to the city. It was inaugurated in 1914.

Carmelite Church (Templo del Carmen). – *Av. Sur 9 and Oriente 4.* This church was built in the 18C and is characterized by a baroque stone facade and painted plasterwork. The right side door is flanked by *estípites* finely carved in stone with busts of monks and molded jambs with stylized feline heads.

Concord Church (Templo de la Concordia). – *Av. Oriente 4 and Sur 23.* The Churrigueresque facade of this 18C church was worked in stucco. The central relief of the second section shows the Virgin of Guadalupe carved in stone. On the inside, the altar has a painting of this Virgin that is a replica of an 18C work by Nicolás Rodríguez Juárez.

EXCURSION

Córdoba. – *22 km – 13.7 miles to the east on highway nº150 D.*
On the drive to this city, the highway offers awesome views of the Metlac Ravine, in particular when crossing the bridge, where the vegetation is rich and many-hued. Córdoba was founded at the beginning of the 17C by authorization of Viceroy Diego Fernández de Córdoba. The early inhabitants gave it a chessboard design of broad, rectilinear streets around a large central square.

Although provincial in atmosphere, this city is a sugar and coffee production center of utmost importance for the state's economy. Within the city, the shaded square and the main arcade – which in 1687 were part of the house, and later hotel, of Captain José Manuel Zevallos – are to be noted. In August of 1821, the Act of Mexican Independence was signed in this house by General Agustín de Iturbide and the Spanish Viceroy, Juan O'Donojú. In 1914 this same house served as barracks for the Constitutional Army, led by General Venustiano Carranza *(see p 33).*

PACHUCA Hidalgo   ◆◆◆◆

Map of Principal Sights p 6

Amidst a varied topography of mountains and deserts stands this once wealthy mining city, where neoclassical and modern styles of architecture predominate. A stroll along its narrow, winding cobble and paving stone streets will lead to picturesque little plazas, gardens and parks. The town offers the visitor pre-Hispanic style dishes and drinks, such as ant eggs *(escamoles),* spicy meat or chicken wrapped in maguey leaves *(mixiotes),* a fermented cactus drink *(pulque),* as well as the traditional *pastes* brought by the English miners in the 19C. In its vicinity, there are magnificent ecclesiastical buildings of the 16C, which give an idea of the arduous task of evangelization carried out by the Augustinians and Franciscans in the region. In this zone is found 25% of the Indian population of the country.

Mining. – The rich mines of this region have been exploited since pre-Hispanic times. During the colonial period, mining expanded greatly, owing to the new system of amalgamation, discovered by Bartolomé de Medina. In the 18C, this industry reached its climax. Pedro Romero de Terreros, First Count of Regla promoted mining in Pachuca as well as in other cities. He owned the most important mines in New Spain and was a great benefactor. Today the mines belong to state corporations and continue producing silver. Their offices are located in the **Royal Treasury** (Cajas Reales).

CENTER OF THE CITY *time: 1/2 day*

Hidalgo Cultural Center (Centro Cultural Hidalgo). – Saint Francis Monastery (Exconvento de San Francisco). *Arista 200.* This center operates in a large colonial building, completely remodeled, which houses interesting exhibition halls, auditoriums, a library, the Hidalgo Fine Arts Institute (Instituto Hidalguense de Bellas Artes) and the main offices of the National Institute for Anthropology and History (Instituto Nacional de Antropología e Historia). This enormous architectural group is surrounded by graceful gardens and plazas in the former atrium and orchard.

Saint Francis' Church (Templo de San Francisco). – In the sacristy of this church, stands a wash basin carved from a single block of volcanic rock; and, in the ante-sacristy, another enormous wash basin is to be found. Its original design includes two carved stones and six pretty Talavera tiles from Puebla.

Our Lady of the Light Chapel (Capilla de Nuestra Señora de la Luz). – *Behind the church.* This chapel is an example of the sober baroque style. It includes a small retiring patio that serves as an atrium. Inside are found the four large oil paintings that belonged to the original **Stations of the Cross** in Saint Francis' Church, and the 18C Churrigueresque **altarpiece** dedicated to Our Lady of the Light. At the center of this altarpiece is a canvas of the Virgin, surrounded by valuable ornamented sculptures of Franciscan saints carved in wood.

Photography Museum (Museo de Fotografía). – A selection of the finest photographs in the museum's holdings are on exhibit. The core of the **photographic archive★★★** was the Casasola collection, one of the richest photography collections covering the Revolutionary era in Mexico. Today the collection is the largest photographic archive in Latin America. The archive's reproduction department is open to the public.

Regional Historical Museum (Museo Histórico Regional). – This building, which previously housed a school for miners, has been converted into a museum that presents the history of the region from pre-Hispanic times to the present by means of objects, documents, photographs and models.

★ **Monumental Clock (Reloj Monumental). –** *Plaza Independencia.* In the center of the square stands this attractive tower 40 m – 131 ft high, adorned with very imposing sculptures that exalt Mexican nationalism. In the tower, different styles are blended, with the neoclassical predominating. The carillon of this clock is a replica of London's Big Ben. This work by the architect Tomás Cordes was inaugurated to celebrate the centennial of Independence and has become a symbol of the city.

Efrén Rebolledo Cultural Forum (Foro Cultural Efrén Rebolledo). – General Cravioto's House (Casa del General Cravioto). *Bravo nº8.* This lovely 19C mansion was built in a mixture of styles, with a predominant neoclassical flavor. The purpose of this forum is to promote the rich culture of Hidalgo state.

ADDITIONAL SIGHT

ⓥ **Rule House** (Casa Rule). – **Residence of Judicial Power** (Residencia del Poder Judicial). *Plaza de la Veracruz*. This elegant residence in the French style was built during the regime of Porfirio Díaz. The house belonged to a wealthy Englishman, Francisco Rule, and is an example of the sumptuous buildings constructed during the mining boom.

EXCURSIONS

★ **Huasca.** – *33 km – 20.5 miles to the northeast. Description p 93.*

★ **Epazoyucan; Tulancingo.** – *49 km – 30.4 miles. Estimate 3 hours. Go southeast from Pachuca on highway nº 130 toward Tulancingo and after 17 km – 10.6 miles, turn right for 3 km – 1.9 miles to reach Epazoyucan.*

★ **Epazoyucan.** – An impressive **monastery** of the fortress type, built by the Augustinians in
ⓥ the 16C, from which a pleasant view of the surrounding semi-arid plains can be admired. Up a flight of steps, lies the huge atrium, which forms a gracious ensemble with the *posas* or corner chapels, and the beautiful **facade** of **Saint Andrew's Church** (Templo de San Andrés), flanked by the open-air chapel.

Cloister (Exclaustro). – On the first floor, the cloister is decorated with capitals, carved with acanthus-like leaves. In the beamed passageways of the lower cloister are found the remarkable **mural paintings**★★★ of *Ecce Homo, Christ carrying the Cross (Cristo cargando la Cruz), The Crucifixion, The Descent from the Cross (El Descendimiento de la Cruz)* and *The Death of the Virgin (El Tránsito de la Virgen)*. Owing to their fine quality, these paintings are regarded as the most important 16C frescoes in America.

Return to highway nº 130 and continue 29 km – 18 miles to reach Tulancingo.

Tulancingo. – This is a provincial town set on the slopes of a hill and surrounded by a great industrial park.

Cathedral. – *Av. Manuel F. Soto*. In this very large structure, the monumental neoclassical facade is worthy of note, as are the altars within. In the 16C this was the church of the Franciscan monastery that was reconstructed by José Damián Ortiz de Castro at the end of the 18C. The gardens were converted into a pretty cobblestone plaza with large trees called the **Grove** (La Floresta) – an excellent vantage point from which to appreciate the cathedral.

Tepeapulco. – *52 km – 32.3 miles. Go southeast from Pachuca on the highway to Ciudad Sahagún and after 43 km – 26.7 miles, turn left and continue 9 km – 5.6 miles, to reach Tepeapulco.*

ⓥ **Saint Francis' Monastery** (Exconvento de San Francisco). – *Av. Hidalgo*. This is a 16C structure, where the famous Friar **Bernardino de Sahagún** began his work, *The General History of the Things of New Spain (La Historia de las Cosas de la Nueva España)*. The monastery was built on a pre-Hispanic temple and although it has been greatly modified, the church has retained its marvelous facade with popular ornamental figures, where the Indians' candor is clearly expressed. The **atrial cross,** decorated with symbols of the Passion and affixed to the facade is also to be noted; and, in the lower
ⓥ cloister, there is a small **exhibit room** with archeological objects.

Reservoirs (Cajas de Agua). – *Av. Hidalgo, unnumbered*. This picturesque 16C Franciscan structure marked the spot where the aqueduct that brought water to the town came to an end. The lion-shaped spouts have been carrying water to the pool with public wash basins for the last four centuries.

Actopan; Ixmiquilpan. – *76 km – 47.2 miles. Estimate 1/2 day. Go northwest from Pachuca on highway nº 85 towards Nuevo Laredo and after 36 km – 22.4 miles you will arrive at Actopan.*

Actopan. – This town, with cobblestone streets, has a large plaza surrounded by arcades; the main one leads to the atrium of the former monastery.

★ **Monastery of San Nicolás Tolentino** (Exconvento de San Nicolás Tolentino). – *Plaza Juárez*.
ⓥ This monumental 16C Augustinian complex – with the structure of a fort – harmoniously combines the Gothic style of the church's vaults and the lower cloister, the Mudejar lines of its high **tower,** the **facade's** rich Plateresque design and the Renaissance-style upper cloister.
The sacristy, next to the chancel, is connected by two depressed arches with the spacious **baptistery.** This area has a groined vault and walls decorated with frescoes; in the middle of this enclosure stands the monumental stone baptismal font, made of one solid block, the half-spherical wooden cover of which has a lovely little sculpture of Saint John the Baptist. In some of the convent cells there are paintings, sculptures and altar fragments of the period on display. The murals that decorate the convent are excellently preserved; the **frescoes**★★★ of the stairway are especially noteworthy for their beauty and quality. They represent in detail saints and leading figures of the Augustinian order; each one is identified by name and depicted studying inside his respective cell.

★ **Open-air Chapel** (Capilla Abierta). – This chapel, on the left side of the church, is one of the largest in New Spain. Its vault is decorated with appealing fresco-painted coffers, and its three walls present Biblical scenes, such as the Creation of Man and the Last Judgment, mixing European models with pre-Hispanic codices.

Continue on highway nº 85 and after 40 km – 24.9 miles you will arrive at Ixmiquilpan.

Ixmiquilpan. – It is a pleasant town with the characteristic uneventfulness of a provincial Mexican village.

Monastery of the Archangel Michael (Exconvento de San Miguel Arcángel). – *Plaza Juárez. On one side of the Plaza Principal.* This fortress-like architectural complex is similar to the monastery in Actopan, also built by Friar Andrés de Mata.
The enormous church with a Plateresque facade has a Moorish-style tower, separating the church from the portico. Both in the portico's ogival arches and in the cloisters, remnants of Gothic style can be observed.

Church Interior. – The ample baseboard, decorated with **frescoes** of mythological and war scenes, has a mixture of European and pre-Hispanic motifs. This work, done in vivid colors by Indian artists, is considered to be the last pre-Hispanic codex or the first Mexican mural painting. In the sacristy, a valuable series of frescoes on the life of Christ is preserved.

⊙ **Carmelite Church** (Iglesia del Carmen). – *Francisco Javier Mina, unnumbered.* This is a small church with a rather large atrium, built in the 18C with funds from wealthy miners of the region. Its **facade** is in the Churrigueresque style, as are the five **altarpieces** inside the church.

Puente de la Otra Banda. – This simple rubblework bridge, surrounded by beautiful old coniferous trees, was built over the Tula River in the middle of the 16C. It is believed to have been the first bridge in New Spain.

★★★ **Teotihuacán Archeological Site.** – *70 km – 43.5 miles to the south. Description p 193.*

★★ PACIFIC COAST

Map of Principal Sights p 5

This extensive region runs parallel to the Pacific Ocean from Bahía de Banderas on the northwest to Puerto Angel at the southeastern tip of Oaxaca, covering more than 1 500 km – 932 miles of abrupt mountains and coastal plains. Between the mountains, there are numerous valleys covered with luxuriant tropical vegetation and capricious broken rock formations – giving the impression that the mountains are sinking into the sea. In some places the irregular topography moves inland, giving way to the straight shoreline of gently sloping beaches with golden sands and palm trees. The proximity of the Sierra Madre has led to the formation of many short rivers that run down the mountains shaping on their way fertile valleys with exuberant growth. In this warm, humid climate, it is common to find tidelands, mangrove swamps and lagoons of fascinating charm resulting from their dense vegetation and the varied fauna.

★★★CENTRAL PACIFIC COAST

From Puerto Vallarta to Lázaro Cárdenas
721 km – 448 miles – 10 days – Follow highway nº 200

Steep seacoast with many sunny coves surrounded by high cliffs.

★★ **Puerto Vallarta.** – *Description p 172.*

Chamela; Barra de Navidad. – *212 km – 131.7 miles to the southeast of Puerto Vallarta.*
This is a journey that offers contrasting landscapes ranging from tropical forest to temperate woods. For the first 60 km – 37.3 miles the winding road climbs between mountains and ravines through the Tuito Sierra, to come down to the sea through a dazzling succession of beautiful small bays, surrounded by high cliffs bathed by the sea, such as **Cala Careyitos, El Tecuán, La Tenacatita** and **Melaque.** Lovely lagoons with warm quiet waters can also be found here.
Boat rides and a great variety of water sports are available in an exotic setting of coconut palms bordering smooth sandy beaches with gentle waves. *In most of these places there are tourist facilities.*

Manzanillo. – *64 km – 39.8 miles from Bära de Navidad. Description p 98.*

★ **Michoacán Coast** (Costa de Michoacán). – *326 km – 202.6 miles southeast of Manzanillo to Lázaro Cárdenas.*
The imposing presence of the Sierra de Coalcoman commonly called the Sierra Madre del Sur is felt in the spectacularly abrupt changes in altitude all the way down to the sea. Beginning in Doca de Apiza, the drive offers many views of the ocean and of places where thick jungle foliage blankets the deep gorges and sea-washed cliffs. Numerous small rock islands dot the frothy waters. The highway design is a work of daring engineering. Especially impressive are the series of winding corniches that overlook the ocean from precipices, in some cases 300 m – 984 ft high. In a stretch of about 200 km – 124.3 miles, there is a chain of idyllic beaches, such as: **Maruata, Faro de Bucerías, Caleta de Campos, Las Peñas** and **Azul,** near the mouth of the Balsas River. This waterway marks the borderline of Guerrero state, where the highway crosses the imposing José María Morelos Dam (Presa), one of the largest hydraulic projects in this region. From here **Ciudad Industrial Lázaro Cárdenas** can be sighted in the distance; the enormous structures of this important steel manufacturing complex rise from a plain of green palm groves.

★★ SOUTHERN PACIFIC COAST

From Ixtapa to Bahías de Huatulco
748 km – 464.8 miles – 12 days – Follow highway n° 200

A seacoast of extensive palm grove plains, alternating with bays and rocky cliffs.

Ixtapa. – This modern tourist center is set in a broad plain covered with coconut palms, protected by jungle-clad hills, with long beaches and strong surf. 4 km – 2.5 miles to the northwest is Punta Ixtapa, a rocky point reaching into the sea, where large beaches are enclosed by steep cliffs, like **Las Cuatas**, of unforgettable charm, and **Quieta**. From the latter, boats leave for **Ixtapa Island** *(10-minute crossing),* a very attractive spot on account of its small, rocky beaches with transparent water, ideal for diving and enjoying the unspoiled marine flora.

Zihuatanejo. – *5 km – 3.1 miles from Ixtapa.*
This bay was formed by mountains that converge at its mouth; it has enticing beaches with gentle surf – an invitation to enjoy the fresh sea breeze under the shade of the palms. The most popular beaches are: **La Madera, La Ropa** and **Las Gatas** *(the latter can be reached by launch from the port's main wharf).* In its rustic center, there are restaurants, where seafood specialities such as clams and lobster are served.

Papanoa. – *75 km – 46.6 miles southeast of Zihuatanejo.*
A lovely spot surrounded by low hills with fruit orchards; the beaches, right next to the highway, are equipped with arbors for enjoying the sea view.

★★★ Acapulco. – *Description p 54*

Marquelia. – *142 km – 88.2 miles southeast of Acapulco, turn right and continue 3 km – 1.9 miles on an unpaved road.*
Marquelia's beautiful and wild natural setting, is composed of a sandbar – formed by the river of the same name – estuaries, dense mangrove swamps and inviting beaches.

Puerto Escondido; Puerto Angelito; Puerto Ángel. – *394 km – 244.8 miles southeast of Acapulco you reach Puerto Escondido.*
These are small bays flanked by hills and rocky cliffs, which are part of the exotic and still unspoiled Oaxaca coasts. Very inviting, calm beaches appear amid the dense vegetation, such as the little rocky cove of **Puerto Angelito**, a miniature bay that serves as a natural swimming pool, offering facilities for water sports lovers.
60 km – 37.3 miles to the southeast (turn right at the 7 km – 4.3 miles sign) lies the beautiful bay of **Puerto Ángel**, with high cliffs and mountains surrounding the tranquil turquoise blue waters and golden sand beaches.

★★ Chacahua Lagoons National Park (Parque Nacional Lagunas de Chacahua). – *65 km – 40.4 miles west of Puerto Escondido, turn left and continue 4 km – 2.5 miles on an unpaved road to Zapotalito. It is recommended to make an early start so as to sleep in Puerto Escondido.*
From Zapotalito a boat can be taken around the exotic **Pastoría** and **Chacahua Lagoons** through natural canals that cross a thick jungle, to observe the varied fauna of this natural reserve. The visit ends in Punta Galera, where the lagoon's waters are luke-warm and transparent. A few steps from the lagoon, an interesting lizard nursery – managed by the national agency responsible for urban and environmental planning (SEDUE) – is open to the public.

★ Bahías de Huatulco. – *At 40 km – 24.9 miles from Puerto Angel, turn right and continue for 5 km – 3.1 miles.*
A beautiful series of bays with placid, crystalline waters and beaches with fine sands and rocky bottoms, such as **Santa Cruz** and **Chahue**.
The construction of a large international tourist complex is being planned for this area.

★★★ PALENQUE Chiapas

Map of Principal Sights p 6 – 150 km–93.2 miles to the northeast of San Cristóbal de Las Casas.

Palenque lies near the mountains of northern Chiapas, in the middle of a tropical jungle so dense that the treetops are not visible from the ground. On account of its mysterious beauty and archeological significance, it constitutes one of the most extraordinary ruins of the Maya culture. The ceremonial center occupies a strategically situated plateau: on one side rise the high, lush hills; on the other, vast prairies, crisscrossed by rivers and lagoons, where the peasant population settled.
As the sun falls on these mystic ruins, the visitor can contemplate the aesthetic and religious experiences that inspired them during Palenque's heyday (6-8C AD). The temples and buildings are a yellowish white hue, softened by the passing centuries, that highlights their elegant architecture against the green background of the jungle. Palenque is the site where the most sumptuous secret **crypt** within a pyramid has been found. It is also the city where stucco modeling reached great artistic heights; in sum, it is a unique jewel among the cultural legacies of ancient America.

⏱ ARCHEOLOGICAL SITE *time: 3 1/2 hours*

The monuments stand atop a series of enormous esplanades, with no apparent overall plan. At a distance, the structures seem light and very similar, but at closer range, the impression of their solidity increases and a quantity of details that merit closer scrutiny come into focus.

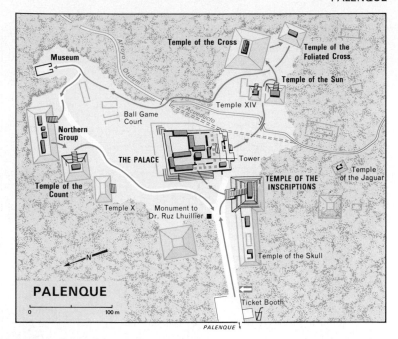

Temple of the Cross
Temple of the Foliated Cross
Temple of the Sun
Museum
Temple XIV
Ball Game Court
Northern Group
THE PALACE
Tower
Temple of the Jaguar
Temple of the Count
TEMPLE OF THE INSCRIPTIONS
Temple X
Monument to Dr. Ruz Lhuillier ■
Temple of the Skull
N
PALENQUE
0   100 m
Ticket Booth

PALENQUE ↓

Temple of the Inscriptions (Templo de las Inscripciones). – It is estimated that this majestic pyramid, constructed at the end of the 7C took no more than ten years to complete. The rapidity with which the pyramid was built is attributed to the proximity of the quarries, an abundant labor force and the use of an existent hill to obviate the need for much fill. The upper part of the structure is roofed with a Maya arch (see p 37), in which each side is independently supported.
Within the shrine there are three panels with hieroglyphic inscriptions, not completely deciphered, wherefrom the building took its name. The rear gallery provides access to the **royal tomb.**

Discovery of the Secret Crypt. – In 1949, the archeologist **Alberto Ruz Lhuillier,** from the National Institute of Anthropology and History of Mexico, while cleaning off the rubble from the Temple of the Inscriptions, noticed that the floor had a cracked paving stone. He dug down one side and found steps. Working very hard to remove the massive rocks and the mud obstructing the entrance, the archeologist eventually found an underground staircase.
In 1951 he uncovered a box containing valuable ceramic, shell and jade offerings, attached to a wall that closed the passage. When he knocked down this thick barrier, Ruz Lhuillier reached a small room containing six skeletons with skull deformations and dental mutilation – ornamental practices very common among the Mayas.
As he reviewed the hall carefully, Ruz Lhuillier saw a stone set into one of the walls. When he moved it a few centimeters, he had a marvelous vision of the chamber that seemed to be carved in ice, owing to the limestone formations from the filtrations through the vaults and walls. Delicate stalactites hung like tapers while thick stalagmites seemed to be extinguished candles. At the center shone a relief on a great stone and when the floor was illuminated, two faces made of stucco glowed forth. He raised the stone and discovered another one below, with four stone caps.
On withdrawing it, he could see in the dim light what had been hidden for more than a millenium: the skeleton of a luxuriously attired man with a mask made of 200 fragments of jade, shell and obsidian – obviously a person of great importance to the inhabitants of Palenque.
Later studies suggested the possibility that the man entombed in the main chamber had commissioned the pyramid, and that the six skeletons in the antechamber were servants, who were sacrificed to accompany the great lord in his life beyond the tomb.
After the burial (683 AD), the Maya priests sealed the access to the crypt.

⊘**Royal Tomb** (Tumba Real). – From the temple's rear gallery, a narrow inner staircase leads down to the crypt. In the mysterious dim light, an imposing chamber is revealed, 7 m – 23 ft long by 3.75 m – 12 ft wide and 7 m – 23 ft high, with a Maya vault reinforced by thick beams of yellow-veined blackish stone. The sarcophagus, a 13-ton monolith, occupies nearly the entire area.

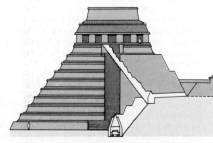

Palenque. Temple of the Inscriptions, cross section

The floor is made of enormous flagstones, perfectly cut, polished and fitted. The tombstone is particularly striking. The relief of the upper face shows, in the foreground, the mask of the earth monster and god of death; at the center, there is a youth with his chest and head thrown back and his right leg partially lifted, looking towards a cross, associated with corn, rain and sun. All these elements meant that, like the buried grain, the dead man deposited in the earth would germinate and spring forth anew. On the walls of the crypt, there are nine stucco figures representing priests who watch over and protect the resurrection of the buried man. An excellent reproduction of this tomb may be seen in the National Anthropological Museum *(p 128)* in Mexico City.

The Palace (El Palacio). – On high and tiered trapezoidal foundations stands the greatest exponent of Palenque's civil architecture, the palace. It was the residence of eminent personalities with important religious and administrative functions. The walls exhibit the most exquisite stucco reliefs of the area, an ornamentation that also appears surrounding some T-shaped openings, which symbolize the wind.

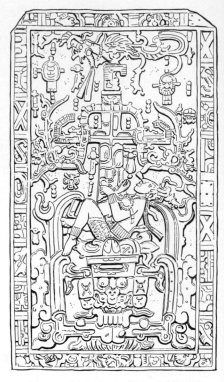

Palenque. Temple of the Inscriptions, tombstone

Behind a series of porticos, in a complicated arrangement of patios and buildings, is found the slendor tower (15 m – 49 ft) that lends an air of distinction to the whole complex.

From the top, the intricacy of this group of buildings, which resulted from several remodelings, can be appreciated. The rooms are distributed around four courtyards of different sizes.

In the eastern one, the largest, there are carved stone figures 3 m – 10 ft high, drawn with an elegant line, representing kneeling chieftains, in a clear expression of submission and surrender.

The south side of the building has various underground chambers, adorned with mythological motifs. These probably belong to the first phase of the palace.

Beyond the aqueduct and the Otulum Brook, is an intimate little square bordered by three temples, that still seem inhabited by the profound reflexions of Maya priests.

Temple of the Sun (Templo del Sol). – The Temple of the Sun was erected on a pyramidal foundation and crowned by a handsome crest that strengthens the vertical thrust of the structure. This ornamental roof structure is composed of two light wedge-shaped rubble walls that were intended to indicate to the crowds the location of the religious ceremonies.

The sanctuary itself constitutes a small temple within the temple. The sun panel at its rear was carved of limestone in a dazzling display of skill. At the center is a mask of the sun above two crossed lances and at each side, a standing priest with an elongated face caused by skull deformation. Four columns of hieroglyphics complement the composition.

Temple of the Cross (Templo de la Cruz). – The upper shrine was decorated at the center with the Panel of the Cross (Tablero de la Cruz), presently on view at the National Anthropological Museum, and the two lateral reliefs that are conserved in the shrine. These are veritable stone drawings of the young Jaguar-Serpent and of a deity from the netherworld. The extreme refinement of all the details, including the folds of its robes, should be noted.

From the temple, a magnificent **panorama** of the area facilitates an understanding of the architectural revolution produced in Palenque: the interior spaces have expanded without detriment to the monumentality of the buildings, and respect for human proportions has triumphed over the overpowering feeling produced by the pyramids of other pre-Hispanic cities.

Temple of the Foliated Cross (Templo de la Cruz Foliada). – Atop a pyramid covered with vegetation, facing a thick curtain of shrubs, ceibas and ficuses stands the white ruin of this temple. Its main facade, along with the better part of its crest, have fallen down, revealing the double corridor typical of Palenque.

The **panel** that gave the temple its name represents corn, in a cross pattern, emerging from the earth. Two figures in profile and various cones of glyphs complete the high relief.

Museum (Museo). – The select collection of clay figurines exhibited in this museum reveals the customs, attire and even the personalities of some Maya rulers. The showcases holding jade, shell, mother of pearl and obsidian jewels demonstrate the luxury in which they lived. Several stucco heads that reveal the Maya society's ideals of physical beauty, such as the slanting forehead, almond-shaped eyes, elongated nose and receding chin, complement this display.

Northern Group (Grupo del Norte). – Local construction techniques are apparent in the five temples composing this complex. The material used was limestone, joined with mud at the interstices; the surfaces were smoothed over with lime and a bit of sand. The wonderful **panorama** from the top of the platform discloses the ingenious adaptation of the buildings to the uneven terrain.

Temple of the Count (Templo del Conde). – The stairway that leads to the temple, the structure's balanced proportions and the surrounding landscape, make this pyramid a fitting finale. From its summit, many still-unexplored mounds can be discerned.
At the beginning of the 9C, Palenque entered into decline. The enormous abyss between the ruling elites and the people unleashed bitter wars that irrevocably destroyed the delicate balance achieved during the Classic Maya period. When the city was abandoned, the temples fell silent under the encroaching jungle.

EXCURSION

★★ **Agua Azul.** – *54 km – 33.6 miles southeast of the town of Palenque. Description p 57.*

★ PAQUIMÉ Chihuahua

Map of Principal Sights p 4 – 6 km–3.7 miles southwest of Nuevo Casas Grandes.

In the Valley of Casas Grandes, by the river of the same name, lies Paquimé, the most important archeological site in northern Mexico. It belongs to the Casas Grandes culture, which is considered to be a branch of the group that settled in the southwestern part of the United States, with roots going back to hunting and gathering communities. These are part of the groups known as the Desert Cultures, whose evolution contrasts with the great cultural progress of Mesoamerica. The highest point of this culture was reached during the Paquimé phase (1205-1261 AD).

⊙ ARCHEOLOGICAL SITE

The remains of the city of Paquimé reveal the degree of progress reached by its population. It is an urban center with ceremonial structures oriented southwest-northwest. Some of these buildings display a clear Mesoamerican influence, such as the ball game courts in the northeast and south of the city and the serpent mound in the northwest. It has a **central plaza** and the remains of **communal housing units** with running water supplied through underground canals. They include many patios and rooms on different levels, constructed by a system unique to Mexico: for the walls, mud was stuck to a basic skeletal structure which was added to, bit by bit, as the wall rose. Special mention should be made of the houses' T-shaped doors, which were presumably meant to facilitate their insulation in winter and their defense. To the north of the city, it is important to note the **Mound of the Cross,** oriented according to the stars and probably related to the agricultural activity of Paquimé, which was developed on the basis of a terrace system. These early Mexicans paid particular attention to tropical bird raising, perhaps for ornamental purposes. This would explain why a series of small cages have been found on the walls of the courtyards in the **Macaw House** (Casa de las Guacamayas) to the southwest of the central plaza.
But it was in **ceramics** that the sensitivity of this culture found its best expression, first in monochrome pottery and later on, in combinations of black and red on white and cream, with geometric designs. About 1340, the city was sacked and burned, although the causes have not as yet been established.

PARRAS DE LA FUENTE Coahuila ◆◆◆

Map of Principal Sights p 5

Parras de la Fuente – called Villa de Santa María de Parras in the 16C – is reached by a route that crosses a desert of thorny thickets, istle and catkins. It is famous for the excellent quality of the light tweed-type cloth it produces.

SIGHTS

⊙ **Saint Ignatius of Loyola Church (Templo de San Ignacio de Loyola).** – *Treviño and Madero.* The church has a beamed ceiling and a grand 18C baroque altarpiece, with attractive wood carvings of Jesuit saints. There is also a valuable parrochial archive from 1605.

Guadalupe Shrine (Santuario de Guadalupe). – Built in the first half of the 18C, this structure is noteworthy for its austere interior and ornate altarpieces..

⊙ **San Lorenzo Hacienda (Hacienda de San Lorenzo).** – *9 km – 5.6 miles towards Pailas.* On a 45-minute tour of this remarkable white-walled structure, the enormous installations and vats belonging to the wine company installed there can be seen.

Map of Principal Sights p 5

The picturesque village of Pátzcuaro, with its colonial aura and sloped, winding cobblestone streets, receives its name and its refreshing breezes from the lovely lake beside it. Its simple architecture takes advantage of the setting's topography. Owing to its geographical location and climatic characteristics, the layout and finishing of its buildings are unusual. Red adobe walls, burnished by time and rain, contrast with the pitched tile roofs. Protruding eaves shelter lovely balconies and slendor wooden columns frame the porticos.

To watch the many craftsmen from the outlying towns converge in Pátzcuaro with their **handicrafts★** is a pleasant and enlightening experience. The city is also famous for its cuisine, based on such delicacies as the indigenous lake fish.

★★ **Festival of the Dead (Fiesta de Muertos).** – The Festival of the Dead in Pátzcuaro and in many other regions of Michoacán alters the rhythm of everyday life. The 1st of November, at midnight, everything seems to vibrate; the craftsmen concentrate on funerary themes and even pastry takes on macabre shapes. The mere fact that the ceremony is called a festival emphasizes the contradiction between life and death. At midnight, the lake processions reach the shores and beautiful offerings are made in the small local cemeteries, like those in Tzintzuntzan *(p 211),* Pátzcuaro itself and the island of Janitzio.

In the dark of the night, the invincible spirit of death permeates the silence of the town and its mysterious lake, with the bitter perfume of the departed; and the pain of the bereaved spills over the humble tombs covered with yellow flowers and surrounded by offerings of the departed's favorite foods, covered with finely embroidered cloths. The impassive Indian faces, illuminated by the wan light of thousands of lamps, complete the picture.

HISTORICAL NOTES

The ancient Tarascan inhabitants of the Michoacán lake region seem to have been related to the Chichimec tribes *(p 37),* that penetrated the region at the end of the 12C and the early 13C. They settled on the highlands towards the northwest of Lake Pátzcuaro and gradually established political and cultural links with the agricultural and fishing peoples along the lake shore. By the mid-14C, these groups were unified under a central power installed in Pátzcuaro, together with two smaller power centers: Tzintzuntzan *(p 211)* and Ihuatzio. This group managed to expand its cultural influence to other zones of western Mexico and to hold off the constant attacks of the Aztec empire, without ever falling under its military control.

The present city was founded in 1534 as capital of the province of Michoacán. The protests and rebellions of the Indians against Spanish abuses caused the intervention of the colonial authorities, who sent **Vasco de Quiroga** as a member of the second *Audiencia* to investigate the situation. In 1537, on orders from the Queen of Spain, Quiroga took over the Bishopric of Tzintzuntzan and moved it to Pátzcuaro. That same year, he founded the College of Saint Nicholas (Colegio de San Nicolás). He was called by the Tarascans *Tata Vasco; tata* is, a term conveying reverence and great respect that means "father". He established hospitals that operated as communities and schools where Indians and *mestizos* were educated and worked for the general good, receiving fair pay for their labor. The organization had a triple purpose: hospital care and aid for the poor, education for youths, and the training of bilingual monks for evangelical work.

Pátzcuaro witnessed important events during the War of Independence, in which the rebels Gertrudis Bocanegra and Father Manuel de la Torre Lloreda distinguished themselves. The Pátzcuaro population also participated in the armed struggle of 1910. The technical and cultural progress of the 20C have not diminished the beauty of this city.

★★★ CENTER OF THE CITY *time: 1 day*

★★ **Plaza Vasco de Quiroga.** – This broad square has a circular central fountain with a bronze statue of the city's revered benefactor, Vasco de Quiroga.

House of the Eleven Courtyards (Casa de los Once Patios). – Convent of the Dominican Nuns (Exconvento de Monjas Dominicas). *Entrance between calles Lerín and José María Coss.* This convent from the middle of the 17C was the only one established by the Dominican order in Pátzcuaro. The building originally had eleven patios assigned to the various conventual activities. However, when the side roads were opened, the convent was broken up and only five courtyards remain.

The complex is lovely because of its simple architecture and layout, based on the patio-chamber so important in the daily life of the cloister. In one of these courtyards there is a small enclosure used as the novices' bath. The vestibule has an arch of small wreathed columns with Corinthian capitals. The keystone is adorned with a shell and the rest of the arch, with small grotesques. Beyond the arch is a hollowed out stone bathtub, and on the rear wall, two supernatural beings serve as water spouts. An octagonal window on the left wall dimly lights the enclosure. In various patio rooms, handicrafts are sold.

Jesuit Church (Templo de la Compañía). – *Calles Portugal and Lerín.* The side entrance to this simple 16C church, which served as a cathedral until 1566, when the Jesuits took it over, is reached by a steep street that leads to the front of the main square. The interior has a Latin cross layout with a barrel vault that is made of wood, as is the choir. On the outside, the finial of the pitched roof is noteworthy. The side and front facades exhibit a very unassuming baroque style, and the tower retains an old clock, which, it is said, was a gift to the city from the King of Spain, Philip II.

★ **Museum of Popular Arts** (Museo de Artes Populares). – **Saint Nicholas School** (Excolegio de
ⓥ San Nicolás). *Facing the Jesuit Church.* This simple construction has an octagonal
portal. It was founded by Vasco de Quiroga in August of 1538, and in 1573 the Jesuits
took the school under their charge. The building now houses a museum. On the street,
to the right of the entrance door, a graceful water tank crowned by an octagonal
pedestal holding a niche with the sculpture of the Virgin, is to be noted. Legend has
it that Vasco de Quiroga made a spring appear to supply the population with water in
1540, when he struck the ground with his pastoral staff. At the same time, the
monument commemorates the date General Lázaro Cárdenas *(see p 33)*, president of
the Republic, ordered that the spring water be piped.

Facade. – The lintel finishes in a molded cornice, on top of which two empty niches flank
a memorial plaque referring to the foundation of the Saint Nicholas School. The finial
rises in three small arches that must have contained sculptures.

Interior. – The hexagonal vestibule contains two stone sculptures: one pre-Hispanic and
the other colonial. The patio is graceful and the disposition of the arcades is especially
appealing, as one arch is lined up with both the door and the vestibule.

Museum (Museo). – The museum proper, which comprises nine rooms opening onto a
central patio, contains a broad sampling of Michoacán handicrafts and popular art.
Among the pieces on display are a large **collection** of textiles, palmfrond objects,
sugarpaste Christs, paintings, ornamented sculptures, ceramics, 19C wax figures,
washtubs, gourds and wooden objects.

ⓥ **Gertrudis Bocanegra Public Library** (Biblioteca Pública). – **Saint Augustine's Church**
(Templo de San Agustín). *Calle Degollado and Zaragoza.* This library occupies the
locale of the old Augustinian monastery, reputedly founded in 1576. The edifice today
houses a library dating back to the 18C, and it has a very austere baroque facade.

Interior. – The spacious interior consists of one nave with a barrel vault designed in the
manner typical of the region: with long planks of wood on slim arches that rest against
the walls. Vast windows illuminate the space. At the end of the nave, on the former
site of the altar, there is a large and splendid **mural★★** painted by the master Juan
O'Gorman in 1942. In it he depicts the history and conquest of Michoacán, with
episodes concerning the Independence and the Revolution of Mexico, imbued with a
profound nationalist sentiment. Facing the library, there is a garden, called by the inhabitants of Pátzcuaro, **Plaza Chica**, meaning "small square" to distinguish it from Plaza
Vasco de Quiroga. In the center of the square that also bears her name, stands the
bronze statue of Gertrudis Bocanegra. To the left side of the library, thrives a bustling
market, which increases its activity on Fridays, with the great influx of craftsmen,
farmers and fishermen.

ⓥ**LAKE PÁTZCUARO** (Lago de Pátzcuaro) *time: 1/2 day on a motor launch*

Starting from the edge of the city, the tour of Lake Pátzcuaro leads to a series of
pleasant villages that bear complicated names. Crewmen of the launches tell stories
of fabulous treasures that are sunken at the bottom of the lake, or of bewitched
women who, on moonlit nights, lure the passersby. The small islands of **Janitzio**
(dominated by a colossal
statue of José María
Morelos), **Tecuén, Yunuén**
and **Pacanda** preserve the
old secrets of the fishermen, who still manage to
catch some of the lake's
precious products.

VOLCÁN DEL ESTRIBO GRANDE

4 km – 2.5 miles
time : 1 hour

*At the corner of the city
hall (Palacio Municipal),
turn right onto calle
Ponce de León and con-
tinue straight ahead for
4 km – 2.5 miles.*

A long and winding
cobblestone road, lined
by age-old oaks, climbs
to this lovely lookout,
where there is a sensa-
tional **view★★** of the distant, ondulating shore-
lines of Lake Pátzcuaro
and its little islands. The
nearby city of Pátzcuaro
spreads out over the hillside in a plethora of red
tile roofs.

(Photo BOTTIN/Paris)

Tarascan fisherman on Lake Pátzcuaro

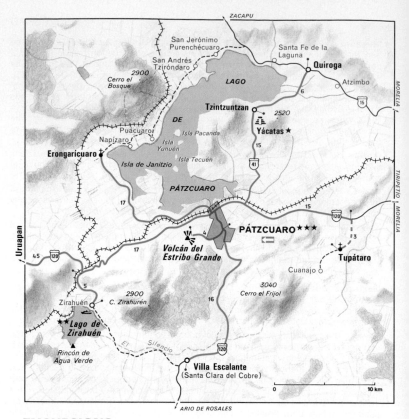

EXCURSIONS

Villa Escalante. – **Santa Clara del Cobre.** *16 km – 9.9 miles south on highway nº 120 towards Ario de Rosales.*

Villa Escalante is an attractive town with tile-roofed adobe houses that stand out against the surrounding green vegetation. This is a center for **coppersmithing**, resulting from the mastery of this metal by the pre-Hispanic inhabitants of Michoacán. Their artistry is apparent in archeological remains of fine copper pieces, such as bracelets, pincers, hatchets and bells. This town won the National Handicraft Prize in 1985.

★ **National Copper Museum** (Museo Nacional del Cobre). – In this museum, precious objects that have won competitions and exhibits are shown: ladles, platters, trays, vessels and pitchers. Among the pitchers there are some shaped like pumpkins, in keeping with the Indian tradition to emulate natural forms. There are also lovely pieces with geometric motifs.

Erongarícuaro. – *17 km – 10.6 miles. Go northwest from Pátzcuaro on the State highway following the signs for Uruapuan; at the junction with the highway to Uruapan continue straight ahead, cross the railway line and take the exit marked Jarácuaro-Erongarícuaro.*

Franciscan Monastery of the Virgin of the Assumption (Exconvento Franciscano de la Virgen de la Asunción). – This is a rather small architectural complex.

Facade. – This facade is designed in a sober Plateresque style with a robust semicircular arch framed in a band adorned with large shells; this decorative element is repeated on the framing of a pair of windows on the second floor.

Church Interior. – The roofing of the church has a trapezoidal shape with strong wooden beams, supported by three rows of thick lintels along the nave. An enormous arch separates the chancel from the rest of the nave.

Monastery. – To the right of the church runs the arcade which forms a small portal; in its arches the beautiful **capitals** are shaped as lambs with angels and fruit and vegetable motifs atop elegant fluted columns. In the center of this portal is the open-air chapel, which has a depressed arch on thick jambs with vigorous moldings. Flanking the chapel, there are slim columns that support a frieze decorated with religious symbols.

Cloister. – *Entrance at the left of the chapel.* Through a plainly decorated stone entrance, a simple two-level cloister can be seen, with a beautiful combination of stone and *tezontle,* blending with the roofings and eaves.

Tupátaro. – *18 km – 11.2 miles. Go east from Pátzcuaro on highway nº 120 towards Tiripetío and after 15 km – 9.3 miles, turn right; continue 3 km – 1.9 miles towards Cuanajo on an unpaved road.*

Facade. – At the sides of the church door, there are two stone tablets, with a sun at the right and a moon at the left – symbols of Jesus and Mary respectively.

Interior. – On entering the church, the astonishing **roofing**★★ catches the eye. It is made up of large wooden planks that form a trapezoid, the slanted sides of which rest on the walls; spanning the width are two broad crossbeams. The wooden panels were covered with a fine coating of stucco and painted in vivid colors. The eye jumps from archangels with the symbols of the Passion of Christ on the slanted sides of the ceiling, to scenes from the life of Jesus in the central part. The beams that cross the nave have also been finely decorated. At the front of the nave, the apse ends with a charming altarpiece in Churrigueresque baroque style.

★★ **Zirahuén Lake** (Lago de Zirahuén). – *22 km – 13.7 miles. Go west from Pátzcuaro on highway n° 120 toward Uruapan and at 17 km – 10.6 miles, turn left and continue 5 km – 3.1 miles to the site.*
This splendid lagoon, beside a picturesque village, is noted for its deep blue waters. Surrounded by low wooded hills, it is a very inviting spot. It is possible to take a boat ride around the lake. At its southern end, find a little cove called **Rincón de Agua Verde,** so named for the intense emerald hue of its clear waters.

Tzintzuntzan, Quiroga. – *21 km – 13 miles. Go northeast from Pátzcuaro on highway n° 120 toward Morelia and turn left onto highway n° 41. Description p 211.*

Uruapan. – *62 km – 38.5 miles to the west. Description p 212.*

La PAZ (Baja California Sur) ◆◆◆

Map of Principal Sights p 4

This state capital, named the Port and Bay of Santa Cruz *(puerto y bahía de Santa Cruz)* by Hernán Cortés in the 16C, was famous during many years for the pearls found in the vicinity. Today it offers the calm of a provincial city that seems to awaken under the impact of modern tourism, in search of beaches and leisure spots. Baja California Sur has **beaches★** to offer, such as **Coromuel** *(3 km – 1.9 miles on a road which is a northern extension of Malecón Drive),* **Tesoro** *(12 km – 7.5 miles),* **Pichilingue** *(17 km – 10.6 miles) – starting here, the road is unpaved –* and the attractive beaches of **Balandra** *(8 km – 5 miles)* and the **Tecolote** *(9 km – 5.6 miles),* where the surf is quieter.
In La Paz, a great variety of imported articles are on sale.

⊙ **Anthropological Museum of Baja California Sur** (Museo Antropológico de Baja California Sur). – *Calles Ignacio Altamirano and 5 de Mayo.* This rather simple museum has photographs of the rupestrian paintings of Baja California and also features the different economic activities of the region.

EXCURSIONS

★★ **Cabo San Lucas.** – *161 km – 100 miles. Go south on highway n° 1, and at km 29 – 18 miles, take exit to the right and continue 132 km – 82 miles on highway n° 19.*
This is an attractive resort with lovely golden beaches at the southern tip of the peninsula, featuring unusual rock formations shaped by wind and waves. Cabo San Lucas is internationally renowned as a center for sport fishing.
At this meeting point of the Pacific Ocean and the Gulf of California, the waters have
⊙ created the beach called **Amor** (Playa del Amor), between steep cliffs of volcanic rock. Note the spectacular **natural arch★** caused by complicated geological fractures within the gigantic blocks of rock.

San José del Cabo. – *33 km – 20.5 miles to the northeast of Cabo San Lucas on highway n° 1.*
In the heart of this small trading and tourist center is a church built in the style of the missions. Its main attractions are the tropical vegetation and the nearby beaches.

(Photo Guillermo Aldana/Mexico)

La Paz. Natural arch at Cabo San Lucas

Majestic volcanoes such as Popocatépetl and Iztaccíhuatl constitute one of the most representative features of Mexican geography – a beautiful landscape of snow-capped peaks dominating deep green forests.

Geographical Notes. – These two volcanoes belong to the **Sierra Nevada** system, which is the gigantic volcanic formation that shaped the Valley of Mexico. Its geological origin dates back to the end of the Tertiary period. Popocatépetl is 5 465 m – 17 930 ft high, making it the second highest peak in the country, while Iztaccíhuatl, at 5 230 m – 17 159 ft, ranks third in altitude. Consequently, both have predominantly cold climates.

Volcanic Idyll. – Legend relates that these two volcanoes represent a love story between an Indian princess and an Aztec warrior. The maiden's father set as a condition for permission to marry his daughter that the brave warrior should defeat one of the most fearful enemies of the tribe and bring back his head as proof of the deed. The warrior fulfilled his promise and returned triumphant to the tribe, only to find that, while they were ready to celebrate his victory, the maiden had died, perhaps of sadness. Taking her lifeless body in his arms, the warrior placed his beloved on a mound, lit a torch and remained forever kneeling beside her to watch over her eternal sleep.

From this romantic legend comes the popular names of the volcanoes: **Iztaccíhuatl-Sleeping Woman** (Mujer Dormida) since the silhouette resembles a woman's figure and **Popocatépetl-Lord of the Lighted Torch** (Señor de la Tea Encendida) or Smoky Mountain, which resembles a kneeling man.

Historical Notes. – Around 1519, when Cortés passed between the two volcanoes on his way to Great México-Tenochtitlán, he sent an expedition under Diego de Ordaz to climb to the crater of one of the volcanoes to get the sulphur needed for making gunpowder.

According to Bernal Díaz del Castillo, in his work, *The True History of the Conquest of New Spain (La Verdadera Historia de la Conquista de Nueva España)*, it was from there that the Spaniards first caught a glimpse of the Great Tenochtitlán as a whole, which created the impression of a silver-covered city emerging from the lakes. *At present the smog usually blocks this view of the valley.*

Approach. – *Go east from Mexico City on highway nº 150 toward Puebla and after 33 km – 20.5 miles, turn right onto the exit for Chalco, continue 4 km – 2.5 miles until you see the sign Amecameca-Chalco, continue 22 km – 13.7 miles on highway nº 115 until reaching Amecameca.*

FROM AMECAMECA TO TLAMACAS 30 km – 18.6 miles – 1/2 day

Go south from Amecameca on highway nº 115 toward Cuautla, continue 2 km – 1.2 miles, turn left and follow the signs to Tlamacas. The distances are calculated starting in Amecameca. It is recommended to plan your visit before 1 PM for better visibility.

From the Chalco-Amecameca junction, the two colossal volcanoes can be discerned looming above their farmland setting.

⊙ **Izta-Popo National Park (Parque Nacional).** – *21 km – 13 miles.* The park comprises an area of 25 679 hectares – 63 426 acres. During the ride from Amecameca, the road winds between densely forested ravines, along the flank of the volcano, where greater detail of the odd glacier formations and brilliant whiteness of the peaks can be glimpsed through the leaves.

★★ **Cortés Pass** (Paso de Cortés). – *23 km – 14.3 miles.* At this spot there is a monument commemorating the feat of Cortés' men and the last of the woods can be seen, before the volcanic ash fossils and snow area begin. From here, the view north takes in the segment called Feet of the Sleeping Woman *(see above)* and part of the figure's chest.

⊙ **Tlamacas.** – *28 km – 17.4 miles.* This is the last point that can be reached by road; from here the view of the imposing summit and the upper rim of the crater is clear. Occasionally rising fumaroles may be observed. To one side lies **El Ventorrillo** – a great dark grey basalt mountain, on which some small glaciers may be detected. Towards the east, there is a panoramic view of the Puebla Valley, with some mountains on its horizon, like Cofre de Perote and La Malinche volcano. From this site mountain-climbers begin their ascent to the crater, using the Tlamacas hostel (3 960 m – 12 992 ft) as a base.

EXCURSION

Tlalmanalco. – *10 km – 6.2 miles to the northwest of Amecameca.*
In the middle of the present town, on the main square, stands the former 16C Franciscan convent of Tlalmanalco. Its church contains some excellent baroque altarpieces and colonial paintings.

★★ **Open-air Chapel** (Capilla Abierta). – *Adjoining the church.* This chapel is among the most beautiful in the whole country. On the five stone arches that form its facade, a delicate decoration was carved, where Romanesque, Gothic and Plateresque elements are skillfully blended. Supernatural figures are masterfully combined with vegetal, animal and human forms, the latter in some cases being veritable portraits.

Without doubt, Puebla is Mexico's best-preserved colonial city. As it is built on a plain, the three great volcanoes – Pico de Orizaba, Popocatépetl and Iztaccíhuatl – as well as the smaller La Malinche volcano, are visible from whatever direction you approach the city.

Its brick, mortar and tile buildings give Puebla a special polychromy, enriched by its numerous churches with walls and vaults covered with golden plasterwork decoration. The beauty of its houses and streets makes Puebla a feast of light and color. Puebla's illustrious past is reflected in the present-day character of this distinguished city.

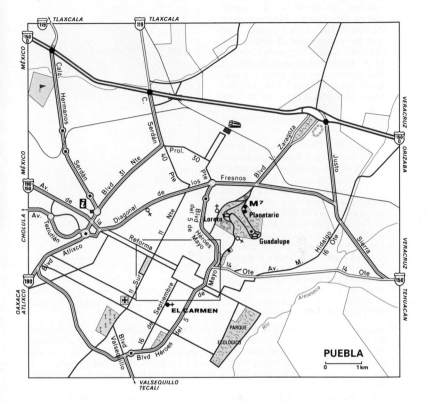

HISTORICAL NOTES

The city of Puebla was founded in 1530 in the location known as Cuetlaxcoapa, which in the Náhuatl language means "snake river". It was the first city founded according to a plan laid down by the Spanish Crown, which chose a strategic spot from which the important Indian cities of Tlaxcala, Cholula, Huejotzingo and Tepeaca could be controlled.

In addition, Puebla was on the Veracruz-Mexico and Veracruz-Oaxaca-Central America trade routes. In 1570 it had about 800 inhabitants and by 1600, the population had reached 1500.

Puebla in the 18C. By this century, Puebla was already renowned as a producer of high quality wheat and flour. Hundreds of mills were established on the banks of the Atoyac River and the surplus production was exported to the Antilles and to Central America. Sheep raising was another important industry: wool was in demand for the many workshops that became the backbone of the Mexican economy. Alongside these, other industries developed, like those of cotton goods, soap, hats, leathergoods, copper and iron objects and, above all its very famous and renowned Talavera-style ceramics – industries that exist to this day.

Heroic Resistance. – The French Army, led by General Lorencez, attacked Forts Loreto and Guadalupe at Puebla on May 5th, 1862. However, the French were badly beaten by the forces of General Ignacio Zaragoza, who died shortly thereafter. For this reason, President Juárez ordered Puebla to adopt the name of its defender. On March 16th, 1863, the French General Forey laid siege to the city; the forces of General Jesús González Ortega defended the town, fighting from house to house, although they were finally forced to surrender for lack of supplies and ammunition. On the 20th of May, one year and 15 days after the first attack, the forces of General Forey occupied Puebla.

The city was practically reduced to rubble, but was quickly restored by its devoted inhabitants, as indeed Puebla's population is fiercely attached to its customs and traditions.

At present it is a modern and progressive city, notwithstanding a deep respect for its old colonial core.

★★★ CENTER OF THE CITY
time: 2 1/2 days – Plan p 167

Cathedral
and Surroundings
time: 1 day

★★ **Plaza Principal.** – This is not among the largest squares of the country, although it is one of the most distinguished. It has many shade trees and well-kept gardens; at its center stands **Saint Michael's Fountain** (Fuente de San Miguel) – the Archangel that was the patron saint of Puebla and Tlaxcala. This 17C carving contributes a note of freshness. Bordering this square are the main colonial buildings: on the south, the cathedral compound, and at the other cardinal points, churches, palaces and buildings that are still used for city government.

★★ **Cathedral.** – From the higher areas ⊙ of the city, the tall, well-proportioned towers of the cathedral are prominent. This is the most slender of the Herreran-style churches erected in New Spain. It was begun in 1575 and finished during the Bishopry of Juan de Palafox y Mendoza. The interior is ample, with high, baroque vaults and two lateral naves lined by chapels where baroque altarpieces and paintings are preserved. Outstanding features are the canopy over the high altar, by Manuel Tolsá, and the **Kings' Chapel★** (Capilla de los Reyes) where Cristóbal de Villalpando painted a mural in oil on the vault of the cupola. The **sacristy★** contains a large number of 18C baroque paintings.

⊙ **José Luis Bello y González Art Museum (Museo de Arte) (M¹).** – This museum exhibits an excellent collection of European painting; magnificent terra cotta, alabaster and marble sculptures; ivories; and Chinese, Sevres, Limoges and Meissen porcelain. It also displays important examples of Mexican art: paintings by Agustín Arrieta (19C); Mexican earthenware made in Puebla in the 19C; a **kitchen★** covered in brick and tiles with a panel portraying San Pascual Bailón, the patron of kitchens; wrought-iron spurs; **furniture★** inlaid with mother of pearl; ancient **musical instruments★**; and a hall filled with religious ornaments.

⊙ **Casa del Deán.** – This 16C dwelling preserves splendid **mural paintings,★★** portraying the Sibyls – twelve pagan priestesses who predicted passages of Christ's life. In the frieze, grotesques of animals such as rabbits, opossums and snakes typical of the region, are represented. These Renaissance-style murals are anonymous.

★★ **Palafoxian Library (Biblioteca Palafoxiana).** – **Bibliographic Museum** (Museo Bibliográfico).
⊙ This library occupies a splendid hall. Its walls are covered by wooden book shelves, with baroque decoration carved by order of Bishop Francisco Fabián. In 1773 the bishop selected this hall in the Tridentine School for the seat of the library that had been donated by the Bishop of Puebla and former Viceroy of New Spain, Juan de Palafox y Mendoza. In the inital donation, there were 5000 volumes, later to reach 40000, making this the most important library in Latin America on Theology, Philosophy, Holy Scriptures, Christian Doctrine and languages like Latin, Greek, Sanscrit, Hebrew and Chaldean. Among these books, there are many European and American incunabula, which may be consulted by specialists.

House of the Man Who Killed the Animal (Casa del que Mató al Animal). – This house has a beautiful facade and an unusual medieval air. The two **reliefs★** depict figures clothed in the fashion of that period, holding ferocious dogs that are attacking fawns and rabbits. The name of the house comes from a legend of a youth who killed a dragon that was devouring the city's inhabitants. Most likely, this story is simply a modified version of Saint George and the Dragon, transplanted to Puebla.

Church of Solitude (Templo de la Soledad). – The slendor lines of the church and its cupola adorned with black and white tiles are striking. Originally it was a chapel dedicated to the Virgin of Solitude (Virgen de la Soledad), which later became a nuns' convent, with the original chapel used as the Virgin's dressing room *(camarín)*.
The baroque **altarpieces★** in the transept are among the best in the city. The exceptionally rich **sacristy★** retains its 18C altarpieces as well as paintings of the same period.

★ **Church and Convent of the Carmelites (Templo y Exconvento del Carmen).** – *Map p 165.* The atrium of the Carmen has been considered one of the most romantic in Puebla, particularly in the afternoon, when the cypress trees cast their shadows on the gleaming tiles of the 18C facade.

■ Casas de Balcón de Ángulo

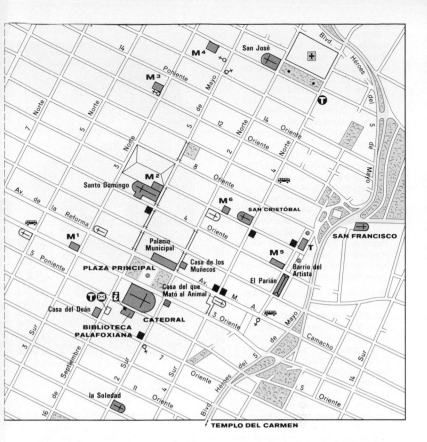

TEMPLO DEL CARMEN

The church has preserved colonial paintings by anonymous artists, although it has a number of other important features. Worth noting are: the **side chapel's**★ oval design; and the chancel, that juts out toward the north, in which the high altar has been replaced by an inlaid **wooden chest of drawers**★ *(cajonera)*. The best paintings are kept in this part of the church.

Church of Santo Domingo (Templo de Santo Domingo) and Surroundings

time: 1 day

Casa de los Muñecos. – This structure has the typical **facade**★ of the Puebla house, faced with brick with mortar and tiles. The facade is adorned with panels showing a series of unidentified characters. They may be related to Hercules and his twelve labors.

City Hall (Palacio Municipal). – Among the old colonial buildings, the city hall is distinguished by its fine neo-Renaissance style. Its severe facade contrasts with those around it since it is made entirely of stone, without the tiles or mortarwork so common in the city of Puebla. In the small interior patio, there is a Carrara marble staircase.

Church of Santo Domingo (Templo de Santo Domingo). – Inside this stark church with its Herreran facade, some fine altarpieces have been preserved, including the 18C high altar of carved and gilded wood.

★★★ **Rosary Chapel** (Capilla del Rosario). – Since its opening for public worship the 16th of April, 1690, this extraordinary chapel has been called the Eighth Wonder of the World, because of its ornate and colorful plasterwork. From the entrance it resembles a grotto, due to the quantity of decorations on ceilings and walls. Amidst the foliage, there are animals, angels, children, saints and the young martyrs accompanying the Virgin, who is sheltered by the canopy on the high altar.

The chapel's beauty is heightened by the almost supernatural light that penetrates the cupola's lantern, giving a special lustre to the gilded plasterwork.

A band of very fine 18C tiles runs all around the church, with small reliefs of cherubs. It should be noted that each sector refers to a different iconographic theme related to the Virgin. For example, on the cupola drum are depicted eight young virgins and martrys who are the eternal companions of Mary.

★ **José Luis Bello y Zetina Museum (Museo) (M²).** – This museum has a rich collection of European paintings. Some of the important ones are *Saint Peter (San Pedro)* by Zurbarán (1598-1664), a male torso by Gericault (1791-1824) and a drawing by Goya (1746-1828).

Among the Mexican painters exhibited here, Julio Ruelas, Miguel Cabrera, Manuel Coro, Juan Tinoco and Francisco Vallejo must be cited. The collection includes furniture, ivory, sculptures, Italian and French crystal of different eras. There is also a library open to the public.

⏱ **Puebla Popular Art Museum** (Museo de Arte Popular Poblano) (M³). – **Convent of Saint Rose** (Exconvento de Santa Rosa). – In this museum we find the most beautiful **kitchen★★** of colonial Mexico. This was founded in 1740 as a beguine convent – for devout women who did not take the vows – but in time it became a full-fledged convent. It retains its 18C **patio★★**, covered with bricks and tiles. The museum has a good collection of handicrafts made in the state of Puebla. Two pieces of wooden **furniture★★** inlaid with mother of pearl should be noted: a dressing table and a desk with 36 drawers. There is also a series of very imaginative **piñatas★** that range from a seven-pointed star to characters from everyday life.

(Photo Ignacio Urquiza/Mexico)

Puebla. Kitchen cupboard
in the Convent of Saint Rose

⏱ **Museum of Religious Art** (Museo de Arte Religioso) (M⁴). – **Convent of Saint Mónica** (Exconvento de Santa Mónica). Behind an austere facade, a good museum of colonial painting, especially by Puebla artists, has been set up in the Santa Mónica Convent. This convent was founded by Bishop Fernández Cruz in 1682 for Augustinian cloistered nuns, who were secularized in 1934. The museum was founded with the unclaimed objects from the convent. Thus it contains works by Juan de Villalobos and Juan Correa (17C), Miguel Cabrera, Pascual Pérez and Xavier Santander (18C), the Zendejas (18C and 19C) and Rafael Morante (19C), who made five large paintings on velvet. Also included in the collection are works by several anonymous painters. On the second floor of this museum, the heart of the founding bishop, which he donated to the convent, is exhibited.

Saint Joseph Parish Church (Parroquia de San José). – This is one of the few churches that retains all of its baroque altarpieces (17-18C).

In 1595 the chapel was finished; it was so small that today it serves as a vestibule to the church that was built in 1628. In the transept of this basilica plan church, the Chapel of Solitude (Capilla de la Soledad) that has preserved its plasterwork, should be noticed. The church has a good collection of colonial paintings among which those located in the Calvary Chapel (Capilla del Calvario) by Zendejas (1724-1815), as well as the *Saint Christopher (San Cristóbal)* in the vestibule, deserve mention.

San Francisco and Surroundings *time: 1/2 day*

★ **Saint Francis' Church** (Templo de San Francisco). – The force and grandeur of its **facade★★** are overwhelming; in it the stonework of the central section, pedestals, niches and sculptures combines with the red brick and the beautiful, multicolored tiles.

The excellent design of the latter attests to the mastery reached by the Puebla ceramists in the 18C. The side portal of this church dates back to the 16C and is presumably the oldest in the city.

Interior. – Within the church, the Gothic style ribbed vaults have been preserved, and in the sacristy there is a painting by the 18C Puebla artist, Cristóbal de Talavera. To the left of the high altar, in the chapel, the preserved body of the Devout Sebastián de Aparicio (Beato Sebastián de Aparicio) is the object of deep veneration, since he is popularly considered a miraculous saint. He introduced carts to New Spain, and a modern monument commemorating his contribution has been erected in the atrium of the church.

⏱ **Theater** (Teatro Principal) (T). – Tradition has it that this theater was the first to be built in mainland America in a horseshoe shape, like that of the Spanish Corral de la Pacheca. On the upper part of the facade, the coat of arms of Castilla and León have been carved in stone.

The square in front of the theater has in its center a large fountain, which comes to life around sunset, because of the young people who gather there.

⏱ **El Parián.** – This is an old market built in 1796 for the sale of used clothing and other articles, which has been converted into a state-run handicraft market, specializing in the alabaster objects from Tecali.

⏱ **Artists' Quarter** (Barrio del Artista). – This city quarter is made up of small locales where Puebla painters work and sell their paintings directly to the buyer, who can watch them at their work.

ⓒ **Regional and Ceramic Museum** (Museo Regional y de Cerámica) (M⁵). – Casa del Alfeñique. The splendid **facade★★★** of this building has baroque mortarwork designs that make it appear to be made of marzipan, or *alfeñique* – hence the house's name. It was inaugurated as a museum in 1926. The museum possesses a series of original colonial codices, some pre-Hispanic objects, carriages of different eras, portraits of state leaders, and a chapel which, although not original, gives an idea of what the chapels of Puebla colonial houses were like. The patio is very lovely, with a fountain in the center and mortarwork decoration on the borders.

★ **Saint Christopher's Church** (Templo de San Cristóbal). – This is a splendid church with a stone facade and two towers which emphasize the building's vertical lines. Inside, note the excellent Saint Christopher carved in wood. The vaults are covered by refined **plasterwork★** that is older than the famous decoration in the Rosary Chapel (Capilla del Rosario) *(p 167)*.

ⓒ **Museum of the Mexican Revolution** (Museo de la Revolución Mexicana) (M⁶) – The Serdán Brothers' House (Casa de los Hermanos Serdán). The house where this museum is installed is an interesting reconstruction of a Puebla house from the beginning of the century. The Revolution of 1910 began here on November 8th, when a conspiracy was discovered and the house was assaulted by the Federal Army. The Serdán brothers, Aquiles and Máximo, were killed while Carmen was saved. The museum displays photographs of leaders and battles of the Revolution. All that remains of the original structure and furniture, are the mirror full of bullet holes and the room in which Aquiles was shot.

In this old part of the city, there are many shops selling *camote,* the local dessert made from sweet potatoes. This Puebla specialty was reputedly invented in the Convent of Santa Clara *(facing the Museum of the Mexican Revolution).*

ADDITIONAL SIGHTS – Map p 165

Forts Loreto and Guadalupe (Fuertes). – The battlements of these moated forts crown the hills where the din of the battle of May 5th, 1862 still seems to resound.

ⓒ **Fort Loreto.** – In front of the main patio is the Chapel of Our Lady of Loreto (Nuestra Señora de Loreto), in which stands the Holy House (Santa Casa), with its traditional dressing room *(camarín).* Both were erected in 1659 and today are part of a museum, which exhibits photographs of leaders who participated in the war against the French (19C), uniforms and arms of both armies and a model of the assault on these fortifications.

ⓒ **Fort Guadalupe.** – This is today an austere ruin which, together with Fort Loreto, contributed to the defense of the city of Puebla, during the attack by the forces of Napoleon III. The moat and the outer walls are intact, and the fort's pentagonal design is visible.

ⓒ **Planetarium** (Planetario). – Within a modern complex of buildings, rises the high dome that houses the planetarium, where films on astronomy are shown. It is equipped with a projector that reproduces the firmament with more than 10 000 stars. In the adjoining rooms, temporary exhibits are displayed.

ⓒ **Natural History Museum** (Museo de Historia Natural) (M⁷). – This museum has a rich collection, particularly of African animals, presented in the form of dioramas that reproduce their habitats. The museum houses the donation from the hunter, Juan Naude Córdoba, which includes lions, tigers, polar bears, wild boars, birds, zebras and many other species. There are also fossils and a mural containing Martín de la Cruz's herbarium, called the Códice Badiano.

EXCURSIONS

★ **Cholula.** – *12 km – 7.5 miles to the west. Description p 72.*

★★ **Huejotzingo.** – *30 km – 18.6 miles to the northwest. Description p 94.*

Africam Safari; Valsequillo Lagoon (Laguna)**; Tecali de Herrera.** – *45 km – 28 miles. Estimate 1/2 day. Go south from Puebla on the state highway toward Tecali, and at 18 km – 11.2 miles turn right, continue for 2 km – 1.2 miles to reach Africam Safari.*

ⓒ **Africam Safari.** – This open-air zoo spans 34 hectares – 84 acres of land beside the Manuel Avila Camacho Dam. The animals are unconfined, and the tour may be made either by car or in the zoo buses. Among the animals, giraffes, lions, bears, flamingos, tigers, antelopes and others may be observed. At the first stop, boat rides are available through the canals behind the dam in a lovely setting covered with water lilies. At the children's zoo, where some specimens are kept in captivity, there are also amusement rides for children and a refreshment stand.

Continue 2 km – 1.2 miles to Laguna de Valsequillo.

Valsequillo Lagoon (Laguna). – This is, in fact, the reservoir of the **Manuel Avila Camacho Dam.** On its shores, the well-to-do from Puebla have built weekend houses. This is a favorite spot for fishing, waterskiing and sailing.

Return to the highway and continue 19 km – 11.8 miles to Tecali de Herrera.

Tecali. – The **basilica★** is an imposing ruin with a lovely facade, built in the purest Renaissance style by the Franciscan monks who evangelized the region in the 16C. Inside the church, the double row of columns that used to support a pitched roof has been preserved. The dimensions and the outbuildings of the unroofed cloister are impressive. In it there are remains of mural paintings and an exquisite stone baptismal font from the 16C.

Parish Church (Parroquia). – The magnificent altarpieces in gilded wood that belonged to the basilica are found in this church. The baroque pieces in the transept are especially lovely. This parish church also houses a monolithic 16C stoup, or holy water fountain, carved with emblems of Christ and a caption in the Náhuatl language.

★ **Acatzingo.** – *47 km – 29.2 miles. Go northeast from Puebla on highway n° 150 D towards Orizaba, turn left 2 km – 1.2 miles to the northeast on highway n° 140 towards Xalapa.*
In the main square of this town on Mondays and Tuesdays, one of the most important markets in the state is held, selling lettuce, turnips, radishes, cabbages and other produce, in a festival of colors and scents. On the south side there is a long 19C arcade.

⏱**Franciscan Monastery** (Convento Franciscano). – The most striking feature of this convent is its resemblance, although on a smaller scale, to the monastery at Tepeaca *(see below)*. While it preserves only vestiges of altarpieces and a few paintings, its stone-carved holy water stoup from the 16C is exceptionally elegant.

Parish Church (Parroquia). – *To the north of the square.* – The atrium has a fountain with pre-Hispanic emblems of Acatzingo. The facade is ornamented with bricks, tiles and mortarwork. The interior layout of the church is a Latin cross; on the high altar two paintings by Miguel Jerónimo Zendejas are to be admired. On the right side, the **Chapel of the Virgin of Sorrows★**(Capilla de la Virgen de los Dolores) has three elegant baroque altarpieces with sculptures and paintings by the same artist; in addition, a band of beautiful tiles runs around the walls. The silver facade of the altar is also notable (1761). The Chapel of the Virgin of Solitude (Capilla de la Soledad), in the atrium, also contains works by Zendejas.

Tepeaca; Tecamachalco. – *60 km – 37.3 miles. Go east from Puebla on highway n° 150 towards Tehuacán, until Tepeaca (38 km – 23.6 miles).*

⏱**Tepeaca.** – The most important buildings of this town are situated around a gigantic square. On the east side, a produce market is set up on Sundays. Opposite it stands the massive, fortress-like **monastery** erected by the Franciscans in the 16C. Its main features are the sentry walks that circle the building and pierce walls and buttresses. The abundance of Isabelline *pomas* used here as a decorative motif is striking.

El Rollo. – This solid tower is octagonal in design, with mullioned windows on the second floor decorated with dog-faced baboon figures. Reportedly the structure served as a courtroom for passing and executing sentences, although it may have been only a watchtower.

Cortés' House (La Casa de Cortés). – According to legend, this is the house where Hernán Cortés wrote the *Second Letter Reporting the Discovery and Conquest of New Spain (Segunda Carta de Relación sobre el Descubrimiento y Conquista de la Nueva España)* to Emperor Charles V of Spain, but it is evident that the house was built after the 16C, inasmuch as brick, mortar and tiles were used in its construction. To the southwest, there are other interesting houses faced with brick and tiles.

Continue 22 km – 13.7 miles on highway n° 150.

⏱**Tecamachalco.** – The **Franciscan Monastery** of this town, built in the 16C, possesses the most important **mural paintings★★** of the era. They were painted on amate, or ficus bark, paper and then glued on the interstices of the lower choir ribbing. They are the work of the Indian artist Juan Gersón, who copied, in 1562, the Old Testament themes from European bibles. Also noteworthy is the 16C holy water stoup sculpted with archangels and vegetable forms. The main facade is stark, with a multi-lobed ogee arch. At the base of the tower there is a striking relief of an eagle with an Indian *copilli*.

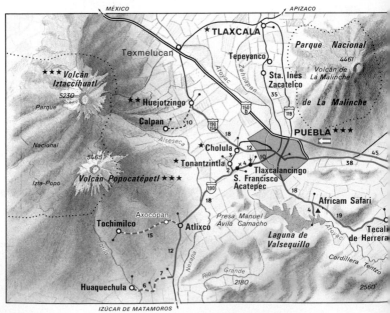

Atlixco; Tochimilco; Huaque-chula. – 87 km – 54.1 miles. *Estimate 1 day. Go southwest from Puebla on highway n° 190 toward Atlixco.*

Tlaxcalancingo. – *Description p 73.*

San Franciso Acatepec. – *Description p 73.*

Atlixco. – During the colonial period, Atlixco was called Villa de Carrión. It is surrounded by haciendas and orchards that have earned it the deserved reputation of producing the tastiest avocado pears (aguacates) in Mexico. Equally renowned are the medicinal waters from its spring at Axocopan, that have been compared to those of Vichy in France. The Franciscan monastery was erected atop Saint Michael's Hill (Cerro San Miguel) – a superb stone mass that can be seen several kilometers outside the town. It dates from the early years of the Conquest and conserves some fine altarpieces, as well as vestiges of mural painting in the cloister.

(Photo Michelin)

Atlixco. Chapel of the Third Order, detail of the facade

Chapel of the Third Order (Capilla de la Tercera Orden). – The facade of this gem of popular art is fashioned of mortarwork that is repainted every year in vivid colors. Most notable are the arabesques on the second level and two large mermaids with vegetable tails. Inside the chapel there are fine gilded wooden altarpieces and some fairly good paintings.

Saint John of God Municipal Hospital of Atlixco (Hospital de San Juan de Dios de Atlixco). – This is one of the few hospitals of the colonial period that still functions today. It possesses a handsome patio with a fountain, the base of which is a figure that has been confused with Hercules because it is patting a lion. In fact, it is a beautiful stone sculpture of Saint Adrian (San Adrián). Inside several altarpieces and baroque paintings remain, as well as a carved stone pulpit with medieval forms.

Parish Church (Parroquia). – Two features stand out in this church: an ungilded altarpiece and the beautiful choir banister, made by Higinio López, "Master of Zacualpan".

In Atlixco, follow Calle 2 Sur, Calz. del Carmen and Av. del Trabajo until it runs into the state highway; turn left, continue 3 km – 1.9 miles to Axocopan, turn right, continue 1 km – 0.6 miles, then turn left and continue 11 km – 6.8 miles.

Tochimilco. – This town lies on the slopes of Popocatépetl Volcano. In the main square, there is a 16C fountain which used to supply water to the town. The fountain is octagonal, with a spout in the form of lions' heads and inscriptions in Náhuatl.

Franciscan Convent (Convento Franciscano). – This convent is housed in a solid stone construction with an austere Renaissance facade and a double Mudejar window crowned with crenellations. The interior has a single nave and contains 17C and 18C altarpieces with colonial paintings. The entrance to the cloister is through the gatehouse, where the balcony-type open-air chapel was installed.

Return to Atlixco and head south, continue 12 km – 7.5 miles on highway n° 190 toward Izúcar de Matamoros, turn right, 7 km – 4.3 miles, turn right again and continue 6 km – 3.7 miles on an unpaved road.

Huaquechula. – In the main square of this small town several pre-Hispanic monoliths with calendar reliefs and a 10C stone cross that originally stood in the convent's atrium have been conserved.

Franciscan Monastery (Convento Franciscano). – An imposing mass of stone, this 16C complex has a rich facade, where Gothic and Plateresque forms combine. The **lateral facade★★** is unusual for its medieval flavor; in the jambs, the images of Saint Peter and Saint Paul (San Pedro y San Pablo) and above, Christ Almighty (Cristo Pantocrátor), accompanied by angels announcing the Last Judgement. Inside the church there are still several altarpieces and baroque paintings, as well as a medieval-style carved stone pulpit.

★★ PUERTO VALLARTA Jalisco ◆◆◆

Map of Principal Sights p 5

This famed vacation spot is wedged in the center of the Bahía de Banderas, at the edge of cliffs and hills covered by thick jungle. The town of Puerto Vallarta has narrow cobblestone streets and small red tile-roofed houses in contrast with the large hotel complexes installed along the beaches.

Towards the south on highway n° 200 there are beautiful vistas of the famous **stone arches** (arcos de piedra), which are rocky islets 25 m – 82 ft high – a symbol of Puerto Vallarta's natural beauty. An evening stroll is particularly pleasant along the Rio Caule, which runs through the city.

Beaches (Playas). – Mismaloya, Boca de Tomatlán and **Yelapa** are among the main beaches, and their charm is enhanced by their location at the foot of rocky cliffs around the mouths of mountain brooks. These short, broad beaches are noted for their warm waters and exotic aquatic plants.

EXCURSIONS

Nuevo Vallarta. – *11.5 km – 7.1 miles. Go north from Puerto Vallarta on highway n° 200. Follow the signs to Nuevo Vallarta.*
This is an attractive landscape of estuaries formed by the waters of the Ameca River, which bring together a series of small islets creating intricate canals parallel to the Pacific coast. There are nearly 5 km – 3.1 miles of magnificent beaches with inviting sands.

Guayabitos; Peñita de Jaltemba. – *75 km – 46.6 miles north on highway n° 200 toward Tepic.*
These paradise-like coves include **Ayala Beach** (Playa de Ayala), with soft waves suited for canoeing, sailing and skin diving and **Guayabitos Beach★** (Playa Guayabitos), which has a group of colonial-style houses with white facades and austere wooden gates at the edge of the beach. Cobblestone streets and small squares adorned with lampposts, flowering jacarandas and poincianas complete the picture.
Situated 2 km – 1.2 miles north is **Peñita de Jaltemba★**, a picturesque little coastal town set on an ample rocky bay, with some islets that make for pleasant seascapes.

★ PUUC ARCHEOLOGICAL ZONE Yucatán

Map of Principal Sights p 6

In the hills of northwest Yucatán, covered by a low jungle that takes on the aspect of thorny underbrush during the dry season, are found impressive Maya ceremonial centers built between the 6C and 9C AD. In these centers, the theocratic states promoted extraordinary development in the arts, especially architecture, in which the Puuc style – "highland" in Maya – attained its peak.

Puuc style buildings have plain walls, with a prolific upper ornamentation in which stucco plays a complementary role to the admirable execution in stone. Outstanding among the decorative elements are the hook-nosed mask, symbolizing Chac, the rain god, and the small columns built into the facade, which are the stone reproduction of the ancient wooden tie beams that formed the walls of the Maya huts.

ARCHEOLOGICAL SITES
38 km – 23.6 miles leaving from Uxmal – 1 1/2 days

★★★**Uxmal Archeological Site. –** *Description p 213.*

> To the south of Uxmal take highway n° 261 towards Hopelchén.

★**Kabah Archeological Site. –** *21 km – 13 miles. Description p 96.*

> Continue 5 km – 3.1 miles on the same highway and turn left 4 km – 2.5 miles to Sayil.

Sayil. – In a leafy setting, stands the most elegant and best-preserved building of this archeological site: **the Palace★** (El Palacio). To judge by its size – 85 chambers distributed in three tiered sections – this might have been the public administration center. The ruinous condition of the lower level and the sobriety of the upper enhance the richness of the intermediate level, where double columned porticos alternate with access bays leading to narrow passageways. The decoration of the walls is striking: small columns and masks of Chac, together with two fantastic reptiles that flank a strange upside-down figure. Further along the sidewalk there are various other buildings, temples and a ball game court – all in a dilapidated state.

> Continue 5 km – 3.1 miles to the east.

Xlapak. – The main building – a rectangular structure with nine chambers on a single level – is situated 90 m – 295 ft from the ticket window. The subtlety of the lower decorations – smooth interwall bands and discreet strips of little drums around the base of the walls and on the central and upper cornices – sets off the vertical facade panels. There, a baroque exuberance holds sway, with several large, superimposed masks of the long-nosed deity in high relief; in their years of splendor, these were painted in vivid colors.

> Continue 3 km – 1.9 miles to the east.

Labná. – This site is not very large. The main buildings are distributed in two groups connected by a *sacbé,* or white road.

The Palace (El Palacio). – *First building on the left.* – This construction is made up of a series of rooms that continue around the square. At the sides of the rooms there are groups of three columns built into the walls, that emphasize the verticality of the structure – an effect that is reinforced by the broad friezes.

The Lookout (El Mirador). – *At the rear of the site.* On top of a ruined pyramid stands the upper temple with an elegant crest. From the summit, a panoramic view of the mountains reveals that there are no surface rivers or lagoons, which explains the importance of the cenotes *(p 23)* and the construction of the irrigation canals.

★★★ **Monumental Arch** (Arco Monumental). – *To the right of the lookout.* This arch linked two sectors of the most exclusive residential area of Labná. Its importance lies in the fact that it is by far the most profusely decorated arch known in Maya architecture. The side facing the lookout is most austere, since its ornamentation is limited to two frets joined by square stones that form a V. The composition becomes more complex on the main side, in which two trapezoidal side doors enlarge the arch. The central cornice has stylized snake mo-

(Photo Bob Schalkwijk/Mexico)

Puuc Archeological Zone. Monumental Arch at Labná

tifs, and above the grid friezes there are two huts built of stone. The false bays of these served as niches for two seated sculptures, long since disappeared. This superb monument is topped with the remains of three stepped and pierced roof crests.

EXCURSION

★★ **Loltún Grottos** (Grutas de Loltún). – *20 km – 12.4 miles. Time: 2 hours. 15 km – 9.3 miles beyond Labná, turn left and continue 5 km – 3.1 miles.*
⊘ This is an enormous cavern with rupestrian paintings and intriguing archeological remains. In the pre-Hispanic period, it was an important clay deposit and stone quarry, a place of worship of deities and a source of water. It has ancient barricades that the neighbors say were hideouts for the Indians during the Caste War. The colored lighting enhances the delicacy of numerous limestone formations.
On the wall to the left of the entrance are a Maya bas relief and the so-called Cathedral Galleries (Galerías de la Catedral), the Child's Room (el Cuarto del Infante) and the Grand Canyon (Gran Cañon). The better part of the paintings, still undated, is to be found in the Room of the Inscriptions (Sala de Inscripciones).

★★ QUERÉTARO Querétaro   ♦♦♦♦♦

Map of Principal Sights p 6

From the hill known as Cuesta China, the visitor can appreciate a fine view of Querétaro neatly framed by its monumental aqueduct. This colonial city is situated in the Bajío, one of the most fertile regions of Mexico. On both sides of its straight, narrow streets there are magnificent palaces, old convents, schools and simple houses where time has left its patina on stone and beautiful, intricately wrought ironwork. The baroque and the French-influenced neoclassical styles mesh with modern architecture, without changing the city's provincial and colonial air.
Querétaro is a crossroads that, due to its privileged location, has witnessed important historical events; today the state of Querétaro is undergoing rapid industrialization.

HISTORICAL NOTES

The founding of Querétaro in the middle of the 16C is attributed to the Utomi Indian, Conin, who took the Christian name, Fernando de Tapia. A century later, thanks to the prosperity derived from its fertile soil, it was ranked as the third city of New Spain, with the title of **Very Noble and Loyal City of Santiago de Querétaro** (Muy Noble y Leal Ciudad de Santiago de Querétaro). In the 18C, the city reached its economic, social and artistic peak. In the 19C, it was the scene of important events that marked a radical change in the history of Mexico. In 1808, under the cover of literary meetings, the **Querétaro Conspiracy** was organized against Spanish power, headed by Epigmenio González and the Mayor, or *Corregidora,* **Josefa Ortiz de Dominguez.** Despite the fact that the conspiracy was discovered and its leaders placed under arrest, the Independence Movement was proclaimed not far from there, in Dolores Hidalgo, on September 16th, 1810.

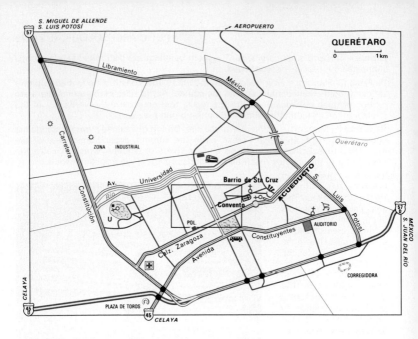

In 1847, when the city of Querétaro was the provisional capital of the Mexican Republic, the treaty that terminated the war with the United States, know as the Treaty of Guadalupe Hidalgo, was ratified there. In 1867, Emperor **Maximilian of Habsburg** was executed by a firing squad in Querétaro, together with the Mexican Generals Miguel de Miramón and Tomás Mejía, on the **Cerro de las Campanas,** thus putting an end to the Second Empire. Half a century later, in 1917, for the second time, Querétaro became the provisional capital of the Republic, according to a decision by Venustiano Carranza, and in 1917 the **Constitution** that still rules the Mexican Republic was promulgated there.

★ CENTER OF THE CITY *time: 1 day – Plan p 175*

Obregón Garden (Jardín Obregón). – Zenea Garden (Jardín Zenea). This laurel-shaded garden was built in honor of Colonel Benito Zenea, on the land belonging to a ruined Franciscan convent. It is surrounded by 18C buildings and, at its center are a stone fountain dedicated to the goddess Hebe and a typical bandstand – two characteristic features of Mexican gardens.

Regional Museum (Museo Regional) (M) – Monastery of Saint Francis (Exconvento de San Francisco). This museum presents a survey of Querétaro's history. It is housed in what was a 17C convent. The **main courtyard** is supported by sober molded arches and fluted columns; the pleasant **novices's courtyard,** and the **orange garden,** with strong buttresses and a murmuring fountain, complete the ensemble, which still preserves mystic reminders of its original function.

Lower Floor. – In this area furniture, paintings and tools of the War of Independence era are displayed.

Upper Floor. – On this level there is a rich painting collection from the 16C to the 19C with works by distinguished masters, like Echave, Páez and Villalpando.
To the right of the staircase, there is a beautiful Churrigueresque **altarpiece** with many paintings by Juan Correa; while in the **main hall** richly carved wardrobes, an enormous 17C gate and Saint Prisco in ceremonial robes are noteworthy.

★ **Plaza de Armas or Independencia. –** This is a charming square bordered by graceful old buildings and planted with leafy Indian laurels. Note the statue of the Marquis de la Villa del Villar del Águila, who brought water to Querétaro.

Federal Government Palace (Palacio del Gobierno Federal) (PG). – Treasury, Prison and Mansion of Doña Josefa Ortiz de Dominguez (Casas Reales, Cárcel y Mansión de Doña Josefa Ortiz de Dominguez). This is a handsome two-story 18C palace with high walls. Its facade is crowned by sturdy urns, which highlight its imposing bulk. It was the residence of the illustrious *Corregidora* de Querétaro who, with the help of the prison warden, managed to warn Miguel Hidalgo that the Independence conspiracy had been discovered.

★ **Offices for the Comprehensive Development of the Family (Oficinas del Desarrollo Integral de la Familia) DIF (K). – House of the Marquis of Ecala** (Casa del Marqués de Ecala). – The **facade★** of this stately 18C house is striking for the sumptuous elegance of its balconies, covered in calligraphic ironwork. Iron and stone were treated as deftly as malleable mortar.

Corregidora Garden (Jardín de la Corregidora). – This is an inviting nook where the **Friendship Tree** (Árbol de la Amistad) is found, preceded by the romantic **monument★** to the **Corregidora,** Josefa Ortiz de Dominguez. In the surrounding countryside, picturesque inns provide pleasant spots to rest or have a meal.

Theater of the Republic (Teatro de la República) **(T)**. – There is a graceful little square in front of this historic edifice, built under the sponsorship of the Junta de Vergara in the mid-19C. Maximilian of Habsburg was sentenced to death here in 1867 by a court martial; and in 1917 the Mexican Congress signed the new Constitution in these very halls.

In recent years, this theater has staged outstanding national and international cultural productions.

⊙ **Cultural Center** (Casa de la Cultura). – House of the Marquise de la Villa del Villar del Águila (Casa de la Marquesa). This stately 18C baroque house, designed by the talented Cornelio, a Querétaro architect, presents a distinguished facade worked in stone, with grilles and a large entrance hall.

Inside, there is a small Mudejar style **patio**★ with a striking Islamic arcade. In this flowery setting cultural performances take place.

★ **Saint Clare's Church** (Templo de Santa Clara). – This plain 17C building was erected, thanks to a donation from Diego de Tapia. The front garden, formerly the orchard, contains a sculpture of Neptune by the Mexican artist, Francisco Eduardo Tresguerras (1759-1833). The severe construction of the exterior enhances the richly ornamented altarpieces preserved in the single nave of the church.

Interior. – In the dim light of the nave, six splendid 18C carved and gilded wooden altarpieces, which still have paintings of Miguel Cabrera and José de Páez, are to be seen. The exuberant Baroque decoration of the **doors** and the **pulpit** has been attributed to Mariano de las Casas. The **choir screen** is most exquisite, with its play of transparencies and glints of light; it partially conceals the organ, which, from a distance, resembles a wooden crysanthemum.

★ **Querétaro Art Museum** (Museo de Arte Queretano) **(G)**. – Augustinian monastery (Exconvento
⊙ de San Augustín). This collection of national and European art contains important works by Mexican artists. The museum is housed in the monastery's magnificent baroque **cloister**★★, richly adorned with remarkable stonework including caryatids, pelicans and floral decoration.

Saint Augustine's Church (Templo de San Agustín). – This handsome 18C church, also built by Ignacio Mariano de las Casas and Fray Luis Martínez Lucio, was erected atop a large stepped platform. Its truncated tower was never finished, and the great tile-covered cupola seems to be escorted by a band of angels. The **facade**★ recalls the structure of an altarpiece, framed by wreathed columns that guard the sculptures of the order's saints, whose habits resemble Gothic drapery.

★★ **Saint Rose of Viterbo Church** (Templo de Santa Rosa de Viterbo). – This sumptuous 18C church is the masterpiece of **Ignacio Mariano de las Casas,** who left a profound mark throughout Querétaro. The sober and stern church looks like a fortress built to protect the nuns. A Mudejar influence is apparent in the cupola and the slim tower. The pier and flying buttresses are accompanied by odd pyramidal pinnacles that are the product of the architect's fancy.

Interior. – The six majestic 18C altarpieces are veritable jewels of baroque art. One is dedicated to the Virgin of Guadalupe (Virgen de Guadalupe) and the others, to different saints. They are covered with draperies, crowns, vines, and countless angels in varying postures. Their gilding glows in the candlelight. The **screen** of the double choir ends in a fan-shaped lattice, decorated with painted medallions.

Sacristy (Sacristía). – The vast hall that is used as a sacristy houses a small painting collection, with works by famous artists. Outstanding among them are the huge painting of a walled orchard by José de Páez (18C) and two magnificent paintings by Miguel Cabrera (1695-1768) of Captain Velázquez de Lorea. The 18C round carved wooden table is also noteworthy.

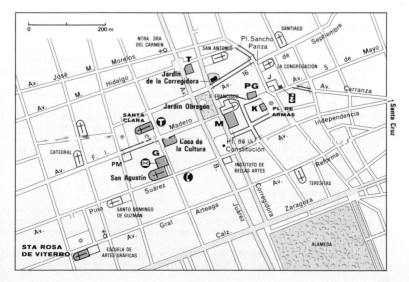

AQUEDUCT AND SURROUNDINGS

time: 2 hours – Map p 174

★★ **Aqueduct (Acueducto).** – This is an imposing 18C construction and was erected thanks to Antonio de Urrutia y Arana, Marquis of la Villa del Villar del Águila. This handsome aqueduct is the symbol of Querétaro and has been considered one of the most admirable works of civil engineering on the American continent. It combines aesthetic and technical skills in a monumental arcade 1 280 m – 4 200 ft long, which reaches a height of 23 m – 76 ft.

Holy Cross District (Barrio de Santa Cruz). – *Independencia and Reforma.* This district set on Sangemal Hill is full of historical reminiscences preserved in its buildings. The site offers a splendid panorama of the colonial city. On this spot, Hernando de Tapia defeated the Indian diehards who continued to defy Spanish authority, thus establishing the Villa de Santiago de Querétaro.

⊙ **Holy Cross Convent** (Convento de la Santa Cruz). – This is a simple, but solid, 16C construction. Here, at the end of the 17C Fray Antonio Lináez established the Apostolic College for the Propagation of the Faith (Colegio Apostólico de Propaganda Fide) from which the great missionaries went forth to carry the faith and Western culture to the northern regions. Within the convent, there is a graceful patio surrounded by a stone wall, that still has the popular **thorn trees,** so called because their branches fill with cross-shaped thorns that, according to legend, descend from the cane belonging to Fray Margil de Jesús, a dedicated evangelizer of saintly reputation.

EXCURSIONS

Celaya. – *42 km – 26.1 miles to the west on highway nº 45 D towards León.*
This industrial city is famous for its traditional custards *(dulces de leche),* caramels *(cajeta),* toffees *(chiclosos)* and sugar bars *(jamoncillos).*
In the 19C, Lucas Alamán established here the first textile factory on an English model. During the Mexican Revolution, Celaya witnessed a great deal of fighting between Generals Francisco Villa and Alvaro Obregón, in which the latter triumphed. From then on, Obregón was nicknamed the One-Armed Man of Celaya (Manco de Celaya), having lost an arm in the battle. Some of the major attractions of the city are the works left by the architect, **Francisco Eduardo Tresguerras,** a native of Celaya.

★ **Church of the Carmelites** (Templo del Carmen). – *Diagonally across from the corner of calles Alvaro Obregón and El Carmen.* This is one of the region's most graceful neoclassical churches; it has a high tile-covered cupola and a well-proportioned tower. The Latin cross design interior is outstanding for its gold and white decoration that blends with the Versaillesque chandelier, the solemn sculptures and the simplicity of the organ. In the **Chapel of the Brotherhood** (Capilla de Cofrades) hangs an enormous painting of scenes from the Last Judgement, attributed to Tresguerras (1759-1833).

San Juan del Río. – *54 km – 33.6 miles to the southeast on highway nº 57 D.*
This is a flourishing industrial town set on a hill of limestone and building rock, surrounded by the ancient leafy savins of the bank of Rio San Juan. The town is famous for its reed and precious stone **handicrafts.** The old walls of inns and some ancient constructions like the 17C **Santo Domingo Parish Church** (Parroquia de Santo Domingo) contribute to the city's architectural importance, both civil and religious. Since the late 1970s, San Juan has developed its dairy industry, especially cheeses, and has promoted its wine industry as well. However, the production of handicrafts continues to be its leading sector.
On **Avenida Juárez** are found the most renowned stores that sell lovely basketry resembling a filigree of bamboo and rush fibers. On the same street there are also shops where craftsmen's skillful hands and ingenuity turn opals and other semiprecious stones into beautiful jewels that capture the glitter of San Juan del Río's sun.

★ REAL DE CATORCE San Luis Potosí   ◆

Map of Principal Sights p 5

257 km – 159.7 miles north of San Luis Potosí. Take highway nº 57 until Matehuala (191 km – 118.7 miles), continue on the same road 6 km – 3.7 miles and turn left; 29 km – 18 miles and turn left again, 31 km – 19.3 miles to Real de Catorce.
After passing through the 19C **Ogarrio Tunnel,** the road comes to a ghost town, full of empty and decaying stone houses, with imposing mountains on the horizon. This place was world famous during the great mining boom; today it attracts thousands of pilgrims who come to fulfill promises and leave offerings to Saint Francis of Assisi. Another time-honored ceremony occurs every year during the winter months: the Huichol Indians walk more than 550 km – 341.8 miles from Nayarit to Catorce, which they call the Holy Mountain, or *Wirikuta,* to celebrate their communal ritual with the hallucinogen, peyote.

HISTORICAL NOTES

In the 17C fourteen members of the Viceroyal Expeditionary Forces died in an unsuccessful attempt to pacify the Indians here. Consequently, the place was named to honor the fourteen *(catorce)* victims. A century later it had the third largest mining production in Mexico.
The changes brought by the Mexican Revolution in the mining enterprises forced the town's inhabitants to leave; the resulting silence pervades even the mine shafts.

SIGHTS

🕑 **Parish Museum (Museo Parroquial).** – *Lanzagorta, unnumbered.* This is a humble house in which there are reminders of the great boom of the Real, the remains of its electric tramway, photographs, machinery, mining tools and coins.

Parish Church of the Conception (Templo Parroquial de la Purísima Concepción). – *To the east of the plaza principal.* This is a monumental church from the end of the 18C. The interior follows the Latin cross design; it retains a lovely picture of the Virgin of Guadalupe with a carved gold frame, attributed to José de Alcíbar, and two pretty sculptures: *The Holy Patroness of the Church* and the miraculous sculpture of *Saint Francis of Assisi.*

🕑 **Mint (Casa de Moneda).** – *To the east of the parish church.* This simple 19C construction, built by Santos de la Maza, has three levels. Here were cast silver coins sought today by collectors.

🕑 **Cockfight Arena** (Palenque de Gallos). – *Northwest of the plaza principal.* This unusual mid-19C structure was designed in the manner of a Roman amphitheater. It was reconstructed during the present century and is used for civic and cultural events.

Bullfight Ring (Plaza de Toros). – *To the north of the Palenque de Gallos.* This is a magnificent building from the mid-19C. The arena is constructed of rose-colored stone and creates a magical impression, to be attributed in part to its extraordinary acoustics. From the plaza, there is a dramatic view of the valley and an enormous ravine.

★ RIO BEC Campeche

Map of Principal Sights p 6

In the southern central part of the Yucatan Peninsula, to the west of Chetumal *(p 65),* there are three splendid sites that developed between the 4C BC and 11C AD. These belong to a region with common cultural traits and reflect the marked influence exerted by the Tikal civilization at its peak. In this era of prosperity, a series of architectural elements were revived in this area – known to researchers as the Rio Bec style – that distinguish it from other Maya regions. The distinctive features of this style are: high towers flanking temples; structures on broad platforms; large structures with rounded corners; buildings with openwork crests; marvelous, profusely decorated portals, simulating reptiles with open jaws; and richly adorned friezes and bands. The overwhelming natural setting of thick tropical rain forest that envelopes this area encroaches on the monuments and creates subtle clashes between the varied greens of the foliage and the white stucco and stone ruins.

ARCHEOLOGICAL SITES

146 km – 90.7 miles starting from Chetumal – 1/2 day

> *West of Chetumal take highway n° 186 to Escárcega, at 59 km – 36.7 miles turn left, 9 km – 5.6 miles to Kohunlich.*

Kohunlich Archeological Site. – *Description – p 65.*

> *Return to highway n° 186, turn left, at 59 km – 36.7 miles, turn right; 100 m – 328 ft off the highway you find Xpuhil.*

🕑 **Xpuhil.** – This handsome group of eroded high towers can be seen from afar. Atop a broad platform, the three towers have frontal staircases – decorated in the center with large, expressive masks – that formerly surrounded a lower temple with a triple portal. The pyramidal remains of the towers can still be discerned. At the sides of the temple portals, there are vestiges of stucco ornamentations representing the rain gods. The style of construction must have had great visual impact, as it combined the vertical aspects of the towers with the horizontal lines of the temple building.

> *Return to highway n° 186 and continue 6 km – 3.7 miles straight ahead, 600 m – 1 969 ft to the right of the highway, you will find Becán.*

🕑 **Becán.** – In what was formerly a large city protected by a moat, the remains of four great structures are laid out around a plaza, almost engulfed by the jungle. The ruins include pyramids with rounded corners and stairways. Their small crowns reveal incipient tower structures resembling temples; some vestiges of large masks and panels can be observed, with geometric lattices in charming stucco combinations, distributed over the stairways of the four buildings.

> *Return to highway n° 186 and continue 2 km – 1.2 miles, turn left and continue 700 m – 2 297 ft on an unpaved road to Chicanná.*

🕑 **Chicanná.** – In a small plaza to the left side of the site entrance stands a simple structure composed of three portals surrounded by lovely geometric stucco decorations. In the center, the eye is drawn to the refined **ornamentation★**, which uses the door opening to simulate the open jaws of a serpent, the fangs of which hang down menacingly from the lintel. Behind this building there is a structure with a striking openwork crest, which rises between the ceiba trees and thick vegetation. Discrete stucco decorations are scattered on the sides of the portal – a pale reminder of their original Maya splendor.

Map of Principal Sights p 5

Saltillo, the capital of the state of Coahuila, is framed by the arid mountains of the Sierra Madre Oriental. It is a major industrial center, producing automobiles and steel, as well as an agricultural and trading hub, famous for its multicolored sarapes. It was founded in 1577 by Captain Alberto del Canto and in 1591, the east of the city was repopulated with Tlaxcaltec families by Francisco de Urdiñola, in order to stop the frequent invasions by the nomad northern tribes. Saltillo was the capital of Coahuila and Texas from 1835 to 1847, when the Texas territory was lost.

SIGHTS

⊘ **Cathedral.** – *Calle Hidalgo and Juárez*. This cathedral was built over different periods and consequently presents a mixture of styles. Its lovely 18C baroque **facade**★ features a rich ornamentation of plant motifs, in combination with paired wreathed columns in the first section and *estípites* in the second. The entrance arch is topped by an enormous shell, which is repeated in the niches decorating the ensemble.

Interior. – In the discreetly decorated interior with a Latin cross layout, the salient artistic elements are: the painting of the Virgin of Guadalupe by José de Alcíbar in the baptistry; a handsome baroque wreathed and gilded altarpiece with a painting of the Holy Family In the right transept; and, at the foot of the latter, a fine wrought-silver frontal. To the right of this altarpiece, the **pulpit** covered in gold leaf is also worth noting.

Chapel (Capilla). – This plain chapel, built in 1762, houses an image of Christ brought from Spain in 1608, noted for the numerous legends with which it is associated.

⊘ **Rubén Herrera Museum** (Museo). – *Bravo Norte nº 342*. This was the residence of Rubén Herrera, the painter (1888-1933), who studied with Antonio Fabrés in Rome. The museum contains over 400 of the artist's works, the majority of which represent Italian landscapes and scenes of daily life. The lovely furniture in the house is original.

⊘ **Ateneo Fuente.** – *Av. Echeverría and Universidad*. This is a charming construction of the Thirties, in Art Deco style. Its academic tradition can be traced back to the origins of Coahuila University. Today it is a preparatory school and the right wing of the first floor houses the Museum of Natural History (Museo de Historia Natural), containing a **collection** of stuffed animal specimens and a sampling of rocks and fossils.
⊘ In the opposite wing, the **painting collection** exhibited includes **works**★ by Mexican and foreign artists. Most important among them are *Saint Peter (San Pedro)* by Juan Rodríguez Juárez, *The Flight of Lot (La Huida de Lot)* by Rubens and *The Legend of the Volcanoes (La Leyenda de los Volcanes)* by Saturnino Herrán.

★★★ SAN CRISTÓBAL DE LAS CASAS Chiapas ♦♦♦

Map of Principal Sights p 6

San Cristóbal de Las Casas is a charming city that seems to be living in the 18C. It is located in the midst of Indian country in a small valley between pine-forested hills. It was founded in 1528 by the Spaniards and was the capital of the region, which then belonged to the General Captaincy of Guatemala. Along its rather quiet stone paved streets, lined by wide-eaved houses, there are splendid religious monuments that amalgamate the cultural influences of both the Viceroyalty of New Spain and the General Captaincy of Guatemala.

SIGHTS

★★ **Central Market** (Mercado Central Lic. José Castillo Tiellmans). – *Beside the Church of Santo*
⊘ *Domingo*. The Indians from the mountains come to this great trading center. The splendid variety of fruits and vegetables, as well as the coloring of the clothing articles constitute a true feast for the eyes. The tremendous cacophony of different native tongues that fill the air, might seem astonishing, but the market is also a social gathering.
It is recommended to visit this lively site on Saturdays, when even the adjacent streets are lined with stands teeming with medicinal herbs, flowers, firewood, hens, turkeys, used clothing and other items for sale.

San Cristóbal de las Casas. Woman from the Chiapas highlands

★ **Church of Santo Domingo (Templo de Santo Domingo).** – *Corner of Calz. Lázaro Cárdenas and Nicaragua.* This church is a solid 16C structure, with very fine 18C baroque-style ornamentation. The magnificent stucco facade adjoining the wall and framed by two heavy towers is a veritable outdoor altarpiece in three sections with Solomonic columns. In the main pediment, there are bas reliefs with two-headed eagles – the emblem of the House of Austria – next to Santo Domingo de Guzmán. The vast interior contains remarkable panelling and an outstanding gold-leaf covered **pulpit**★.

⊘ **Na-Bolom Museum (Museo).** – *Av. Vicente Guerrero n° 33.* Inside an old privately owned mansion, marvelously decorated with regional handicrafts, is an exhibit of Maya ceramics and everyday objects. On display are willow traps, arrows, drums and articles of the **Lacandon** Indians who live in the dense jungle of the eastern part of the state. The **library** is specialized in the Maya culture (15000 volumes).

⊘ **Cathedral.** – *Plaza 31 de Marzo.* Its stark facade is early baroque, one of the most widespread styles in 18C Central America. Within the church, two **paintings**★ – *Virgin of Sorrows (Virgen Dolorosa)* by Juan Correa, to the left of the altar, and, inside the sacristy, *The Magdalena* by Miguel Cabrera – are remarkable.

EXCURSIONS

★★ **Yaxchilán and Bonampak Archeological Sites.** – *Access by light aircraft (1 hour). Description p 221.*

⊘ **San Cristóbal Grottos (Grutas de San Cristóbal).** – *9 km – 5.6 miles to the southeast on highway n° 190, turn right 700 m – 2297 ft on unpaved road. Guided tour 30 minutes.* Hidden in a pine forest, the entrance to the cavern was discovered in 1960. The strange forms of the stalactites and stalagmites become fantastic in the spacious so-called Golden Room (Salón de Oro), where the 500 m – 1640 ft tour ends. The rest of the underground cavern is a mysterious labyrinth, not totally explored.

San Juan Chamula; Zinacantán. – *15 km – 9.3 miles. Estimate 3 hours. Go northwest from San Cristóbal de Las Casas toward Zinacantán, and after 7 km – 4.3 miles turn right and continue 4 km – 2.5 miles on an unpaved road.*

San Juan Chamula. – In the square of this town, the clothing worn by the people merits keen observation. Their dress is not only charming and colorful, but, in addition, denotes the matrimonial status and social standing of the wearer. Single men wear a kind of shawl drawn between the legs; those who cover their heads with a red handkerchief and a black cloth hat are city officials; and the poorest may be detected by the thin soles on their sandals.

The first thing to do is to purchase a ticket (pase) at the Tourist Department on the lower floor of the town hall. For religious reasons pertaining to the Chamulas' traditions, photographing inside the church is not permitted.

⊘ **Saint John's Church** (Templo de San Juan). – Every Sunday its dark interior is faintly lit by hundreds of candles and more than 40 images are thus worshipped. In this unique atmosphere, magic **religious celebrations**★★, with pre-Hispanic influences, are carried out in the Totzil language. Besides strengthening the communal feeling, these celebrations serve to reinforce the social autonomy of the local ethnic group.

Returning to the junction, continue 4 km – 2.5 miles to Zinacantán

Zinacantán. – This small town surrounded by mountains and springs considered sacred
⊘ by the local people, is built around the **Church of San Lorenzo** (Iglesia de San Lorenzo) and the **Hermitage of the Lord of the Esquipulas** (Ermita del Señor de las Esquipulas). Each Sunday the worshippers converge on both these churches, wearing their elegant pink flowered garb and blue shawls, flooding the town with color.

Photographing is strictly forbidden in the churches and in the town.

★ SAN LUIS POTOSÍ San Luis Potosí ◆◆◆◆◆

Map of Principal Sights p 5

San Luis Potosí was founded on a wind-swept and sun-parched plain. Its narrow streets retain a good number of elaborate colonial mansions, built in ochre-colored stone, as well as Porfirista-style residences – some of which are today occupied by businesses – alongside examples of modern architecture. The city was the home of distinguished cultural leaders such as Manuel José Othón, Francisco González Bocanegra, Julián Carrillo and Francisco de la Maza.

HISTORICAL NOTES

In 1592 the discovery of gold and silver ores on San Pedro's Hill (Cerro de San Pedro) prompted the foundation of San Luis Minas de Potosí. The momentum generated by this find, in addition to the prosperous livestock haciendas of the region, turned San Luis Potosí into the fourth most important city in the Viceroyalty of Mexico. Evidence of this past wealth can still be seen in the churches and monuments of the city.

Confronting the French Intervention, in 1863, President Juárez made San Luis Potosí the provisional capital of the Republic. Five years later, during a stay in this town, Juárez refused to pardon Emperor Maximilian of Habsburg and Generals Miramón and Mejía, who were shot in Querétaro *(see p 174).*

In 1910, Francisco I. Madero was held prisoner in this city and subsequently fled to San Antonio, Texas. From there he issued the Plan of San Luis Potosí, arousing the Mexican people to rebel against President Porfirio Díaz.

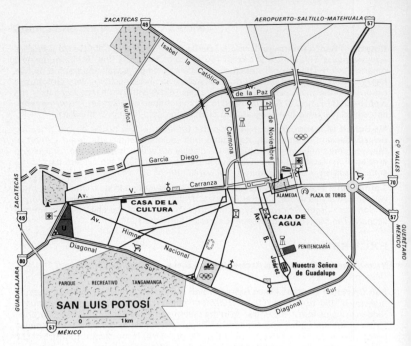

★ CENTER OF THE CITY *time: 1 day – Plan below*

Founders' Square (Plaza de los Fundadores). – **Small Square of the Jesuits** (Plazuela de la Compañía). This was the first area of the city to be settled at the end of the 16C. Today it is bordered by severe constructions belonging to different eras. On the north side stand the **University**, with a simple 17C facade, and the **Loreto Chapel** (Capilla de Loreto), the facade of which is worked in Solomonic baroque style; and on the west side, the **Ipiña Building**, from the beginning of this century, displays its monumental arcade.

Plaza de Armas. – **Hidalgo Garden** (Jardín Hidalgo). This is a lively place, full of trees and shrubbery, with a pink bandstand in its center, where Mexican music is played. This park is surrounded by distinguished constructions of past centuries: the Government Palace, city hall and the Cathedral.

⊙ **Government Palace (Palacio de Gobierno) (PG).** – **Consistorial Palace and New Royal Houses** (Expalacio Consistorial y Nuevas Casas Reales). This is a rather austere building that took over 150 years to construct. In 1815 Agustín de Iturbide lived there and later various presidents of the Republic resided there as well, such as Antonio López de Santa Anna and Benito Juárez. On the first floor, the chamber in which the Princess of Salm-Salm pleaded for the pardon of Emperor Maximilian has been preserved.

Cathedral. – The facade of this impressive mid-17C edifice resembles a Chinese screen with two exuberantly decorated buttresses standing out. Its **facade** combines Solomonic and baroque components; note the marble sculptures of the Apostles – copies in smaller size of the ones Bernini carved for the Basilica of Saint John Lateran in Rome. The **interior** has a basilica form with three naves and an enormous cupola that illuminates the high altar. The latter is covered by a lovely canopy. Some 18C paintings by José de Páez and Rodríguez Juárez can also be seen here.

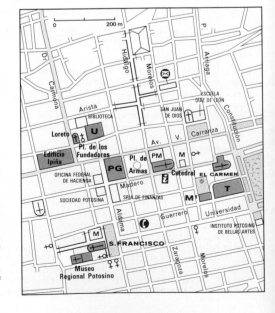

★ Carmelite Church (Templo del Carmen). –

Facing one of the prettiest squares in San Luis stands this magnificent church, which was built in the mid-18C thanks to the will of Nicolás Fernando Torres. Its **facade** is one of the richest in New Spain, worked in the Churrigueresque baroque style, combined with wreathed supports that are decorated in plant motifs. Male and female saints of the Carmelite order are represented there. In the upper central sector is a lovely niche, containing a solemn sculpture of the Virgin of Carmen.

Interior. – This church has only one nave and its transept is prolonged to the right by the sacristy and to the left by the Chapel of the Most Holy (Capilla del Santísimo). In the nave the two altars nearest the transept have been carved in stone and gilded.

Chapel of the Most Holy (Capilla del Santísimo). – Its harmonious facade, carved in many-colored stone, is dedicated to the archangels and adorned with superb mortarwork decoration. The chapel serves as a dressing room for the Virgin of Carmen, and its altarpiece is richly worked in wood and entirely covered in gold leaf. It was rebuilt in this century, reproducing the original colonial style.

Sacristy. – This vast hall is covered with large mural canvases by the colonial painter, Francisco Antonio Vallejo (1713-1756).

Peace Theater (Teatro de la Paz) (T). – The architect José Noriega designed and built this elegant neoclassical building in the mid-19C. A grand flight of steps leads to the pink stone **facade,** with its aristocratic porch supported by columns. The horseshoe-shaped **interior** is a good example of the numerous theaters built on the pattern of the Paris Opera.

★ **National Mask Museum and Telegraph Office** (Museo Nacional de la Máscara y Oficinas de Telégrafos) (M[1]). – **Federal Palace** (Antiguo Palacio Federal) formerly the **Mansion of Ramón Martí** (Mansión del señor Ramón Martí). In this baronial residence from the beginning of the century, more than 700 masks, in a great variety of materials and colors, are featured. The majority reflect the sacred character that the Mexican Indians confer on the forces of nature during their traditional ceremonies. A selection of European and Asiatic masks completes the collection.

★ **Saint Francis' Church** (Templo de San Francisco). – This structure from the second half ⊙ of the 17C was built on the handsome square of the same name. It possesses an admirable baroque facade, combining harmoniously Doric and Solomonic columns; among them are several sculptures of Franciscan saints. The Saint Francis in the second section is especially noteworthy. In the third section on either side, are fixed the emblems of the Franciscan order.

Interior. – The interior has a Latin cross layout and paintings by Miguel Cabrera, Antonio de Torres and Francisco Martínez with scenes of Saint Francis' life. At the center of the apse hangs a handsome chandelier in the shape of a ship made of fine prisms, which, according to legend, was donated by a survivor of a shipwreck.

★★ **Sacristy.** – This vast chamber occupies the entire rear section of the chancel – a characteristic of San Luis Potosí architecture. In it, sturdy pilasters and great mural canvases by Pedro Calderón and Antonio de Torres are outstanding. In the splay of the door leading to the east chamber, there is a lovely 18C **relief** representing the stigmatization of Saint Francis, within a bucolic landscape of abundant water and vegetation, with a solicitous squirrel that has witnessed the miracle.

Meditation Room (Sala de Profundis). – This room, located beyond the door with the above-mentioned relief, contains a reproduction of an ancient altarpiece from the high altar, worked in the baroque style.

⊙ **San Luis Potosí Regional Museum** (Museo Regional Potosino). – Franciscan Convent (Exconvento Franciscano). This simple construction from the mid-17C has thick walls that enclose a warm spiritual atmosphere.

Lower Floor. – A survey of San Luis Potosí's Huastec culture, through archeological pieces, sculptures and vessels, is exhibited here. One of the most beautiful pieces is the copy of the sculpture known as the *Huastec Youth (adolescente huasteco).* In another room, there are fine wrought-iron pieces from the 16C and 17C.

★ **Aranzazú Chapel** (Capilla de Aranzazú). – The chapel of the Franciscans, today divested of its treasures, is located on the second floor. The buttresses include enormous Churrigueresque pilasters, ornamented with applications of mortarwork, and the vaults are decorated with plasterwork. The entire surface is gilded and painted in many hues. Particularly noteworthy is the rich plasterwork of the cupola, where some fairly good anonymous paintings, as well as a Christ made of cornstalks, have been conserved.

CALZADA DE GUADALUPE *(Av. B. Juárez)*

time: 1 hour – Area map p 180

This is one of the broadest avenues in the city, with a wide, tree-shaded central strip cooled by fountains and bordered by several important buildings.

★ **Reservoir (Caja de Agua).** – This is a splendid 19C work, today a national monument, built by the engineer Juan Sanabria. It was fashioned with all the wealth of the era, ornamented in finely cut stone. This reservoir distributed throughout the city the water coming from the ravine known as Cañada del Lobo.

Our Lady of Guadalupe Sanctuary (Santuario de Nuestra Señora de Guadalupe). – This church goes back to the middle of the 17C. It displays an elegant facade with very fine towers that dominate the city.

The facade features an interplay of baroque elements, with girdled Solomonic and Ionic columns among scattered foliage. In the center, an enormous sculpture of the Archangel Gabriel seems to be holding the Virgin of Guadalupe.

Its **interior** adheres to the Latin cross design and has been decorated with neoclassical elegance by the Italian masters, Claudio Molina and José Campiani.

Sacristy. – Here a good number of enormous canvases can be seen, among them a collection of the Stations of the Cross, attributed to Francisco de P. Herrera.

ADDITIONAL SIGHT *Area map p 180*

★ **Cultural Center (Casa de la Cultura). Vista Hermosa Mansion of Gerardi Meade.** – This elegant mansion, whose name means "lovely view", was built at the beginning of the 20C. The edifice has the overall appearance of a stately European residence. Objects from the Huastec culture, valuable 18C Mexican paintings as well as furniture from the 16C and 17C are on display.

On the **second floor,** there is a collection of works by anonymous painters, crucifixes and handicrafts from San Luis Potosí, the famous local *rebozos* and inlaid boxes from Santa María del Río. The remarkable **Gothic Chapel** houses a splendid gold altarpiece.

★★ SAN MIGUEL DE ALLENDE Guanajuato ◆◆◆

Map of Principal Sights p 5

This is one of the most beautiful mountain cities of Mexico. From the higher altitudes, San Miguel de Allende resembles a giant Nativity scene. At night it seems to have been invaded by fireflies. Its narrow cobblestone streets are lined by rustic houses, elegant mansions and many churches.

San Miguel is a very busy trading center, particularly in handicrafts, such as jewelry, wooden furniture, pottery, tin articles, textiles among many others. There are also shops selling antiques and reproductions. No less active is its cultural life; there are many art galleries where young painters' works are on exhibit, since San Miguel has a large artist colony.

HISTORICAL NOTES

In 1542, Fray Juan de San Miguel founded the town of San Miguel in honor of the Archangel. Years later, according to legend, the town was moved to the northeast, to a place the Indians called Fundación Itzcuinapan Río de Perros or River of the Dogs, because wild animals used to come to the river to drink. This spot is now known as El Chorro.

It was in this city in the 18C that Father Benito Díaz de Gamarra produced a revolution in Mexican thinking by introducing Cartesian rationalism into his philosophy courses. At this same period the installation of factories, tanneries and other industries, turned San Miguel el Grande into an important economic center. At the beginning of the 20C, the Act of Foundation was modified to honor Captain Ignacio Allende, who was born in this town and participated in the War of Independence.

★ CENTER OF THE CITY *time: 1 day*

Plaza Allende. – This square was laid out on a rose-colored platform. Shaded by laurel trees, this is an inviting spot to rest and to contemplate the 18C portals and the old constructions that border it.

Parish Church (Parroquia). – The voluminous parish church can be seen from any vantage point in San Miguel de Allende. It was built at the beginning of this century in neo-Gothic style by Zeferino Gutiérrez. This enormous mass was superimposed on the 17C colonial church, without modifying its interior, which is still based on a Latin cross. The only change was in the original facade. Within the church, several paintings attributed to Juan Rodríguez Juárez have been preserved.

Regional Museum (Museo Regional) (M). – House of Ignacio Allende (Casa de Ignacio Allende). This mid-18C residence, with a baroque facade, was the birthplace and home of Captain Ignacio Allende y Unzaga, hero of the War of Independence. The interior is used for temporary exhibits.

★ **House of the Counts of la Canal (Casa de los Condes de la Canal) (A).** – **Banco Nacíonal de México.** This is a lovely example of the noble family residences of the 18C.

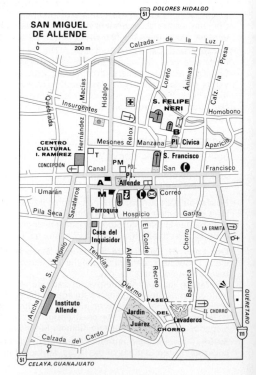

The side portal, *(on calle Real)* designed in the neoclassical style reinforces the aristocratic character of the building; its sturdy **outer door★** is embellished with panels in high relief. The arch keystone is inscribed with an eagle, symbolizing the standard-bearing rank accorded to José Marino de la Canal y Hervás.

⊘**Saint Francis' Church (Templo de San Francisco).** – This handsome church, dating back to the 18C, is set on a small square full of vendors' stalls with all sorts of goods, especially regional sweets. The venerable laurel trees of the square partially hide the church's Churrigueresque facade, where the fine, slender *estípites,* typical of the Guanajuato baroque school, stand out. This is topped by an effigy of Saint Francis. In its spacious neoclassical interior, there are paintings portraying the death of Saint Francis attributed to Juan Rodríguez Juárez and, in the sacristy, works by Juan Correa (17C) and a *Transfiguration* by Salvador Fajardo (18C).

Civic Plaza (Plaza Cívica). – This enormous esplanade was dedicated to Captain Ignacio Allende. On the northeast side, is the market, where fruits, flowers and some handicrafts are sold.

Church of Our Lady of Salvation (Templo de Nuestra Señora de la Salud) (B). – This splendid 18C building formed part of the Old College of Saint Francis de Sales (Antiguo Colegio de San Francisco de Sales). It features a simple Churrigueresque facade with sculptures of the Immaculate Conception, San Joaquín and Saint Anne (Santa Ana). The delicate carved *estípites* are protected by an ample shell, which is uncommon in this region.

★**Saint Philip Neri's Prayer Hall (Oratorio de San Felipe Neri).** – In front of a small, ⊘irregularly-shaped atrium stands this gracious church, which was known in the 17C as the mulattos' church. In the 18C, Saint Philip's followers remodeled it, adding a pink stone baroque facade, which shows a strong Indian influence, and dedicated it to Our Lady of Solitude (Nuestra Señora de la Soledad), who appears accompanied by the sculptures of five apostles. To the right, can be seen the Cross of Caravaca (better known as the Cross of Lorraine) and the medallion of Saint Philip Neri. The church has a slender tower decorated with mortarwork.

Interior. – The interior, based on a Latin cross design, has neoclassical altars and paintings by Miguel Cabrera. The canvas of the Virgin of Guadalupe, on the right transept altar, is particularly distinguished. A notable collection of 33 oil paintings representing various scenes of Saint Philip Neri's life is exposed in the nave.

Sacristy. – A huge 18C chest of drawers with fine marquetry and, above it, a large canvas with scenes from the Old Testament and the *Feast of the Passover (Cena Pascual)*, attributed to Andrés López, are memorable. There is also a stunning painting by Juan Rodríguez Juárez representing the *Immaculate Conception (la Purísima)*.

★★**The Holy House of Loreto** (Santa Casa de Loreto). – This austere 18C chapel was built thanks ⊘to donations from Manuel Tomás de la Canal; it copies the Holy House of the Virgin (Santa Casa de la Virgen) which is found in Loreto, Italy. Its large baroque front faces the left transept of the oratory. Most noticeable on it are two pairs of ondulating Solomonic columns. Within the chapel, floors and walls are covered by colored tiles made in China, Valencia and Puebla. On the side walls of the altar there are two sculptures depicting the benefactor in prayer.

★★**Dressing Room** (Camarín). – This lovely diminutive octagonal room is decorated with ⊘exuberant gilded altarpieces, all of which are baroque except for that of Saint Joseph (San José), which belongs to the neoclassical style. The walls are adorned with many-colored plasterwork motifs. Especially notable are the altarpiece of San Joaquín and the sculpture of the Apostle James. This dressing room is the crowning glory of the Holy House of Loreto (Santa Casa de Loreto), since it is the chamber dedicated to the Virgin.

★**Ignacio Ramírez Cultural Center (Centro Cultural Ignacio Ramírez) – The Sorcerer (El** ⊘**Nigromante). – Convent of the Conceptionist Nuns** (Exconvento de la Concepción). The patio of this convent is probably the largest of its kind built in New Spain. It is full of age-old trees that shade the central fountain. It has been transformed into a cultural center where classes are given in painting, literature and other subjects.

★**SAN MIGUEL HOUSES (CASAS SAN MIGUELENSES)**

time: 1 hour

The San Miguel de Allende houses, famous for their history and their elegance, infuse a certain grace and urban harmony into the town, while glimpses of lively and colorful inner patios add a note of gaiety.

Inquisitioner's House (Casa del Inquisidor). – This small house from the end of the 18C is striking for its ostentatious and intricate French-style facade. On the second level the elaborate wrought-iron balconies add color to the whole. The name derives from the fact that a commissioner of the Holy Office lived there.

⊘ **Allende Institute (Instituto Allende). – Country Mansion of Don Tomás de la Canal y Bueno de Baeza** (Mansión de Campo). This is an elegant ancestral mansion from the middle of the 18C. Its facade is a prominent stone structure; inside, the spaciousness of its courtyards, as well as its grand arcade, are impressive. From its beautiful tree-shaded gardens there is a lovely view of the city.
In the chapel, part of the original frescoes has been preserved, as well as a statue of Christ crafted by the Indians, a polychrome chest of drawers and an 18C arcade. At present it houses an educational establishment.

★ PASEO DEL CHORRO *time: 1 hour*

On this pleasant walk along winding cobblestone streets, there are old mansions with massive front gates framed with stone jambs and windows protected by whimsical wrought-iron grilles. This promenade leads to the pleasant spot that once was the seat of Itzcuinapan.

From there a path goes down to the pink stone **laundry basins** from colonial times. The walk ends in the charming **Juárez Garden** (Jardín Juárez) whose venerable trees make it a favorite resting spot.

EXCURSION

⊙ **Atotonilco Sanctuary (Santuario de Atotonilco).** – *17 km – 10.6 miles. Go north from San Miguel de Allende on highway n° 51 toward Dolores and after 14 km – 8.7 miles turn left and continue 3 km – 1.9 miles on an unpaved road.*

In an arid countryside burned by the sun, where trees are only rarely seen, stands the Atotonilco Sanctuary, a pilgrimage site during the colonial period. It was from this sanctuary that, in 1810, the priest Miguel Hidalgo took the standard bearing the image of the Virgin of Guadalupe, which was adopted as the flag of the pro-Independence armies.

The fortress-like sanctuary contains a striking **screen★★** entirely decorated with oil painted panels depicting scenes from the lives of various saints. Immediately beyond, there is a colossal Saint Christopher (San Cristóbal) carved in wood and painted in many colors. The walls are covered in **mural paintings★★**, as is the vault, with scenes from the life of Christ that date from the end of the 18C.

In this sanctuary, some popular paintings, attributed to Antonio Martínez Pocasangre, and others, attributed to Juan Correa, have been preserved. In the right hand chapel, numerous 18C paintings on glass should be seen.

★ SIERRA GORDA MISSIONS Querétaro

Map of Principal Sights p 5

Five main evangelizing missions (Jalpan, Landa de Matamoros, Tilaco, Tancoyol and Concá) lie in a setting of unforgettable charm. They are located in the region known as the Sierra Gorda, which is a mountain range to the east of the Sierra Madre Oriental, running north to south, that borders on the states of Querétaro, Hidalgo, Guanajuato and San Luis Potosí.

HISTORICAL NOTES

For over two centuries, the drive for **evangelization** was hampered by the indomitable nature of the indigenous populations. In this area there were numerous old and scattered settlements of Chichimecs, dedicated to agriculture, given the gentle climate and abundant water from the Moctezuma, Jalpan and Concá Rivers, which cut through the craggy topography.

It was only in the mid-18C that José de Escandón reorganized the humble chapels and missions. At that time he was asked to establish the new missions and to hand over the existing ones to the College of Saint Ferdinand (Colegio de San Fernando). The renowned missionary, **Junípero Serra,** who arrived in 1750 and settled in Jalpan, together with Friars Francisco Palau and Miguel Molina, accomplished great evangelizing work and promoted the economic and agricultural development of the region.

★ MISSIONS *174 km – 108.1 miles starting from Jalpan – 1 day*

⊙ The five above-mentioned missions, built in the middle of the 18C, are unique examples of Latin American baroque architecture. In these buildings, elements of 16C architecture *(p 39)* have been preserved, along with a mixture of styles, such as the Renaissance and the baroque. Indian craftsmanship added a particular stamp to them, which is apparent on the facades, towers and cupolas, where mortarwork and polychromy play an important role. The mission interiors all follow the Latin cross layout.

Jalpan. – This enchanting mission, dedicated to the Apostle James, was the first and largest of the five. It was built by **Fray Junípero Serra,** who succeeded in putting together a complex with balanced proportions and rich ornamentation. The **facade★** adorned in mortarwork presents an interesting combination of plant motifs and complicated iconography, in which the Mexican Virgin of Guadalupe shares the central motifs with the Spanish Virgin of the Pillar (Virgen del Pilar). There are frequent Gothic touches, like those in the lower riches.

Follow 20 km – 12.4 miles on highway n° 120 toward Xilitla, turn left and continue 300 m – 984 ft on a stone paved road.

Landa de Matamoros. – This mission is named after Mariano Matamoros, one of the most important leaders of the Morelos army in the War of Independence in 1810, who was allegedly a priest here.

The church's regal **facade★** honors the Virgin Mary. Striking images of Duns Escoto and Sor María de Agreda, historical figures both devoted to the Virgin, are placed at the sides of the windows.

Leave Landa de Matamoros on highway n° 120 and at 10 km – 6.2 miles turn right and continue 4 km – 2.5 miles on a paved road and 12 km – 7.5 miles on an unpaved road.

Tilaco. – On the **facade★** the play of chiaroscuro is enhanced by the shadows of various projecting architectural elements.

On the polychrome facade, the eye is drawn to the image of Saint Francis, the shield, and the little blond mermaids who seem to support the cornice – all intertwined in rich decorations of plant motifs.

Return to highway n° 120 and at 7 km – 4.3 miles, turn left and continue 4 km – 2.5 miles on a paved road and 12 km – 7.5 miles on an unpaved one.

Tancoyol. – This mission is located at the bottom of a fertile valley, surrounded by mountains covered in oaks and ferns, where solitary deer are occasionally sighted. In front of a broad atrium, which has preserved the remains of the *posas* or corner chapels and the pedestal of the atrial cross, rises the beautiful mission dedicated to the Holy Cross (Santa Cruz). Both in size and in ornamentation, its **facade★** recalls that of the Jalpan mission. A relief depicts the stigmatization of Saint Francis, and all the empty spaces are occupied by vines hung with thick bunches of grapes.

Return to Jalpan and take highway n° 62 toward Río Verde and at 34 km – 21.1 miles, turn left for 1 km – 0.6 miles on a cobblestone road.

Concá. – This exquisite mission is reached by crossing a modern bridge over the Santa María and Jalpan Rivers, which have the peculiarity of having different colored waters. For a few meters, the waters remain separated thus creating a fascinating polychromy.

On the **facade★** of this mission of Saint Michael

(Photo Lourdes Grobet/Mexico)

Sierra Gorda. Concá, Mission of Saint Michael

(Misión de San Miguel), the door has a broken-edged arch with spandrels covered in acanthus leaves. On the upper part, the sculpture of Saint Michael with his sword aloft, tramples on a horrible four-footed monster that appears to beg for mercy.

SOMBRERETE Zacatecas ◆

Map of Principal Sights p 5

Wedged in the shadow of Sombreretillo Hill (Cerro del Sombreretillo), from which it takes its name, the old mining city of Villa de San Juan Bautista de Llerena retains its colonial air. Particularly worth mentioning are the religious constructions like the 18C church and monastery of **Saint Francis** (Templo y Convento de San Francisco) and the **Chapel of the Third Order** (Capilla Anexa de la Tercera Orden), with an elliptical layout that is extremely rare in Mexico. The church of Santo Domingo (Templo de Santo Domingo) retain good samples of colonial painting, and the imposing parish church is a prominent feature of the town's architectural landscape.

EXCURSION

★★**Sierra de los Órganos.** – *33 km – 20.5 miles. Go northwest from Sombrerete on highway n° 45 and at 25 km – 15.5 miles, turn right and continue 8 km – 5 miles to San Francisco de los Órganos on an unpaved road.*
This extraordinary natural site, extending over a 25 km^2 – 9.7 square mile area, is situated between a pine valley and a desert plain. It is renowned for its strange **basalt rock formations** that resemble organ cactuses, hence the site's name. The spectacular landscapes attract mountain climbers as well as film directors in search of impressive settings for Westerns.

If you are puzzled by an abbreviation or a symbol in the text or on the maps, consult the key on p 52.

Map of Principal Sights p 6 – *17 km–10.5 miles east of Tuxtla Gutiérrez*

This is one of the most spectacular geological faults in America; it splits the mountain mass flanking Tuxtla Gutiérrez. The gigantic crack was formed 12 million years ago and at present is an oasis of vegetation under the scorching sun. Its nearly vertical walls plunge almost 1 300 m – 4 265 ft to where the Grijalva River runs through the bottom of the gorge, providing a habitat for ducks, herons and pelicans.

At the end of the canyon, is one of the largest hydraulic works in Latin America, the **Manuel Moreno Torres Dam (Chicoasén)**, inaugurated in 1980. Because of its proximity to a seismic zone, and due to regional faults, the dam has a retaining wall with a flexible central core 262 m – 860 ft high.

★★★ **Boat trip (Recorrido en lancha).** – *Time: 2 1/2 hours. Boarding at the dock in Chiapa de Corzo.*

The beginning of the trip offers an impressive panorama, with Cahauré Island in the background flanked by various limestone hills. Beyond the Panamerican Highway Bridge, the corn and banana plantations begin to thin out, as the mountains close in and the river bed narrows. As the boat rounds a curve, an imposing vertical wall, seems to block the way. The marvelous cliffs ahead are marked by ancient strata in white, pink and grey tonalities, which are particularly noteworthy in the **Cave of Colors** (Cueva de Colores).

Further along, on the right side, the eye is drawn to the so-called **Christmas Tree** (Arbol de Navidad), an impressive rock formation made of moss-blanketed flagstones behind a waterfall.

At the end of the gorge lies the reservoir. Under its waters rests the ancient town of Usumacinta, whose inhabitants moved to the right river bank when the water level began to rise. The monument in the background portrays a driller, a mason and a peon beside Manuel Moreno, the engineer who built the dam.

Automobile ride (Recorrido en automobile). – *Time: 2 hours. In Tuxtla Gutiérrez, follow calle 11a. Oriente Norte. 17 km – 10.6 miles beyond the entrance booth.* After 2.5 km – 1.6 miles, at the **Ceiba Lookout** (Mirador La Ceiba), the entrance to the canyon can be glimpsed, although its impressive beauty unfolds 9 km – 5.6 miles farther on, at the **Coyota Lookout** (Mirador La Coyota), where the view plunges down the cliffs all the way to the riverbed. Continuing 5 km – 3.1 miles, the **Tepehuaje Lookout** (Mirador El Tepehuaje) is reached, from which there is a close view of the cliff faces where bits of grass and a few trees cling to the rocky walls. Farther along (1 km – 0.6 miles), the highway ends at an altitude of 1 200 m – 3 937 ft. From this point, the **view★★★** of the profound Sumidero abyss is overwhelming.

You will find a selection of regional tours on pp 7 to 15.

Plan your route with the help of the map of principal sights on pp 4 to 6.

Map of Principal Sights p 5

Between the Cazones and the Tecolutla Rivers, set in a terrain richly endowed with flora and fauna, are situated the ruins of El Tajín, which was the main urban settlement and ceremonial center of Veracruz.

The Totonac Indians named the site El Tajin, which means "the city of the thunder gods". The site's history dates back to the 4C BC, but it was after the 6C AD that the Indians began to build the fastuous temples and buildings for which the city was renowned.

ARCHEOLOGICAL SITE time: 1/2 day

The site is divided into two parts: El Tajín proper comprising the monuments on the plain, and El Tajín Chico, made up of the constructions erected on the small flattened mounds.

Site Museum (Museo de Sitio). – In this museum fragments of the stone drums that constituted the column shafts from the Palace of the Colums (Edificios de las Columnas) are on exhibit. These finely carved pieces demonstrate the Indians' extraordinary masonry skills.

Volador's Dance (Danza del Volador). – Next to the entrance of the ceremonial center, rises the **pole** for the traditional dance of the *volador* or flyer, an impressive and dangerous ritual with pre-Hispanic origins in which a dancer at the top of the pole plays a flute and a little drum while four others, tied by ropes to the top of the pole, hang in space and begin to descend in ever larger circles until they reach the ground. It takes 52 rotations – which correspond to the number of years in the Indians' mythological cycle – to complete this dizzying feat.

A few steps further lies a path flanked by exuberant vegetation that allows a glimpse of several unexplored mounds, as though nature were unwilling to reveal their mysteries. After a small winding stretch, suddenly a surprising landscape opens up and the first outstanding complex of El Tajín appears.

South Ball Game Court (Juego de Pelota Sur). – In this rectangular courtyard 60 m – 197 ft long by 10 m – 33 ft wide, there are six remarkably carved **panels,** constituting one of the few pieces of concrete evidence regarding certain details of this most important Mesoamerican ritual.

Present-day research has not yet succeeded in construing a comprehensive interpretation of this ritual.

First Panel (1). – This shows a human sacrifice related to the game. One figure holds a player locked in his arms while the other is cutting his chest open with a knife. At one end there is a skeletal figure that symbolizes the netherworld.

Second Panel (2). – The *pulque* ceremony is depicted here. Four figures in different poses and a maguey plant fill the interior space.

Third Panel (3). – This scene portrays a human figure disguised as an eagle, facing another reclining figure, accompanied by two musicians, one playing on a tortoise shell and the other shaking a rattle.

Fourth Panel (4). – This relief faces the previous one and depicts a ritual to the rain god involving three persons.

Fifth Panel (5). – In the upper part of the relief, there is an interesting composition of a human face formed by the profiles of two joined heads.

Sixth Panel (6). – This panel depicts a ceremony between two ball game players. Both are standing and each has the symbol for a word before its mouth, which means that they are conversing. Two more figures watch the ritual; one of them is in a semi-kneeling position and has a coyote mask covering his head.

Building 5 (Edificio 5). – This truncated pyramid 12 m – 39 ft tall was built in five stages. There is a marked contrast between the simplicity of its sloping sides and the profusion of niches in the panels and in the beveled cornice. The two sets of niches at the summit are decorated on the inside with a fret pattern called **xicalcoliuhqui,** composed of the geometric representation of a serpent – a very common symbol in pre-Hispanic art.

Pyramid of the Niches
(Pirámide de los Nichos). – This building is the most spectacular monument constructed by the Totonacs. As the sun strikes it, the strong contrast between its surfaces and openings creates a vivid play of chiaroscuro enhancing its air of majesty.

The principal facade, looking to the east, has a broad staircase bordered by ramps that are decorated with the **xicalcoliuhqui** fret.

The 325 niches on its panels, added to those that decorate the stairway altars and those that are hidden under it, total 364. Adding the opening of the entrance that the upper temple used to have, the grand total is 365, which leads to the hypothesis that this structure could have served to count the days of the year and to calculate astronomical positions. Unfortunately, these and other niches of the site have collapsed many times, partially owing to poor construction techniques and insufficient foundation consolidation. The isolated blocks of stone placed in front of the east facade probably held banners.

(Photo Guillermo Aldana/Mexico)

El Tajín. Pyramid of the Niches

North Ball Game Court (Juego de Pelota Norte). – This court is smaller than the southern one. Despite its advanced state of deterioration, its panels still bear witness to a highly developed artistic sensitivity, as can be seen in the friezes of interlaced serpentine forms running along the top of the walls.

Following the uphill path, you reach to the second sector.

Once again the path barely manages to open a way through the ever-present undergrowth on this site. At the **Plaza of Tajín Chico,** suddenly a new group of buildings appears.

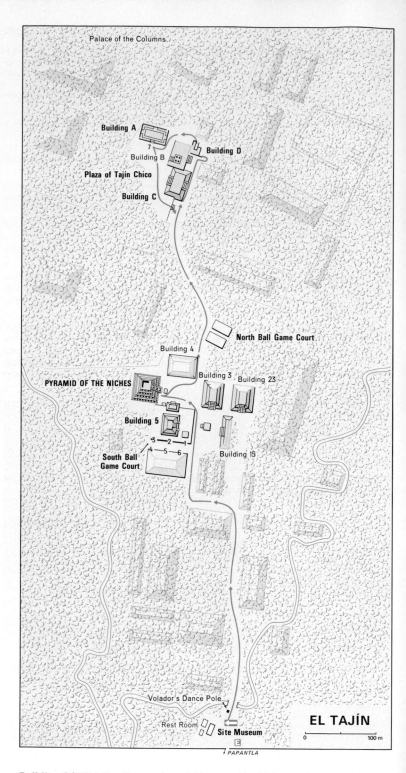

PAPANTLA

Building C (Edificio C). – The rear face of this pyramid, which dates from the early post-Classic period, is decorated with a series of frets designed to simulate niches.

Turn right and go down the hill following the steps set into the slope.

Building D (Edificio D). – In order to make the best possible use of the available space, this building was erected on the slope of a terrace. A narrow tunnel was constructed to connect the two levels by a covered stairway.

Go through the underground passage and up the nine steps.

The main entrance on the upper platform is decorated with intertwined rhomboidal motifs.

Building A (Edificio A). – In the principal facade of this imposing palace, the entrance is formed by a **Maya arch** ( ) *(p 37)*.

Go up the stairs and turn left.

In the passageway around the central structure, there is a double interlaced fret that resembles a swastica.

Go up the stairs at the southwest corner.

In the upper part, the symmetrical layout of this residence that once lodged the families of the most notable priests in this area becomes apparent. The entrances to the rooms are on the east side and the corridor, on the west. The rooms are separated by terraces, which also served as sources of ventilation. During the archeological excavation it was discovered that this enormous complex was entirely covered by a roof made of lime, sea shells and sand, mixed with pumice powder and fragments of pottery. Apparently this mixture was cast over a curved and polished framework.

The decline and eventual abandonment of El Tajín (12C) was principally due to wars, socio-political disorganization and the breakdown of trading alliances.

EXCURSIONS

Papantla. – *13 km – 8.1 miles to the east.*
Palm straw hats protect the Indians from the abundant rains and the intense sun that beat down on this typical Gulf coast village. The land is ideal for cultivating the native orchids and the vanilla beans that brought them prosperity before the artificial essence was developed.

The special atmosphere of Papantla combines the presence of the Western world with the pre-Hispanic past. The monumental sculpted panel in front of the town's main park (Parque Central) attests to this peculiarity, by integrating the Pyramid of the Niches with modern oil rigs and representations of local dances.

From the atrium of the Saint Mary of the Assumption Parish Church, (Parroquia de Santa María de Asunción) where they perform the **Volador's Dance** (Danza del Volador), a magnificent **view** of the locality can be enjoyed.

Teayo. – *66 km – 41 miles. Go north from Papantla 24 km – 14.9 miles on highway n° 180 to Poza Rica; continue 20 km – 12.4 miles on towards the north on highway n° 130 and in Tihuatlán turn left and follow a road in fair condition 21 km – 13 miles toward Metlaltoyuca (entrance is not marked).*
Crossing one of the most fertile regions of the country, the visitor can appreciate the burgeoning agricultural production of sugar cane, potatoes, citric fruits and bananas and also catch an occasional glimpse of the vents for the oil pipeline that runs under this petroleum-rich soil.

Teayo Castle (Castillo de Teayo). – In the main square of the isolated town of Teayo, there is a three-level **pyramid,** popularly called the Castle. Built of large flagstones joined with lime and sand mortar, it is one of the few monuments, excluding those of the Maya zone, that still retains remnants of its upper temple, even though the present roof is not authentic. The monument dates from the post-Classic period of the Huastec culture *(p 37).*

Statuary (Estatuaria). – *Behind the Castle, next to the basketball court.* Behind a simple grille are twenty sculptures – mainly standing figures with flat surfaces – that bear witness to one of the few phallic cults in Mesoamerica.

TAMPICO Tamaulipas ◆◆◆◆◆

Map of Principal Sights p 5

At the mouth of the Pánuco River, the towns of Tampico and Madero have merged into one city. After various attempts frustrated by pirate raids, the city was officially founded on April 12th, 1823. Its port is of vital importance for the oil industry.

SIGHTS

⊘**Museum of Huastec Culture** (Museo de la Cultura Huasteca). – *7 km – 4.3 miles on Av. Hidalgo and Ejército Nacional, turn right 700 m – 2 297 ft on the grounds of the Madero City Technological Institute (Instituto Tecnológico de Ciudad Madero).* This museum presents a worthwhile exhibit of numerous pieces and objects belonging to the Huastec culture; it includes obsidian arrowheads (10 000-3 000C BC) from the nomads, as well as clay figures, pottery and sculptures (11C BC to 15C AD). Most striking of these is the replica of the *Huastec Youth, (adolescente huasteco)* the original of which is displayed in the National Anthropological Museum in Mexico City.

Miramar Beaches (Playas de Miramar). – *Go north on Blvd. López Mateos 15 km – 9.3 miles and turn right.*
These long beaches with fine, soft sand are bathed by the warm waters of the Gulf of Mexico. From the southern end of the ocean drive, the playful dolphins can be seen swimming near the river's mouth.

For further tourist information while in Mexico call the 24–hour English language hot line operated by the Mexican Government Tourist Office ☎ (5) 250-0123 or (5) 230-0151.

Built on the sides of the mountains and the edge of the cliffs, Taxco is one of the most fascinating colonial cities in Mexico. The white walls of its buildings bring out the clear blue of the skies. The silhouette of **Saint Prisca** Parish Church (Parroquia de Santa Prisca) can be sighted miles off on the serpentine road leading to the city. Taxco's old cobblestone streets wind over the hills, disappear in mysterious nooks and often lead to romantic little squares that are bordered by simple whitewashed houses with red tile roofs.

But Taxco is not only a quaint historic town; it is also a renowned center for the production of silver objects, enlivened with the bustling activity of its silversmith workshops.

HISTORICAL NOTES

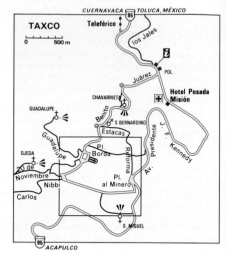

In 1524 the Spaniards reached Taxco, where they found silver mines in the place today known as Old Taxco (Taxco Viejo) 12 km – 7.5 miles to the northwest. Years later the town was moved to Bermejo Hill – the ancient village of Telancingo – which contained still larger deposits of tin, and came to be called the **King's Gallery** (Socavón del Rey).

Mines of the Past. – Captains Rodrigo de Castañeda and Miguel Díaz de Auz took the Indians to work in the mines, founding the districts of Tlachcotecapan and Acayotlas or San Miguel and Guadalupe, as they are known today *(see map opposite)*. There the Franciscans built two chapels to evangelize the Indians. At the beginning of the 18C, José de la Borda came to Taxco to work the mines on a larger scale, thus giving a great boost to the area; at that moment the town received the name of Taxco, which in the Náhuatl language means "in the ball game".

Today's Mines. – At the beginning of this century, with the opening of new roads, the city reawakened, thanks to the mining of silver, copper, zinc, lead and the famous fluorite mines – Azul and Gavilán – as well as the mercury mine of Huehuetoca. In addition, William Spratling, a North American who had fallen in love with the city, taught silversmithing in a workshop that brought international fame to Taxco and earned it the designation of National Monument.

It is advisable to leave the car at or near Plaza Borda and to visit the city on foot, for which comfortable shoes are indispensable.

SAINT PRISCA AND ITS SURROUNDINGS
time: 1/2 day – Plan p 191

This jewel of Mexican architecture is located on the east side of the city's main square, which is full of street vendors and tourists. Many artistic, cultural and religious events also take place in this square; for example, it is the gathering point for the famous **Holy Thursday★** procession, in which the penitents carry candles and heavy thorny burdens through the steep streets of the city.

★★★**Parish Church of Saint Prisca and Saint Sebastian (Parroquia de Santa Prisca y San** ⊘ **Sebastián).** – This is an outstanding example of 18C baroque art. The work was sponsored by the wealthy miner, José de la Borda, who thus thanked Providence for bestowing on him the riches that came out of his mines and, by the same token, provided his son, Manuel, with a church where he could practice his vocation.

The parish church was dedicated to two Roman martyrs, Prisca and Sebastián. In 1748, the work began under the direction of the architect, Miguel Custodio Durán, assisted by the master builder, Juan Caballero. They finished their work in 1758. The altarpieces were commissioned to Isidoro Vicente Balbás, son of the renowned architect, Jerónimo de Balbás, who designed the altarpiece in the Chapel of the Kings in the Metropolitan Cathedral of Mexico City *(p 107).*

Facade. – From the atrium grille, the structure's enormous height and volume can be appreciated. The facade displays a cluster of baroque adornments, and the tower tops seem to disappear in the clouds. Paired columns frame the sturdy wooden door decorated with geometric designs. Between the columns are the images of **Saint Peter** and **Saint Paul.**

The upper level has Solomonic columns in fine spiral carving, which accompany the images of the titular saints, **Saint Prisca** and **Saint Sebastián** (Santa Prisca and San Sebastián). At the center, there is a medallion with a magnificent relief representing the baptism of Christ in the presence of the Holy Father, the Holy Spirit and a cloud of angels and cherubs.

Taxco. Parish church of Saint Prisca

This relief is the center of the composition and a splendid example of Mexican colonial sculpture. The cornice stands boldly on columns, only to retreat under the choir window. A railing, interrupted by the clock, crowns the facade. Above the clock are found the images of the Immaculate Conception (Purísima Concepción) flanked by Saint John (San Juan) with the eagle and Saint Mathew (San Mateo) with the angel. At closer range, decorative elements typical of baroque art, such as masks, volutes, plant garlands, shells, fruits and little angels that climb out on the overhangs like naughty children can be observed.

Nave Altarpieces. – In the Latin cross layout of the interior, all the original carved and gilded baroque altarpieces have been preserved. They are paired and are identical in style but each altarpiece is dedicated to a different saint. In the left side chapel, devoted to Our Father Jesus of Nazareth (Nuestro Padre Jesús Nazareno), three more very beautiful pieces are located, dedicated to the Virgin, on the right; the Passion of Christ, on the left; and the Souls in Purgatory, in the center. The latter has a fine painting in which the Archangel Michael is outstanding.

High Altarpiece. – This is a magnificent baroque work, with very fine sculpted ornamentation, including the sculptures of the Immaculate Conception (La Purísima) and of the Holy Patrons (Santos Patrones).

The Immaculate Conception, in the center, is superbly carved in wood, with expressive movement suggested in the fabric of the Virgin's robes. Above this stands the sculpture of Saint Peter, the first of many popes depicted in this piece. The ornamental summit is particularly striking: it is pyramidal in shape, with myriad ascending moldings from which cherubs emerge, surrounded by foliage.

Sacristy. – This is a wonderful structure composed of three sections, divided by panel-led pilasters. Between them there are huge paintings by Miguel Cabrera, the most notable artist of the 18C, representing scenes from the Virgin's life, from the Annunciation to the Assumption. Also some pieces of furniture and an excellent sculpture of the Virgin of Sorrows (Virgen de los Dolores) with glass eyes and human teeth have been preserved here.

City Hall (Palacio Municipal) **(PM). – House of Don José de la Borda.** This is a distinguished 18C mansion with a pleasant and harmonious layout. Due to the site's topography, the structure has only one floor facing the main square, but four floors on the rear side.

House of the Painter, Fidel Figueroa (Casa del Pintor) (M¹). – This simple 18C house belonged to the Count of La Cadena and was called the **House of Tears** (Casa de Lágrimas) because legend relates that during its construction, the Indian workers, who were paying their tributes with their labor, were cruelly treated.

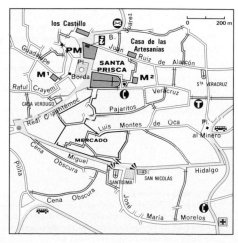

TAXCO ★★★

◷ **The Castillo Family** (Los Castillo). – **Handicraft Workshop** (Taller Artesanal). The facade of this typical colonial house is covered with green plants. It houses the workshop of these well-known silversmiths, where the different procedures and materials involved in fashioning beautiful silver and precious stone jewelry pieces and other objects can be observed.

◷ **Handicrafts House** (Casa de las Artesanías). – **House of Baron Alexander von Humboldt**. It is the most beautiful mansion from the end of the 18C and has a Mudejar-style facade, ornamented with mortarwork arabesques. In 1803 Alexander von Humboldt *(see p 19)* stayed here for a time. Legend relates that in this house there were mirrors that corrected the physical defects of the image reflected.

Spratling Museum (Museo Spratling) (M²). – The museum presents a historical survey of Taxco and a collection of pre-Hispanic pieces donated to the city by William Spratling. Some are authentic; others are reproductions. Prominent among them are bone and shell necklaces, pectorals made of precious stones, vessels and small animal figures belonging to the early Olmec and Maya cultures.

◷ **Market** (Mercado). – A picturesque trading and meeting place, this market is a veritable labyrinth, where fruits and other foods in addition to multicolored fabrics, basketry, ceramics and other articles abound. This market becomes particularly colorful on Saturdays and Sundays when many craftsmen and traders come in from the surrounding areas to sell their products.

ADDITIONAL SIGHTS

◷ **Cable Car** (Teleférico). – **Quarry Mountain** (Montaña la Cantera). This cable car across the mountains and gorges filled with greenery, affords a magnificent **view★** of Taxco in all its splendor, one of the most beautiful cities in Mexico.

◷ **O'Gorman Mural.** – **Hotel Posada Misión**. In the 1950s, an interesting mosaic of colored stone and glass was inlaid on the retaining wall in the hotel garden by the architect Juan O'Gorman. In it the artist portrayed Cuauhtémoc, the last Mexican king, using pre-Hispanic symbols.

EXCURSION

★★★ **Cacahuamilpa Grottos** (Grutas). – *31 km – 19.3 miles and 1 1/2 hour guided tour. Go*
◷ *north from Taxco on highway n° 95 toward Cuernavaca and at 22 km – 13.7 miles, turn left and after 9 km – 5.6 miles, turn right to reach the grotto entrance.* This monumental grotto, wedged between mountains and thick tropical vegetation, contains myriad natural forms. This limestone cavern is covered with stalactites, stalagmites and other formations. Metallic oxides have colored many of these shapes pink, green and blue. These ancient forms create the impression of having taken a journey through a world of fantasy.
The tour covers 2 km – 1.2 miles through 20 enormous caves, fabulously lit so as to create different settings, resembling a forest, organ pipes, alabaster domes or fine curtains hung from the cave vaults, as well as other scenes.

TEHUANTEPEC Oaxaca ◆◆

Map of Principal Sights p 6

Tehuantepec means "the hill of the beasts" in the Náhuatl language. Due to its proximity to the coast, its activities are closely linked to shipping. This pleasant city is divided into two parts by the river of the same name and still preserves the original layout of its old quarters.

Market (Mercado). – *Av. Hidalgo.* In this colorful market, which comes alive in the early hours of the morning, there is a large variety of products brought to town by the inhabitants of the mountains of Veracruz, Tabasco and Chiapas. They bring mostly farm produce and live animals of various sorts. The cries of these animals and the presence of the enigmatic **Tehuantepec women** with their rich tunics and striking headdresses, amicably chatting in their native tongue, lend an exotic touch.

◷ **Cultural Center** (Casa de la Cultura). – **Dominican Monastery** (Exconvento Dominico). *Guerrero and Guadalupe Victoria.* This 16C structure still retains a great part of its original architecture. Inside there are vestiges of mural painting.

Information in this guide
is based on tourist data provided at the time of going to press.
Improvements in tourist facilities and fluctuations
in the cost of living may account for certain discrepancies.
We hope our readers will bear with us.

Map of Principal Sights p 6

⊙ Discovering the serene majesty of Teotihuacán, the "place of the gods" and the most important city of Mesoamerica *(p 36)* in the Classic period, constitutes an unforgettable experience. But Teotihuacán is something more than a fabulous **archeological site;** it is the center and the axis of a major part of Mexican mythology – the meeting place of the gods, the heavens, the earth and man, intimately bound by the inexorable laws of the universe.

The importance of the ceremonial center surpasses its mere beauty, and reaches beyond time and space. It inspired and directed the life of many other religious centers spread over the vast Mexican territory, both in the form and in the contents of their constructions.

To appreciate Teotihuacán's greatness it is necessary to penetrate its mysteries through the rich symbols that appear throughout the complex.

HISTORICAL NOTES

Although this area had been populated during millennia by agricultural communities, Teotihuacán appeared between the years 200 and 150 BC. It reached the climax of its development between 200 and 500 AD, when its social and cultural organization was consolidated in a theocracy, in which the high priests controlled the religious, scientific and political secrets.

When its decline began in the 8C, the city was populated by about 200 000 inhabitants. Overexploitation of natural resources, social upheavals and general deterioration of the governing systems explain why the city, much to the surprise of the Spaniards, had been abandoned at least five centuries before their arrival. Nevertheless, the Aztecs had been using it as a center for prayer and source of some of their myths.

CEREMONIAL CENTER *time: 4 hours*

Nothing was left to chance in the design of the center. The Avenue of the Dead is an impressive artery more than 2 kilometers – 1.2 miles long, forming a deeply symbolic north-south axis with a deviation of 17° aligned on the west facade of the great Pyramid of the Sun (Pirámide del Sol). The quadrangular layout of the complex reflects the four cardinal points.

To the north, behind the Pyramid of the Moon (Pirámide de la Luna), rises Cerro Gordo, the hill that is believed to be the abode of Tláloc, the god of water, who rules the forces that fertilize the earth. According to the original plan of the city, the river, which has since dried up, cut across the central axis, marking the borderline between the north and south of the city.

Site Museum (Museo de Sitio). – It is advisable to begin the visit in this museum, which contains exhibits that will facilitate the understanding of the different Teotihuacán eras. In particular, it displays a model that clarifies the general layout of the buildings and surroundings of the city. This museum occupies the site where, according to some researchers, the main market once stood.

The Citadel (La Ciudadela). – When the Spaniards saw the enormous plaza (400 m – 1 312 ft on each side) and the four platforms that enclose it, which were topped by small temples, they thought it was a military structure, so they called it the Citadel. It is large enough to serve as an atrium to the great temple that occupies the eastern side.

Temple of Quetzalcóatl and Tlaloc (Templo). – This building, which best exemplifies the expressive force of Teotihuacán sculpture, is one of the most fascinating of the complex. The temple's reliefs (originally totaling 365) establish a link between the earth and the heavens – a complementarity reflected in the two gods: Tlaloc represented as a deity with enormous goggles; and Quetzalcóatl depicted as the feathered serpent – in a constant duality of the material

(Photo Kuligowski/VLOO/Paris)

Teotihuacán. Head of the Feathered Serpent

and the immaterial. From the flower, symbolizing plenitude, emerge serpents and masks among rattlesnakes that slither over snails and shells. The architectural details – slope, panel and stairway, flanked by ramps – are almost overshadowed by the beautiful decoration. Two clearly distinct construction periods are visible in the complex. A small passageway between the two makes it possible to see the entire facade of the first building, which had been covered by the second. Only four of the six tiers that presumably completed the pyramidal structure have been preserved.

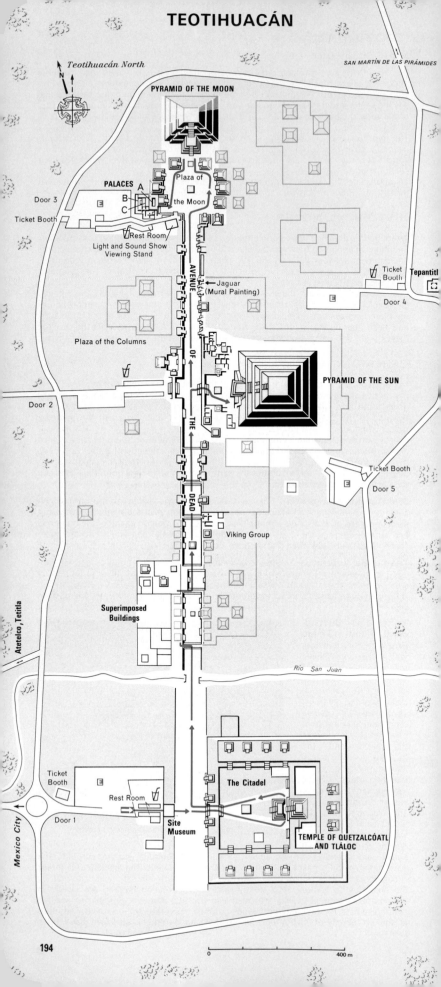

TEOTIHUACÁN

Teotihuacán North

SAN MARTÍN DE LAS PIRÁMIDES

PYRAMID OF THE MOON

Plaza of
the Moon

PALACES
A
B
C

Door 3

Ticket Booth

Rest Room

Light and Sound Show
Viewing Stand

Jaguar
(Mural Painting)

AVENUE

Ticket
Booth

Tepantitl

Door 4

Plaza of the Columns

OF

PYRAMID OF THE SUN

Door 2

THE

Ticket Booth

DEAD

Door 5

Viking Group

Superimposed
Buildings

Atetelco, Tetitla

Río San Juan

Ticket Booth

Mexico City

Rest Room

Door 1

Site
Museum

The Citadel

TEMPLE OF QUETZALCÓATL
AND TLÁLOC

0   400 m

Avenue of the Dead (Calle de los Muertos). – The Aztecs gave this name to the street because its sides were lined with mounds – the ruins of the ancient buildings – that gave the impression of a great avenue flanked by tombs.

With the Great Pyramid of the Sun presiding over its center, the Avenue of the Dead is the channel that enables man to become part of the superhuman world of Teotihuacán. From south to north, from light to shadow, man progresses toward the gods, thereby repeating the never-ending cycle of life beyond death. The avenue is 2.3 km – 1.4 miles long and 40 m – 131 ft wide. It rises an imperceptible 30 m – 98 ft and culminates at the foot of the Pyramid of the Moon, which, by means of this artful optical illusion, appears taller than it actually is.

Superimposed Buildings (Edificios Superpuestos). – On the left side of the Avenue of the Dead, some 300 m – 984 ft from the bridge over the bed of the Rio San Juan, is the complex of superimposed buildings that served as housing for the priestly classes. So as not to damage the outer structures, the exploration was carried out through a system of tunnels, revealing the manner in which the design of the ceremonial center was altered in different periods. The intriguing remains of staircases, floors, rooms and paintings can be seen in these passageways.

Pyramid of the Sun (Pirámide del Sol). – This silent witness to Teotihuacán's former glory is the site's most ancient structure and one of the most astonishing structures of the pre-Hispanic world. The Pyramid of the Sun embodies the sum of the astronomical knowledge possessed by the inhabitants of the fabulous ancient city and was designed with a remarkable precision that continues to astound archeologists and scientists.

Constructed along the Avenue of the Dead, the pyramid faces west, where according to pre-Hispanic mythology, the sun is transformed into a jaguar that plunges into darkness – the symbol of death. The pyramid's facade is aligned with the point on the horizon where the sun sets on the 19th of May and the 25th of July – the two days of the year in which the sun is exactly over the peak of the pyramid at noon. This special orientation explains the 17° deviation of the Avenue of the Dead.

The impressive Pyramid of the Sun, 225 m – 738 ft on each side and 65 m – 213 ft high, was constructed with successive layers of mud, covered with blocks of stone. It has five tiers, four of them with sloping sides and one with a small panel on the slope. Like most pre-Hispanic pyramids, this structure was completely painted and was crowned with a temple. In spite of its gigantic proportions, the structure is strikingly well balanced.

The ascent – 242 stairs with narrow steps and high risers arranged in flights of steps and landings – is quite taxing, but the visitor is fully rewarded at the summit by the magnificent **view★★** of the entire ceremonial center. From this vantage point, it is possible to imagine the grandeur of the city at the height of its glory.

Plaza of the Moon (Plaza de la Luna). – The long pilgrimage up the Avenue of the Dead ends in this intriguing plaza, bordered by a group of temples that form a striking ensemble, presumably used for esoteric and specialized ceremonies.

Pyramid of the Moon (Pirámide de la Luna). – The night goddess, who holds sway over the earth's waters and the movement of the tides, has been attributed a place of honor at Teotihuacán. The pyramid devoted to the goddess is situated at the end of the great avenue and acts as a mystical link between the city and the lovely setting of Cerro Gordo.

The pyramid's base measures approximately 150 m – 492 ft on each side, and the structure is 42 m – 138 ft high. Although not as tall as the Pyramid of the Sun, the summits of the two pyramids attain the same height because the Pyramid of the Moon stands on the highest spot of the site. The structure is four-tiered with sloping sides. The lower section contains a *talud-tablero* structure *(see p 35)* with a central stairway flanked by relatively small ramps. From the top platform, looking towards the south, the visitor can admire the impressive layout of the complex as well as its harmonious integration with the surrounding landscape.

Quetzalpapálotl Palace (Palacio de Quetzalpapálotl) (A). – This palace also known as the Quetzal-Mariposa (meaning "butterfly" in the Náhuatl language) was part of the priests' residential complex. It has been completely restored from scattered remains found by archeological expeditions. The palace is situated on the southwest corner of the Plaza of the Moon. A staircase leads to a rectangular chamber – a sort of small vestibule with square columns – at the rear of which is the entrance to the palace proper.

The palace consists of a square courtyard with thick pillars that form a small roofed passageway between the courtyard and the exterior walls of the surrounding rooms. On these walls traces of paintings can be detected. Noteworthy are the carved crests stones crowning the roof and the pillars, which are adorned with unusual low reliefs depicting a bird called *quetzalmariposa*. It is thought that the eye sockets were inlaid with obsidian and that these fanciful animals were painted.

Jaguar Palace (Palacio de los Jaguares) (B). – *To the west of the Quetzalpapálotl Palace.* The Jaguar Palace is made up of small passageways connected to a square courtyard. On the east side of this patio there is a small staircase which leads to the temple entrance.

In the rear on the left side, there are some chambers arranged according to the characteristic layout of Teotihuacán's constructions. On the exterior walls of these rooms, looking towards the courtyard, there are paintings representing enormous, beautifully stylized jaguars wearing feathers and holding in one paw a conch into which they are blowing and from which emerges a sign that symbolizes a sound.

Palace of the Feathered Snails (Palacio de los Caracoles Enplumados) ( ). – *To the right of the wall paintings in the Jaguar Palace, there is a small passageway that leads to the Palace of the Feathered Snails.* This palace consists of a small temple set on a simple *talud-tablero* structure, in which the best-preserved examples of Teotihuacán painting can be admired. The two doors of the temple are framed with bands decorated in low relief with motifs of snails, feathers and four-petalled flowers, on which vestiges of red paint have been preserved. Probably the entire temple was originally decorated in this way. On the panels, the pictorial effect is achieved with all sorts of beautiful tropical birds, masterfully drawn and vividly colored. This complex is situated directly below the Quetzalpapálotl Palace and belonged to an older substructure.

ADDITIONAL SIGHTS

Go back to the starting point. By automobile, following the belt highway (periférico) of the area, you can visit three interesting archeological (residential) sites. At 600 m – 1 969 ft turn left on an unpaved road and continue 800 m – 2 625 ft to the first palace.

Tetitla. – This is a group of rooms that served as lodgings for the priests; it has several patios, passageways and traces of painting on the outer walls. In the rear patio, to the right, there are walls with pictures of the god, Tláloc, as well as abstract designs and bird motifs related to the symbol of the sun.

Leaving Tetitla, continue east 700 m – 2 297 ft on the unpaved road to Atetelco.

Atetelco. – In one of the courtyards of this building, there is a small pyramid built to scale, with its stairway and sections in a *talud-tablero* configuration, crowned by a small temple surrounded by Teotihuacán-style crenellations. Around this central structure, at the sides of the courtyard, there are four temples with vestiges of painting around their entrance doors. These remains have been studied and are gradually being rebuilt.

Return to the belt-highway and turn left, follow 3 km – 1.9 miles on a stone-paved road, turn left and continue 100 m – 328 ft.

Tepantitla. – One intriguing feature of these ruins is the wall that contains an interpretation of the elements comprising the *Tlalocan*, or paradise of the god Tláloc, over which the god himself presides, on the upper part of the wall. Due to their ruinous condition, it is very difficult to perceive the details of the paintings. Therefore, it is recommended to see the excellent reproduction of this mural in the Teotihuacán Room of the National Anthropological Museum *(p 126).*

GREEN TOURIST GUIDES
Picturesque scenery, buildings
Attractive routes
Automobile tours
Plans of towns and buildings.

TEPIC Nayarit   ◆◆◆◆

Map of Principal Sights p 5

Tepic, the present capital of Nayarit state, is set in the valley of Matatipac, surrounded by volcanoes, which amply justifies its name, "a place among mountains". Their peaks cut a clear profile against the blue sky, with the Sangangüey volcano standing out most prominently because of its height and peculiar shape.

HISTORICAL NOTES

This city was founded by Nuño Beltrán de Guzmán at the beginning of the 16C. Originally called Santiago Compostela, Tepic was given its present name two centuries later. As a strategic base for the conquest of the northwest of New Spain, it was the starting point for the Franciscan evangelizing missions towards the kingdom of the *Calafias* (California), led in the 18C by Fray Junípero Serra.

SIGHTS

Regional Anthropological Museum (Museo Regional de Antropología). – **House of the Counts of Miravalle** (Casa de los Condes de Miravalle). This 18C mansion houses a museum, installed in several rooms around a central patio enclosed by a neoclassical arcade. One room displays items belonging to the Cora-Huichol-Tepehuan ethnic group, offering ethnographic information and exhibiting animal-shaped pottery, among other interesting objects. Another section that merits attention is the one dedicated to the **Ixtlán del Río** ceremonial center *(p 197),* the focal point of which is the circular temple of Quetzalcóatl.

Convent of the Cross (Exconvento de la Cruz). – This former convent was built in the 17C around a very curious phenomenon: the formation in a hayfield of a 3 m – 10 ft long cross, which is neither watered nor pruned, yet has remained thus since the 16C. Since that time it has been considered a miraculous site.

Santa Cruz; Matanchén Bay (Bahía de Matanchén). – *58 km – 36 miles. Estimate 1 day. Go west from Tepic on highway n° 66 to Santa Cruz and from there towards the north following the signs for San Blas.*

From Tepic to Los Cocos Bay (Ensenada de los Cocos). – *48 km – 29.8 miles.* The journey offers fascinating contrasts in landscapes, since in a few minutes it changes from temperate-zone oak forests to intermediate tropical rainforests. The route runs through the area where the mountain range gives way to the coastal plain and the sea. The steep, winding road provides a chance to enjoy spectacular landscapes – a mixture of mountain, jungle and beach – in a 40 km – 24.9 mile stretch, until sea level is reached at Los Cocos Bay.

★ **From Los Cocos Bay to Matanchén Bay.** – *10 km – 6.2 miles. It is advisable to use insect repellent for protection from gnats and mosquitos that are particularly bothersome in the late afternoon.*

This attractive shore offers quiet beaches and strong waves, good for surfing. The palm-lined coastal drive offers beautiful seascapes. To the south of Los Cocos Bay lies **Miramar,** famous for seafood dishes. This is an ideal spot to view the bay and enjoy the Santa Cruz beaches.

Continuing north 8 km – 4.9 miles, the road reaches Matanchén, a lovely bay with a calm sea, where the Las Islitas Beach, made up of three small coves with shallow, crystal-clear waters, is located. This is a typical landscape of the tropical Pacific coast, with exuberant vegetation and rocks where the waves break. Fray Junípero Serra set out from here to establish the California missions in the middle of the 18C, aboard the ship, *Purísima Concepción.*

★★ **Puerto de San Blas.** – *65 km – 40.4 miles. Estimate 1 day. Go west from Tepic on highway n° 66, following the signs to San Blas.*

This port lies at the southern end of the Río Santiago delta, on the spurs of the Sierra Madre Occidental and the plain. It has the characteristic coastal village houses and seems to hide among the mangrove swamps, the estuary and the palm groves. It was a key port for the Philippine trade, which led to pirate raids and motivated the construction of Spanish fortifications on Cerro de la Contaduría. The ruins of an 18C Spanish fort and the baroque Church of Our Lady the Seafarer (Nuestra Señora La Marinera) are still standing.

★★ **La Tovara.** – At the entrance to the town of San Blas, at the foot of Cerro de la Contaduría, ⊙ lies the wharf where boat rides depart for a tour around La Tovara, a series of natural canals, between jungle and mangrove swamps, where innumerable sea birds may be seen; at times the boat goes through tunnels of vegetation where the sun hardly ever penetrates. This beautiful natural setting has been used many times in films. At the end of the ride lies the spring called Limestone Water Eye (Ojo de Agua de Piedra Caliza), which is the meaning of Tovara. There eating facilities are available, and swimming is allowed in these warm and translucent waters.

Lake Santa Maria (Lago de Santa María); **Ceboruco Volcano; Ixtlán del Río.** – *131 km – 81.4 miles. Estimate 1 day. Head out of Tepic toward Guadalajara and after 35 km – 21.7 miles turn left at the turn-off to Santa María del Oro, 20 km – 12.4 miles to the lake.*

This ride presents a unique landscape made up of volcanic cones and tablelands, in what is geologically a tectonic depression. Along the way, Sangangüey Volcano will be easily sighted, with the peculiar rounded basalt formation on its summit.

Lake Santa Maria (Lago de Santa María). – Along the road there are spectacular glimpses of the volcanic crater lake, between the winding curves and the dense foliage. The road makes an abrupt descent to the oval-shaped rim of the *axalapasco* (crater lake), which is approximately 2 km – 1.2 miles in diameter. Its warm transparent waters are ideal for all kinds of water sports.

Return to highway n° 15, turn left and continue 52 km – 32.3 miles to Ixtlán del Río.

Ceboruco Volcano (Volcán Ceboruco). – During the first 25 kilometers – 15.5 miles the scenery undergoes brusque changes. The stately oak forests and cultivated farms give way to an inhospitable, stony landscape bereft of vegetation and composed of rough, dark grey basaltic spills of volcanic origin. These are the result of eruptions of Ceboruco Volcano, the outline of which can seen in the distance to the left of the road.

Go east from Ixtlán del Río on the same highway 4 km – 2.5 miles.

Ixtlán del Río Archeological Site. – Here a series of simple buildings and pyramid foundations can be seen. The most interesting is the circular pyramid dedicated to Quetzalcóatl, composed of several layers of construction.

(Excolegio de San Francisco Javier) México

Map of Principal Sights p 6

The small town of Tepotzotlán is dominated by the majestic architectural complex of the Saint Francis Xavier Seminary. The rich facade of the church, the tree-lined atrium and the enormous orchard bear witness to the wealth of the seminary, which has retained the distinctive beauty and the mystery of great religious institutions.

HISTORICAL NOTES

Although the first evangelists of this Otomí town were Franciscans, at the end of the 16C Tepotzotlán was given to the Jesuit order with the mission of converting the children of the Indian chiefs and forming new generations of Jesuits. In 1591, the novitiate was transferred to Puebla, and in 1606 it returned to Tepotzotlán. The Jesuit order received important donations, such as that of the Merchant Pedro Ruiz Ahumada, which were used towards the building of the school.

After the Jesuits' expulsion in 1767, the building stood vacant for years, until it was given to the secular clergy for their Royal College Training Seminary (Real Colegio Seminario de Instrucción), which continued until the 19C. The Jesuits reoccupied the college, until 1914.

⊙ **VISIT** time: 3 hours

At present renovation work is in progress to house the site museum, the Colonial Arts Museum and the Colonial Museum (museos de Sitio, de las Artes Virreinales y del Virreinato).

Plaza Hidalgo or Atrium (Plaza Hidalgo o Atrio). – This square has a shaded garden and a large esplanade that unifies the complex, with a pretty stone-carved **atrial cross** bearing symbols of the Passion.

Church. – The construction of the church began in 1670, and it was completed in the middle of the 18C. In 1760, Father Rector Pedro Reales ordered the modernization of the facade, the tower and the altarpieces.

★★ **Facade.** – The splendid facade carved in stone is considered the most outstanding Churrigueresque-style work in Mexico. It sets off a marvelous play of light and shadow that produces differing tonalities in the stone. Its ornamental wealth and the Jesuit iconography on the outside are echoed in the altarpieces on the inside. The tower is richly decorated with double *estípites*.

Aljibes Cloister (Claustro de los Aljibes). – *Through the tree-filled atrium, you reach the entrance to the seminary.* The first thing that stands out in this former seminary is an austere cloister, ornamented with a series of **paintings★** by **Cristóbal de Villalpando** (1649-1714) that depict scenes from the life of Saint Ignatius of Loyola (San Ignacio de Loyola).

★★★ **Interior of the Church.** – *Coming down on one side of the Aljibes Cloister, you reach the entrance to the church.* Inside this church, the gilded altarpieces glistening in the light penetrating through the openings of the dome, together with the vivid red rugs, cause an indelible impression.

The five Churrigueresque altarpieces adorning the church walls are remarkable for their richness and fine craftsmanship. The high altar is dedicated to Saint Francis Xavier (San Francisco Javier); the one on the left side, to the Virgin of Guadalupe; the right-hand one, to Saint Ignatius (San Ignacio); and the ones in the nave, to Saint Joseph (San José) and to the Virgin of Light (Virgen de la Luz). All are embellished with beautiful sculptures.

On the walls of the lower choir, there are two paintings by Miguel Cabrera: *The Patronage of Jesus Christ of the Souls in Purgatory (El Patrocinio de Jesucristo a las Almas del Purgatorio)* and *The Patronage of the Virgin Mary to the Jesuit Order (El Patrocinio de la Virgen María a la Compañía de Jesús).*

★★ **The Virgin's Dressing Room** (Camarín de la Virgen). – *Preceded by the Chapel of the Virgin of Loreto (Capilla de la Virgen de Loreto).* The Virgin's Dressing Room, or *Camarín de la Virgen,* is a small inner chamber used to change the Virgin's robes for processions. This dressing room is a unique jewel of Mexican baroque interior decoration.

In this small space, the walls of which are completely covered with multicolored mortarwork, classical baroque features are combined with local elements, such as mirrors, caryatids with Indian traits and rich coloring.

★ **Domestic Chapel** (Capilla Doméstica). – *Between the two cloisters.* This chapel contains a naive and striking altarpiece, gaily decorated with mirrors, relics, paintings and small ivory figures, which attracted the young novices.

Kitchens. – Around the patio, which has an unusual water spigot, the visitor can appreciate the layout of the seminary's old kitchen, with its cellar, pantry and cold room.

Orange Cloister (Claustro de los Naranjos). – In this cloister an attractive stone-carved fountain stands amid inviting orange trees, surrounded by a graceful arcade. Adjoining the cloister is a lovely **orchard,** where a small, picturesque **hermitage** has been preserved.

EXCURSIONS

Cuautitlán de Romero Rubio. – *8 km – 5 miles. Go east from Tepotzotlán toward Tlacatelpan and after 3 km – 1.9 miles turn right and continue 5 km – 3.1 miles towards Cuautitlán.*
In the main square, which was part of the old convent, stands the beautiful **atrial cross★★,** containing fine **high reliefs** of the symbols of Christ's Passion. On the high altar of the cathedral *(east side of the square)* there are four excellent **paintings★** of Saint Peter and Saint Paul *(San Pedro y San Pablo)* by the Flemish artist, **Martín de Vos** (16C).

★ **Arcos del Sitio.** – *26 km – 16.2 miles to the west, towards Villa del Carbón.*
This **aqueduct,** which is nearly 60 m – 197 ft high, is one of the tallest in the country. It consists of four levels of arches in the deepest part of the ravine and was built in the 18C by the Jesuits to supply their school with water.

★ TEPOZTLÁN Morelos   ◆

Map of Principal Sights p 6 – Local map p 77

Tepoztlán is a delightful small town situated at the foot of an enormous **mountain range★★.** Its geological formation is unusual, due to the frequent combination of volcanic and sedimentary deposits caused by ancient floods, which result in curiously twisted grey cliffs and crags that stand out against the green landscape.
The region's temperate climate creates a favorable habitat for the goldfinches, poincianas, plum trees and jacarandas that fill the town's streets with color. The famed Tepoztlán Mardi Gras includes much festivity and merry-making, such as the chinelos' hop dance *(danza del brinco),* recalling the christening of the local Indian king. The early inhabitants of the region were related to the Chichimecs and were subjected by the Spaniards in 1521, before the conquest of Tenochtitlán. North of the town, at the summit of the hill called Tepozteco in memory of a local god of the ancient Indians, there is an **archeological site,** which can be reached after an exacting climb *(1 hour by foot)* over steep rocks *(opening days are uncertain).* In the mid-16C, the Dominicans built a church and a convent here. Tepoztlán owes its development to the paper industry; however, between 1813 and 1833 the town suffered a series of epidemics that took a heavy toll on its population.

⊙ **Church and Convent of the Nativity of the Virgin Mary (Templo y Exconvento de la Natividad de la Virgen María).** – *In the center of town.* This robust 16C structure, resembling a fortress, stands out against its lovely setting.

Atrium. – Vestiges of its **posas** *(p 39)* are preserved in the corners of this large structure that blends Gothic and Renaissance styles. The one on the left side of the church facade has peculiar layout and functions as chapel and convent gatehouse. To the right, the remains of the open-air chapel, with its trapezoidal plan can be observed.

Church. – On its lovely stone-carved **facade,** the entrance arch is profusely decorated; the triangular pediment depicts the Virgin and Child (Virgen con el Niño) flanked by Saint Dominic and Saint Catherine (Santo Domingo and Santa Catalina). The adornments show the Indian craftsman's touch and a clear medieval influence. The salient elements of the church's interior are the arch of the lower choir and the groined vaults of the chancel.

Convent. – Despite its massive dimensions, this convent possesses the basic forms of the Renaissance style. There are also traces of **painting** visible on its humid walls, which have suffered over time. There is a beautiful **washstand** in the lower cloister refectory and a **vantage point** in the upper cloister from which a splendid **view** of the Tepoztlán Valley can be enjoyed.

TIJUANA Baja California Norte   ◆◆◆◆◆

Map of Principal Sights p 4

Tijuana is the most visited city on the United States border. Its dynamic growth has made it one of the major urban centers of the country. Thousands of persons cross this border every day to visit Mexico and to enjoy the attractions of the city, such as greyhound races, horse races, jai alai games, bullfights, and lively nightclubs. This is a good starting point for a tour south along the coast to discover the lovely beaches and landscapes of Mexico.

Tijuana Cultural Center (Centro Cultural Tijuana). – *Paseo de los Héroes and Mina.* This fine example of contemporary architecture was designed by Pedro Ramirez Vázquez
⊙ and Manuel Rosen as a setting for the **Museum of Mexican Cultures** *(Museo de Identidades Mexicanas).* The museum displays replicas of pre-Hispanic sculptures and ceramics, and numerous documents and objects illustrating the history and ethnography of the
⊙ country. The museum also hosts temporary exhibits. The **planetarium★★** is equipped with a very sophisticated projection system that produces spectacular visual and sound effects.

*Plan your own itinerary by consulting the map
of the principal sights (pp 4 to 6).*

★ TLAXCALA Tlaxcala

Map of Principal Sights p 6

Tlaxcala is a pleasant city where the buildings' different hues of red, the tree-lined plaza and the provincial streets make for an inviting atmosphere. This city is the capital of one of the smallest states of the Republic of Mexico; its diversified economy centers on the agricultural produce from the fertile valleys of Huamantla, the fierce bulls from the wild zones of Terrenate and Tlaxco, and the textile manufactures from the region of Santa Ana Chiautempan. To further its development, factories have been established in the Apizaco zone, and a wide industrial corridor has been created toward the northwest region of the state.

Because of Tlaxcala's proximity to Puebla, local architecture has been mainly influenced by the Puebla baroque style, as evidenced in the facades covered with brick, tiles and mortarwork and the church interiors decorated with plasterwork. Especially noteworthy is the large number of fine baroque altarpieces to be found even in the most modest villages – a reflection of the inhabitants' devotion.

HISTORICAL NOTES

When the Spaniards arrived, Tlaxcala consisted of four dominions: Tepeticpac, Quiahuiztlán, Ocotelulco and Tizatlán, which were located near the present capital. These territories maintained a strong rivalry with México-Tenochtitlán. This led the Tlaxcaltecs to establish an alliance with the Conquistadors. Their chieftain **Xicoténcatl,** who first fought against the Spaniards, eventually assisted them in capturing the capital of the Mexican empire.

The city of Tlaxcala as such was founded by the Spaniards (1519-1524), who did not consider the locations of the ancient pre-Hispanic domains adequate. The population grew rapidly, and by 1635 it received from Charles V of Spain the title of Loyal City, as well as a coat of arms.

CENTER OF THE CITY *time: 1/2 day*

★ **Plaza de la Constitución.** – This broad, shaded square has an charming bandstand and an octagonal fountain – a gift from the Spanish King, Philip III. The main buildings of the city border this square.

⊙**Palace of Justice (Palacio de Justicia).** – **Royal Chapel** (Antigua Capilla Real). *West side of the plaza.* At the base of the baroque facade of this 18C building, there are two handsome low reliefs: one representing the coat of arms of the Kingdoms of Castille and Leon with the *Plus Ultra*; and the other the Royal House of Austria's coat of arms containing a two-headed eagle.

⊙**Cathedral.** – **Former Parish Church of Saint Joseph** (Antigua Parroquia de San José). *At the southeast side of the plaza.* Although this is a 16C building, it has undergone modifications during the 18C and 19C. In the cathedral's interior there are good colonial paintings and the silver frontal of the high altar is beautifully wrought. The Chapel of Saint Joseph (Capilla de San José), on the left side of the chancel, with vaults ornamented in plasterwork and very fine altarpieces, deserves special mention.

⊙**Government Palace (Palacio de Gobierno).** – *North side of the plaza.* Originally this building, constructed after 1545, was used as the seat of the Viceroyalty and of the city government (Casas Reales y Consistoriales). Its facades, delicately carved in grey stone, convey a serene beauty, strikingly set off by the shady green trees on the square. Within are some **mural paintings** by Desiderio Hernández Xochitiotzin, a contemporary artist from Tlaxcala, which relate the history of the Tlaxcaltec people from their first settlements to the Conquest.

★ **Convent of the Assumption (Exconvento de la Asunción).** – *To the southeast of the plaza.* This convent was erected by the Franciscans between 1537 and 1540. In the atrium entrance, on the north side, rises the free-standing tower, that was probably used as a watchtower, since it connects with the convent by a passageway that crosses the atrium entrance. The church facade was worked in Renaissance style. From the atrium you can watch the bullfights in the ring below.

Interior. – The church's fine **ceiling** in Mudejar-style carved wood (restored) is worth noting, as are several good paintings and, above all, the gilded high altarpiece with its 17C paintings.

Chapel of the Third Order (Capilla de la Tercera Orden). – *To the right of the chancel.* The painting depicting **The Baptism of the Tlaxcala Chieftains** (El Bautizo de los Caciques de Tlaxcala), as well as a rich collection of altarpieces are noteworthy. In the sacristy there are two paintings attributed to Zurbarán: *Saint Francis (San Francisco)* and *Saint Dominic (Santo Domingo).* The museum is in the old cloister, connected to the church.

★ **Open-Air Chapel** (Capilla Abierta). – *Enter by the staircase in front of the facade.* This is a charming structure built in Gothic style with pointed arches.

★★★ SANCTUARY OF THE VIRGIN OF OCOTLÁN

(SANTUARIO DE LA VIRGEN DE OCOTLÁN) *3 km – 1.9 miles – 1 hour*

Go east from Tlaxcala on the old highway n° 119 toward Puebla and at 1 km – ⊙*0.6 miles, turn left and continue 2 km – 1.2 miles.* This magnificent sanctuary (17-18C) stands at the top of a hill that affords a marvelous view of Tlaxcala. It is representative of the Puebla-Tlaxcalan baroque style and was erected to honor the Virgin who, according to legend, appeared there to the Indian, Juan Diego Bernardino, in 1541.

★ **Facade.** – The facade is very tall, with slender white towers, decorated in fine mortarwork. The lovely portal is adorned with images of the Virgin, Saint Francis and the archangels.

Interior. – The chancel virtually swirls with the golden glints from the 18C **altarpieces★★**, made by the Indian **Francisco Miguel Tlayotehuanitzin**. The central urn, containing the image of Our Lady of Ocotlán (Nuestra Señora de Ocotlán), is a fine example of goldsmithing, as are the altar table and the lamps.

Sacristy. – This room contains six large canvases by José Joaquín Magón (18C) narrating Christ's Passion.

★★ **Dressing Room** (Camarín). – The sacristy connects with the dressing room, an octagonal chamber used to change the Virgin's robes. The abundant baroque **decoration** on the walls and the cupola (the work of Francisco Miguel Tlayotehuanitzin) is an explosion of color. On all sides, figures of angels and saints are skillfully intertwined with garlands. There is also a good series of paintings by Juan de Villalobos (18C) that depict scenes from the Virgin's life.

EXCURSIONS

Tepeyanco; Santa Inés Zacatelco. – *12 km – 7.5 miles. Estimate 1/2 a day. Go south from Tlaxcala and continue 7 km – 4.3 miles on old highway n° 119, toward Puebla.*

Tepeyanco de las Flores. – This simple village lies in a small depression, where the majestic ruins of the 16C **Franciscan monastery** stand guard. To the left of the church, is the open-air chapel whose columns support semicircular arches.

Saint Francis Parish Church (Parroquia de San Francisco). – Southwest of the monastery. The 17C facade of this construction reminiscent of the colorful Puebla churches with their characteristic combination of tiles, brick and mortarwork. The interior houses an excellent series of **altarpieces★** (17-18C), depicting scenes from the lives of Christ and the Virgin.

Continue 5 km – 3.1 miles south to Santa Inés Zacatelco.

Santa Inés Zacatelco. – On the main square of this small trading town stands Sanat Inés Parish Church, distinguished by its tall stone facade and its slendor tower. Toward the right side, the remains of the primitive temple are visible. The church houses various important works, such as the paintings below the choir, depicting some of the Indians' activities during colonial times, the monolithic **holy water stoup** *(left side of the nave)* and the huge **high altarpiece★** (18C) devoted to Santa Inés. The latter has robust columns decorated with paintings of archangels. In the courtyard of the priest's house, note the 16C stone sculpture with medieval features, representing the Virgin.

Santa Cruz Tlaxcala; La Trinidad. – *14 km – 8.7 miles. Estimate 2 hours. Go east from Tlaxcala to Santa Ana Chiautempan (6 km – 3.7 miles), continue 8 km – 5 miles, following the signs IMSS-LA TRINIDAD to Santa Cruz Tlaxcala.*

Santa Cruz Tlaxcala. – This church contains a rich collection of gilded **altarpieces** (17-18C). In the one depicting the souls in purgatory, **Indians** appear in the ceremonies for the dead. On the high altar there is an unusual 17C **painting★**: Adam and Eve are shown almost life size, half naked and surrounded by medallions representing the capital sins, with captions in the Náhuatl language.

La Trinidad. – *500 m – 1 640 ft north of Santa Cruz Tlaxcala.* This vacation spot occupies the premises of an old textile mill that operated until the beginning of this century. The small houses for workers have been turned into lodgings. The large turbine which produced power for the factory can also be visited.

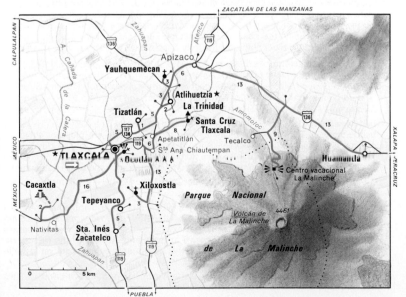

Xiloxostla. – *16 km – 9.9 miles. Estimate 1 hour. Go east from Tlaxcala toward Santa Ana Chiautempan, turn right and continue south on the new highway n° 119 towards Puebla, turn right and continue 3 km – 1.9 miles to Xiloxostla.*

⊘ **Saint Isabel Parish Church** (Parroquia de Santa Isabel). – This church possesses one of the loveliest **interiors★** in Tlaxcala. The nave walls as well as the vaults are covered with fine lace-like **plasterwork**. The **high altarpiece★★** (18C) is a fine example of the wreathed Solomonic baroque style. It contains, in the central niche, a graceful ornamented **sculptural group**, showing the visitation of the Virgin to Saint Isabel.

⊘ **Cacaxtla Archeological Site.** – *18 km – 11.2 miles. Estimate 1/2 day. Go south from Tlaxcala and turn right on the state highway toward Nativitas (16 km – 9.9 miles), turn right and continue 2 km – 1.2 miles to the site parking area. From there walk 1 km – 0.6 miles to the site.*

Built in the 7C AD, this was the seat of an important ethnic group known as the Olmec Xicalancs, whose commercial activity extended throughout the valley of Tlaxcala. The city was built as a fortress atop a natural promontory, reinforced with retaining walls arranged in terraces. On the upper part, there is a series of chambers and palaces around a rectangular plaza.

★★★ **Mural Paintings** (Pinturas). – In front of the plaza note the impressive **Battle Mural** (Mural de ⊘ la Batalla), the largest fresco discovered to date (22 m – 72 ft long). This colorful work portrays a multitude of richly dressed persons engaged in a brutal battle. To the right of this wall, under the protection of a shed, there are other **frescoes** adorning the porch of a temple; these are very realistic and represent persons attired in elegant religious robes. On one of the jambs, there is a red-painted stucco relief, which reveals a surprising and marked influence of the Maya and Teotihuacán cultures.

Tizatlán; Atlihuetzía★; Yauhquemecan. – *20 km – 12.4 miles. Estimate 1/2 day. Go northwest from Tlaxcala on highway n° 117, turn right on highway n° 136 towards Apizaco and after 5 km – 3.1 miles, turn left 1 km – 0.6 miles to Tizatlán.*

⊘ **Tizatlán.** – This was one of the domains of the Republic of Tlaxcala that was ruled by Xicoténcatl *(see p 200)*, when the Spaniards arrived. Two small altars with mural paintings belonging to this period have been preserved in front of the church atrium.

⊘ **Open-Air Chapel** (Capilla Abierta). – One section of this 16C chapel, enclosed by the outer wall of the church apse, contains a painting that depicts the baptism of the Tlaxcaltec chieftains. The chapel also contains the vestiges of mural painting.

Return to the same highway and at 5 km – 3.1 miles turn right; 2 km – 1.2 miles to Atlihuetzía.

★ **Atlihuetzía.** – The beautiful waterfall that gave this spot its name – Atlihuetzía means "place where the water falls" in Náhuatl – can be seen 1 km – 0.6 miles before reaching this old town. *Turn to the right. The waterfall is on the grounds of the Hotel Misión.*

⊘ At a distance, dominating the town, rises the huge old church of the 16C **Franciscan monastery** (Convento Franciscano). The **interior★**, with the high roofless walls, seems to dwarf the visitor.

⊘ **Immaculate Conception Parish Church** (Parroquia de la Inmaculada Concepción). – *North of the monastery.* The parish church conserves two paintings (18-19C) illustrating the martyrdom of the Tlaxcaltec children, who were sacrificed for having collaborated with the evangelization during the early years of the colonial period. Also worth seeing is a good collection of **altarpieces★** (17-18C), especially the central one with its delicate ornamental sculptures.

Go straight on and after 3 km – 1.9 miles turn left at the junction with highway n° 136 toward Calpulalpan and continue 2 km – 1.2 miles, turn right; 1 km – 0.6 miles to Yauhquemecan.

Yauhquemecan. – The **Saint Denis Parish Church** (Parroquia de San Dionisio) has a simple stone facade (18C), lightened by a slendor tower with mortarwork decorations. A large carved wooden door leads to the interior, which houses a splendid **high altarpiece★** (18C). In the sacristy, the painting by Cayetano Pérez (18C) of the Last Supper *(La Última Cena)* and a silver stand for the Holy Sacrament are noteworthy.

La Malinche National Park (Parque Nacional de la Malinche); **Huamantla.** – *63 km – 39.1 miles. Go northwest from Tlaxcala on highway n° 117, turn right on highway n° 136 until Apizaco (19 km – 11.8 miles), go through town and continue 13 km – 8.1 miles east on highway n° 136 towards Veracruz, turn right and continue 9 km – 5.6 miles, following the signs for IMSS-La Malinche.*

⊘ **La Malinche National Park.** – The visitor enters these pine woods by a road that climbs the gentle slope of La Malinche Volcano. Along the road there are pleasant spots for outings and excellent views of the Apizaco region. At the end of the ride lies La Malinche Vacation Center (Centro Vacacional la Malinche), a starting point for the ascent to the volcano's summit, which takes four hours with the proper equipment.

Return to highway n° 136 toward Veracruz and after 13 km – 8.1 miles, you reach Huamantla.

Huamantla. – This town is famous for its **August Fair★** (Feria de Agosto), when the main streets exhibit their showy **flower and sawdust rugs** (tapetes de serrín y flores), which are made during the night, to be destroyed the next day as the Virgin's procession passes over them. In August, many visitors arrive in Huamantla to attend the **huamantlada**, during which, the bulls that will be used in that afternoon's bullfight are set loose in the streets of the town.

Saint Louis Parish Church (Parroquia de San Luis). – *Northwest of the plaza principal.* This 17C structure conserves three 18C altarpieces.

Map of Principal Sights p 6

This city, which is the capital of the state of México, is reached by a highway lined by pine trees, crossing farming and industrial districts. The city itself is set in a pretty valley bordered by lovely mountains.

Toluca is known for its varied production of **sausages, creams, cheeses** and **butter** and for its traditional handicrafts that have survived the city's intense industrial development.

HISTORICAL NOTES

Since pre-Hispanic times Toluca has been a major settling place for **Otomís, Mazahuas** and **Matlatzincs,** who have left important ceremonial centers such as Calixtlahuaca *(p 204)* and Teotenango *(p 205).* As a result of the Spanish Conquest, Toluca was given to Hernán Cortés as a part of the Marquisate of the Valley (Marquesado del Valle). In 1677 its status as a city was recognized.

At the beginning of the 19C, Toluca played an important role in the Independence Movement against the Spanish Crown, having participated in the Machete Conspiracy (Conjura de los Machetes). In the War of Independence, the priest Hidalgo arrived in the city in 1810 and organized an army. The population took an active part and was defeated only after 99 Indians were shot in the main square. These are known as the Independence Martyrs.

In 1831 the city was declared capital of the state of México and on the 14th of November, 1861, its name was changed to Toluca de Lerdo, in honor of Miguel Lerdo de Tejada.

CENTER OF THE CITY *time: 1 day*

Plaza Cívica. – **Plaza of the Martyrs** (Plaza de los Mártires). This large esplanade is bordered by a series of arcades that were begun in 1832 and continued in various stages. Along the arcades, are stalls selling regional sweets in various shapes and colors, as well as of the typical drink, called *mosquitos,* made of firewater and orange liqueur.

Cathedral. – The original baroque facade for Saint Francis' Church (Templo de San Francisco) is used as the altarpiece in this cathedral.

⊙**Fine Arts Museum (Museo de Bellas Artes).** – **Carmelite Convent** (Exconvento del Carmen). *Santos Degollado n° 102 Poniente.* This is a striking colonial building that still retains, in some areas, ornamental vestiges from the 18C and, in others, 19C neoclassical elements. Within, it houses an important collection of academic painting, including the works of Cristóbal de Villalpando, José Juárez, Felipe Gutiérrez, Pelegrín Clavé and José María Velasco are noteworthy.

Carmelite Church (Templo del Carmen). – *Santos Degollado in front of Plaza España.* Built in the 17C and remodeled in the 19C, this structure, with its pleasant atrium and simple facade, is one of the few examples of colonial architecture in the city of Toluca.

★★ **Cosmovitral and Botanical Garden** (Jardín Botánico). – **September 16th Market** (Mercado ⊙16 de Septiembre). *Facing the Plaza España.* This Art Nouveau style iron structure was built between 1909 and 1933. In its spacious interior, there are more than one thousand varieties of plants from different parts of the world, in an area of 3500 m² – 37674 square ft.

Completing the architectural complex, there are 48 stained glass windows, begun in 1978 by the Tolucan artist, Leopoldo Flores. The leadwork was also executed by local artisans.

★★ MEXIQUENSE CULTURAL CENTER
(CENTRO CULTURAL MEXIQUENSE) *10 km – 6.2 miles – 1/2 day*

⊙*From Toluca take Vía Venustiano Carranza toward Temascaltepec 8 km – 5 miles southeast, turn right and continue 2 km – 1.2 miles, following the signs.*

This impressive complex was designed to shelter a great cultural and recreational center. Amid broad green areas and simple paths, modern architecture is juxtaposed with the remains of an old hacienda, while the open landscape is complemented by the distant view of the snow-capped peak, el Nevado de Toluca.

Museum of Modern Art (Museo de Arte Moderno). – *First building to the left.* This museum occupies an unfinished planetarium that has been remodeled and modernized. The collection includes works of Mexican painters from 1920 to the present, with numerous pieces by artists from the state of Mexico. Among the artists represented are Carlos Mérida, Roberto Montenegro and Alfredo Zalce. At the left of the entrance is a mural made of volcanic rock by Luis Nishizahua.

Museum of Popular Cultures (Museo de Culturas Populares). – **Hacienda of La Pila** (Ex-hacienda de la Pila). *Second building to the right. Start the tour to the right.* In what must have been the silos and barns of the former hacienda, there is a simple exhibit of the state's most representative handicrafts, in ceramics, textiles, blown glass and rush. In a second room there is an example of a typical house and furniture from the state of México. In the main courtyard, stands an original wooden granary with a shingle roof; now it houses temporary handicraft exhibits. The tour ends with the Dove Patio (Patio de las Palomas), which still has the original dovecotes along the hacienda walls.

Charrería Museum (Museo de la Charrería). – *Behind the Patio de las Palomas.* This is a fascinating exhibit devoted to the regional Mexican horsemen *(charros),* including clothing, spurs, arms, saddles, hats and wooden or wrought-iron stirrups. Along the walls, a series of popular sayings and paintings referring to horses and horsemen are on display.

Main Public Library (Biblioteca Pública Central). – *Facing the Museo de Culturas Populares.* The architect of this project was Pedro Ramírez Vázquez. It houses various cultural services: children's reading rooms, a reading and consultation room for adults, a video cassette library, a newspaper library, computer services for children, computerized bibliographic information terminals connected with five countries, as well as a substantial number of books and special editions. At the entrance of the library there is a striking mural in enameled clay with pre-Hispanic motifs, by Luis Nishizahua.

Anthropological and Historical Museum of the State of México (Museo de Antropología e Historia del Estado de México). – *Building located at the rear of the complex. Start the tour to the right.* This structure was also designed by the architect Ramírez Vázquez. In a series of five rooms, different aspects of the region are shown, such as its ecology and archeological remains. Among the ceramic pieces are: the stone **statue** of the wind god Ehécatl, found in the excavations of the archeological site at Calixtlahuaca; and the ceremonial **drum** carved from a tree trunk from Malinalco. Another series of rooms present important phases of the state history's.

The room to the left of the museum entrance is devoted to rotating and temporary exhibits.

ADDITIONAL SIGHT

⊘ **Casart.** – *700 Paseo Tollocan Oriente.* Built as an outlet for the handicrafts of the region, this construction also accommodates temporary and permanent exhibits. A comprehensive description of the different communities engaged in handicraft production is provided.

EXCURSIONS

⊘ **Church and Convent of San Miguel Zinacantepec** (Iglesia y Convento de San Miguel Zinacantepec). – **Colonial Museum of Toluca Valley** (Museo Virreinal del Valle de Toluca). *Go west from Toluca on highway nº 15 towards the Valle de Bravo and Morelia 8 km – 5 miles, then turn left and continue 1 km – 0.6 miles.* Among the large trees shading this spacious atrium is a completely dry Mexican conifer, called *ahuehuete,* which is known as the grandfather of the town and predated the Franciscans' 16C construction. The lovely open-air chapel still preserves a simple 17C altarpiece, with paintings of the period. On the side walls there are several frescoes with scenes of Saint Francis' life. The baptistry has a handsome **font★** from the 16C, which is a curious mixture of elements from the iconography and craftsmanship of the Indians of the region and motifs copied from European books. The convent conserves remains of mural paintings as well as a collection of canvases, furniture, incunabula and household equipment that illustrate various aspects of colonial monastic life.

Calixtlahuaca; Tecaxic. – *19 km – 11.8 miles. Estimate 1 1/2 hours. Go north from Toluca on highway nº 55 towards Querétaro and after 12 km – 7.5 miles, turn left, continue 2 km – 1.2 miles and turn left again on an unpaved road.*

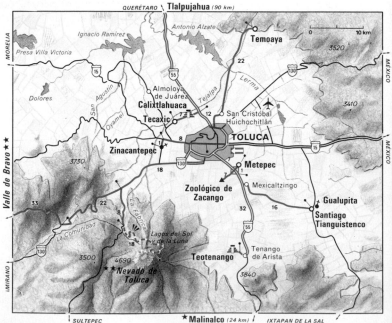

Ⓥ **Calixtlahuaca Archeological Site.** – This is a ceremonial center situated at the summit of Tanismó Hill (Cerro de Tanismó). Its ruins reveal the presence of Teotihuacán, Matlazinc and Aztec cultures. It includes seventeen monuments scattered over various terraces (three have been restored).

Quetzalcóatl Temple (Templo de Quetzalcóatl). – *To the right.* On this circular plan, there are four superimposed buildings from different eras. The sculpture of the wind god Ehécatl, now exhibited in the Anthropological and Historical Museum *(above),* was discovered at the foot of this temple.

Tzompantli or Skull Wall (Muro de los Cráneos). – This cruciform structure was designed to hold the heads of the enemies defeated in battle.

Calmecac or Row of Houses (Hilera de Casas). – This has a series of interconnected patios with rooms on different levels. The building was used to house the children who were being educated as future leaders.

Retrace the 100 m – 328 ft of unpaved road, turn left and continue 5 km – 3.1 miles.

Ⓥ **Tecaxic.** – An ancient town with pre-Hispanic settlements, Tecaxic has a pleasant baroque **Franciscan monastery** (Convento Franciscano) housing a collection of canvases of the period. In the church atrium a 16C sundial can be seen.

Ⓥ **Temoaya.** – *22 km – 13.7 miles to the north on highway n° 55 toward Querétaro, turn right toward San Cristóbal Huichochitlán.*
Temoaya is an important handicraft center, where the famous small woolen rugs, or *tapetes,* are hand woven using either original designs or those based on traditional Indian forms and frets. It is interesting to visit the factory, where 150 artisans weave 140 000 knots of wool per square meter, thus creating polychrome surfaces that are veritable jewels of textile art.

Metepec; Zacango Zoo (Zoológico de Zacango)**; Santiago Tianguistenco; Gualupita.**
– 39 km – 24.2 miles. Estimate 1 day. Go southeast from Toluca on highway n° 55 toward Ixtapan de la Sal,· after 7 km – 4.3 miles, turn left, continue 1 km – 0.6 miles to Metepec.

Metepec. – The mestizo population of Metepec has managed to preserve, in their home workshops, a deep-rooted potters' tradition as a family industry passed down from father to son. Exuberant and colorful forms emerge from the clay under their gifted hands, such as **Trees of Life** (Árboles de la Vida), Nativity Scenes, candle-holders and toys.
These original pieces may be purchased every Monday in the market *(tianguis)* that is set up in the main square.

Go back to highway n° 55, cross it and continue 7 km – 4.3 miles, on the turn-off for the zoo (Zoológico).

Zacango Zoo. – This zoo accommodates a number of attractions in the natural setting of the old Zacango hacienda, home of Franciscan friars in the 16C.

The Zoo. – This entertaining site has been specially designed to simulate the natural habitats of more than 40 different species of animals. Especially attractive are the African section, with the white rhinoceros, the gorilla and the orangutang, and the serpent section, with specimens from all parts of the world.

Museum. – Visitor can see a number of wild life dioramas and a projection room where documentary films on ecological subjects are shown. A regional handicraft center has been set up in this museum.

Cri-Cri Plaza. – This is an area where children's games are organized; it is dedicated to the characters created by the Mexican composer, Gabilondo Soler, who sang to the Mexican children.

Return to highway n° 55 and continue 4 km – 2.5 miles to Mexicaltzingo, turn left and follow 12 km – 7.5 miles to Santiago Tianguistenco.

Santiago Tianguistenco. – This town was given as an *encomienda* (an estate consisting of land or mines and subjects granted by the Crown in the colonial period to Spanish settlers in America) to Juan Gutiérrez Altamirano in 1528 and inherited by the counts of Calimaya (Condes de Calimaya) in 1683. At present it is an important commercial center. On Tuesdays there is a bustling market where regional handicrafts are sold. The outstanding architectural feature is the Parish Church of Santa María del Buen Suceso.

Gualupita. – Part of the urban complex of Santiago Tianguistenco, Gualupita is famous for its woolen products. On Tuesdays and Sundays, the weavers leave their modest workshops, usually installed in the patios of their own homes, to sell their products.

Ⓥ **Teotenango Archeological Site.** – *39 km – 24.2 miles south on highway n° 55 toward Ixtapan de la Sal and take the turn-off toward the town of Tenango de Arista, following the signs to the site.*
This walled site is noted for its elegant architectural remains and its extraordinary location, which affords a panoramic view of the surroundings.

Archeological Museum of the State of México – Doctor Román Piña Chán (Museo Arqueológico del Estado de México – Doctor Román Piña Chán). – The collection comprises pieces from the Toluca Valley.
Recent explorations in the area have aimed principally at restoring the architectural complex known as the Northern System (Sistema del Norte), which belongs to the Classic period.

Plaza of the Jaguar (Plaza del Jaguar). – This is a broad esplanade bordered by several platforms and a stairway leading to the ceremonial center.

Temazcal. – *Up the stairway to the right.* Ritual baths were carried out here. On both sides there are rectangular structures that were used as priests' rooms.

Ball Game Court (Juego de Pelota). – *At the rear.* This I-shaped court contains a reproduction of a ball marker.

Serpent Foundation (Basamento de la Serpiente). – *Behind the Temazcal.* This large structure 120 m – 394 ft long owes its name to the snake carved on one of its ramps.

★★ **Nevado de Toluca.** – *44 km – 27.3 miles. Go southwest from Toluca on highway n° 130 18 km – 11.2 miles, turn left towards Sultepec-Nevado, continue 8 km – 5 miles, turn left again and continue 18 km – 11.2 miles on an unpaved road.*
The Nevado de Toluca is a majestic volcano 4 690 m – 15 387 ft high; it has a peculiarly shaped crater, which gives the impression that its cap was ripped off, leaving various jagged points. This is the origin of its name, *Xinantécatl,* which means "the place of the nine snow peaks".

Junction (Entronque) **Sultepec-Nevado.** – The route crosses a dense oak and fir tree forest, where the volcano's silhouette intermittently appears.

Interior Crater and Lakes. – After a winding ride between sands and snowy mountainsides, the upper rim of the crater is reached. The two **crater lakes** named after the sun and the moon, have diameters of approximately 400 m – 1 312 ft and 200 m – 656 ft respectively. This site was used for pre-Hispanic religious worship, evidenced by the copal offerings and vessels of different forms that have been rescued from the bottoms of the lakes.

★★ **Valle de Bravo.** – *107 km – 66.5 miles. Go southwest from Toluca on highway n° 130 and after 40 km – 24.9 miles, turn right and continue 33 km – 20.5 miles.*
In this valley there is a lovely artificial lake, surrounded by pine and oak trees formed by the **Miguel Alemán Dam** (20 km^2 – 7.7 square miles). In the reservoir a number of water sports are practiced such as sailing, fishing, skiing and, in the hills, hang-gliding. The town still preserves its rustic touch with red tile roofs and stone-paved streets.

North Shore. – *22 km – 13.7 miles.* This ride offers marvelous views of the lake; after crossing the dam, the road descends sharply, leaving on the right the small Tilostoc Dam (Presa Tilostoc), finally leading to another artificial lake, where the higher temperature produces a different sort of vegetation.

South Shore. – *12 km – 7.5 miles.* This route also affords magnificent panoramic views of the lake and the lovely waterfalls beside the highway. At the end of this drive, there is a golf club in a residential complex reminiscent of Switzerland.

El Oro; Tlalpujahua. – *102 km – 63.4 miles. Estimate a day. Go northwest from Toluca on highway n° 55 to Atlacomulco and after 64 km – 39.8 miles turn left and continue 30 km – 18.6 miles to the west on the state highway to El Oro.*

El Oro. – This town was founded in 1787 on a mining property owned by the Tultenango Hacienda. Despite its mining boom, El Oro is a peaceful place that has tried to preserve the French-style manners of the Porfirista era.

Town Hall (Palacio Municipal). – This graceful neoclassical structure is flanked by small towers. The spacious rooms of the second floor are luxuriously decorated with hardwood floors, furniture and soft velvet curtains.

Juárez Theater (Teatro Juárez). – *To the right of the town call.* This neoclassical structure is enhanced by its narrow entrance arches and the small vestibule with beautiful carved wooden doors and balconies.

Go through the town of El Oro and continue 8 km – 5 miles west to Tlalpujahua.

Tlalpujahua. – Set on a steep hill, the town's zinc roofs glisten in the sun.

Parish Church of SS. Peter and Paul (Parroquia de San Pedro y San Pablo). – *On the left side of the town hall.* Its rich 18C baroque facade has thick octagonal Solomonic columns, decorated with strong flutes that catch the light. The bases of the columns on the first level are decorated with supernatural figures; the finial is ornamented with a double niche holding sculptures of the patron saints. Its interior is adorned with great imagination in pastel-colored plasterwork that combines floral and geometric motifs with clear popular overtones. On the nave arches, the decoration takes on a Moorish flavor.

★ **Malinalco Archeological Site.** – *63 km – 39.1 miles. Go south from Toluca on highway n° 55 toward Ixtapan de la Sal and in Tenancingo turn left and continue 14 km – 8.7 miles to Malinalco. Description p 97.*

(From photo Arturo Cháirez/Mexico)

Tlalpujahua. Parish church
of SS. Peter and Paul

Torreón is set in the busy Lake District (Comarca Lagunera) close to the desert. The region's hot summers and mild winters are ideal for cotton and dairy production.
Torreón has preserved a wealth of civil architecture, with beautiful mansions decorated in Art Nouveau style. One notable example is the **Central Market.**
Its strategic location made this city the scenario for numerous battles: in 1913 and 1914, **Pancho Villa** defeated Victoriano Huerta's army here.

SIGHTS

Isauro Martínez Theater (Teatro). – *Matamoros and Galeana.* Because of its interior decoration, this theater is considered the second loveliest in the Republic. It was built in 1930 by the Valencian artist, Agustín Tarazona.
The plain facade, which has a Moorish arch with a mullioned window, belies its lavishly ornamented interior.

★★★ **Interior.** – One of its main attractions is the proscenium arch covered in fine openwork plasterwork with scenes from Hindu mythology. The lighting of the hall creates the impression that the arch is carved in ivory.
At both sides of the stage, there are scenes of street festivals with dancers and tumblers accompanied by elephants; these are visible from the boxes where aristocratic gentlemen sit with their wives.
The center of the ceiling opens into a cupola 5 m – 16 ft in diameter, richly decorated with plasterwork in intricate arabesques, that surround the painting of a poet visited by the muses.

Laguna Regional Museum (Museo Regional de la Laguna). – *Av. Juárez Oriente and Cuauhtémoc.* This museum contains valuable pieces of jewelry and pottery from the archeological sites of the region; the Ethnography Room features an exhibit of typical dress from the different states of the Republic.

EXCURSIONS

Bilbao Dunes (Dunas de Bilbao). – *69 km – 42.9 miles. Go east from Torreón on highway n° 40 to Ejido Zapata and after 53 km – 32.9 miles turn right and continue 16 km – 9.9 miles.*
This awesome desert with its ondulating dunes is reminiscent of Africa.

★ **Ojuela Bridge (Puente de Ojuela).** – *75 km – 46.6 miles. Go west from Torreón, through the town of Gómez Palacio, continue northwest on highway n° 49 39 km – 24.2 miles, after passing Bermejillo, turn left, continue 20 km – 12.4 miles toward Mapimí, turn left and continue 7 km – 4.3 miles on an unpaved road.*
This is a gigantic suspension bridge constructed of wood and steel cables, more than 100 m – 328 ft long and approximately 300 m – 984 ft high. From the bridge, a splendid panorama of the arid canyon unfolds and from the lookout, a lovely **view★** of the valley.

★ **Silence Zone (Zona de Silencio).** – *140 km – 87 miles to the northwest on highway n° 49. At the entrance to Ceballos.* This mysterious desert owes its name to the common belief that there are zones where radio waves cannot be transmitted. The area is the habitat of enormous turtles and thousands of hares. Marine fossils and fragments of aerolites abound. The view of the firmament is dazzling; myriad stars and even the artifical satellites can be seen. The prickly pear plants are purple on the side facing the morning sun and green on the other side.

TULA Hidalgo

Map of Principal Sights p 6

On a plain rich in limestone, magueys, prickly pears and cactuses stand the vestiges of the Toltec capital, the principal heir to the knowledge and traditions of legendary Teotihuacán *(p 193).* In order to solve the problems derived from the aridity of the land, the Toltecs organized a powerful theocratic military government, which expanded its borders by conquering neighboring peoples. They exacted high tributes and exploited the work force for the extraction of obsidian, a black volcanic glass used for making knives, arrow points and other instruments.

HISTORICAL NOTES

At the beginning of the 10C AD, the inhabitants of the area were conquered by the son of Chimalma and Mixcóatl, a Toltec hero who bore the name of one of the principal gods: Ce Ácatl Topiltzin Quetzalcóatl.
By sanctifying warfare and proliferating cults that required human sacrifices, this powerful ruler created a climate of tension that ultimately unleashed a confrontation with his neighbors to the north. These semi-nomadic groups set Tula's temples and palaces afire forcing the Toltecs to emigrate south in the year 1165.
Owing to the power that the Toltec civilization was to exercise over Chichén Itzá *(p 66)* and to the admiration which, centuries later, it aroused among the Aztecs (who went so far as to confuse Hernán Cortés' arrival with that of Quetzalcóatl), the Toltecs revolutionized the life of Mesoamerica during the post-Classic period.

⏱ **ARCHEOLOGICAL SITE** *time: 1 1/2 hours*

⏱ **Museum (Museo).** – The ceramics and sculptures from this site are on exhibit in this modern building. Most striking is the reclining statue of Chac-Mool, the intermediary between gods and men, with a vessel in his hands to receive offerings.

Continue along the path.

Coatepantli. – This is a fragment of the wall that protected the ceremonial center. The decoration is the same on both sides, finished off with a motif representing fragmented snail shells. The central frieze shows rattlesnakes that devour fleshless human faces – a fearsome representation intended to frighten Tula's enemies.

(Photo Ignacio Urquiza/Mexico)

Tula. "Atlantes"

Temple of Tlahuizcalpantecuhtli (Templo). – *Immediately behind the wall.* This pyramid has five tiers with protruding stones on the facing. Some of these slabs still display low reliefs depicting buzzards and eagles devouring hearts, as well as walking jaguars and coyotes. These mythical animals are associated with the planet Venus – the main object of veneration of this temple.

On the summit there are four monumental columns in the shape of soldiers, known as **atlantes★**. The one at the extreme left is a replica, replacing the original, which is on exhibit in the National Anthropological Museum in Mexico City. Each one weighs 8.5 tons and consists of four stone blocks assembled by the tongue and groove system. They wear feathers and butterfly-shaped breastplates, and, on their backs, a large brooch in the form of a sun. In the right hand they carry dart-throwers and, in the left, resin bags.

The **view** from this point encompasses the hills and plains that were populated by as many as 85 000 Toltecs.

Burned Palace (Palacio Quemado). – *To the left of the previous one.* This structure consists of a series of vestibules with numerous pillars that supported roofs made of perishable materials. Remains of the benches set in the walls have survived; these are adorned with low reliefs of processions of warriors that conserve their original colors. It is thought that this area was used for the most important religious ceremonies or for the bustling markets, where traders brought cotton, cacao and feathers from the tropical region, precious shells and snails from the coasts and fruits and resins from the colder areas.

Temple of the Sun (Templo del Sol). – *The very large building.* Originally, this structure was decorated with slabs in low reliefs like those on the Temple of Tlahuizcalpantecuhtli *(see above).* Near the stairway there is a mound that was built during the Aztec occupation.

Join us in our never ending task of keeping our guides up to date.

Please send us your comments and suggestions.

**Michelin Travel Publications/Michelin Tire Corporation
One Parkway South
Greenville, South Carolina 29615 – USA.**

Map of Principal Sights p 6

The Maya ceremonial center of Tulum stands upon a cliff 12 m – 39 ft high, facing the Caribbean Sea – a brilliant mirror of blues and greens through which the corals and sands of the bottom can be seen. The temples, palaces and lookout points are surrounded by a stone fortification, which was built on account of the constant wars stemming from the region's political instability, during the period in which the site was occupied – the three centuries preceding the Spanish Conquest.

The remains of that troubled era stand today in a peaceful setting of gardens and palm trees, swayed by the sea breeze.

ARCHEOLOGICAL SITE *time: 2 hours*

This consists mainly of a rectangular area bordered on one side by the sea coast and by a thick wall on the other three sides, with five roofed passageways that constitute the entrances. The most important buildings are clustered in the center.

Funeral Platform (Plataforma Funeraria). – *First structure in the front.* At the center of this structure there is a cruciform tomb, in which a skeleton was discovered, surrounded by the remains of shark, iguana and lizard, among other sacred foods.

Temple of the Frescoes (Templo de los Frescos). – *Behind the previous structure.* The principal facade, 8 m – 59 ft long, has an elegant portico with four thick columns that support a frieze decorated with stucco masks in the corners and three niches. In the middle one, the remains of an idol, very prevalent in Tulum, are visible: the **Descending God** (Dios Descendente), associated with the planet Venus, guardian of the east coast and commerce. This was an important activity which brought great prestige to the city, since it controlled the sea lanes around the Yucatan Peninsula from Tabasco to Honduras. On the second level of the building, there is a temple superimposed on an older one, which now appears like an inner room on the lower floor, behind the passageway. This older structure conserves paintings in a bluish-green color on a black background, representing scenes of offerings to the gods that are very similar to those sketched in the codices.

The Castle (El Castillo). – *The taller structure facing the sea.* The rich traders commissioned the best artists to build this breathtaking religious complex, which was completed in various stages. The mural paintings did not survive the effects of time, contrary to the stucco work of the upper temple, where the Descending God is again prominent. The two columns at the entrance to the sanctuary resemble serpents – an animal worshipped by the merchant elite and the astronomer-priests alike.

From the rear of the sanctuary, a magnificent **view★★** of the coral reefs and the Caribbean Sea unfolds.

(Photo Guillermo Aldana/Mexico)

Tulum

EXCURSION

Cobá. – *44 km – 27.3 miles. Go northwest from Tulum, continuing until you find highway n° 307 to Chetumal, turn left, continue 2 km – 1.2 miles, turn right and continue 42 km – 26.1 miles.*

On this hot plain stood Cobá, one of the major Maya cities, which is now in a ruinous state, covered by a thick jungle full of deer, monkeys and wild boar, and surrounded by five natural lakes where turtles, herons and multicolored fish abound.

Because of its strategic position, between the coastal ceremonial centers and the cities of the interior, Cobá secured economic control over the region between the 4 and 11C AD, through a network of stone roads, the longest of which covered 100 km – 62.1 miles.

TULUM★★

Amidst the ball game courts, palaces, temples and residential complexes hidden by the exuberant vegetation, two pyramids dominate the scene. They were built with rough-hewn stone blocks and were finished in polychrome stucco.

The Church (La Iglesia). – In front of a large square, at the foot of the steep slope of the monument's foundation, 24 m – 79 ft high, rises a stela at which the present-day Maya peasants leave offerings and light candles in the hope of improving their harvests.

Nohoch Mul. – This is the most massive and tallest (42 m – 138 ft) pyramid in the northern part of the Yucatan peninsula. At its summit, the Descending God is represented on the temple facade. From this vantage point, a fine view opens over the region.

TUXTLA GUTIÉRREZ Chiapas   ◆◆◆◆

Map of Principal Sights p 6

The modern capital of Chiapas state, Tuxtla Gutiérrez, is located in a hot, fertile valley. It is a major trading center for the products of the region.

The economic and commercial leadership of the city emerged during the troubled 19C, when Tuxtla Gutiérrez headed the state's Independence Movement from Spain and from Guatemala and, later on, favored its voluntary annexation to the Republic of Mexico.

SIGHTS

★★★ **Miguel Alvarez del Toro Zoo (Zoológico).** – *Follow the signs from the Libramiento Sur.*
⊙ This famous zoo and ecological conservation park, situated in the Cerro Hueco jungle, hosts only animals indigenous to Chiapas state. Those animals that are not dangerous (squirrels, lizards, a species of ape) roam in complete freedom amid the luxuriant vegetation. On its grounds (25 hectares – 62 acres), 110 species are kept in spacious reservations: the largest feline in America – the jaguar – reigns unchallenged in a closed area of $1\,000\ m^2$ – 10764 square ft.

Note the tapirs and the showy peacocks (the emblem of the zoo), which are difficult to raise in captivity, and the royal eagle.

Serpent House (Serpentario). – Behind large glass cases, the colors, habits and size of the boas, *nauyacas,* coral snakes, rattlesnakes and other indigenous serpents can be observed.

Insect House (Vivario). – The zoo includes a series of terrariums, with insects and spiders, like tarantulas and black widows.

There are numerous signs identifying the animals and explaining the threats to their survival, placed along the shaded paths of the park.

⊙ **Chiapas Regional Museum (Museo Regional de Chiapas).** – *Calzada de los Hombres Ilustres unnumbered.* This brick, marble and glass **construction★** (1982) by the renowned architect, Pedro Ramírez Vaquez, juxtaposes wall surfaces with large vestibules and flower boxes in an interesting play of volumes.

Archeological Room (Sala de Arqueología). – *Lower floor.* A large variety of original objects from the Olmec and Maya civilizations are on exhibit. Special attention should be paid to the jewels, textiles and multicolored utensils found in different tombs of the region.

EXCURSIONS

★★ **Yaxchilán and Bonampak Archeological Sites.** – *Accessible by light aircraft (1 hour 15 minutes). Description p 221.*

★★ **Sumidero Canyon.** – *Tour by automobile. Description p 186.*

Chiapa de Corzo. – *17 km – 10.6 miles to the east on highway n° 190.*
In the 16C the Spaniards founded this city beside the Rio Grijalva. At the center of the plaza, they built an enormous Mudejar-style **fountain★**, with majestic arcades that are shaped like the Catholic Kings' crown. The bricks surmounting the towers are fashioned to imitate diamonds.

★★★ **Boat Ride through Sumidero Canyon.** – *Description – p 186.*

⊙ **Regional Lacquer Museum** (Museo Regional de la Laca). – *On one side of the plaza.* Attractive and colorful handicrafts made of wood and tree bark are exhibited here. Their waterproofing and decoration is based on the same technique used in pre-Columbian Mexico. The collection includes a small sample of lacquerwork from China, Thailand and Japan.

Santo Domingo Parish Church (Parroquia de Santo Domingo). – *One block towards the river.* This is a basilica plan 16C church, with three large naves divided by massive pillars. The transepts are roofed in the Gothic manner, and a long row of windows on the side walls provides abundant light. The tower to the left of the apse has preserved a great **bell**, which weighs 5 168 kg – 11 393 lbs and is made of an alloy of gold, silver and copper.

★★★ **San Cristóbal de Las Casas.** – *85 km – 52.8 miles to the east. Description p 178.*

Map of Principal Sights p 6

Situated south of Veracruz between the sea and the coastal plains of the Gulf of Mexico, the **Sierra de los Tuxtlas** constitutes a lush volcanic region irrigated by a dense network of rivers and springs.

The winding road *(highway n° 180)* unfolds varying landscapes that range from the teeming tropical rainforest inhabited by spider monkeys, racoons and armadillos, to the bucolic pastures dotted with livestock, passing through the fields of beans, corn, coffee, tobacco and sugar cane.

From Santiago Tuxtla to Catemaco. – *23 km – 14.3 miles east of Santiago Tuxtla on highway n° 180 – 1 day.*

★★ **Santiago Tuxtla.** – This is a picturesque village that rises in steps up the mountain. After the Conquest, it was one of the sites the Spaniards chose for livestock farms and sugar plantations, owing to its abundant resources.

Juárez Park (Parque Juárez). – In this tree-filled park rests the colossal **Olmec head** (cabeza olmeca) *(see p 37)* of Cobata, a stone sculpture weighing 45 tons.

★ **Tuxtleco Museum** (Museo Tuxtleco). – *At one side of the park.* This contains a selection
⊙ of regional objects, including El Negro, a monumental Olmec bust to which the local population attributes magic powers.

Continue 13 km – 8.1 miles from Santiago Tuxtla.

San Andrés Tuxtla (San Andrés Tuxtla). – The dynamic activity of this city to the south of Saint Martin Volcano (Volcán de San Martín) can be attributed to the leading economic and commercial role it plays as a business center for this fertile mountain region. In addition, it has various high-quality cigar factories.

Continue 10 km – 6.2 miles from San Andrés Tuxtla.

Catemaco. – The startling atmosphere of this lakeside town may derive from the strange beliefs of its inhabitants, whose origins stem from a mixture of various races and cultures of Mexico, Spain and Africa.

In the silent streets of the suburbs, witch-doctors' offices can be glimpsed. Secret ceremonies, with black cats, candles and monotonous prayers, involving mysterious legends and traditions, are performed there.

★ **Lake Catemaco** (Lago de Catemaco). – A large basin fed by filtrations and mineral water springs forms this lake, which is bordered with tropical vegetation, rich in fruit trees and striking flowers. It has several crater lakes and two islets inhabited by white herons and monkeys.

TZINTZUNTZAN Michoacán ◆

Map of Principal Sights p 5 – Local map p 162

In the Tarascan language, its name means "place of hummingbirds". As one of the most important capitals of the Tarasc empire, in the 15C AD it became a very influential government center. In this period it expanded and achieved a complex social organization. The town settled on the shores of Lake Pátzcuaro, and its typical architecture of tile roofs and eaves lends it a distinctive provincial flavor. Its commercial activity is based on regional handicrafts, principally clay and straw articles.

SIGHTS

★ **Yácatas Archeological Site.** – *1 km – 0.6 miles south of the town.* An impressive
⊙ group of five pyramids rises from rectangular platform 400 m – 1 312 ft long by 25 m – 82 ft wide, with retaining walls facing the lake. The buildings are composed of one rectangular section connected to a semicircular section, built of superimposed stone slabs, and faced with thick blocks of stone used as mosaics. At the summit of the circular sections there used to be temples made of wood and straw. On the platform facing the lake, there was a wide stairway with ramps, and on the other side, a large plaza, possibly for ceremonial rites.

Saint Francis' Church (Templo de San Francisco). – *To the left of the handicraft market.* Inside a broad atrium adorned with olive trees, stands this church, which was founded in the 16C and built in the 17C. Its Plateresque facade displays balustraded columns, a double-arched choir window, and a huge shell. To the left of the church is the elegantly ornamented Plateresque open-air chapel. At the right corner of the atrium is the Church of the Virgin of Solitude (Templo de la Virgen de la Soledad), where a 16C jointed statue of Christ made of cane paste is displayed. In the adjoining courtyard, there is another open-air chapel dating back to the 17C, which belonged to the old hospital.

EXCURSION

Quiroga. – *7 km – 4.3 miles north on highway n° 15 to Morelia.*
Along the sides of this road there are many stands selling the varied regional handicrafts from Michoacán State. The town of Quiroga, which bears the name of the province's benefactor, **Vasco de Quiroga** *(see p 160),* is enlivened by the constant to-and-fro of tourists, shopping among the wares of the local craftsmen including clay pots, leather, wood, tin and copper goods, guitars and colorful washtubs.

URUAPAN Michoacán ◆◆◆◆

Situated on the Tarascan plateau amidst rich vegetation and varied landscapes, Uruapan was founded in 1533 on the site of an old Indian village. The city was designed like a chessboard, despite the irregularities of the terrain.

Its friendly atmosphere is propitious for business, agriculture, cattle-raising and forestry.

SIGHTS

★★ Eduardo Ruiz National Park (Parque Nacional Eduardo Ruiz). – *Calzada La Quinta. The* ⊙ *visit should be made in a clockwise direction.* This national park is also called Barranca del Cupatitzio, for the river of the same name that originates there. *Cupatitzio* means "river that sings through its falls". The park is especially pleasant because it is the source of so much vegetation and water. The many small cascades have been used to make fountains. Popular fantasy has given some of them Indian names like *Tzintzun*, "hummingbird fountain", and *Cutzi*, "half moon", which was the name of a Tarascan princess. The sound of falling water and the bird songs add enchantment to the spot.

At the end of the tour, a small spring named Rodilla del Diablo "Devil's Knee" appears; it is the source of the river that some kilometers farther along, fed by other springs, becomes a powerful waterfall, called Cascada Tzaráracua.

★ Huatapera. – *Facing the plaza principal.* This 16C construction was founded by Friar Juan de San Miguel to house a hospital for the Indians. Its Plateresque-style facade, with visible Mudejar influence, hosts a profusion of grotesques and plant motifs that bear witness to skillful Indian craftsmanship. To the right of the facade, there is a spacious courtyard. The windows along its corridors were designed in a lovely Mudejar style. Within, there is a good collection of handicrafts from different regions of the state.

EXCURSIONS

Tzaráracua Waterfall (Cascada Tzaráracua). – *7 km – 4.3 miles south on highway n° 37 to Apatzingán.*

A gentle slope of over 800 m – 2 625 ft leads down to the end of the ravine where, with a drop of 40 m – 131 ft, the torrential Cupatitzio River takes a deafening leap from the rocks.

Angahuan. – *Go north from Uruapan on highway n° 37 to Carapán 13 km – 8.1 miles, then turn left and continue 20 km – 12.4 miles on an unpaved road.*

Angahuan is an unusual village of simple shingle-roofed frame houses. Its gray surroundings recall the long standing volcanic activity that deposited ashes over a radius of many kilometers.

Señor Santiago Parish Church (Parroquia del Señor Santiago). – *At the town entrance.* This church has an uncommon **facade★★** in beautiful Mudejar style. Its three sections are adorned with rectangular frames in the Arab manner, called *alfices*. The ornamentation also shows an Indian influence.

Paricutín Volcano. – *Time: 2 1/2 hours by horseback. No guide is required since the horses are accustomed to doing the tour. As the road is very stony, it is not advisable to walk.* The old village of **San Juan Parangaricútiro★**, a place that was buried by lava in 1943, can be reached from Angahuan.

An unusual natural formation created by the twisted wrinkles in the igneous rock surrounds the remains of what used to be the temple. From there the cone of the extinct volcano is clearly visible.

Tingambato Archeological Site. – *Go east from Uruapan on highway n° 120 toward Pátzcuaro 27 km – 16.8 miles then turn right and continue 1 km – 0.6 miles to the parking area.*

This is a simple ceremonial center, of moderate size, that flourished in the post-Classic period. In its architecture, the *talud-tablero* configuration prevailed, recalling the Teotihuacán style.

Particularly notable are a six-tier pyramid on a square base and, among the small courtyards and rooms, an unusual ball game court, flanked at the ends by low walls with stairways.

The symbol ⊙ placed in the left margin beside a sight description indicates that specific visitor information can be found in the Opening Hours and Admission Charges section at the end of this guide.

The sights are listed alphabetically in this section either under the place – town, village or area – in which they are situated or under their proper name.

Map of Principal Sights p 6 – Local map p 102

In an undulating terrain which conceals one of the richest archeological sites on the American continent, amidst vines, trunks and branches, rises the fantastic Maya city of Uxmal, with its regal buildings that turn golden in the setting sun.

The facades of monumental pyramids, temples and palaces constitute eloquent examples of the Maya civilization's artistic genius. This architectural achievement was all the more remarkable, since it was accomplished without metal tools, beasts of burden or the wheel.

The silence and solitude that today envelope these ruins contrast with the activity that this city must have witnessed during its years of glory (7-10C AD), when an elite of priests, chieftains, astronomers, engineers and architects controlled the political and economic life of the surrounding region, including **Kabah** *(p 96)* and the **Puuc Archeological Zone** *(p 72)*.

⏱ ARCHEOLOGICAL SITE *time: 3 hours*

From the very outset, the visitor is impressed by the majesty of these low and elongated buildings, which seem to mirror the horizontal lines of the surrounding natural landscape.

The landscape and the great architectural complexes, grouped in the center, provide an idea of the region's fertility, devoted today to citrus fruit cultivation. The lack of rivers and lakes was compensated by the Mayas through the use of waterproofed natural cisterns and bottle-shaped wells, like the one to be seen at the entrance of the ceremonial center.

Pyramid of the Soothsayer (Pirámide del Adivino). – This is an overwhelming oval-shaped structure nearly 28 m – 92 ft tall.

Go up the staircase that faces east.

Near the top, there is a great hole pierced recently by archeologists. It leads to an ancient temple that was closed when the Mayas enlarged the building.

Upper Temple. – This temple has three rooms; the central one faces west, the principal cardinal point in pre-Hispanic mythology. The priests who prayed in these bays had to make careful observations of the stars and planets in order to validate their holy predictions and divinations.

(Photo Michelin)

Uxmal. Maya arch

The **view★★** from the temple is breathtaking. The strange and penetrating light reflecting off the pale ruins offers a unique spectacle. The temple's majesty is further enhanced by the stone ornamentation, resembling interwomen matting, adorning the principal facade.

On the first landing of the very steep staircase, there is a temple faced with exquisitely carved stone masks of **Chac,** the rain god. The temple's entrance is shaped like Chac's mouth.

Down on the esplanade, masks representing the same deity occupy the spaces generally reserved for the ramps. Also to be noted are the passageway below the staircase, and, on the lower part of the facade, the vestiges of frets, columns and rattlesnakes that belonged to an earlier structure.

The Quadrangle of the Nuns (Cuadrángulo de las Monjas). – This is a group of four large buildings, each with a distinct design, arranged around a broad courtyard. The impressions of delicateness and purity that the fine facade reliefs elicit, together with the rows of solitary rooms, led the 16C Spanish conquerors to imagine that this architectural complex was inhabited by Maya priestesses – which explains its name.

East Building. – The facade is adorned with a frieze resembling snake scales and punctuated by six large trapezoid motifs that are framed by a series of serpent's heads and crowned with the head of an owl – an animal associated with death. Above the central door and on the corners of the edifice, there are large masks of the popular god Chac, represented with his characteristic long nose and fangs.

North Building. – This elegant structure consists of a high platform with a series of 26 rooms aligned in a horizontal sequence. The frieze that runs above the room entrances is adorned with frets and representations of human figures, birds, monkeys and stylized traditional Maya huts. This intricate stone lacework is enriched by seven roof combs, consisting of Chac masks and representations of Tlaloc, the water god, who was revered by the agricultural communities.

Two small annexes at the courtyard level further enhance the beauty of the complex: the construction on the left side, dedicated to the planet Venus, is outstanding for its monolithic fluted columns.

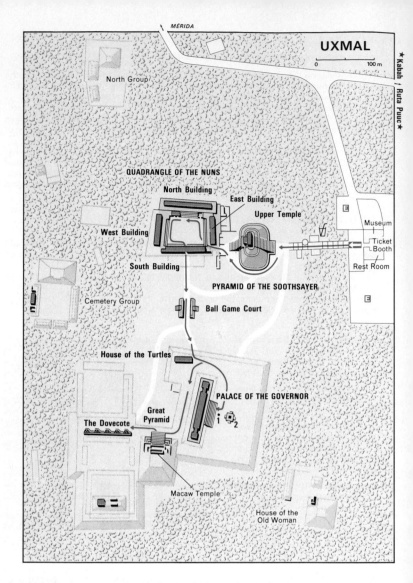

UXMAL

0   100 m

★Kabah / Ruta Puuc★

North Group

QUADRANGLE OF THE NUNS

North Building

East Building

Upper Temple

West Building

E

Museum

Ticket
Booth

South Building

Rest Room

PYRAMID OF THE SOOTHSAYER

Cemetery Group

Ball Game Court

E

House of the Turtles

PALACE OF THE GOVERNOR

Great
Pyramid

1   2

The Dovecote

Macaw Temple

House of the
Old Woman

West Building. – The wide band that adorns the upper part of the facade is an intricate stone mosaic with bulky superimposed figures. A striking figure above the central door probably represents an old dignitary associated with the turtle cult, under an ostentatious feather ornament.

The two feathered rattlesnakes that slither between the frets were added at a later period. From their fangs emerges the divine face of Quetzalcóatl-Kukulcán, the wind.

South Building. – The skillful stonecutting and the stately presentation of the frieze elements, reflect the order and moderation that distinguished the Uxmal theocracy. The ornamentation, which enlivens the facade, consists of smooth panels with groups of three columns, reminiscent of the interlaced poles that form the sides of Maya huts. Among these ornamental features are the gridded panels – a distinctive trait of residential constructions – as well as crestings of feathers and masks of Chac, without his long nose, but with waves that spring from his eyes, symbolizing rainfall.

This long structure is abruptly interrupted by a wide vaulted passage, formerly covered in polychrome stucco. When this coating fell off, two red hands painted on the wall became visible – a strange sign that is repeated elsewhere in the mounds of this site.

Beyond the quadrangle's great arch, unfolds an impressive **panoramic view** of the rest of the ceremonial center, sunk in the abundant vegetation as though it were part of the earth.

Ball Game Court (Juego de Pelota). – This ball game court is a small enclosure where teams competed in a ritual test of strength. The few spectators that attended the event climbed the outer stairs of the two thick walls, which had stone rings built-in on the inner surface of either side, through which the rubber ball was supposed to pass. These walls bore hieroglyphic inscriptions and reliefs of feathered serpents.

House of the Turtles (Casa de las Tortugas). – This plain rectangular stone temple, with entrances on its four sides, is noted for the small turtle sculptures that decorate the upper lintel. It is thought that representations of turtle shells were related to the Maya rain-invoking rituals. From this site there is a splendid view of the Pyramid of the Southsayer and the Quadrangle of the Nuns.

Palace of the Governor (Palacio del Gobernador). – On a gigantic platform made from 358 000 m³ – over 12.6 million cubic feet of stone, rises this extraordinary building, almost 100 m – 328 ft long, 12 m – 39 ft wide, and 9 m – 30 ft high, considered one of the architectural masterpieces of ancient Mexico.

Its exquisite facade illustrates the arcane ceremonial and civic life that took place in its 24 chambers.

On the socle, decorated with small columns, rests a smooth wall perforated by the entrance openings. Its extreme simplicity serves to enhances the rich geometric patterns of the frieze, rigorously framed by a double cornice, the upper one in the form of an undulating serpent. The ornamental band repeats the intricate design of a snakeskin. To this scene is added the omnipresent of Chac, slithering between stepped frets and dice patterns, and adorning the corners. Above the central door, appears the stunning figure of a ruler, with a showy feather as a backrest, and crowned by a trapezoidal composition of two-headed serpents.

Two vaulted passageways, later closed off by the Mayas, divide the palace into three sections. The large arches that mark the passage entrances have slightly convex sides, which convey greater elegance to the ensemble.

Facing this structure, there is a **phallic column (1)** and, further on, a **two-headed jaguar (2)** stands guard on a little platform. Beyond this begins the 18 km – 11.2 mile *sacbé*, the road that leads to Kabah *(p 96)*. The *sacbé* was principally used to import basalt and obsidian.

Great Pyramid (Gran Pirámide). – The broad front stairway leads to the **Macaw Temple** (Templo de las Guacamayas) on the upper level, so-named because this colorful bird, associated with the sun, is the main decorative motif on the facade.

The Dovecote (El Palomar). – The nine openwork triangles that form the crest of this ruinous architectural complex seem to receive all the wandering doves in their cubbyholes, hence the name of this quadrangle.

As in the other buildings, these facades were painted in vivid colors.

★★★ **Light and Sound Show (Luz y Sonido).** – Every night, under the same stars that ruled
⊙ the destinies of the Mayas, a show is presented that transports the visitor to the glorious era of Uxmal, reviving authentic legends, whose drama and tragedy enhance the fascination of the site.

EXCURSIONS

★ **Kabah Archeological Site.** – *21 km to the southeast on highway n° 180 towards Hopelchén. Description p 96.*

★ **Puuc Archeological Zone.** – *This includes the archeological sites of Sayil, Xlapak and Labná. Description p 72.*

★ **VERACRUZ** Veracruz   ◆◆◆◆◆

Map of Principal Sights p 5

A tropical coastal city, rich in tradition, Veracruz proudly conserves its squares and buildings from the early part of the century. Built upon a broad plain under a burning sun, it was the first deep-sea traffic port of Mexico.

Veracruz is the heart of a rich agricultural region, a great commercial center and a dynamic industrial hub noted for its metallurgy, naval base, shipyards and tobacco production.

In this busy city the famous **Mardi Gras★** (Carnaval) is celebrated, in a whirlwind of excitment and fantasy that runs through the city to the tune of its merry local music *(jarocha)*.

HISTORICAL NOTES

On Holy Friday in 1519, the Day of the True Cross (Día de la Vera Cruz), Hernán Cortés and his men landed directly across from Sacrifice Island (Isla de los Sacrificios), and founded the town of Villa Rica de la Vera Cruz. The conquest of New Spain thus began.

Veracruz became the gateway to the New World. Its wharfs witnessed the continuous flow of ships that brought men and merchandise from overseas and sailed to Spain loaded with treasure. Soon many hostelries and enormous wooden storehouses were erected. The so-called Plank City (Ciudad de Tablas) came to know the greed of corsairs and pirates.

To defend the vulnerable port, Fort San Juan de Ulúa (1600) was constructed. By the end of the century, the city was walled and protected by seven bastions. However, a number of factors including the increased population, composed of various races and strata, the lack of sanitation and the frequent epidemics, eventually led to the demolition of the stone walls, which suffocated the city and stunted its growth.

At the end of the 19C, the railroad gave a new boost to the city's port, which was enlarged and modernized, with important engineering works that reclaimed land from the sea.

The Heroic City. – Veracruz was born Spanish but learned to be Mexican; it received the title of "Heroic" in recognition for the people's resistance to the Spanish (1825), French (1839), and North American (1847 and 1914) invasions.

CENTER OF THE CITY *time: 1/2 day – Plan p 217*

Cathedral. – The pediment of the building's neoclassical facade bears an inscription from 1721, the year in which construction began. When the cathedral was completed nearly one century later, the national coat of arms of the newly founded Republic was added.

Inside the cathedral, there are four sumptuous Baccarat candelabra.

Plaza de Armas. – This square flanked by arcades is situated in the center of the city. The most lively spot is the northeast corner with its popular restaurants, cafés and bars, where musicians and street vendors abound.

Walk through the arcades towards the sea.

Plaza de la Reforma. – There are several interesting buildings on this enormous esplanade.

⊘ **Reforma Sanctuary** (Santuario de la Reforma). – **Church of the Saint Francis Convent** (Extemplo del Convento de San Francisco). In this hall, the first section of the Reform Laws *(see p 31)* was promulgated.

Its cold and solemn interior houses eight monumental statues of prominent men from this movement, presided by Benito Juárez in the apse.

⊘ **Civil Registry** (Registro Civil). – The main vestibule of this public building is decorated with a mosaic depicting the first birth certificate to be inscribed in the Mexican Civil Registry. This historic certificate, which is dated October 10th 1860, was issued to Jerónima Francisca Juárez, the daughter of President Benito Juárez and his wife Margarita Maza.

⊘ **Postal, Telegraph and Maritime Customs Offices** (Oficinas de Correos, Telégrafos y de la Aduana Marítima). – These buildings reflect the architectural trends of the Porfirio Diaz dictatorship *(p 31)*. They were built of cement at the beginning of this century on land reclaimed from the sea.

Their neoclassical style has severe and majestic lines with imposing pediments and stone busts of Veracruz leaders.

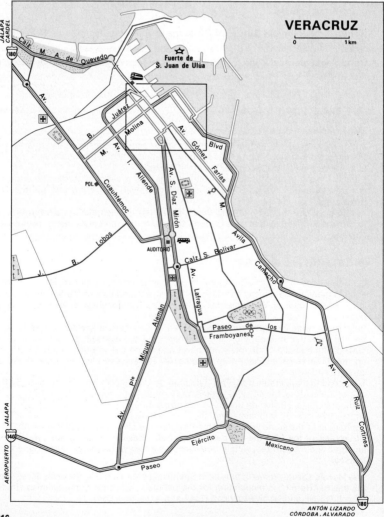

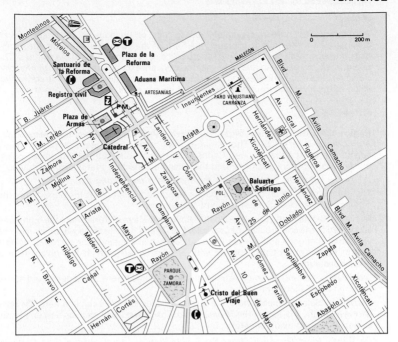

⊘FORT SAN JUAN DE ULÚA (FUERTE DE SAN JUAN DE ULÚA)

time: 1 hour – Plan p 216

This great fortress (16-18C) was built on an islet, now connected to the mainland by a paved road, to secure the naval routes and protect the port of entrance to New Spain, which had suffered repeated pirate attacks.

This colossal construction, shrouded in mysterious legends, was built of coral rock. It has retained a moat, a ramp, five bastions and a large number of dungeons. In one of the latter, an **information center** (museum) has been installed, with objects and sketches that help to reconstruct the site's history. The fort also served during some years as a trading center, jail, garrison and naval service center. On two occasions, under Juárez and Carranza, the main house served as a presidential residence.

ADDITIONAL SIGHTS *Plan above*

⊘ **Santiago Bastion (Baluarte de Santiago).** – Built at the beginning of the 17C, this is the only vestige remaining of the wall that protected the city. Its strong lines and austere sloping sides suggest a medieval influence in the military architecture of the day.
To enter, cross the drawbridge over the moat. Above the entrance opening there is a relief of *Señor Santiago*. Straight ahead is a small museum with temporary exhibits. A visit to the tower's twelve cannons is also worthwhile.

Chapel of Christ of the Safe Journey (Capilla del Cristo del Buen Viaje). – In this simple 16C parish church, a black Christ is worshipped, in remembrance of the mulatto fishermen who originally lived in the neighborhood, and who prayed before setting out to sea.

EXCURSIONS

Antón Lizardo Point (Punta). – *Leave Veracruz on highway n° 180 toward Alvarado and after 15 km – 9.3 miles, passing Boca del Río, turn off to the left on highway n° 140 towards Mandinga and Antón Lizardo.*
On the way to the point, the road goes through two small villages, **Boca del Río** *(12 km – 7.5 miles)* and **Mandinga** *(19 km – 11.8 miles),* both known throughout the region for the quality of their fresh shellfish. The road ends at Antón Lizardo Point, which is a formation made of sediments deposited on the reefs by the Gulf currents.

⊙ **Heroic Naval Military Academy** (Heroica Escuela Naval Militar). The academy was built in 1952 on this strategic point. Interesting features of the main building are the Flag
⊘ Room (Sala de Banderas) and, next to the gymnasium, the **Naval Museum,** exhibiting uniforms, weapons and a splendid collection of scale models of the Mexican navy's ships.

Cempoala Archeological Site. – *41 km – 25.5 miles. Go northwest from Veracruz on highway n° 180 to Cardel; continue north on highway n° 180 and after 8 km – 5 miles turn left. Description p 65.*

The maps and plans are orientated with north at the top.

Villahermosa, the modern capital of Tabasco state, on the banks of the Grijalva River, is situated in a region that contains one third of the country's hydraulic resources. In its museums, the city conserves superb relics of the Olmec and Maya cultures. The unexpected oil boom in the area has caused an exceptional growth of the city. However, this modernization has not frightened away the legions of grackles that settle noisily every afternoon in the colorful foliage of the royal poinciana trees.

SIGHTS

★★ Regional Anthropological Museum – Carlos Pellicer (Museo Regional de Antropología).
🕐 *Av. Carlos Pellicer n° 511.* The statue in front of this concrete and glass building depicts the great Tabasco poet, Carlos Pellicer, who directed the old archeological museum for 26 years and organized the splendid collection that is displayed here.

To the left of the vestibule, take the elevator to the second floor.

The visit begins with an exhibit of graphs and pictures that cover the period from the settling of America to the formation of Mesoamerica.

First Floor. – In this room, dedicated to the Olmec and Maya cultures, note the high-relief **bricks** used in the construction of **Comalcalco** *(p 219)* and the **urns of Tapijulapa,** clay filigrees with images of gods and priests. As these pieces had remained for centuries inside a grotto, some are partially covered with lime carbonate, which has given them a mysterious aura.

Lower Floor. – Among the monumental pieces displayed here are jaguars and stelae from the Maya Classic period.

Mezzanine. – Selected pieces from the museum collection are exhibited here. **The Teapa Urn★** evokes the majesty of the Maya priests. The **Pellicer Vase★** depicts a ruler and his subjects, in a profusion of color.

★La Venta Park-Museum (Parque-Museo de La Venta). – *Blvd. Adolfo Ruiz Cortines,*
🕐 *unnumbered.* Carlos Pellicer founded this innovative park-museum in the 1950s in order to protect the Olmec works of art discovered at the La Venta archeological site, which was subsequently transformed into an oil field. To this end, he recreated a landscape that resembled the original site, as a repository for the Olmec sculptures. The **Introductory Room** presents an overview of various aspects of the Olmec culture and features some objects from La Venta as well as a model of the site. Next to this room is an enormous cage containing two jaguars.

The visit continues counterclockwise.

In the midst of lush tropical plants, each carefully labeled, the visitor discovers several outstanding relics: several altars with frontal niches, which are thought to represent the cave through which man emerged from the earth (numbers 6, 16, 29 and 30); the stela with a man wearing a false beard (21); the famous **monumental heads ★★★** sculptured in stone (11, 27 and 25), executed in a strikingly realistic manner; the imposing **jaguar cage** (27), composed of 44 basalt columns; and the **mosaic** (8), portraying the stylized face of a jaguar, with approximately 500 tiles carved in serpentine forms.

🕐 **Popular Culture Museum** (Museo de Cultura Popular). – *Zaragoza n° 810.* In this typical house there are exhibits of masks, musical instruments and the attractive costumes that the Chontal Indians of Tabasco wear for their dances. An annex room displays their daily utensils, where carved gourds hold a prominent place. This museum is completed by a replica of a typical dwelling inhabited by the Chontal Indians, who constitute the state's largest ethnic group.

(Photo Ignacio Urquiza/Mexico)

Villahermosa. Olmec head in La Venta Park

EXCURSIONS

Cupilco; Comalcalco. – *55 km – 34.2 miles. Go northwest from Villahermosa towards Comalcalco and after 44 km – 27.3 miles you arrive in Cupilco.*
The road crosses the most populated region of Tabasco: La Chontalpa – a broad plain with swamps, lagoons and intermittent spots of jungle. Numerous Indian communities take advantage of the scarce firm ground for pastureland and for growing cacao.

Cupilco. – In this town, the picturesque **facade**★ of the Church of Our Lady of the Assumption (Nuestra Señora de la Asunción) cannot be overlooked. Its bright colors reflect the freshness of the environment and are a vivid example of popular art. Above the entrance opening, there is a candid high relief that portrays Juan Diego receiving flowers from the Virgin of Guadalupe *(see p 129).*

Follow on 9 km – 5.6 miles to the village of Comalcalco, continue 3 km – 1.9 miles, turn right and 900 m – 2 953 ft ahead is the archeological site.

⊘ **Comalcalco Archeological Site.** – Comalcalco was the most westerly Maya city. It reached the peak of its grandeur between 800 and 1250 AD. The site reveals the ingenuity employed in substituting the traditional construction materials (there is no stone in the region) for bricks baked in the sun and joined with a mixture of sand and clay with burnt and ground oyster shells.

Museum. – In a palm shed, some bricks with high reliefs are displayed.

Great Acropolis (Gran Acrópolis). – This is a group of religious, public and residential buildings, where the large stucco masks are finely detailed, especially those found in the Tomb of the Nine Figures (La Tumba de los Nueve Personajes).

⊘ **Grottos of Coconá (Grutas de Coconá).** – *57 km – 35.4 miles. Estimate a 1 hour visit. Go south from Villahermosa to Teapa and after 54 km – 33.6 miles turn left and continue on a narrow paved road 3 km – 1.9 miles.*
In the mountains of northern Chiapas, which has one of the highest annual rainfalls in the world, lie these 492 m – 1 614 ft long grottos. All eight halls have intriguing white and red formations, but they can be best appreciated in the **Hall of the Blind Fish Well** (Sala del Cenote de los Peces Ciegos).

★★★ **Palenque Archeological Site.** – *144 km – 89.5 miles to the southeast on highway n° 186. Description p 156.*

XALAPA Veracruz ◆◆◆◆

Map of Principal Sights p 5

Xalapa, the capital of the state of Veracruz, is located on the slope of Macuiltépetl Hill. In the 18C, it became the center for overseas trade, replacing the port of Veracruz, which then was suffering domestic turmoil and pirate raids.
The prosperity of that era set the character of the city, which still endures in the neoclassical architecture of its churches and public buildings. In the vicinity, there are numerous older houses with red tile roofs scattered over the city's uneven terrain. Endowed with artificial lakes and handsome parks, Xalapa at present offers opportunities for many cultural and recreational activities.

SIGHTS

★★★ **Xalapa Archeological Museum** (Museo de Arqueología de Xalapa). – *The corner of Av. Xalapa and 1° de Mayo.* This modern (1986) stone complex consists of a series of long, elegant buildings, facing a large garden. The buildings' volume is broken up by numerous small openings that admit abundant sunshine. These interstices also serve to incorporate plant-filled patios, enlivening the 3 500 m – 11 483 ft of exhibit space. The museum features remains of the three cultures that developed in Veracruz during the pre-Hispanic era: Olmec, Center of the Gulf and Huaxtec.
A gigantic **Olmec head** in the vestibule, weighing almost 20 tons, invariably impresses visitors on account of its markedly realistic expression. This head was carved in the pre-Classic period and probably represents a god created after man's image, a deified ruler or a ball game player.

Olmec Exhibit. – The region south of the Gulf of Mexico was the cradle of Mesoamerican civilizations. As early as the 18C BC the Olmecs made offerings to their gods in order to obtain divine mercy – the jaguar being their symbol of the absolute.
From the monumental heads to the children figurines in the showcases (the style is called "baby face"), all display a feline mouth – an distinctive trait reflecting their desire to be linked with the gods. On display at the entrance to room 2 is the **Priest of the Limas** (Sacerdote de las Limas) (5C BC – 1C AD) – a jade sculpture 55 cm – 22 inches tall, representing a scarred human figure holding the body of the sun child.

Center of the Gulf Exhibit. – This collection is mainly composed of archeological remains from four ceremonial centers (Remojadas, Tajín, Higueras and Zapotal). Among the ceramic pieces, the Smiling Faces (Caritas Sonrientes) in terra cotta, associated with dance, music, sun and happiness, are most attractive.
The jade, coral and bone jewelry is exquisitely crafted, while the fragments of mural painting from the Higueras center exalt their deities. This search for technical perfection in order to express the darkest mysteries of life as interpreted by their religion was masterfully achieved in the *Cihuateteos*, or women who died in childbirth, and the *Mictlantecuhtli*, or Lord of the Dead, from the Zapotal center. These are superb examples of this culture's ceramics from the 6C to 9C AD.

Huastec Exhibit. – The cultures from the northern area of the Gulf reached their peak in the centuries immediately preceding the Spanish Conquest. The elegant simplicity of their sculptures carved in pale sandstone reflect the character of this peaceful people.

⊘ **Juárez Park (Parque Juárez).** – *Beside the Government Palace.* This is a pleasant, tree-lined spot with a lookout that offers a splendid view of San Marcos Hill (Cerro de San Marcos). The rocky outcropping of Cofre de Perote covered with evergreens, and the Pico de Orizaba's spectacular alpine landscape are visible to the west.

Xalitic Wash House (Lavaderos de Xalitic). – *Revolución and Victoria.* These washbasins were built at the beginning of the 19C in the picturesque King's District (Barrio del Rey), taking advantage of the springwater coming from the ravine. The gallery, supported on slendor columns and covered with a pitched roof of beams and brick, has been preserved. Still today the neighborhood women come to this little square in the early hours of the morning with their great baskets of laundry.

EXCURSIONS

★ **Francisco Javier Clavijero Botanical Garden (Jardín Botánico).** – *2.5 km – 1.5 miles south on the old highway to Coatepec.*
⊘ This botanical garden exhibits more than 1 500 labelled plants, showing the great variety of Veracruz flora, ranging from jungle vegetation to evergreen woods.
The garden is set in a peaceful area of 9 hectares – 22 acres that includes a formal garden with decorative flowers, an artificial lake for aquatic plants, and a section demonstrating traditional methods of vegetable-growing. In the remaining areas there are rich forests, palm groves and pine woods. The careful maintenance and didactic approach of this garden enhance its attraction.

Xico Waterfall (Cascada de Xico). – *21 km – 13 miles. Go south from Xalapa toward Xico on the new highway that crosses Coatepec (18 km – 11.2 miles). At the entrance to the town, turn left and after the church turn left again and continue 3 km – 1.9 miles on a cobblestone road.* This is a very pretty cascade with three crystalline falls. From the simple iron bridge built in 1908, the bottom of the ravine and the winding river can be seen. In front of the bridge, one of the falls carries its waters down the face of the cliff and on the left, from a small lookout, the roar of the largest cascade can be heard, while observing the bottom of the gorge, amid rocks and exuberant foliage.

Cempoala Archeological Site. – *76 km – 47.2 miles. Go southeast from Xalapa toward Veracruz and 50 km – 31.1 miles ahead turn left toward Cardel; go 8 km – 5 miles towards the north on highway n° 180 and turn left. Description p 65.*

★★ XOCHICALCO Morelos

Map of Principal Sights p 6 – Local map p 77

⊘ This **archeological site** is situated on a high hill that was terraced to accommodate the buildings. In the Náhuatl language, *Xochicalco* means "house of the flowers". Its peak was reached between 750 and 900 AD and it is considered one of the most important sites of the late Classic period. The site's architecture combines the salient Meso-american styles of the time, such as Teotihuacán, Zapotec and Maya. It is believed that the site was planned as a center for calendar and astronomic studies.

Observatory (Observatorio). – *On the west side of the site.* There is a tunnel that leads to a vaulted chamber with a small circular hole in the roof. On the 14th of May, at noon, the sun reaches its zenith directly above this opening, flooding the chamber with light.

Pyramid of the Feathered Serpent (Pirámide de la Serpiente Emplumada). – *On the first plaza after the climb.* The architectural elements of this *talud-tablero* building include an attractive **ornamentation★** of serpents, frets and, on the panels, seated persons with Maya traits. To the left of the stairway, note the fabulous serpent, which frames a **relief** bearing a calendar correction.

(From photo by Arturo Cháirez/Mexico)

Xochicalco. Relief from the Pyramid of the Feathered Serpent

Stelae Temple (Templo de las Estelas). – *At the opposite end of the entrance courtyard.* This temple was built on a platform and consists of a set of palaces around a small pyramidal temple, called "stelae" because of the carved pieces found on the temple floor during the archeological excavation.

Two-Glyph Stela Plaza (Plaza de la Estela de Dos Glifos). – *To the right of the Stelae Temple, go down the walk.* At the foot of a ruinous staircase that belonged to an enormous pyramid, lies a square bordered by two temples, facing each other. These frame a shrine from which the stela emerges – hence the plaza's name.

From the rear of the plaza, there is a **view★** of the **Rodeo Lagoon** (Laguna del Rodeo) and, to the right, behind one of the temples, a rise overlooking an unusual **ball game court.** Its stylized slopes attest to its former architectural magnificence. To the left of this structure, there are the remains of priests' living quarters; and, to the rear, a broad platform overlooks the valley around Xochicalco.

★★ YAXCHILÁN Chiapas

Map of Principal Sights p 6

⊙ *Air travel is the only advisable means of access to the site.*

The archeological site of Yaxchilán is situated on the left bank of the Usumacinta River. The jungle that engulfs the area seems to hold the luxurious palaces and many temples under a mute spell. Only the birds and monkeys break this stony silence. Taking off after the morning fog has lifted, the flight affords a splendid **panoramic view★★**. As the aircraft crosses the Central Plateau of Chiapas, the Tzeltal and Tzotzil settlements can be seen, with their traditional palm- or straw-roofed houses. At the edge of the tropical zone, the jungle begins – a veritable treasure-house of precious hardwoods growing on the hills. Suddenly turquoise blue lakes appear. This rugged land is inhabited by the **Lacandons,** who go barefoot and wear long hair. A few minutes later, the plane reaches the Usumacinta River, which forms the boundary with Guatemala. As the plane descends, the first Maya monuments begin to emerge.

⊙ **ARCHEOLOGICAL SITE** *time: 2 hours*

This great Maya metropolis adopted the contour of the terrain. The tour begins on a walk flanked by various jungle-covered mounds, leading to a dark tunnel through a intricately designed temple. At the end of the tunnel, a courtyard appears among the ceiba and ficus trees, surrounded by ceremonial platforms and stairways, within a mysterious world of engraved lintels, hieroglyphic inscriptions and large stelae.

Left-Hand Complex (Conjunto de la Izquierda). – Walking clockwise, it is easy to imagine the procession of the rulers, with their retinue, passing through this area of luxurious shrines and residences during the heyday of the city (6-7C AD).

Right-Hand Complex (Conjunto de la Derecha). – The fine **carved lintels★★** over its three doors distinguish the Temple of the Bird Offerings (Templo de Ofrendas de Aves) – the first on the slope. The luxuriously attired figures of gods, priests and women produce an interesting play of light and shadow. The next shrine, at present protected by metal roofing, was severely damaged when a grave robber cut into the stone carvings. The third monument on this platform has two passageways roofed with stepped vaults, a sophisticated elaboration on the **Maya arch** *(see p 37).*

Great Acropolis (Gran Acrópolis). – At the summit of the steep slope behind the Right-Hand Complex, rises a structure with very large chambers. Its facade decoration is based on highly stylized snake heads.

Structure 33 (Estructura 33). – *Climb the hill behind the temple protected by sheet metal roofing.* Behind a leafy curtain stands one of the best-preserved buildings of the site. It is crowned by an elegant and light openwork crest. Inside, there is a sculpture representing a deity with very strange features: the head is broken and separated from the body. At present, the Lacandons worship this image and believe that when the head returns to its place, the whole world will collapse.

South Acropolis (Acrópolis del Sur). – *300 m – 984 ft southwest of Structure 33. Across a field.*
This acropolis is composed of three shrines preceded by circular altars and several skillfully carved stelae.

EXCURSION

⊙ **Bonampak.** – *15 minutes by plane towards the south starting from Yaxchilán.*
This is an archeological site incrusted in the jungle where, in 1946, the largest painting of the Maya civilization was found. It occupies the walls and vaults of the three rooms in the **Temple of the Paintings** (Templo de las Pinturas) at the right end of the first platform.

★★ **Room nº 1 (Cuarto nº 1).** – The pre-war rituals are portrayed in a broad gamut of richly nuanced colors, which physically envelope the visitor – such is the power of this work of art. Social stratification is symbolized by the person's distance from the floor and the amount of empty space surrounding him. At the top of the vault are the symbols of the gods. The two following rooms feature the battle and the victory celebration, although, unlike the previous room, they still have the lime deposit which has preserved these extraordinary works since the 8C AD, but which, regrettably, makes these paintings difficult to see. The National Anthropological Museum of Mexico City *(see p 128)* exhibits an excellent life-size reproduction of the temple and its frescoes.

★★ YURIRIA MONASTERY Guanajuato

Map of Principal Sights p 5

This Augustinian monastery, built in the 16C, stands in the middle of an open area that enhances the impact of the complex's architectural volume.

Church Facade. – Amid an exuberance of symmetrical volutes, its broad facade rises three levels with exquisite ornamentation. The contrast between this and the simplicity of the tower, also three-level, and the bell gable, is surprising. The architectural composition is very similar to that of the church at Acolman (p 56), but in Yuriria the builder's ingenuity admirably treated the empty spaces and highlighted the building's elegant Plateresque style. The right side door of the church displays the same style in a more discreet form.

Interior. – The church comprises one nave with a Latin cross layout and coffered barrel vaulting. The vaults of the transept and the chancel are masterfully built with ribbings that are Gothic in character.

⊙ **Monastery.** – To the left of the church stands the solid porch with its four arches. Four rooms on the lower floor of the cloister are occupied by a modest museum, displaying pre-Hispanic and colonial objects, as well as religious paintings and sculptures from the 17C and 18C. The delicacy of the arches that rest on slender fluted columns and the ribbing of the vaults over the passageway are remarkable. There are also vestiges of paintings here. In the patio, gargoyles in the form of fantastic animals and the stairway, covered with a double ribbed vault, should be noted. In the upper cloister, the passageway is separated from the cells by an inner corridor covered by a barrel vault with arched skylights and round windows. The monastery's library contains approximately 4000 volumes dating from the 16C to the beginning of the 20C.

Exept where otherwise stated, all recommended itineraries in towns, are designed as walks.

The main parking facilities are indicated on the town plans.

★★ ZACATECAS Zacatecas ◆◆◆

Map of Principal Sights p 5

Zacatecas lies at the foot of **Cerro de la Bufa** in an arid region dotted with cactuses and prickly pears. It is the capital of the state of Zacatecas.
Strolling through Zacatecas' cobblestone streets – sometimes a taxing experience because of the city's hilly terrain – the visitor discovers elegant mansions of rose-colored stone with fanciful wrought-iron grilles as well as handsome colonial churches that date back to the 18C, when gold and silver mining brought prosperity to the area.

HISTORICAL NOTES

Zacatecas was founded in the 16C by Juan de Tolosa, Diego de Ibarra, Cristóbal de Oñate and Baltazar Temiño de Bañuelos. The mineral wealth of Zacatecas made it an ostentatious city of luxurious residences and lovely baroque churches.
In 1914, in a much celebrated battle, Francisco Villa seized the city and liberated it from the Federal army led by Victoriano Huerta.

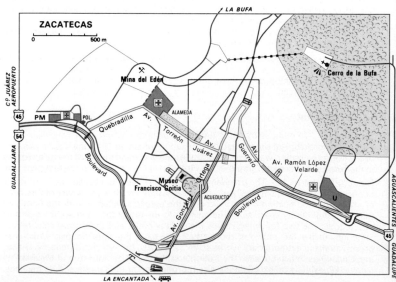

★★ CATHEDRAL AND SURROUNDINGS
time: 1/2 day – Plan below

★ **Cathedral.** – This opulent construction, built in the Mexican baroque style, is considered by historians to be one of the finest examples of Hispanic-American architecture. Built in the 17C as a parish church, the edifice had to be reconstructed in the following century owing to its poor state of conservation. In 1864 the church was elevated to the rank of cathedral. The 17C **south facade,** dedicated to Our Lady Patroness of Zacatecs (Nuestra Señora del Patrocinio) is designed in a sober baroque style. The **north facade** seems to have been altered, since the arms of the caryatids show clearly that a section was added to support the capitals.

★★★ **Principal Facade.** – This beautiful stone facade resembles a rich lace mantle. It is carved in plant motifs, garlands of flowers and acanthus leaves, as though to compensate for the lack of this sort of vegetation in the region. Seen from the side and at a distance, the facade resembles a bishop's miter or a noble's coat of arms. The enormous rose window, which resembles a crown of thorns, illuminates the choir. Among the sculptures adorning the facade are cherubs, angels and the Doctors of the Church – Sts Gregory, Jerome, Ambrose and Augustine. The Apostles stand on richly adorned baroque pedestals.

Interior. – The tone of the inside is set by its soft pink stone and the simple design of its columns and cupola, making up a harmonious ensemble. The finely carved keystones are particularly noteworthy.

Palace of Justice (Palacio de Justicia) **(J)**. – **Mala Noche Palace** (Palacio de la Mala Noche). – This old mansion dates back to the 18C and bears the name Mala Noche or "bad night" because, so it is told, its owner, Manuel Reategui, having lost all his money, was contemplating suicide, on the very night that he learned that a rich vein had been struck in his mine. This house has retained its back door *(on Callejón Veyna),* which the miner reputedly used, to come and go unobserved with his riches.

Government Palace (Palacio de Gobierno) (PG). – The original edifice as well as the site belonged to the Maestre del Campo Don Vicente Saldivar. The building was enlarged and embellished by the first Count de Santiago de la Laguna and subsequently remodeled in a splendid fashion by the second Count de Santiago de la Laguna. This plain 18C palace has a facade with heavy, though not unattractive, forms. In 1867, Benito Juárez resided in what is now the reception hall.

○ **González Ortega Market (Mercado).** – Until a few years ago, this was the most centrally located market in the city. In view of its considerable architectural value, it has been restored, and adapted as an outlet for handicrafts.

Calderón Theater (Teatro Calderón) **(T)**. – Begun in 1891, this elegant neoclassical construction, which towers above the surrounding buildings, is visible from various points in the city. Its interior has conserved the flavor of 19C theaters. At present, the theater hosts major cultural events.

★ **Church of Santo Domingo** (Templo de Santo Domingo). – This plain baroque-style structure was erected on an enormous foundation, to compensate for the unevenness of the terrain. It dates back to the middle of the 18C. Note the church's **eight altarpieces** of gilded wood. This is the richest church in the city.

Sacristy (Sacristía). – The sacristy, constructed on an octagonal plan, has one of the few authentically baroque layouts. Displayed on its recessed walls are eight paintings by Francisco Martínez depicting different scenes from the Passion of Christ.

★★ **Pedro Coronel Museum.** – College of San Luis Gonzaga (Excolegio de San Luis Gonzaga).
○ Built as a school for young men, this impressive construction today houses one of Mexico's finest museums, featuring the rich collection of the renowned Zacatecas painter, Pedro Coronel. The **pre-Hispanic collection** includes outstanding examples of the Mescal style from the state of Guerrero. The exhibit of **colonial works** features an 18C painting of the Christ of Chalma by Miguel Herrara and some 17C wooden relic cases. Among the works in the collection of **European-masters** are the superb **series★** of etchings by Francisco Goya – *The Bullfight (La Tauromaquia)* and the *Proverbs (Los Proverbios).* The collection also includes works by Hogarth, Piranesi, Daumier and several 20C artists like Miró, Picasso and Vasarely.
This splendid collection is completed by marvelous African masks and fine examples of Chinese, Japanese and ancient Greek art.

ZACATECAS★★

⊙**Saint Augustine's Church (Templo de San Agustín).** – Consecrated in 1782, this church, which was partially destroyed in the 19C, has recently been restored. Its large and impressive **lateral facade★★** with strong vertical lines, is framed by two enormous Churrigueresque niche pilasters.

The facade's center is dominated by a relief depicting Saint Augustine in the garden of the house where his conversion took place. The saint is accompanied by the sun and angel musiciens.

The church's huge solemn nave is crowned by an octagonal cupola decorated with stone floral motifs and angel atlantes. On the sides, note the two large carved stone arches.

⊙**EDÉN MINE (MINA DEL EDÉN)** *time: 1 hour – Plan p 222*

One of the oldest mines in Zacatecas (16C), Edén Mine originally named after San Eligio, reached its apex in the 18C. The guided tour allows visitors to explore approximately 2 km – 1.2 miles of the underground mine network (1,6 km – 1 mile – by small train and 400 m – 1 312 ft – on foot). Some shafts are flooded with apparently pure water which is, in fact, poisoned by different mineral substances. The adventurous may cross a hanging bridge over one of the shafts and see the mineral's glint in some places.

ADDITIONAL SIGHTS   *Plan p 222*

Cerro de la Bufa. – *Take the scenic highway to La Bufa.* This mountain is shaped like a bucking horse. Its summit, which offers a wonderful **view** of the entire city, is crowned by the Chapel of Our Lady of Zacatecs (Capilla de Nuestra Señora de los Zacatecos), a renowned pilgrimage site. Behind the chapel stands the Meteorological Observatory (Observatorio Meteorológico). The mausoleum dedicated to the city's illustrious men (Mausoleo de los Hombres Ilustres Zacatecanos) is situated on an elevated site in front of the chapel.

★**Francisco Goitia Museum.** – *Calle General Enrique Estrada n° 102.* This is a
⊙handsome mansion built of pink stone in the neoclassical style, with an attractive interior and surrounded by rose gardens. The museum displays works by Zacatecan artists who have gained recognition outside Mexico. The collection of etchings, oils, watercolors, temperas, silk-screenings and sculptures by Francisco Goitia, Julio Ruelas, Manuel Felguérez, Pedro Coronel, José Kuri Breña and Rafael Coronel, offer a colorful survey of 90 years of Zacatecan art.

EXCURSIONS

★**Convent of Guadalupe (Exconvento de Guadalupe).** – *Go southeast from Zacatecas on highway n° 45 and after 6 km – 3.7 miles turn right, continue 500 m – 1 640 ft and turn left on calle Begoña, a cobblestone road in front of the Plaza Principal.*
This old construction is located in a small suburb of Zacatecas. In its colonial origins, it was an important evangelizing center, since it was the School for the Propagation of the Faith (Colegio de Propaganda Fide), from which many friars set out to proselytize the north of Mexico during the 18C.

★★**Museum.** – This museum houses one of the finest collections of Mexican colonial art,
⊙including works by renowned artists such as Andrés López, Cristóbal de Villalpando, Nicolás Rodríguez Juárez, Ibarra, Gabriel José de Ovalle, Antonio de Torres and Miguel Cabrera. The Gallery of Colonial Art (Galería de Arte Virreinal) situated in the upper cloister features Cabrera's series of 14 oval paintings depicting themes from the life of the Virgin, as well as noteworthy works by Villalpando and Morlete Ruiz. A fine collection of engravings and lithographs and important pieces of sculpture are also on display.

The choir, situated on the upper level to the left of the staircase, has conserved its carved wood stalls. In the center of the room, a jointed effigy of Saint Francis is exposed.

Other points of interest include the library and the collection of apothecary jars, which belonged to the pharmacy of the School for the Propagation of the Faith *(see above).*

★★**Naples Chapel** (Capilla de Nápoles). – The walls of this wonderful 19C chapel are covered with gilded stuccowork. Other notable features are the extremely tall cupola with plasterwork ornamentation and the floor made of rare woods in a compass design that also indicates the months of the year.

⊙**Regional Historical Museum** (Museo Regional de Historia). – Built as an annex to the convent, this building was transformed into a boarding school in the 19C. In the room devoted to the history of transportation in Mexico, a fine collection of carriages and other types of vehicles is on display.

⊙**Ruins of Chicomostoc.** – **La Quemada.** *47 km – 29.2 miles. Go west from Zacatecas on highway n° 54 toward Guadalajara and after 44 km – 27.3 miles turn left, continue 3 km – 1.9 miles from the junction on a paved road.*
This imposing pre-Hispanic center was a fortress; it is situated on a mountain summit, from which the green valley of Villanueva can be admired. The ceremonial and residential centers were built of flagstone and mortar. Particularly noteworthy in this complex are the **Room of the Columns** (Salón de las Columnas) and the **Votive Pyramid** (Pirámide Votiva).

Jerez. – *47 km – 29.2 miles. Go west from Zacatecas on highway n° 54 toward Guadalajara, and after 25 km – 15.5 miles turn right at Malpaso and continue 22 km – 13.7 miles towards Tlaltenango.*
Jerez de Zacatecas is a romantic village, where the memory of the poet, **Ramón López Velarde,** is still present. The town has preserved beautiful private houses with patios shaded with orange trees and stone-curbed fresh water wells.
Two churches are still standing: the **Old Parish Church** (Vieja Parroquia) and the **Sanctuary of Solitude** (Santuario de la Soledad), designed in an eclectic style with neoclassical and neo-Gothic features.
The magnificent old **Hinojosa Theater★** (Teatro Hinojosa), built on a horseshoe layout, preserves a romantic flavor. The cistern below the proscenium that was designed to improve the acoustics, has remained intact. Other interesting points in this village are the neo-Gothic **La Torre School** (Colegio de la Torre) and the house of the poet López Velarde, where an attempt has been made to recreate the atmosphere in which he lived. Velarde's poems are exhibited among his furniture and personal belongings. The local handicrafts industry produces fine leather articles.

ZAMORA Michoacán ◆◆◆◆

Map of Principal Sights p 5

Founded in 1540, this city was named after the charming Spanish medieval town. With a simple layout, it is located beside the Lerma River, which flows into the Chapala Lagoon (Laguna de Chapala). Its main economic activities are agriculture and livestock-raising, in addition to intensive trade with the western region of the state.

★★ **Unfinished Cathedral** (Catedral Inconclusa). – *Justo Sierra and Av. 5 de Mayo.* This monumental edifice overlooking a large garden, has remained unfinished to this day. In this neo-Gothic cathedral, the ample ogee arches have large triangular pediments with stone-carved rose windows. The visitor is struck by the spaciousness of the interior, wich comprises 3 naves and is filled with the abundant light pouring into the roofless central nave.

EXCURSIONS

Lake Camécuaro (Lago de Camécuaro) *12 km – 7.5 miles southeast on highway n° 15 toward Morelia.*
This small lake bordered by weeping willows is a popular place for weekend outings.

★ **Ixtlán de los Hervores.** – *26 km – 16.2 miles to the northwest on highway n° 16 toward La Barca.*
Here a powerful natural **geyser** spouts more than 30 m – 98 ft into the air; it is caused by an escape of sulphurous volcanic gases, which, on contact with underground currents and springs, produce dense steam flows that spews forth under great pressure at temperatures near 96°C – 204.8°F.

Jiquilpan. – *54 km – 33.6 miles to the west on highway n° 15 toward Sahuayo.*

General **Lázaro Cárdenas** *(see p 33)* was born in this town. Jiquilpan exudes a calm atmosphere, where the new and the old gracefully mingled.

Lázaro Cárdenas Museum. – It contains important exhibits concerning the life of the illustrious president as politician and statesman.

Licenciado Gabino Ortiz Public Library (Biblioteca Pública). – *On the main street, facing the bus terminal.* This is a small single-nave chapel with a handsome bronze door adorned with relief busts of great Latin American thinkers and writers. The interior contains fascinating mural **paintings★★** by José Clemente Orozco *(p 41),* completed in 1940. The colorful mural at the end of the nave is particularly striking. Expressive images in black and white, representing struggles, mutinies and shootings, adorn the side walls.

Practical information

BEFORE LEAVING

Mexican Government Tourist Offices. – For information, brochures, maps and assistance in planning your trip apply to the official tourist office in your country.

United States

Chicago – 70 East Lake Street, Suite 1413, Chicago, Ill. 60601 ☎ (312) 606-9015.
New York – 405 Park Ave., Suite 1002, New York, N. Y. 10022 ☎ (212) 755-7261.
Houston – 2707 North Loop W., Suite 450, Houston, Texas 77008 ☎ (713) 880-5153.
Los Angeles – 10100 Santa Monica Blvd., Suite 224, Los Angeles, Cal. 90067 ☎ (213) 203-8350.
Mexican Government Tourist Information hot line ☎ (800) 262-8900 (toll-free number in the US).

Canada

Montreal – 1 Place Ville Marie, Suite 2409, Montreal, Que H3B 3M9 ☎ (514) 871-1052.
Toronto – 181 University Ave., Suite 1112, Toronto, Ontario M5H 3M7 ☎ (416) 364-4139.

Great Britain

London – 7 Cork St, London W1X 1PB ☎ (01) 734-1058.

ENTERING MEXICO

Visitors entering Mexico must be in possession of a valid passport or other proof of citizenship (birth or naturalization certificate).

Tourist Card. – All visitors planning to remain in Mexico more than 72 hours are required to obtain a tourist card *(tarjeta de turista).* Single-entry cards are valid up to 90 days. Multiple-entry cards allow a maximum stay of 6 months.
Upon presentation of proof of citizenship, tourist cards are issued free of charge by Mexican Government Tourist Offices *(see addresses above),* travel agencies, airlines, or at Mexican border offices at official points of entry. Visitors must carry the card with them at all times and surrender it upon leaving the country.

Customs. – It is forbidden to enter Mexico with sausages, dairy products, fruits, plants and flowers. Returning US citizens are entitled to a US $400 duty-free exemption (Can $300 for returning Canadian citizens) on items purchased in Mexico.

Automobile Entry. Visitors wishing to enter Mexico with their personal vehicle are required to obtain a **car permit.** The six-month permit ($25 fee) is issued at official points of entry upon presentation of a valid driving license, car registration card and proof of citizenship. A car permit may also serve as a tourist card. As US or Canadian automobile insurance generally does not cover vehicles in Mexico, it is recommended that visitors entering the country with their personal vehicle consult their insurance agent or their automobile association before leaving.

GETTING AROUND

By Plane. – The national carriers, Aeroméxico and Mexicana de Aviacion, fly to 57 domestic destinations. Passengers are required to pay an airport tax, the DUA (Derecho del Uso del Aeropuerto).

By Boat. – Many international ocean liners stop at Mexican ports along the Pacific coast (Puerto Vallarta, Acapulco, Mazatlán, La Paz and Los Cabos), the Gulf of Mexico and the Caribbean (Tampico, Veracruz, Cancún, Cozumel and Playa del Carmen).

By Train. – It is advisable to travel on the routes that have pullman, reserved first class and special service *(see table pp 229-231).*

By bus. – There is first-class bus service to almost all cities, towns and villages; the bus terminals (Central Camionera) in the larger cities provide information about ticket price and schedules.

Car Rental. – Major car rental agencies are located in large airports and cities throughout Mexico.

Highways. – The road system comprises 66 300 km – 41 199 miles of main highways. Direct toll roads receive regular maintenance. They are safe and well marked. For greater safety, it is advisable not to travel by night and it is important to carry a map because many of the smaller roads are poorly marked.

Gas stations are open during the day, but very few have night service. It is recommended to fill the tank before leaving the highway, since many secondary roads have no gas stations.

Emergency Breakdown Assistance. – Major highways are patrolled by a fleet of green tow trucks known as *Angeles Verdes* (Green Angels), which provide mechanical assistance, tourist information and emergency medical aid. This service functions daily from 8:00 AM to 8:00 PM.

THE BASICS

Money. – The unit of currency in Mexico is the peso. Note that the peso symbol ($) resembles the dollar sign.

Exchange. – As the exchange rate varies from day to day, it is advisable to verify it when changing cash or traveler's checks (accepted in almost all the shops in Mexico City). It is a good idea to carry your funds in US dollars, because in many towns and even in Mexico City other currencies are not always accepted.

Banks. – Banks are open Monday to Friday from 9:00 AM to 1:30 PM; some bank branches open for limited operations on Saturdays, Sundays and afternoons on special days.

Credit Cards. – Most shops in the large cities and tourist spots accept US dollars, although at a lower rate than the banks or exchange agencies. In order to avoid difficulties, it is suggested to change your money in the large cities. In the leading stores, hotels and restaurants, international credit cards such as American Express, Diners, Visa and Carte Blanche are accepted.

Taxes and Tips. – Except for some basic products, most consumer goods are subject to a Value Added Tax (VAT), which amounts to 6% for some foods, 15% for most consumer goods, including restaurant, bar and hotel services, and 20% for luxury goods. Foreigners are not exempt from paying the VAT. As a rule, this tax is included in the sales price.

In restaurants and bars, the service is not included, and it is customary to leave a 10% to 15% tip.

Tourist Information. – Federal and state tourist information centers are found in most major cities and towns *(see table pp 229-231)*.

Hotels. – The Ministry of Tourism has established a one-to-five star rating system for hotel accommodations throughout the country. The highest category is *Gran Turismo (GT)*. To register complaints ☏ (5) 250-85-55 and (5) 250-01-51. Peak tourist seasons: December 15th to May 15th and during the months of July and August. Advance reservation is highly recommended especially for beach resorts.

Since small towns often lack proper accommodations, it is recommended to spend the night in nearby cities *(see table pp 229-231)*.

Post Offices. – Post offices are open Monday to Friday 9 AM to 2 PM and 4 to 6 PM, Saturday and Sunday 9 AM to noon.

Telephone. – A local call costs 100 pesos. When calling long distance within Mexico dial "91" followed by the area code. The area code for Mexico City is "5" *(see table pp 229-231 for area codes of principal cities)*.

For international calls dial "95" followed by the code of the country. There is a 40% tax on international calls.

Telegrams. – To send international telegrams by telephone, call *fototelegrafía*, ☏ (5) 519.59.21 through 39.

Electric Current. – 120 volts (60 cycles). Certain appliances may require a transformer. Electrical plugs have flat straight prongs.

Weights and Measures. – In Mexico the metric system is used.

Length	1 meter (m) 3.05	feet
	1 kilometer (km) 0.62	miles
	1 centimeter (cm) 0.39	inches
Weight	1 kilogram (kg) 2.2	pounds
Volume	1 liter (l) 0.264	gallons

EMBASSIES

United States – Paseo de la Reforma 305, Colonia Cuauhtemoc, Mexico City, DF 06500, ☏ (5) 211-0042.

Canada – Schiller 529, Colonia Polanco, Mexico City, DF 11580 ☏ (5) 254-3288.

Great Britain – Río Lerma 71, Colonia Cuauhténoc, Mexico City, DF 06500 ☏ (5) 207-2089.

For the addresses of consulates in other Mexican cities, inquire at your country's embassy in Mexico City.

For further tourist information while in Mexico call the 24-hour English language hot line operated by the Mexican Government Tourist Office ☏ (5) 250-0123 or (5) 230-0151.

FURTHER READING

AZUELA, Mariano. **The Underdogs.** *New York. Buccaneer Books, 1986.*

BERNAL, Ignacio. **A History of Mexican Archeology.** *London. Thames & Hudson, 1980.*

COE, Michael D. **Mexico.** *New York. Thames & Hudson Inc., 1984.*

COE, Michael D. **The Maya.** *New York, Thames & Hudson Inc., 1987.*

FUENTES, Carlos. **The Death of Artemio Cruz.** *New York. Farrar, Strauss & Giroux, 1964.*

GONZALEZ PEA, Carlos. **History of Mexican Literature.** *Dallas, Texas. Southern Methodist University Press, 1968.*

GREENE, Graham. **The Power and the Glory.** *New York, Penguin, 1977.*

HELMS, Mary W. **Middle America.** *Englewood, New Jersey. Prentice Hall, 1975.*

LAWRENCE, D.H. **The Plumed Serpent.** *New York. Random House, 1955.*

MILLER, Mary Ellen, **The Art of Mesoamerica from Olmec to Aztec.** *London. Thames & Hudson Ltd, 1986.*

PAZ, Octavio. **The Labyrinth of Solitude.** *New York. Grove Books, 1985.*

PARKES, Henry Bramford. **A History of Mexico.** *Boston. American Heritage Library, Houghton-Mifflin Co., 1969.*

PRESCOTT, William H. **History of the Conquest of Mexico.** *Chicago. University of Chicago Press, 1986.*

RIDING, Alan. **Distant Neighbors.** *New York. Vintage Books, Random House, 1986.*

VOCABULARY

A selection of foreign terms found in this guide.

avenida	avenue	**iglesia**	church
bahía	bay	**lago**	lake
barranca	canyon, ravine	**jardin**	garden
barrio	quarter, neighborhood	**laguna**	lagoon
cabo	cape, headland	**mercado**	market
calle	street	**mesa**	plateau
calzada	avenue	**mina**	mine
capilla	chapel	**mirador**	lookout
capilla abierta	open-air chapel *(p 39)*	**museo**	museum
capilla posa	corner chapel *(p 39)*	**nevado**	moutain peak
carretera	highway	**palacio municipal**	city hall
casa	house	**palapa**	palm sunshade
cascada	cascade, waterfall	**parroquia**	parish church
cerro	hill	**paseo**	avenue, promenade
cludad	city	**patio**	courtyard
claustro	cloister *(p 39)*	**piso (primer, segundo, tercer)**	floor (1st, 2nd, 3rd)
colegio	school, seminary		
conjunto	architectural complex	**plaza (principal)**	square (main)
convento	convent, monastery	**planta (baja, alta)**	floor (ground, upper)
estípite	*(p 40)*	**portada**	façade or portal
fachada	façade	**sierra**	mountain range
fuente	fountain	**talud-tablero**	*(p 35)*
fuerte	fort	**templo**	church
gruta	grotto	**tezontle**	a pink or red building stone
hacienda	large ranch or farm		
isla	island	**zócalo**	main square *(p 105)*

(Photo Mexican Tourist Office/Paris)

Detail of the state seal of the Mexican Republic

GENERAL TOURIST INFORMATION

ACCESS

✈	By air: commercial flights on local airlines or rental of light aircraft
🚆	By train: Pullman or reserved first-class seats
X	By highway: automobile
🚌	By highway: interurban or interstate bus service
O	By sea: ship or ferry. It is usually possible to embark a car; it is best to make reservations in advance.

SERVICES

G	Gas Stations		
	Accommodations:		Restaurants:
H	Recommended	**R**	Recommended
H	Available	R	Available

TOURIST INFORMATION – TOURIST OFFICES (OFICINAS DE TURISMO)

Federal. – Run by the Tourist Ministry.

State. – Run by the state government.

Area codes are given in parentheses.
Long-distance dialing within Mexico: 91 (area code) + local number.

For information in towns without a tourist office, apply to the *Oficina del Estado* (state house) or to the *Palacio Municipal* (city hall).

LOCALITY	ACCESS	SERVICES	Federal	State
Acapulco Gro.	✈ X 🚌 O	G H R	(748) 5.10.41	
Acolman Méx. (see Teotihuacán)	X 🚌			
Agua Azul Chis. (see Palenque)	X			
Aguascalientes Ags.	✈ 🚆 X 🚌	G H R	(491) 5.11.40.16	(491) 5.11.55
Álamos Son.	X 🚌	G H R		(642) 8.00.53
Bahuichivo Chih. (see Cerocahui)	🚆			
Cabo San Lucas BCS	✈ X 🚌 O	G H R		
Campeche Camp.	✈ 🚆 X 🚌	G H R	(981) 6.31.97	(981) 6.60.68
Cancún Q. Roo	✈ X 🚌	G H R	(988) 4.32.38	
Catemaco Ver.	X 🚌	G H R		
Cempoala Ver. (see Veracruz)	X	G		
Cerocahui Chih.	🚆	H R		
Chetumal Q. Roo	✈ X 🚌 O	G H R		(983) 2.08.55
Chichén Itzá Yuc.	X 🚌	H R		
Chihuahua Chih.	✈ 🚆 X 🚌	G H R		(14) 17.89.72
Cholula Pue.	X 🚌	G H R		
Ciudad Hidalgo Mich. (see San José Purúa)	X 🚌	G		
Ciudad Juárez Chih.	✈ 🚆 X 🚌	G H R	(161) 14.06.07	(161) 15.23.01
Colima Col.	✈ X 🚌	G H R		(331) 2.43.60
Comitán Chis.	X 🚌	G H R		
Cozumel Q. Roo	✈ O	G H R		(987) 2.03.57
Creel Chih.	🚆 X	G H R		
Cuernavaca Mor.	X 🚌	G H R	(731) 2.18.25	(731) 4.38.72
Cuetzalan Pue.	X 🚌	G H R		
Cuitzeo Mich. (see Morelia)	X 🚌	R		
Dolores Hidalgo Gto.	X 🚌	G H R		(468) 2.08.01
Durango Dgo.	✈ X 🚌	G H R	(181) 2.76.44	(181) 1.21.39
Edzná Camp. (see Campeche)	X			
Ensenada BCN	X 🚌 O	G H R		(667) 6.22.22
Fresnillo Zac.	X 🚌	G H R		
Guadalajara Jal.	✈ 🚆 X 🚌	G H R	(36) 14.83.71	(36) 14.86.86
Guanajuato Gto.	X 🚌	G H R	(473) 2.01.23	(473) 2.00.86
Guayabitos Nay.	X 🚌	G H R		
Guaymas Son.	✈ X 🚌 O	G H R		(622) 2.29.32
Guerrero Negro BCS	X 🚌	G H R		
Hermosillo Son.	✈ 🚆 X 🚌	G H R	(621) 7.29.64	(621) 2.35.54
Hidalgo del Parral Chih.	X 🚌	G H R		

LOCALITY	ACCESS	SERVICES	TOURIST INFORMATION Federal	State
Huasca Hgo. (see San Miguel Regla)	X 🚌	G		
Huejotzingo Pue. (see Cholula)	X 🚌	G R		
Irapauto Gto.	🚆 X 🚌	G H R		(462) 6.28.19
Isla Mujeres Q. Roo	✈ O	G H R		(988) 2.01.73
Ixtapa-Zihuatanejo Gro.	✈ X 🚌	G H R	(743) 4.28.35	
Kabah Yuc. (see Uxmal)	X			
Lagos de Moreno Jal.	🚆 X 🚌	G H R		
Léon Gto.	✈ 🚆 X 🚌	G H R		(471) 6.53.10
Loreto BCS	✈ X 🚌	G H R		
Malinalco Méx. (see Toluca)	X 🚌	R		
Manzanillo Col.	✈ X 🚌 O	G H R	(333) 2.01.81	(331) 2.43.60
Matehuala SLP	X 🚌	G H R		
Mazatlán Sin.	✈ 🚆 X 🚌 O	G H R	(678) 5.15.20	
Mérida Yuc.	✈ 🚆 X 🚌	G H R	(992) 4.94.31	(991) 5.00.92
Mexicali BCN	✈ 🚆 X 🚌	G H R		(656) 52.96.95
Mexico City D.F.	✈ 🚆 X 🚌	G H R	(5) 2.50.01.23	
Mitla Oax. (see Oaxaca)	X	G		
Los Mochis Sin.	✈ 🚆 X 🚌	G H R		
Monte Albán Oax. (see Oaxaca)	X			
Montebello Chis. (see Comitán)	X	R		
Monterrey NL	✈ 🚆 X 🚌	G H R	(83) 54.20.44	(83) 45.15.00
Morelia Mich.	✈ 🚆 X 🚌	G H R	(451) 2.05.22	(451) 2.37.10
Mulegé BCS	X 🚌	G H R		
Nuevo Casas Grandes Chih.	🚆 X 🚌	G H R		
Oaxaca Oax.	✈ 🚆 X 🚌	G H R	(951) 6.01.44	(951) 6.48.28
Orizaba Ver.	🚆 X 🚌	G H R		
Pachuca Hgo.	X 🚌	G H R	(771) 3.95.66	(771) 2.32.53
Palenque Chis.	🚆 X	G H R		
Papantla Ver.	X 🚌	G H R		
Paquimé Chih. (see Nuevo Casas Grandes)	X			
Parras de la Fuente Coah.	X 🚌	G H R		
Pátzcuaro Mich.	🚆 X 🚌	G H R		(954) 2.18.88
La Paz BCS	✈ X 🚌 O	G H R	(682) 2.11.90	(682) 2.11.99
Playa Azul Mich.	X 🚌	G H R		
Popocatépetl-Iztaccíhuatl Méx.	X	G H R		
Puebla Pue.	🚆 X 🚌	G H R	(22) 40.92.09	(22) 46.12.85
Puerto Escondido BCS (see Loreto)	X			
Puerto Escondido Oax.	✈ X 🚌	G H R		
Puerto Vallarta Jal.	✈ X 🚌	G H R	(322) 2.25.54	
Puuc Yuc. (see Uxmal)	X			
Querétaro Qro.	🚆 X 🚌	G H R	(463) 4.32.73	(463) 2.82.02
Real de Catorce SLP (see Matehuala)	X 🚌			
Río Bec Camp. (see Chetumal)	X			
Saltillo Coah.	✈ 🚆 X 🚌	G H R	(841) 5.55.71	(841) 5.58.11
San Andrés Tuxtla Ver.	X 🚌	G H R		
San Cristóbal de Las Casas Chis.	X 🚌	G H R		(967) 8.04.14
San Felipe BCN	X 🚌	G H R		
San José del Cabo BCS	✈ X 🚌	G H R		
San José Purúa Mich.	X 🚌	H R		
San Luis Potosi SLP	✈ 🚆 X 🚌	G H R	(481) 4.00.06	(481) 2.31.43

LOCALITY	ACCESS	SERVICES	TOURIST INFORMATION Federal	State
San Miguel de Allende Gto.	🚆 X 🚌	G H R		(465) 2.17.47
San Miguel Regla Hgo.	X 🚌	H R		
San Quintín BCN	X 🚌	G H R		
Santa Rosalia BCS (see Mulegé)	X 🚌 O	G R		
Santiago Tuxtla Ver.	X 🚌	G H R		
Sierra Gorda Qro.	X 🚌	G H R		
Sombrerete Zac. (see Fresnillo)	X 🚌	G		
Sumidero Chis. (see Tuxtla Gutiérrez)	X			
Tajín Ver. (see Papantla)	X			
Tampico Tamps.	✈ X 🚌 O	G H R		(121) 2.00.07
Taxco Gro.	X 🚌	G H R		(732) 2.34.09
Tehuantepec Oax.	X 🚌	G H R		
Teotihuacán Méx.	X 🚌	H R		
Tepic Nay.	🚆 X 🚌	G H R	(321) 3.09.93	(321) 3.07.24
Tepotzotlán Méx. (see Mexico City)	X 🚌	G R		
Tepoztlán Mor.	X 🚌	G H R		
Tijuana BCN	✈ X 🚌	G H R	(66) 82.33.47	(66) 81.94.92
Tlaxcala Tlax.	X 🚌	G H R	(246) 2.36.06	(246) 2.00.27
Toluca Méx.	✈ 🚆 X 🚌	G H R	(721) 3.89.61	(721) 5.21.87
Torreón Coah.	✈ 🚆 X 🚌	G H R		(17) 18.55.30
Tula Hgo.	X 🚌	G H R		
Tulum Q. Roo (see Cancún)	X 🚌	G		
Tuxtla Gutiérrez Chis.	✈ X 🚌	G H R	(961) 2.45.35	(961) 3.48.37
Tzintzuntzan Mich. (see Pátzcuaro)	X 🚌	G		
Uruapan Mich.	✈ 🚆 X 🚌	G H R		(452) 2.06.33
Uxmal Yuc.	X	G H R		
Valle de Bravo Méx.	X 🚌	G H R		
Veracruz Ver.	✈ 🚆 X 🚌 O	G H R	(29) 32.70.26	
Villahermosa Tab.	✈ X 🚌	G H R	(931) 5.04.74	(931) 5.25.68
Xalapa Ver.	X 🚌	G H R		(281) 7.30.30
Xochicalco Mor. (see Cuernavaca)	X			
Yaxchilán Chis. (see Tuxtla Gutiérrez)	✈			
Yuriria Gto. (see Morelia)	X 🚌	R		
Zacatecas Zac.	✈ 🚆 X 🚌	G H R	(492) 2.67.50	(492) 2.01.70
Zamora Mich.	X 🚌	G H R		(351) 2.00.93

Opening hours and admission charges

The following information, based on official tourist data provided at the time of going to press, is subject to change without notice.

Opening Hours and Admission Charges. – Unless otherwise specified in the alphabetical list below, hours and entrance fees are as follows:

Churches, convents, monasteries, chapels and cathedrals. – Open 8 AM to 1 PM and 4 to 6 PM (sometimes later on Sunday). In tropical areas, monuments may open earlier.

Museums. – Open 10 AM to 5 PM, closed on Monday and holidays. Provincial museums may close at lunchtime. Admission ranges between 180 and 750 pesos.

Municipal and Federal Government buildings. – Open daily 8 AM to 8 PM, closed on national holidays.

Archeological sites. – Open daily 8 AM to 5 PM. Admission ranges between 240 and 3000 pesos.

It is recommended to visit **natural sights** in the morning when visibility is best.

In the following pages, all sights, whose hours vary from those given above, are listed alphabetically under the city, village or area in which they are situated. Isolated sights are listed under their proper name. Opening and closing hours are the same throughout the year. Unless otherwise specified, the admission charges quoted apply to individual adults. Many sights offer special rates for students and teachers, as well as for children.

All sights included in the following list are indicated in the main section of this guide by the symbol ⊙ placed in the margin beside the sight description.

HOLIDAYS

January 1st	New Year's Day
February 5th	Constitution Day
February 24th	Flag Day
March 21st	Benito Juárez's Birthday
March-April	Thursday and Friday (Good Friday) before Easter
May 1st	Labor Day
May 5th	Battle of Puebla
September 1st	President's Report
September 16th	Independence Day
November 1st	All Saints' Day
November 2nd	All Souls' Day
November 20th	Revolution Day
December 25th	Christmas

a

ACAPULCO

Fort San Diego. – Tuesday to Sunday 10 AM to 6 PM, 550 pesos. Sundays free from 10 AM to 5 PM. Guided tours in French and English.

Roqueta Island. – 8 AM to 5 PM. Embarcation at Playa Caleta. Fares vary with the seasons. Consult list of fares at the Port Captain's station (Capitanía del Puerto), according to the trip you wish to take. Fares also differ for special trips.

La Quebrada. – Afternoons and evenings. The schedule varies according to the conditions of surf and tide. Information available at the Hotel Mirador, ☎ 311.55 or 312.21.

Coyuca Lagoon. – 10 AM to 6 PM. Embarkation point in front of Pie de la Cuesta Beach. Fares vary with the seasons. Consult list of fares at the Cooperative ticket booth, according to the tour desired.

ACATZINGO

Franciscan Monastery. – The family living in the caretaker's lodge will open the monastery.

ACOLMAN
Saint Augustine's Monastery. – Tuesday to Sunday 10 AM to 5 PM. 550 pesos. Parking: 145 pesos.

ACTOPAN
Monastery of San Nicholás Tolentino. – Tuesday to Sunday 10 AM to 2 PM and 4 to 6 PM. 700 pesos.

AFRICAM SAFARI
Monday to Friday at 10:45 AM, 12:45 PM and 2:45 PM, Saturday and Sunday at 10:45 AM, 12:45 PM, 1:45 PM and 2:45 PM. 7000 pesos. ☏ 35.87.13 or 35.87.00.

AGUASCALIENTES
Cathedral Basilica of the Virgin of the Assumption. – 7 AM to 2 PM and 4 to 9 PM.

Saint Anthony's Church. – 7 AM to 2 PM and 4 to 9 PM.

Aguascalientes Museum. – Tuesday to Sunday 10:30 AM to 2 PM and 4 to 8 PM.

Church of the Oak Tree. – 7 AM to 2 PM and 4 to 9 PM.

Guadalupe Posada Museum. – Tuesday to Sunday 10 AM to 2 PM and 4 to 8 PM.

Saint Mark's Church. – 7 AM to 2 PM and 4 to 9 PM.

Plaza del Vestido. – Monday to Saturday 8 AM to 8 PM, Sunday 8 AM to 4 PM. Closed on national holidays.

Viñedos de San Marcos. – Monday to Saturday 9 AM to 2 PM and 5 to 8 PM.

ANGANGUEO
Monarch Butterfly Sanctuary. – Although butterflies can be seen from November through April, the best time is during February or March. Vehicles can be rented from Angangueo; allow 1 1/2 hours for the drive from Angangueo to the sanctuary. The best route is through Ocampo (7 kms – 4.3 miles before Angangueo). Once at the sanctuary the visitor must go on foot; allow a 1/4 hour walk to reach the start of the trail; wear comfortable shoes as the path is difficult and steep in places. The total distance depends on where the butterflies are that day. 2500 pesos.

ANTÓN LIZARDO (Point)
Heroic Naval Military Academy. – Monday to Friday 1 to 5 PM. A military parade takes place every Thursday.

Naval Museum. – Monday to Friday 1 to 5 PM.

ATLIHUETZIA
Franciscan Monastery. – 8 AM to 8 PM.

Immaculate Conception Parish Church. – 8 AM to 8 PM.

ATLIXCO
Saint John of God Hospital. – Tuesday to Sunday 8 AM to 2 PM. Guided tours.

ATOTONILCO EL GRANDE
Convent of Saint Augustine. – 9 AM to 2 PM and 3 to 5 PM.

ATOTONILCO
Sanctuary. – 7 AM to 8 PM. It is advisable to visit this site in the morning.

BACALAR
Fort San Felipe. – 9 AM to 5 PM.

BAHUICHIVO
Transportation to the lodge is available at Cerocahui. Limited accommodations, advance reservation required.

BAJA CALIFORNIA
Ferry service
Santa Rosalía to Guaymas (crossing: 8 hours). – Tuesday, Thursday and Sunday at 11 PM. Departure from Customs Wharf (muelle de la aduana). Various fares. Information: ☏ 200.13 and 200.14.
Guaymas to Santa Rosalía. – Tuesday, Wednesday, Friday and Sunday at 11 AM. Information: ☏ 223.24.

La Paz to Mazatlán (crossing: 15-17 hours). – Daily at 5 PM. Departure from Pichilingue Terminal. Various fares. Tickets on sale from 8 AM to noon. Information: ☏ 201.09 and 294.85.
Mazatlán to La Paz. – Daily at 5 PM.

La Paz to Topolobampo (crossing: 8 hours). – Wednesday and Sunday at 8 AM. Departure from Pichilingue Terminal. Information: ☏ 294.85 and 234.24. Topolobampo to La Paz. – Monday at 10 AM.

Cabo San Lucas to Puerto Vallarta. – Service suspended.

Puerto Vallarta to Cabo San Lucas. – Service suspended.

BALAMCANCHÉ (Grotto)

Guided tour in English and Spanish (40 min.) Monday to Saturday 8 to 11 AM and 2 to 4 PM, Sundays 8 to 11 AM. 3 250 pesos.

La BARCA

House of la Moreña. – Monday to Sunday 8:30 AM to 9 PM.

BECÁN (Archeological Site)

8 AM to 5 PM. 700 pesos.

BONAMPAK (Archeological Site)

See **YAXCHILÁN.**

CABO SAN LUCAS

Natural Arch and Playa del Amor. – Boats can be rented at the dock. Prices vary according to the season.

CACAHUAMILPA (Grottos)

Guided tour (2 hours) in English and Spanish, every hour, Monday to Saturday 10 AM to 5 PM, Sunday 10 AM to 4 PM. 3 800 pesos.

CACAXTLA (Archeological Site)

Tuesday to Sunday 10 AM to 5 PM. 900 pesos.

Mural Paintings. – Tuesday to Sunday 10 AM to 5 PM.

CALIXTLAHUACA (Archeological Site)

8 AM to 6 PM. 1 000 pesos.

CALPAN

Monastery of San Andrés. – 10 AM to 5 PM.

Parish Church. – 10 AM to 5 PM.

CAMPECHE

Solitude Bastion. – Tuesday to Sunday 8 AM to 8 PM. 1 000 pesos.

Santiago Bastion. – Tuesday to Friday 8 AM to 2 PM and 4 to 8 PM, Saturday and Sunday 8 AM to 2 PM.

Saint Peter Bastion. – Monday to Saturday 8 AM to 8 PM.

Saint Charles Bastion. – 8 AM to 2 PM and 4 to 8 PM.

Cathedral. – 6 AM to 1 PM and 4 to 8:30 PM.

Campeche Regional Museum. – Tuesday to Saturday 9 AM to 8 PM, Sunday 9 AM to 1 PM. 500 pesos. Guided tours.

San Román Church. – 7 AM to 2 PM and 4 to 8 PM.

Fort Saint Michael. – Tuesday to Sunday 8 AM to 8 PM. 1 000 pesos.

CANCÚN

Regional Museum of Anthropology and History. – Open Tuesday to Saturday 10 AM to 5 PM. 600 pesos.

El Rey Archeological Site. – 8 AM to 5 PM. 700 pesos. The site can also be reached by boat.

CELESTÚN

Flamingo Spectacle. – The fare is arranged directly with the fishermen. You must be in Celestún before 10 AM, as the fishermen do not like to go out later than that. Take binoculars and a camera with a telephoto lens, as well as a hat to shade you from the sun.

CEMPOALA (Archeological Site)

8 AM to 6 PM. 700 pesos.

CHACAHUA (Lagoons)

National Park. – 8 AM to 5 PM. Boat crossing from Zapotalillo. Different fare rates. Information at Puerto Escondido.

CHALCATZINGO (Archeological Site)

10 AM to 5 PM.

CHAPINGO

Autonomous University. – Closed for restoration.

CHIAPA DE CORZO

Regional Lacquer Museum. – Sunday and Monday 9 AM to 1 PM and 4 to 7 PM, Tuesday to Saturday 9 AM to 7 PM.

CHICANNÁ (Archeological Site)

8 AM to 4 PM. 1 000 pesos.

CHICHÉN ITZÁ (Archeological Site)
8 AM to 5 PM. 2 950 pesos. Guided tours 8 AM to 4 PM, in Spanish, English, French and German. 55 000 pesos. Light and Sound Show at 7 PM in Spanish, 1 800 pesos and at 9 PM in English, 2 700 pesos.
Inner Temple of the Castle. – 11 AM to 2 PM.
Temple of the Jaguars. – 2 to 3 PM and 4 to 5 PM.

CHICOMOSTOC (Ruins)
Tuesday to Saturday 10 AM to 5 PM. 750 pesos.

CHIHUAHUA
Museum of Popular Art. – Tuesday to Saturday 9 AM to 1 PM and 4 to 7 PM.
Miguel Hidalgo Prison. – Tuesday to Sunday 9 AM to 8 PM. 300 pesos.
Chihuahua Regional Museum. – Tuesday to Sunday 9 AM to 1 PM and 4 to 7 PM. 500 pesos.
Historical Museum of the Revolution in the State of Chihuahua. – 9 AM to 1 PM and 3 to 7 PM. 500 pesos. Guided tours in English.

CHIHUAHUA-PACIFIC RAILROAD Barranca del Cobre (Copper Canyon)
The vista-train leaves Chihuahua every day at 7 AM, arrives at Creel at 11:45 AM (20 585 pesos); Divisadero at 12:57 PM (24 770 pesos); Bahuichivo at 2:17 PM (27 910 pesos); and Los Mochis at 7 PM (45 710 pesos).
It leaves Los Mochis daily at 7 AM; arrives at Bahuichivo at 11:49 AM (17 445 pesos); Divisadero at 12:53 PM (20 940 pesos); Creel at 2:20 PM (24 770 pesos); and Chihuahua at 7:05 PM (45 710 pesos). There is a luxury car attached to the vista-train, called the Expreso Cañón de Cobre, which leaves Chihuahua every day at 7 AM and arrives at Los Mochis at 7 PM (45 710 pesos). The trip takes 12 hours. Reservations: Chihuahua ☎ 15.77.56, Los Mochis ☎ 208.53 or 208.99, Mexico, D.F. ☎ 541.53.25. Information on car transport service in Chihuahua ☎12.22.84, 15.77.56 or 12.38.67.

CHOLULA
Saint Gabriel Monastery. – 10 AM to 5 PM. To visit the cloister, ask the priest for permission.
Open-Air Chapel. – 10 AM to 5 PM.
Archeological Site. – 10:30 AM to 5 PM. 950 pesos.
Museum. – You should see the model of the pyramid before visiting the site.

CIUDAD JUÁREZ
Art Museum. – Tuesday to Sunday 10 AM to 7 PM. 300 pesos.

COCONÁ (Grottos)
10 AM to 6 PM. 500 pesos.

COLIMA
Museum of Western Cultures. – Tuesday to Saturday 8 AM to 7 PM, Sunday 8 AM to 1 PM.
Nevado de Colima and Volcán de Fuego. – 9 AM to 6 PM. It is best to go before noon.

COMALCALCO (Archeological Site)
10 AM to 4 PM. 950 pesos.

COMITÁN
San Caralampio Church. – 9 AM to 5 PM.
Dr. Belisario Domínguez Museum House. – Tuesday to Saturday 10 AM to 1:45 PM and 5 to 6:45 PM, Sunday 9 AM to 12:45 PM. 500 pesos.

COZUMEL
Saint Gervasio Archeological Site. – 8 AM to 5 PM. 700 pesos. Guided tours in Spanish and English.

CREEL
It is advisable to make reservations in advance since accommodations are limited. Also accessible by car.

CUERNAVACA
Cathedral Compiex. – 9 AM to 2 PM and 4 to 7 PM. Sunday services with mariachi music at 11 AM and 8 PM.
Ethnobotanical Garden and Traditional Medicine Museum. – 9 AM to 5 PM.
Studio of David Alfaro Siqueiros. – Closed for restoration.
Shrine of Tlaltenango. – 7 AM to 2 PM and 4 to 7 PM.

CUETZALAN
Calmahuiztic Museum. – Thursday to Monday 10 AM to 2 PM and 3 to 5 PM.
Las Pozas. – Hire a local guide in town.
Las Cascadas. – Hire a local guide in town.

CUILAPAN DE GUERRERO
Monastery. – 9 AM to 5 PM. 360 pesos.

CUITZEO
Monastery. – Monday to Saturday 10 AM to 6 PM. Sunday 10 AM to 5 PM. 270 pesos. Closed on holidays.

DAINZÚ (Archeological Site)
10 AM to 5 PM. 700 pesos.

DESIERTO DE LOS LEONES
Monastery. – Tuesday to Sunday 10 AM to 5 PM. 500 pesos. Bring a flashlight to visit the cellars.

DOLORES HIDALGO
Casa de Visitas. – 9 AM to 2 PM and 4 to 6 PM.
Museum. – Tuesday to Sunday 9 AM to 2 PM and 4 to 7 PM. 500 pesos.

DURANGO
Government Palace. – Monday to Saturday 8 AM to 3 PM and 6 to 8 PM, Sunday 10 AM to 1 PM.
House of the Count of the Valle de Súchil. – Monday to Friday 11:30 AM to 10:30 PM.
Museum of Anthropology and History. – Tuesday to Saturday 10 AM to 1 PM and 3 to 6:30 PM, Sunday 11 AM to 5 PM.

DZIBILCHALTÚN (Archeological Site)
8 AM to 5 PM. 950 pesos.

EDZNÁ (Archeological Site)
8 AM to 4 PM. 1 000 pesos.

ENSENADA
Social, Civic and Cultural Center of Ensenada. – Monday to Saturday 9 AM to 6 PM.

EPAZOYUCAN
Saint Andrew's Monastery. – 9 AM to 2 PM and 3 to 5 PM. Admission to the cloister: 130 pesos.

GUADALAJARA
Cathedral. – 7 AM to 8 PM. Ask for permission to enter the sacristy.
Regional Museum of Guadalajara. – Tuesday to Sunday 9 AM to 3:45 PM. 750 pesos.
Degollado Theater. – Monday to Saturday 10 AM to 1 PM and 4 to 7 PM. Closed holidays.
Cabañas Cultural Institute. – Tuesday to Saturday 10 AM to 6 PM, Sunday 10 AM to 3 PM. 500 pesos. Guided tours in English and French.
Libertad Market. – 6 AM to 7 PM.
Saint Francis' Church. – Monday to Saturday 8 AM to 2 PM and 4 to 8 PM, Sunday 7 AM to 2 PM and 6 to 8 PM.
Chapel of Our Lady of Aranzazú. – Monday to Saturday 8 AM to 2 PM and 4 to 8 PM, Sunday 7 AM to 2 PM and 6 to 8 PM.
Old University. – Closed to the public.
Santa Monica's Church. – Monday to Saturday 10 AM to 12:30 PM and 5 to 7:30 PM, Sunday 8 AM to 1 PM and 5 to 7 PM.
Regional Ceramics Museum. – Tuesday to Saturday 10 AM to 4 PM, Sunday 10 AM to 1 PM.
Independencia Lookout Park. – 7 AM to 7 PM. 100 pesos. Parking 100 pesos. Guided tours in English.
Science and Technological Center and Planetarium. – Tuesday to Sunday 9 AM to 8 PM. Guided tours. 500 pesos.
University of Guadalajara. – Monday to Friday 9 AM to 3 PM and 5 to 8 PM. Closed on holidays.

Archeological Museum of Western Mexico. – Monday to Saturday 10 AM to 7:30 PM, Sunday and holidays noon to 7:30 PM. 200 pesos.

Albarrán Hunting Museum. – Saturday and Sunday 10:30 AM to 2:30 PM.

Dr. Atl Lookout Park. – 7 AM to 7 PM. 100 pesos.

Tequila. – Certain tequila producers open their premises to visitors. Apply in advance: ☎ 13.16.98, 15.69.30 or 30.07.07 in Guadalajara.

GUADALUPE (Convent)

Museum. – Tuesday to Sunday 10 AM to 5 PM. Closed on national holidays.

Regional Historical Museum. – Tuesday to Sunday 10 AM to 4:30 PM.

GUANAJUATO

Minor Basilica of Our Lady of Guanajuato. – 10 AM to 1:30 PM and 4:30 to 8 PM.

Legislative Palace. – Monday to Friday 9 AM to 7 PM.

Hidalgo Market. – 10 AM to 5 PM. Closed last Friday of May and first Friday of October.

Regional Museum. – Tuesday to Sunday 10 AM to 2 PM and 4 to 6 PM. Camera 750 pesos.

Diego Rivera Museum. – Tuesday to Saturday 10 AM to 2 PM and 4 to 7 PM, Sunday 10 AM to 3 PM. 300 pesos. Guided tours in English and Spanish.

Jesuit Church. – 7 AM to 8:30 PM.

Mummy Museum. – 9 AM to 6 PM. 1 500 pesos.

La Valenciana Church. – 7 AM to 8:30 PM.

La Valenciana Mine. – 9 AM to 6 PM. Closed on holidays.

Cata Church. – 7 AM to 8:30 PM.

Museum of the Pedro Domecq Firm. – Tuesday to Sunday 10 AM to 2 PM and 5 to 8 PM.

HERMOSILLO

Sonora Museum. – Wednesday to Saturday 10 AM to 5:30 PM, Sunday 10 AM to 3:30 PM. 700 pesos.

Sonora Ecological Center. – Wednesday to Sunday 8 AM to 5 PM. 1 000 pesos.

HUAQUECHULA

Franciscan Monastery. – 10 AM to 5 PM. If it is closed, apply to the caretaker *(guardián)*.

HUASCA

Church of Saint John the Baptist. – 10 AM to 7 PM.

HUEJOTZINGO

Church of San Diego de Alcalá. – 10 AM to 5 PM.

IRAPUATO

City Hall. – Monday to Friday 9 AM to 3 PM, Saturday 10 AM to 1 PM.

IXMIQUILPAN

Carmelite Church. – Monday to Saturday 9 AM to 2 PM, Sunday 4 to 6 PM. If the church is closed, call Alicia Benítez, ☎ 300.72.

IZAMAL

Monastery. – 0 AM to noon and 1 to 8 PM.

JEREZ

Hinojosa Theater. – 10 AM to 3 PM and 5 to 7 PM.

La Torre School. – Monday to Friday 9 AM to 2 PM and 5 to 8 PM, Saturday 10 AM to 1 PM. Closed on national holidays.

JIQUILPAN

Lázaro Cárdenas Museum. – Tuesday to Saturday 8 AM to 7 PM, Sunday 9 AM to 2 PM and 4 to 7 PM. Guided tours.

Licenciado Gabino Ortiz Public Library. – Monday to Friday 9 AM to 2 PM and 5 to 7 PM.

LAGOS DE MORENO

Rosas Moreno Theater. – Apply to the caretaker.

LAMBITYECO (Archeological Site)

Open from 9 AM to 5 PM. 470 pesos.

LEÓN

Cathedral of the Most Holy Mother of Light. – Monday to Saturday 5:30 AM to 1:30 PM and 4:30 to 8 PM, Sunday 5:30 AM to 9 PM.

LOLTÚN (Grottos)

Guided tours in English and Spanish. Daily 9:30 AM to 3:30 PM. 2500 pesos.

MALINALCO (Archeological Site)

10 AM to 4:30 PM. 500 pesos.

La MALINCHE (National Park)

Weekends: adults 1000 pesos, children 500 pesos, Weekdays: adults 700 pesos, children 350 pesos. Warm clothing is recommended. On Saturday after 8 PM small bonfires are lit.

MAMA

Monastery. – 8 AM to noon and 4 to 8 PM. Guided tours in English and Spanish.

MANI

Monastery. – 8 AM to noon and 4 to 8 PM. Guided tours.

MARFIL

Museum. – Monday to Friday 9 AM to 5:45 PM.

MARQUIS OF JARAL DE BERRIO (Hacienda)

Under restoration, to be converted into a hotel. Open 8 AM to 7 PM.

MAZATLÁN

Sea Shell City. – 8 AM to 6 PM. Guided tours in English and Spanish.

Aquarium. – 10 AM to 6 PM. Adults 3000 pesos, children 1000 pesos. Guided tours in English and Spanish.

MÉRIDA

Convent of the Conceptualist Nuns. – 8 AM to noon and 5 to 8 PM. Apply to the priests for access to the lookout.

Cathedral. – Monday to Saturday 6 AM to noon and 4 to 8 PM, Sunday 6 AM to 1 PM and 4 to 8 PM.

Santiago Parish Church. – 6 to 9 AM and 6 to 8 PM.

Regional Museum of Anthropology. – Closed, to be transferred to new premises.

La Mejorada Monastery. – Monday to Friday 5 to 9 PM, Saturday 9 AM to 1 PM.

Museum of Popular Art. – Tuesday to Saturday 8 AM to 8 PM, Sunday 9 AM to 2 PM.

Saint Christopher's Parish Church. – Monday to Saturday 6 AM to noon and 5 to 8 PM, Sundays 6 to 10 AM and 6 to 9 PM.

Saint John the Baptist Church. – 8 AM to noon and 5 to 8 PM.

Santa Isabel Hermitage. – Monday to Saturday 8 AM to noon and 5 to 8 PM, Sunday 8 to 10 AM and 6 to 8 PM.

MEXICALI

Regional Museum of Baja California University. – Tuesday to Saturday 9 AM to 6 PM, Sunday and holidays 10 AM to 4 PM.

MEXICO CITY

Urban Transport. – In the Federal District there are the following means of transportation: regular taxis, collective vans (jitneys) and regular (Route 100) buses, which crisscross Mexico City and some outlying districts. These complement the subway *(metro)* routes. In addition there are trolleybuses on some of the main arteries. There are 15-day tickets valid for unlimited travel on the subway, buses and trolleybuses.

Historic Center. – New traffic regulations are currently being elaborated by city authorities.

Plaza de la Constitution and Surroundings

Metropolitan Cathedral. – 8 AM to 7 PM. Closed on May 1st, September 15th and 16th and November 20th.

Sacristy of the Cathedral. – 11 AM to 1 PM. Closed on May 1st, September 15th and 16th and November 20th.

Metropolitan Tabernacle (Sagrario). – 8:30 AM to 7:30 PM. Closed on May 1st, September 15th and 16th and November 20th.

Archeological Site and Museum of the Great Temple. – Tuesday to Sunday 9 AM to 5 PM. 750 pesos. Guided tours in English, Spanish, Italian and French. 3 000 pesos. The tour starts with the archeological site and ends in the museum.

Houses of the Mayorazgo de Guerrero. – Ask permission from the *Intendente*. ☎ 522.35.15.

Church of the Most Holy. – 7 AM to 1 PM and 5 to 8 PM.

Cloister of the Most Holy. – Ask permission at calle de la Santísima n° 8.

National School of Fine Arts. – Monday to Friday 8 AM to 3 PM and 5 to 7 PM. Closed two weeks during the Easter season, the first two weeks of July and from December 16th to January 2nd.

National Museum of Cultures. – Tuesday to Saturday 9:30 AM to 5:45 PM, Sunday 9:30 AM to 4 PM. Guided tours in Spanish.

National Palace. – Monday to Friday 9 AM to 6:30 PM, Saturday and Sunday 9 AM to 5 PM. Guided tours in Spanish 9 AM to 6:30 PM and in English 4 to 6:30 PM. For guided tours: ☎ 709.21.47 (Subdirección de Bibliotecas y Museografía).

House of Representatives. – Monday to Friday 9 AM to 6:30 PM.

Juárez Wing. – Monday to Friday 9 AM to 6:30 PM.

Supreme Court. – Monday to Friday 9 AM to 1 PM.

Old Federal District Building. – Monday to Friday 9 AM to 6 PM.

Monte de Piedad. – Monday to Friday 10 AM to 5 PM, Saturday 10 AM to 3 PM.

Santo Domingo and Surroundings

Old Palace of the Inquisition. – Tuesday to Sunday 9:30 AM to 6 PM. Closed two weeks during the Easter season, the first two weeks of July and from December 16th to January 2nd.

Old Custom House. – Monday to Friday 8 AM to 7 PM.

House of Diego y Pedraza. – Monday to Saturday 9 AM to 8 PM.

Department of Public Education. – Monday to Friday 9 AM to 7 PM.

Escuela Nacional Preparatoria. – 8 AM to 6 PM. Closed the first two weeks of July and from December 16th to January 2nd.

El Generalito. – Closed for restoration.

Bolivar Amphitheater. – Tuesday to Thursday noon to 3 PM or when there is a performance. Ask the *Intendente* about the dates.

Abelardo Rodríguez Market. – 8 AM to 6 PM.

Mexico City Museum and Surroundings

Mexico City Museum. – Tuesday to Sunday 9:30 AM to 7 PM. Guided tours in English and Spanish 11 AM to 5 PM.

Jesús Hospital. – 9 AM to 8 PM.

Main Office of the Jesús Hospital. – Monday to Friday 8 AM to 5 PM, Saturday 8 AM to 1 PM. Apply to the Administrative Offices.

Jesús Hospital Church. – 8 AM to 2 PM and 4 to 7 PM. Go during daylight hours so as to see the Orozco paintings, which are rather dark.

Cloister of the Monastery of la Merced. – 8 AM to 2 PM. Ask for permission at the *Intendencia*.

Carretones Glass Factory. – Monday to Friday 10:30 AM to 5 PM, Saturday 10:30 AM to 4 PM.

Residence of the Counts of San Mateo Valparaíso and Surroundings

Residence of the Counts of San Mateo Valparaíso. – Monday to Friday 9 AM to 1:30 PM.

Saint Augustine's Church. – Monday to Friday 9 AM to 8 PM.

Church of Saint Philip Neri. – Monday to Friday 9 AM to 5 PM.

Church and Convent of Saint Jerome. – Monday to Friday 9 AM to 5 PM.

Colegio de las Vizcaínas. – Monday to Friday 10 AM to 1 PM. Ask permission to visit at the Office of the College. ☎ 512.42.67. Closed the week before Easter, July, August and from December 16th to January 2nd.

Opening hours and charges

Madero and Surroundings

Latin American Tower. – 10 AM to 7 PM. 5000 pesos. Use of telescopes: 500 pesos.

House of Tiles. – 7:30 AM to 10 PM.

Monastery of Saint Francis

Church. – 7:30 AM to 8 PM.

Cloister. – Monday to Friday 9 AM to 1 PM and 3 to 6 PM. Ask permission from the caretaker.

Iturbide Palace. – Monday to Friday 9 AM to 1:30 PM.

La Profesa Church. – 8 AM to 1 PM and 4 to 8 PM.

Painting Collection. – Sundays 11 AM to 2 PM. Guided tours in English and Spanish at noon.

Spanish Casino. – Monday to Saturday 10 AM to 5 PM.

Plaza Manuel Tolsá and Surroundings

Minería Palace. – Monday to Friday 9 AM to 2 PM. Closed two weeks during the Easter season, the first two weeks of July and from December 16th to January 2nd.

Central Post Office. – Monday to Saturday 9 AM to 6 PM.

Senate. – Monday to Friday 10 AM to 7 PM.

Old House of Representatives. – Monday to Friday 9 AM to 3 PM.

House of the Counts of Heras y Soto. – Monday to Friday 9 AM to 3 PM and 5 to 8 PM.

Alameda Central and Surroundings

Palace of Fine Arts. – Tuesday to Sunday 10:30 AM to 6:30 PM.

The Crystal Curtain. – This can only be seen during the performances of the National Folkloric Ballet. Present schedule: Wednesday at 9 PM and Sunday at 9:30 AM and 9 PM.

Arts and Crafts Museum. – 10 AM to 6 PM.

Alameda Museum. – Tuesday to Sunday 10 AM to 6 PM.

Viceroyal Painting Collection. – Tuesday to Sunday 9 AM to 5 PM.

The Pantheon of San Fernando. – Monday to Friday 8 AM to 6 PM.

Plaza de la Santa Veracruz and Surroundings

National Museum of Engravings. – Tuesday to Sunday 10 AM to 5 PM.

Franz Mayer Museum. – Tuesday to Sunday 10 AM to 5 PM. 400 pesos. Guided tours in English, Spanish and Italian Tuesday to Saturday 10 AM to 5 PM. 500 pesos. ☏ 518.22.66.

Hospital of San Hipólito. – 10 AM to 10 PM.

San Cosme

National Museum of the Mexican Revolution. – Tuesday to Sunday 9 AM to 5 PM. Guided tours every hour.

San Carlos Museum. – Wednesday to Monday 10 AM to 6 PM. 500 pesos.

University Museum of the Chopo. – Wednesday to Sunday 10 AM to 2 PM and 4 to 7 PM. Closed two weeks during the Easter season, the first two weeks of July and from December 16th to January 2nd.

Paseo de la Reforma

Center for Contemporary Art. – Tuesday to Sunday from 10 AM to 6 PM. 50 pesos.

Chapultepec Forest

Wednesday, Thursday and Friday 10:30 AM to 6 PM, Saturday and Sunday 9:30 AM to 8 PM. In the **First Section,** cars are not allowed.

Zoo. – Wednesday to Sunday 9:30 AM to 4 PM.

Little Train. – Wednesday to Sunday 10:30 AM to 4:30 PM. 50 pesos.

Lake House. – Wednesday, Thursday and Friday 10 AM to 5 PM, Saturday and Sunday 10 AM to 3 PM. .

National Anthropological Museum

Tuesday to Saturday 9 AM to 7 PM, Sunday and holidays 10 AM to 6 PM. 750 pesos. Photographs are not permitted. Guides are available in English, Spanish and French. 1000 pesos per person (one hour), from Tuesday to Saturday 10 AM to 5:30 PM. Free wheelchairs for the elderly or disabled can be requested at the ticket booth.

Tomb of the Temple of the Inscriptions. – Closed for restoration.

Chapultepec Castle and Other Museums

National Historical Museum. – Tuesday to Sunday 9 AM to 5 PM. 750 pesos.

History Gallery. – Tuesday to Sunday 9 AM to 5 PM.

Second and Third Sections of the Park

Natural History Museum. – Tuesday to Saturday 10 AM to 5 PM, Sunday 10 AM to 6 PM. 50 pesos.

Technological Museum. – Tuesday to Saturday 9 AM to 4:45 PM, Sunday 9 AM to 1:45 PM.

Amusement Park. – Wednesday and Thursday 10:30 AM to 5 PM, Saturday 10:30 AM to 7 PM, Sunday 9:30 AM to 1 PM and 3 to 7 PM. 300 pesos. Additional fare for the rides, free on Sunday from 9:30 AM to 1 PM. Roller coaster 1 200 pesos.

Atlantis. – Tuesday to Friday 10 AM to 2:30 PM, Saturday and Sunday 10 AM to 6 PM. Open every day 10 AM to 6 PM during holidays in December, Holy Week and summer. The entrance ticket to the park (7 500 pesos) does not cover the shows.

Tlatelolco and La Villa

Tecpan. – Tuesday, Thursday and Sunday noon to 6 PM.

Villa de Guadalupe

Old Basilica. – Closed for restoration.

Guadalupe Museum. – Tuesday to Sunday 10 AM to 6 PM. 100 pesos.

Churubusco

Museum of Foreign Interventions. – Tuesday to Sunday 9 AM to 6 PM. 550 pesos.

Church of San Diego. – Monday to Thursday 7 to 10 AM, Friday 7 to 10 AM and 5 to 9 PM, Saturday 11 AM to 2 PM and 6:30 to 8 PM, Sunday 8 AM to 2 PM and 6:30 to 8 PM.

Coyoacán

Coyoacán Municipal Hall. – Monday to Friday 8 AM to 9:30 PM, Saturday 8 AM to 2 PM.

Chapel of the Conception. – Open Friday and Saturday for religious ceremonies and Sunday at 10:30 AM.

Frida Kahlo Museum. – Tuesday to Sunday 10 AM to 2 PM and 3 to 6 PM.

San Ángel

Casa del Risco. – Closed for restoration.

Diego Rivera Studio Museum. – Tuesday to Sunday 10 AM to 6 PM.

University Campus

Cultural Center Nezahualcóyotl

Concert Hall. – Open for performances only. Closed two weeks during the Easter season, the first two weeks of July and between December 16th and January 2nd.

Sculpture Area. – 9 AM to 6 PM. Closed two weeks during the Easter season, the first two weeks of July and between December 16th and January 2nd.

Cuicuilco Archeological Site. – Tuesday to Saturday 10 AM to 5 PM, Sunday 10 AM to 4 PM. 700 pesos. Free on Sunday and holidays.

Tlalpan

Casa Chata. – Monday to Friday 9 AM to 3 PM. Closed the week before Easter and from December 16th to January 2nd.

Additional Sights

Azcapotzalco Monastery

Rosary Chapel. – 8 AM to 1 PM and 5 to 7 PM. ☎ 561.04.53.

El Ajusco National Park

College of México. – Monday to Friday 9 AM to 7 PM. Closed two weeks during the Easter season and from December 15th to January 2nd.

Reino Aventura (Amusement Park). – Thursday to Sunday 11 AM to 6 PM; open every day during the summer and during Holy Week and Christmas 10 AM to 8 PM. The ticket costs 20 000 pesos per person and covers the majority of the shows and rides inside the grounds.

Tenayuca Archeological Site. – Tuesday to Sunday 10 AM to 5 PM. 700 pesos.

MITLA (Archeological Site)

8:30 AM to 6:30 PM. 960 pesos.

Frisell Museum. – 9 AM to 6 PM. Guided tours in English, Spanish, French and German.

MONTE ALBÁN (Archeological Site)

8 AM to 5 PM. 960 pesos. Guided tours in English, Spanish and German.

Opening hours and charges

MONTERREY

Church of La Purísima. – Monday to Saturday 8 AM to 8:30 PM, Sunday 10 AM to 8:30 PM.

Monterrey Museum. – Tuesday, Wednesday and Friday 9:30 AM to 5 PM, Thursday 9:30 AM to 10 PM. Saturday and Sunday 10:30 AM to 6 PM.

Alfa Cultural Center. – Tuesday to Sunday 3 to 9:30 PM. 4 000 pesos. Closed on holidays. Free transportation from the Alameda Central every hour starting at 3 PM.

MORELIA

Cathédral. – 7 AM to 9 PM.

Baptistry. – Open Sunday at noon and for christenings.

Michoacán Museum. – Tuesday to Sunday 9 AM to 2 PM and 5 to 7 PM.

State Museum. – 9 AM to 7 PM.

Cultural Center. – Monday to Saturday 9 AM to 2 PM and 5 to 7 PM.

Museum of Colonial Art. – Tuesday to Sunday 9 AM to 2 PM and 5 to 7 PM.

OAXACA

Cathedral. – 6 AM to 8 PM.

Santo Domingo Monastery. – Tuesday to Sunday 10 AM to 5 PM. 950 pesos.

Juárez House. – Tuesday to Friday 10 AM to 2 PM and 4 to 6 PM, Saturday and Sunday 10 AM to 6 PM. 1 500 pesos.

Mexican Pre-Hispanic Art Museum – Rufino Tamayo. – Wednesday to Monday 10 AM to 2 PM and 4 to 7 PM, Sunday 10 AM to 3 PM. Closed on national holidays. 1 000 pesos.

OCOTEPEC

Cemetery. – Generally closed, but the barrier is low, so that it is possible to look at the tombs from the outside.

OXCUTZCAB

Monastery. – 8 AM to noon and 4 to 8 PM. Guided tours.

PACHUCA

Hidalgo Cultural Center

Saint Francis Church. – 7 AM to 1 PM and 4 to 8 PM.

Our Lady of the Light Chapel. – Apply to the Sacristy of Saint Francis's Church.

Photography Museum. – Tuesday to Saturday 10 AM to 6 PM, Sunday 10 AM to 5 PM. Guided tours available.

Photographic Archive. – Monday to Friday 8 AM to 3 PM.

Regional Historical Museum. – Tuesday to Saturday 10 AM to 2 PM and 5 to 7 PM, Sunday 10 AM to 2 PM. Guided tours in Spanish.

Efrén Rebolledo Cultural Forum. – Monday to Saturday 10 AM to 2 PM and 5 to 8 PM. Guided tours in Spanish.

Rule House. – Monday to Friday 8 AM to 2 PM and 5 to 7 PM.

PALENQUE (Archeological Site)

8 AM to 5 PM. 1 000 pesos.

Royal Tomb. – 10 AM to 4 PM.

PAQUIMÉ (Archeological Site)

9 AM to 5 PM. 700 pesos. Closed during heavy rain. Check with the Chihuahua Tourist Office. ☎ 585.01 or 591.24.

PARRAS DE LA FUENTE

Saint Ignatius of Loyola Church. – Open daily but apply in advance.

San Lorenzo Hacienda. – 8 to 11:30 AM and 2 to 5:30 PM. To visit, phone in advance ☎ 201-11.

PÁTZCUARO

Museum of Popular Arts. – Tuesday to Saturday 9 AM to 7 PM, Sunday 9 AM to 3 PM. 550 pesos. Guided tours in English and Spanish.

Gertrudis Bocanegra Public Library. – Monday to Friday 9 AM to 2 PM and 5 to 7 PM.

Lake Pátzcuaro. – Boat departures from 9 AM to 6 PM. See the list of fares at the dock.

LA PAZ

Anthropological Museum of Baja California Sur. – Tuesday to Sunday 9 AM to 1 PM and to 4 to 7 PM.

POPOCATÉPETL-IZTACCÍHUATL (Volcanoes)

Izta-Popo National Park. – Open round the clock, try to visit between 6 AM and 6 PM. Warm clothing is recommended.

Tlamacas. – 24-hour service. Restaurant service and lodgings. Inquire about mountain-climbing guides.

PUEBLA

Cathedral. – 6 AM to noon and 4:30 to 8 PM.

José Luis Bello y González Art Museum. – Tuesday to Sunday 10 AM to 5 PM. Adults 400 pesos, children 200 pesos. Guided tours in English and Spanish.

Casa del Deán. – Tuesday to Sunday 10 AM to 5 PM. 500 pesos.

Palafoxian Library. – Tuesday to Sunday 10 AM to 5 PM. 400 pesos.

City Hall. – Monday to Saturday 8 AM to 3 PM.

Church of Santo Domingo. – 7:30 AM to 8 PM.

Rosary Chapel. – 4 to 8 PM.

José Luis Bello y Zetina Museum. – Tuesday to Sunday 10 AM to 5 PM. Guided tours in Spanish.

Puebla Popular Art Museum. – Tuesday to Sunday 10 AM to 5 PM. 400 pesos. Guided tours.

Museum of Religious Art. – Tuesday to Sunday 10 AM to 5 PM. 500 pesos.

Theater. – 10 AM to 5 PM. No visiting during performances.

El Parián. – 9:30 AM to 8 PM. Bargain before buying in this market.

Artists' Quarter. – Monday to Saturday 10 AM to 8 PM. Sunday 10 AM to 3 PM.

Regional and Ceramic Museum. – Tuesday to Sunday 10 AM to 4 PM. Adults 400 pesos, children 200 pesos.

Museum of the Mexican Revolution. – Tuesday to Sunday 10 AM to 5 PM. Adults 400 pesos, children 200 pesos.

Fort Loreto. – Tuesday to Sunday 10 AM to 5 PM. 550 pesos.

Fort Guadalupe. – Tuesday to Sunday 10 AM to 5 PM. 550 pesos.

Planetarium. – Tuesday to Sunday 10 AM to 5 PM. Adults 1500 pesos, children 700 pesos. Film show.

Natural History Museum. – Tuesday to Sunday 10 AM to 5 PM. Adults 400 pesos, children 200 pesos.

q - r

QUERÉTARO

Regional Museum. – Tuesday to Saturday 9 AM to 4 PM.

Federal Government Palace. – 10 AM to 2 PM. 1000 pesos.

Cultural Center. – Monday to Friday 9 AM to 2 PM.

Querétaro Art Museum. – Monday to Saturday 9 AM to 8 PM.

Holy Cross Convent. – Tuesday to Sunday 9 AM to 2 PM and 4 to 6 PM. Guided tours.

REAL DE CATORCE

Parish Museum. – 10 AM to 2 PM and 4 to 7 PM. 100 pesos.

Mint. – 10 AM to 2 PM and 4 to 7 PM. Closed on national holidays. Apply the Municipal Presidency.

Cockfight Arena. – 10 AM to 2 PM and 4 to 7 PM. Apply the Municipal Presidency.

SALTILLO

Cathedral. – 9 AM to noon and 3:30 to 5:30 PM.

Ruben Herrera Museum. – Wednesday to Monday 9 AM to noon and 3 to 6 PM.

Ateneo Fuente. – 9 AM to 8 PM.

Painting Collection. – 9 AM to 8 PM.

SAN BLAS (Puerto de)

La Tovara. – 8 AM to 5 PM. 50 000 pesos (4 persons), 5 000 pesos for every additional person from La Aguada to La Tovara. 60 000 pesos (4 persons), 5 000 pesos for every additional person from El Conchal to La Tovara. Guided tours in English, Spanish and French, 60 US dollars for a group of 15 to 40 persons.

SAINT CHRISTOPHER (Grottos)

9 AM to 5 PM. 50 pesos. Parking: 50 pesos.

SAN CRISTÓBAL DE LAS CASAS

Market. – Sunday to Friday 7 AM to 2 PM, Saturday 7 AM to 3 PM.

Na-Bolom Museum. – Tuesday to Sunday 4 to 5:30 PM. 2 000 pesos.

Cathedral. – 10 AM to 1 PM and 4 to 8 PM.

SAN FELIPE TORRES MOCHAS

Museum. – Tuesday to Saturday 10 AM to 6 PM, Sunday 10 AM to 5 PM. 550 pesos.

SAN JOSÉ PURÚA

Gorge. – 9 AM to 7 PM.

SAN JOSÉ VISTA HERMOSA (Hacienda)

Guided tours in English and Spanish of the old hacienda. If you eat at the hotel, you may use the swimming pool.

SAN JUAN CHAMULA

Saint John's Church. – 6 to 8 PM. Purchase a pass for 1 000 pesos at the Tourist Office. It is recommended to go on Sunday and not to take photographs.

SAN LUIS POTOSÍ

Government Palace. – Monday to Friday 8 AM to 9 PM, Saturday and Sunday 8 AM to 2 PM.

Saint Francis' Church. – 7 AM to 2 PM and from 4 to 9 PM.
The sacristry is open from 10:30 AM to 12:30 PM and from 4:30 to 6:30 PM. Closed on Wednesday and Sunday.

San Luis Potosí Regional Museum. – Tuesday to Saturday 10 AM to 2 PM and 4 to 6 PM, Sunday 10 AM to 2 PM. 200 pesos. Guided tours in English, Spanish and French.

Cultural Center. – Tuesday to Friday 10 AM to 2 PM and 4 to 6 PM, Saturday 10 AM to 2 PM and 6 to 9 PM, Sunday 10 AM to 2 PM. 200 pesos.

SAN MIGUEL DE ALLENDE

Parish Church. – Tuesday to Saturday 10 AM to 4 PM, Sunday 10 AM to 2 PM.

Regional Museum. – Tuesday to Saturday 10 AM to 4 PM, Sunday 10 AM to 2 PM. No charge.

Saint Francis' Church. – 7 AM to noon and 5:30 to 8 PM.

Saint Philip Neri Prayer Hall. – 6:30 AM to 9:30 PM.

The Holy House of Loreto. – 7:30 AM to 8 PM.

Dressing Room. – 7:30 AM to 8 PM.

Ignacio Ramírez Cultural Center. – Monday to Friday 9 AM to 7 PM, Saturday 9 AM to 6 PM, Sunday 9 AM to 3 PM.

Allende Institute. – Monday to Friday 9 AM to 6 PM.

SAN MIGUEL ZINACANTEPEC

Church and Convent of San Miguel. – Tuesday to Saturday 9 AM to 3 PM, Sunday 9 AM to 2 PM. 250 pesos. Guided tours in English and Spanish.

SANTIAGO TUXTLA

Tuxtleco Museum. – Tuesday to Saturday 9 AM to 7 PM, Sunday 9 AM to 3 PM. 360 pesos.

SIERRA GORDA (Missions)

The five missions are open from 8 AM to 8 PM.

SUMIDERO

Boat trip. – Boarding at Chiapa de Corzo; it is best to go between 10 AM and 2 PM. 63 250 pesos for 10 persons, 2 hours. On Saturday and Sunday, the trips are more frequent.

Automobile ride. – From Tuxtla Gutiérrez. It is advisable to take this ride between 6 AM and 6 PM.

t

El TAJÍN (Archeological Site)

9 AM to 5 PM. 950 pesos. Free on Sunday and holidays.

TAMPICO

Museum of Huastec Culture. – Closed for restoration.

TAXCO

Parish Church of Saint Prisca and Saint Sebastian. – Monday to Saturday 7 AM to 8 PM, Sunday 6 AM to 9 PM.

City Hall. – Monday to Saturday 9 AM to 2 PM and 5 to 7 PM. Closed on Sunday and national holidays.

The Castillo Family. – Monday to Saturday 10 AM to 1 PM and 3 to 7 PM, Sunday 10 AM to 1 PM.

Handicrafts House. – Monday to Saturday 10 AM to 7:30 PM, Sunday 10 AM to 2 PM.

Market. – Monday to Saturday 8 AM to 7 PM, Sunday 7 AM to 5 PM.

Cable Car. – 8 AM to 6 PM. 8000 pesos for a round-trip ticket. Departure every half hour.

O'Gorman Mural. – 8 AM to 6 PM.

TECAMACHALCO

Franciscan Monastery. – Wednesday to Sunday 10 AM to 2 PM. Guided tours in Spanish. If it is closed, apply to the caretaker *(guardián).*

TECAXIC

Franciscan Monastery. – 8 AM to 2 PM and 4 to 6 PM. The cloister is opened on request.

TEHUANTEPEC

Cultural Center. – 9 AM to 9 PM.

TEMOAYA

Factory. – Monday to Saturday 9 AM to noon, Sunday 9 to 11 AM. To visit phone in advance ☎ 275.40.

TEOTENANGO (Archeological Site)

Tuesday to Sunday 9 AM to 5 PM. 1000 pesos. Guided tours in Spanish.

TEOTIHUACAN (Archeological Site)

8 AM to 6 PM. 1000 pesos.

TEPEACA

Monastery. – 10 AM to 5 PM. If it is closed, apply to the caretaker.

TEPEAPULCO

Saint Francis' Monastery. – 10 AM to 2 PM and 4 to 6 PM.

Exhibit Room. – Closed Monday and Tuesday. 250 pesos.

TEPEYANCO DE LAS FLORES

Franciscan Monastery. – Closed for restoration.

Saint Francis Parish Church. – Monday to Saturday 2 to 8 PM. Sunday 6 AM to 6 PM.

TEPOSCOLULA

Open-Air Chapel. – Tuesday to Friday 10 AM to 6 PM, Saturday and Sunday 10 AM to 5 PM.

TEPOTZOTLÁN

Saint Francis Xavier Seminary. – Tuesday to Sunday 11 AM to 6 PM. 750 pesos.

TEPOZTLÁN

Church and Convent of the Nativity of the Virgin Mary. – Tuesday to Saturday 9 AM to 6 PM, Sunday 10 AM to 5 PM. 550 pesos.

TIJUANA

Anthropological and Historical Museum. – Monday to Friday 11 AM to 7 PM, Saturday and Sunday 11 AM to 8 PM. 600 pesos. Guided tours in Spanish and English.

Planetarium. – Monday to Friday 2 to 9 PM, Saturday and Sunday 11 AM to 9 PM. The price varies from 2900 to 4700 pesos depending on the film and includes admission to the Anthropological and Historical Museum.

TIZATLÁN (Archeological Site)

10 AM to 5 PM. 750 pesos.

Open-Air Chapel. – Tuesday to Sunday 10 AM to 5 PM.

TLAXCALA
Palace of Justice. – 8 AM to 3 PM.

Cathedral. – 7 AM to 1 PM and 5 to 8 PM.

Government Palace. – 8 AM to 8 PM. Guided tours in Spanish from 10 AM to 4 PM.

Sanctuary of the Virgin of Ocotlán. – 7 AM to 7 PM.

Dressing Room. – 7 AM to 7 PM. To visit phone a day in advance ☎ 210.73.

TLAYACAPAN
Monastery of Saint John the Baptist. – Church: 7 AM to 6 PM, exhibit hall: Tuesday to Sunday 9 AM to 6 PM. 350 pesos.

TOLUCA
Fine Arts Museum. – Tuesday to Sunday 10 AM to 8 PM. Guided tours.

Cosmovitral and Botanical Garden. – Tuesday to Sunday 9 AM to 4 PM. Adults 200 pesos, children and students 100 pesos. Guided tours.

Mexiquense Cultural Center. – Tuesday to Sunday 10 AM to 6 PM. Guided tours in English and Spanish.

Casart. – 10 AM to 8 PM.

La TRINIDAD
Old Textile Mill. – 10 AM to 6 PM.

TULA (Archeological Site)
Wednesday to Sunday 10 AM to 4 PM. 950 pesos.

Museum. – Wednesday to Sunday 10 AM to 4 PM.

TUXTLA GUTIÉRREZ
Miguel Alvarez del Toro Zoo. – Tuesday to Sunday 8:30 AM to 5:30 PM.

Chiapas Regional Museum. – 8 AM to 4 PM. 1 000 pesos.

TZINTZUNTZAN
Yácatas Archeological Site. – 10 AM to 5 PM. 500 pesos.

URUAPAN
Eduardo Ruiz National Park. – 8 AM to 6 PM. Adults 200 pesos, students 100 pesos. Guided tours in Spanish 11 AM to 3 PM.

UXMAL (Archeological Site)
8 AM to 5 PM. 2 950 pesos. Guided tours 8 AM to 4 PM in English and Spanish. 51 714 pesos, an extra 30% for guided tours in French and Italian.

Light and Sound Show. – 7 PM (2 700 pesos) in Spanish and 9 PM (4 000 pesos) in English.

VERACRUZ
Reforma Sanctuary. – Monday to Saturday 8 AM to 3 PM, Sunday 9 AM to noon.

Civil Registry. – Monday to Friday 9 AM to 3 PM, Saturday 9 AM to noon.

Postal, Telegraph and Maritime Customs Offices. – Monday to Friday 8 AM to 10:30 PM, Saturday 8 AM to 8 PM, Sunday 9 AM to 1 PM.

Fort San Juan de Ulúa. – Tuesday to Sunday 9 AM to 5 PM. 950 pesos. Guided tours in English, Spanish and German.

Santiago Bastion. – Tuesday to Sunday 10 AM to 7 PM. 550 pesos.

VILLA ESCALANTE
National Copper Museum. – Tuesday to Sunday 9 AM to 8 PM. Foreigners 1 000 pesos, Mexicans 200 pesos.

VILLAHERMOSA
Regional Anthropological Museum – Carlos Pellicer. – 9 AM to 8 PM. 1 000 pesos. Closed on national holidays.

La Venta Park-Museum. – 8 AM to 4:30 PM. 500 pesos. Guided tours in Spanish 10 AM to noon and 12:30 to 2:30 PM.

Popular Culture Museum. – 9 AM to 8 PM.

XALAPA

Juárez Park. – Lookout schedule varies. Closed at night.

Francisco Javier Clavijero Botanical Garden. – Tuesday to Saturday 8 AM to 5 PM. 100 pesos.

XEL-HA

Natural Aquarium. – From 8 AM to 5 PM. 1 000 pesos.

XILOXOSTLA

Saint Isabel Parish Church. – Apply to the municipal authority (Presidencia Municipal) or the presbytery.

XOCHICALCO (Archeological Site)

9 AM to 5 PM. 1 000 pesos. Apply to the warden to visit the Observatory.

XPUHIL (Archeological Site)

8 AM to 4 PM. 1 000 pesos.

XTACUMBILXUNÁN (Grottos)

8 AM to 4:30 PM. 1 000 pesos.

YAGUL (Archeological Site)

8 AM to 6 PM. 500 pesos.

YANHUITLÁN

Monastery. – 10 AM to 6 PM. 550 pesos.

YAXCHILÁN

Access by light aircraft to Yaxchilán and Bonampak from San Cristóbal de Las Casas, Comitán and Tuxtla Gutiérrez. Departures vary according to the period and the demand. Check with the Chiapas Tourist Office ☎ 3.51.86, 3.48.37 or 3.48.90. The cost varies from 190 US dollars to 105 US dollars according to the number of passengers.

Archeological Site. – 8 AM to 4 PM. 950 pesos.

Bonampak Archeological Site. – 8 AM to 4 PM. 950 pesos.

YAXCOPOIL (Hacienda)

Open Monday to Saturday 8 AM to 6 PM. Sunday 9 AM to 1 PM. 1 500 pesos. Guided tours.

YECAPIXTLA

Monastery of Saint John the Baptist. – Tuesday to Sunday 9 AM to 6 PM.

YURIRIA

Monastery. – Tuesday to Sunday 10 AM to 2 PM and 3 to 4:45 PM. 550 pesos.

ZAACHILA (Archeological Site)

10:30 AM to 5:30 PM. 500 pesos.

ZACATECAS

González Ortega Market. – 10 AM to 7:30 PM.

Pedro Coronel Museum. – Friday to Wednesday 10 AM to 2 PM and 4 to 7 PM. 1 000 pesos.

Saint Augustine's Church. – Tuesday to Sunday 10 AM to 5 PM.

Edén Mine. – Noon to 7:30 PM. 2 000 pesos. Guided tours in English and Spanish (additional fee).

Francisco Goitia Museum. – Tuesday to Sunday 10 AM to 2 PM and 4 to 7 PM. 1 000 pesos.

ZAMORA

Unfinished Cathedral. – Monday to Saturday 9 AM to 2 PM and 5 to 7 PM.

ZINACANTÁN

Church of San Lorenzo and Hermitage of the Lord of the Esquipulas. – 6 AM to 8 PM.

Index

Monterrey Manche . . . . Cities, sights and tourist region followed by the state *(see state abbreviations p 16).*

Juárez, Benito . . . . Historic names and terms explained in the text.

Isolated sights (lakes, islands, grottos...) are indexed under their proper name.

MANUFACTURE FRANÇAISE DES PNEUMATIQUES MICHELIN
Société en commandite par actions au capital de 875 000 000 de francs
Place des Carmes-Déchaux - 63 Clermont-Ferrand (France)

R.C.S. Clermont-Fd B 855 200 507

© Michelin et Cie, Propriétaires-Éditeurs, 1989

Dépôt légal 1er trim. 90 – ISBN 2.06.015.791-9 – ISSN 0763-1383

Printed in France 12-89-35
Photocomposition : COUPÉ S.A., Sautron - Impression MAURY Imprimeur S.A., Malesherbes n° J89/28175G

This guide was prepared in collaboration with

Guías Turísticas Banamex, S.A. de C.V.

REFORMA Nº 155 3er PISO, LOMAS DE CHAPULTEPEC CP. 11000 MEXICO. D.F. TEL. 540.64.21